DOWDING
AND
CHURCHILL

DOWDING
AND
CHURCHILL

The Dark Side of the Battle of Britain

The Involvement of High Officials of
Government and the Air Ministry
intent on Discrediting
Air Chief Marshal Sir Hugh Dowding

J.E.G. DIXON

O good old man! How well in thee appears
The constant service of the antique world,
When service sweat for duty, not for mead!
Thou art not for the fashion of these times,
Where none will sweat but for promotion,
And having that, do choke their service up
Even with the having.
As You Like It, William Shakespeare

Pen & Sword
MILITARY

First published in Great Britain in 2008 by
Pen & Sword Military
an imprint of
Pen & Sword Books Ltd
47 Church Street
Barnsley
South Yorkshire
S70 2AS

Copyright © J.E.G. Dixon, 2008

ISBN: 978 1 84415 854 6

Typeset by S L Menzies-Earl

Printed and bound in Great Britain by MPG Biddles Ltd

Pen & Sword Books Ltd incorporates the imprints of:
Pen & Sword Aviation, Pen & Sword Maritime, Pen & Sword Military,
Wharncliffe Local History, Pen & Sword Select,
Pen & Sword Military Classics, Leo Cooper, Remember When,
Seaforth Publishing and Frontline Publishing.

For a complete list of Pen & Sword titles please contact:
Pen & Sword Books Limited
47 Church Street, Barnsley, South Yorkshire, S70 2AS, England
E-mail: enquiries@pen-and-sword.co.uk
Website: www.pen-and-sword.co.uk

Contents

Epigraph

*The only commander who won one of the decisive battles in history
and who got sacked for his pains.*
MRAF Sir Arthur Harris

*The peace and happiness of thousands of millions unborn,
through countless generations to come, depended directly on his decisions.*
C.S. Forester

*To him, the people of Great Britain and of the free world
owe largely the way of life and the liberties they enjoy today.*
Inscription on Dowding's statue in The Strand, London

*It is a great pity that the war is so affected by these human considerations,
but there it is.*
Sir Henry Tizard

*For the very first time the continued existence of the Army and the Navy
became totally dependent for their protection upon the RAF.
While the bitterness of their pill may have been masked at the time
by the common threat, the inescapable facts of the Battle of Britain
meant that things would never be the same again.*
Norman F. Dixon

Why did we get rid of Dowding, who did something. . .?
ACM Sir Wilfrid Freeman

It is dangerous to be right when the powers are wrong.
Voltaire

Preface

A Personal Note

When war was declared against Germany on September 3rd 1939, I was a fifteen-year old schoolboy living on the coast of East Kent. As a family we listened to the lugubrious voice of the defeated Neville Chamberlain as it came across the wireless announcing war. Ten minutes later the air raid sirens wailed for the first time, we took the only cover available. Our house and back garden abutted onto a private girls' school. The school was empty for the summer holidays. (As it happened, they never came back and the school closed down.) We knew of a dug-out in the school garden, which had been excavated at the time of the Gotha bombings of the First World War. We all trooped round and sat on mouldy wooden benches in the dank and musty atmosphere, fearful and curious, until the 'all clear' sounded fifteen minutes later.

In December I was forced by family circumstances to leave school, and my mother, now a widow of thirty-seven, had to do something about her five children, aged from seventeen to nine years old. Her solution was to enter me as an apprentice in the RAF, without, so far as I recollect, my having any say in it. That was the way things were done in those days, and it is not necessarily the worst way.

In the intervening nine months I found various makeshift jobs, until the time of Dunkirk when invasion threatened. We had been invaded previously: why not again? All the invasions of England, or attempted invasions, had taken place where I lived, or not far off. One of the many measures taken by the authorities to make invasion difficult for the enemy was the erection of telephone poles in the open fields of southern England, as an obstacle to paratroops and gliders. For the next two months I toiled away for twelve hours a day Monday to Friday, and ten hours on Saturday. We were graciously allowed Sundays off.

When that work terminated I had two weeks left. Mothers being mothers, I was not allowed to idle my time away. A local farmer needed a hand to hoe a field of vegetables: I was sent. The farm turned out to be on the south side of the aerodrome of RAF Station Manston. It was during those two weeks in August that Manston was bombed to smithereens. Episodes such as this brought home to us the reality of war fought almost in our front garden. Everyone knew the odds and what was at stake. We knew that invasion was a likelihood; and we knew with even greater certitude what the consequences would be in the event of our failure. It is true to say that every man, woman and youth was prepared to tackle the enemy with garden forks if any had the audacity to land in their street.

In September I left to join the RAF at Halton. The invasion scare was still alive throughout the country. We apprentices were given a crash course in oxy-acetylene welding, and were put to work to make weapons. The weapons were six-foot lengths of one-inch steel pipe, to one end of which we welded three wedge-shaped pieces of steel plate so that they came together at a point. They were called pikes. We made hundreds of them in the next two weeks, and they were issued to reserve units of the Army, and to elements of the Local Defence Force (the forerunner of the Home Guard, made endearing in the comic tv series, *Dad's Army*). We jokingly boasted that our efforts must have been successful, for there was no invasion.

I thought no more of the Battle of Britain for the following twenty-eight years – until, that is, the showing of the movie. It set me to reading. If there was one thing about the Battle that mystified me it was the removal of Dowding from Fighter Command after he had won the Battle. And not only Dowding, but Park as well.

Some writers, apparently sympathetic to the received version, put out explanations which did not add up. The facts are these: 1) the Battle of Britain was an action which posed a threat to England on a scale unseen since 1066; 2) Dowding and Park were, respectively, the strategist and the tactician who engineered the victory; 3) Dowding and Park were removed from their commands shortly after the Battle had been won, and seen to be won.

In 1988 I began to concentrate my studies on the third item Soon a fourth factor emerged: Dowding and Park were replaced by two men who proceeded to demonstrate their unfitness for their commands. Little by little, a picture began to take shape and substance. I was assailed by a searing sense of injustice. I published the results of my inquiries in 2003 in a paperback with the title, *The Battle of Britain: Victory and Defeat*; the present book is a revised, up-dated, enlarged and partly rewritten version of this. I have pillaged it for material I needed in order to avoid re-writing it. It was, in any event, out-dated, diffuse, unfocused and insufficiently objective.

In the present work I have gone beyond my early findings and stress the greatness of Dowding and his struggle against lesser people who, consumed with fear and eaten with ambition, abused their power to denigrate him to their advantage. I also stress the moral divide that separates the loyal men and women in operational roles from the planners and power-brokers in the higher echelons of the Service who, being engaged in 'the race to the top', are more intent on pursuing their own interests than on doing their duty and serving their country. Finally, I feel constrained to dwell on the unwholesome evidence which shows that, whereas the terms of service of the officers and men – and women – working at the 'sharp' end bind them to a personal responsibility for the work they do, the very people 'at the top' who dictate those terms of service are careful to ensure that they are never caught in the trap of accountability. Even more regrettably, I find that Trenchard is the chief agitator behind the campaign to denigrate Dowding and the architect of Dowding's removal.

A word about two contentious issues. At the time of the Battle, defeat in the air seemed a very real possibility, given our inadequate knowledge of the German air force; victory was not inevitable – not any more than winning the war itself was until mid-1944. Secondly, if Fighter Command had been defeated and the German air force established air supremacy over Britain, was defeat *then* inevitable? Defeat by what means? Again, given our defective intelligence of the German capabilities, invasion by sea seemed a distinct threat and possibility. Today we see that it could not have come within a mile of success. But defeat by blockade and starvation was possible, as given time the German High Command would have realized that their air force and their U-Boat fleet could have neutralized or even destroyed the British Fleet...

What then?
Thousands of highly trained and dedicated men and women manned Fighter Command and made it ready to fight the Battle. Two men could have lost it. Today the free world seems little bothered to learn what the Battle of Britain meant, or how much it owes to Dowding and Park.

Introduction

'Here I stand'

Today mention of the Battle of Britain is all too often associated with Winston Churchill. It is true that his speeches that summer stirred and galvanized the nation. Especially, in his speech to the House of Commons on August 20th, one ringing sentence has come to sum up the struggle and to place it in its just historical context: 'Never in the field of human conflict have so many owed so much to so few.'

It is a momentous historical claim to make. He is saying that, throughout the course of human history, *no* war or battle has ever been fought with such immeasurable consequences for good or evil and that most of humanity will be affected by the outcome, decided at this moment by a relatively few fighter pilots. All that is summed up in sixteen words–nay, in eleven brief English words: : 'Never before have so many owed so much to so few.' These 'Few' have been made immortal by Churchill's oratory. But Churchill did not win the Battle of Britain. Of no man can it be said that he alone won the battle: yet, if the seeds of victory in the Battle of Britain can be said to have been sown by any one man, that man was Air Chief Marshal Sir Hugh (later Lord) Dowding. It is fairly safe to say that the Allies could have lost the battle without Dowding; but could it have been won without Churchill? In strictly military terms, the answer is 'yes'. But, as we shall show, if Churchill had not been there to give Dowding his support, the Air Ministry might well have got rid of Dowding, even during the Battle itself. This move could conceivably have lost us not only the battle but the war as well. Yet ironically, later in 1940, Churchill came close to losing us this battle before it had even begun, as we shall relate in due course.

In March 1941, when the Battle of Britain had been over for four months, the Air Ministry issued a slim pamphlet on the Battle and summed it up in these words: 'Such was the Battle of Britain in 1940. Future historians may compare it with Marathon, Trafalgar and the Marne.' Yet the Air Ministry not only removed Dowding summarily from his command in November 1940, without explanation: they also accorded him not even a passing mention in their booklet. Despite establishing the historic significance of the Battle, the Air Ministry ignored the role and the very existence of the chief architect of the victory. Indeed, for most of those four years they regarded him as a thorn in their side rather than, especially in 1939-1940, as Britain's likely only saviour.

The Air Ministry's collective attitude toward Fighter Command was one of endemic superiority, for Fighter Command was but one of many Commands. When it was established in 1936 it played a very second fiddle to Bomber Command, created at the same time. Furthermore, the Air Staff regarded Fighter Command as having very much a local sphere of action, restricted to the British Isles, whereas the Air Ministry was self-consciously aware of its world-wide strategic concerns and responsibilities.

This distinction between the Air Ministry and Fighter Command viewpoints was stressed as recently as 1990 at a conference at the Royal Air Force Staff College to mark the occasion of the Battle's fiftieth anniversary. An Air Ministry historian characterized Dowding's remit as 'parochial' in asserting the better informed global vision of the Air Ministry. 'Newall . . . [he said] as CAS . . . had to take a wider strategic view than the more parochial concerns of a C-in-C.' This judgement was repeated in 1995, in the article on Dowding in the *Oxford Companion to World War II*: 'His [Dowding's] vision, necessarily, was a narrow one and he was no politician.'

Global, strategic, parochial: what do these terms mean? It would be accurate to suggest that they were used more in a geographical and temporal, rather than a strictly military, sense. If this distinction is valid, then global and strategic mean nothing more than remote, and hence perhaps beyond help or interference.

In this sense, if 'parochial' becomes a concern with the immediate situation and what is possible in the present, were Dowding and the Battle of Britain parochial? We must give thanks that there was a man who saw clearly what had to be done and did it. While the air marshals in Whitehall either did not see what had to be done, or, seeing, did nothing, either through fear of their political masters or to protect their positions, Dowding, alone, took a stand on an unshakeable principle. In order to do what he did to create Fighter Command from the ground up, to prepare it for war, and to lead it when war came, he had to tread on many toes and incur unpopularity and even hostility. He fought with the Air Staff; he went over the head of the Chief of the Air Staff; and he stood firm against Churchill and the War Cabinet, at a critical moment when no one else did, when vital issues at stake threatened to weaken his forces and imperil the security of the kingdom.

Dowding conceded that it would have been perfectly possible to have good relations with people on the Air Staff. But in order to realize those cordial relations, Dowding would have had to acquiesce in many recommendations and urgings which he disagreed with for sound reasons. In rejecting or opposing them because their implementation would be wasteful or dangerous, Dowding never lost sight of essential priorities. Always at the heart of his concerns was the security of the base – which amounted to nothing less than the salvation of the British people. All his and Fighter Command's strategic and tactical thinking were devoted to that end.

Dowding's gaze was penetrating and whole. He understood what was happening, and acted upon that understanding. He knew that the first principle of war, as it governed his generalship, was the security of the base. The entire issue at stake in the Battle of Britain was that security. If Britain succumbed everything was lost. He pursued that aim single-mindedly: he let nothing deter or deflect him from that course. If the price of that dedication was to find himself held in disfavour in the Air Council and by the Air Staff, it was a price he was willing to pay. And they certainly made him pay it.

Part I

Past is Prologue

CHAPTER 1

At the Air Ministry: Of Dinosaurs and Ostriches

—︵ᴍᴍ︵—

The Battle of Britain, fought over 'the green and pleasant land' that is England in the summer of 1940, was an aerial engagement involving the German and British air forces that would arguably determine the ultimate outcome of the war. Most of the high commanders in Germany realized it, for with Britain undefeated the war would be long and protracted. Most of the people in Britain – and perhaps a few in the United States – understood what was truly at stake. Pre-eminent among them all was Air Chief Marshal Sir Hugh Dowding, the Air Officer Commanding-in-Chief of Fighter Command. Already, on May 16, 1940, he had written to the Government this prophetic warning:

> I believe that, if an adequate fighter force is kept in this country, if the Fleet remains in being, and if Home Forces are suitably organised to resist invasion, we should be able to carry on the war single handed for some time, if not indefinitely. But, if the Home Defence Force is drained away in desperate attempts to remedy the situation in France, defeat in France will involve the final, complete and irremediable defeat of this country.[i]

The conflict which became known as the Battle of Britain waged aggressively by the Germans was fought out in two major stages. The first stage was an assault whose purpose and aim was the destruction of the British defences and the establishment of aerial supremacy which would permit an invasion by a combined operation involving the German land, sea and air forces. This stage opened on August 13 and lasted until the end of October. The second stage, which comprised heavy bombardments of British cities and ports by night, was carried out with the aim of breaking both the spirit of the British people and their industrial capacity to continue the war. This stage opened on September 7, 1940 and ended on May 27, 1941.

The first stage ended in a victory as momentous as those of the Armada, Trafalgar and Waterloo. The second ended in a stalemate : the Germans failed to cow the British people but the defence forces were powerless to prevent the raids, as we shall have cause to examine later in this narrative. The ways in which both these campaigns were fought, however, were to play a significant role in the fate of Dowding; this will also be examined later, in chapters three and seven.

The Air Ministry decreed that the official opening and closing dates of the Battle would be July 12 and October 31. These dates were chosen for the sole purpose of deciding which aircrews would become eligible to wear the decoration which became known as the Battle of Britain clasp. It seems logical that the Germans, as the aggressors, would determine the dates; but the Air Ministry was to make many more questionable, even offensive, decisions during the period just identified.

*   *   *   *   *

The Royal Air Force is an unparalleled creation. In a real sense its foundations were the work of one man, Hugh Trenchard. In 1928 T.E. Lawrence wrote to him: 'the RAF is the finest individual effort in British history. . ... the RAF is your single work, and it's thanks to your being head and shoulders greater in character than ordinary men that your force, even in its childhood, surpasses the immemorial army and navy.'[ii] (This claim, particularly with respect to the Navy, is not to be taken *à la lettre*, but it harbours nevertheless a substantial grain of truth.)

Among the reasons to be found for Lawrence's claims are that Trenchard insisted on the highest standards of equipment and material; of training, both for the air and the ground; and of selection of officers, airmen and airwomen. It was to be a technical service, even a scientific service, from the beginning, and required a consistent level of education.

Another essential ingredient of that creation is high ideals. The Royal Air Force has attracted, by that very virtue, thousands of men and women of the finest character and ability. One of the many ingredients was the ethos of personal responsibility. This feature of the service was especially prominent, and practiced, at the operational level of things – that is, where the essential work of flying and aircraft maintenance was performed. For example, a tradesman who carried out certain technical work on an aircraft was required to sign a maintenance log which specified what he had done and where and when. Equally, the pilot who took charge of that aircraft made it his business to examine the aircraft visually and to carry out tests before test-flying it, and similarly signed the log to certify his satisfaction with the state of the aircraft before assuming responsibility for it.

No one embodied in his service career a higher devotion to the idealism stated above than Dowding – Air Chief Marshal Sir Hugh Dowding, as he was when this drama opens. It is not open to question to say that Trenchard and Dowding were the two greatest men who ennobled the history of the Royal Air Force. Yet they came together in an irreconcilable conflict, instigated by Trenchard, to his discredit. It is a part of this study to discover how it came about. The story of their relations, which only comes to a head later in this narrative, is at once a national tragedy and a lesson in irony. The tragedy, of almost Greek proportions, is played out even when the Battle of Britain was at its height, and saw Trenchard involved in a cabal intent on ousting Dowding from his command, and agitating covertly, to spur on a colleague to do the dirty work. That colleague was Sir John Salmond, Trenchard's successor as Chief of the Air Staff. What Salmond, for his part, had against Dowding is a mystery – unless one is open to the notion that Trenchard had a compelling way with people, even with strong people such as Salmond.

Other writers have sought 'reasons' for Dowding's removal from his command. We are beyond reasons: we must seek motives, though they are notoriously difficult to fathom. Often people do not even know why they do certain things. But in the case of Trenchard specifically we propose to show that his motives are plain enough.

The whole purpose of the independent Air Force, which became the Royal Air Force on April 1st 1918, was, firstly, to be rid of the ties that bound it to the Navy and Army and to pursue its own *raison d'être*. That reason, which assumed the power of an obsession throughout the 1920s and 1930s, was the conviction that an air force, equipped with bombers of an ever-increasing destructive capacity, would be able to carry war to an enemy and eventually to inflict such devastating damage that the enemy would be unable to continue the war, either because his war-making capacity had been destroyed, or, even better, his morale had been shattered. This conviction, which became known as the 'Trenchard Doctrine', held undisputed sway throughout the period in question, and the faithful came to dominate the councils of power in the Air Ministry. One writer has gone so far as to claim that '[Trenchard's] hold on his subordinates (who were, in due course, to become the leaders of the RAF in the Second World War) was positively hypnotic'.[iii]

Yet, thankfully, history shows that through the thistles and nettles and other weeds a hardy oak will thrust its head, and force its attention upon its surrounds. Such was the career of Dowding, who by sheer ability imposed himself upon his peers and colleagues. In the early years of the new service there was little cause for dispute over strategy; but the mid-1930s, with the rise of Hitler, brought fresh demands upon the military leaders of the West. Most relied on the experience of past wars. A few, very few, recognized the novelty of the threat. The majority, dwelling in the past, redoubled their efforts to counter threat with greater threat. The few began to think: Dowding proved himself to be the most independent thinker of the Royal Air Force. For was the Royal Air Force not now an independent fighting arm?

The irony of the situation in which the Royal Air Force found itself soon after the outbreak of war – and which was not lost on Trenchard – was twofold. If the Royal Air Force had not been created, and the Royal Flying Corps and the Royal Naval Air Service had remained in being, attached to and under the command respectively of the Army and the Navy, the military situation that developed in France in early June 1940 would have resulted in the committing of their air arms lock-stock-and-barrel to the conflict and they would have been destroyed. Their destruction would have laid bare the British Isles to invasion and, subsequently, defeat in the summer of 1940. But the Royal Air Force had been formed; it was independent; and in 1936 Fighter Command had been created, separate from Bomber Command. In 1940 Fighter Command was ready for the battle for which it had been founded and trained, which was lucky given that Bomber Command alone was never powerful enough to realize the fulfilment of the Trenchard Doctrine. The victorious outcome of the Battle of Britain not only gave the Allies, the defenders of our immemorial freedoms, the opportunity to marshal the forces that were to save Western Civilization: it left the Trenchard Doctrine, and much that Trenchard had lived for, in doubt.

If the doctrine of personal responsibility and accountability for the performance of one's duties was a marked feature of the life of the individual at the operational end of the Royal Air Force, we are sadly constrained to state that the further one moved from the operations, and the closer one approached the higher levels of the structure of the organization, that ethos melted away in the heat generated in the corridors of power. One must ask whether it was possible for any man to rise to the top of his profession, serve for six years in those halls and corridors of influence and command, and at the same time develop not only an independent mind but retain the ideals of service that personified the very best of the men and women of the Royal Air Force. If such a man existed, he must not only be a very extraordinary person indeed, but one almost destined to swim upstream, to run against the pack, and – dare we say it? – to kick against the pricks. Nowhere in the Royal Air Force was that idealism, and the morale that it engendered, more in evidence than among the men and women of Fighter Command, under the inspired and unshakeable leadership of its commander-in-chief.

The pall that Trenchard cast over the senior officers of the Air Staff also had far-reaching, though less edifying, consequences: personal advancement hinged on the degree to which they accepted and promoted his ideas, and that those ideas were rooted in a past which was never touched by subsequent experience or modified by later technological advances. The sorry tale we tell in these pages – a tale of the intellectual and moral servility, self-serving irresponsibility and vindictiveness displayed in the higher reaches of the Royal Air Force – is crowned by the extraordinary behaviour of the Prime Minister. For it was Churchill who passed from being Dowding's most loyal admirer and champion for over two years – and who went so far, in July 1940, as to suggest that he should be considered for promotion to the next Chief of the Air Staff – to acquiescing, first, in the appointment of Portal as Chief of the Air Staff without his, Churchill's, being consulted – so far as we are aware –and finally in the removal of Dowding from his command. Churchill was content to listen to, and act on, the criticisms levelled at Dowding by his enemies – led by Sinclair and Portal – without requiring evidence as to the justness of their allegations, and without offering Dowding the opportunity to hear his accusers.

Let us now turn from the operational functions of the Air Force to look at the organization that directed them. The First Volume of the Official History of *The Royal Air Force in the Second World War* by Denis Richards, an historian sympathetic to the Air Ministry, sets out by painting a glowing picture of the Royal Air Force and the Air Ministry as they were in 1939:

> The principle of a unified Air Force . . . had triumphed over all opposition; thanks to that . . . it was possible to fight the air war with efficiency and economy. Up-to-date equipment, sound organization, correct principles – these were all very vital. . . . The Service was well staffed and well led. In the Air Ministry alone there was an enormous array of talent.[iv]

Which of the two pictures we have presented is the reader to believe? We need, for the moment, only to draw attention to one over-riding failure. The entire strategic policy of the 'unified Air Force', a strategy which was known as the 'Trenchard Doctrine', was, as we have seen, anchored on the creation of a bomber force which would strike at the enemy from the moment of the outbreak of war and destroy his war-making capacity and his will to fight. By September 1939 all the Air Force's bombers were twin-engined machines with a short range and small bomb-carrying capacity, and were hopelessly obsolete. Moreover, eighty per cent of the aircrews could not even find a designated 'target' in daylight and in friendly skies. At the time these facts were, of course, concealed from the British public, lest they undermine the trust and faith that the British people had come to place in the Royal Air Force since the earliest days of its history.

The difference between the men on the ground and the men in charge was vast, and may also have contributed to absence of a completely unified air force. Many of the 'brass' would pull out all stops to prevent their being posted away from their cocoons of safety and desks of authority to a position in the field which offered neither of those commodities. These differences created a gap which was difficult to bridge; an alienation difficult to overcome, almost an antipathy. Certainly very different ways of thinking. To the Air Ministry mind, the commands, stations and squadrons feel that their roles are far more important than all the others and should get priority of treatment in supplies and the best people. To the men and women of the squadrons and stations, on the other hand, the Air Ministry – and even at times their own Command Headquarters – are seen as being divorced from reality, out of touch, and unaware of what is going on. It is fairly certain that important disagreements will lead to recrimination on both sides. But perhaps the most significant difference between the people – to use a neutral term – at the fighting end of the arm and the people at the directing end was the question of personal responsibility. It is one of the themes of this narrative to illustrate that the farther one gets from the fighting, and the closer to the high command, the less one feels responsible for his decisions, and the less he is held accountable for his actions.

Air Chief Marshal Sir Hugh Dowding had been, successively, before he became the first head (AOC-in-C) of the new Fighter Command, the Air Member for Supply and Research, 1930-1935, and Air Member for Research and Development, 1935-1936. It was in the former capacity that he signed the Certificate of Airworthiness of the airship R.101, which crashed in France two days later with great loss of life. This matter is introduced here for an important reason. Hough and Richards in their *History of the Battle of Britain* described thus Dowding's dilemma, and his lesson:

> Not all Dowding's decisions between 1930 and 1936 turned out well. Within a few weeks of his first appointment, trusting to the experts, he cleared the airship R.101 for her maiden flight to India. The disaster at Beauvais made him very wary in future of trusting experts without strong proofs of their correctness.

This statement itself lacks 'correctness' and calls for modification. The 'decision', such as it was, was not wholly Dowding's. New as he was to his post, he had not had the time to study the experts' opinions. For the fact is that the best informed opinion was against the flight of the R.101. Charles G. Gray, the author of *A History of the Air Ministry*, is very specific:

> The [R.101] was foredoomed to failure. Its structure and its design had been severely criticised in this and other countries. Its trials had been unsatisfactory. And the Air Ministry had been warned in print that it would come to grief. Unhappily, for political reasons, the ship was ordered to start for India, and the Air Ministry and the RAF had to obey orders.

The Air Ministry and the RAF 'had to obey orders'? Despite the traditions and constitutional requirement subordinating the military to civilian control, the statement calls for examination. First, who had to obey orders? The Air Ministry and the RAF were not abstract organisms brought up to follow orders like trained seals. They were human organizations made up of thinking men and women – especially, at the top, of men who, supposedly, were trained to use their judgment. Who were these men who obeyed orders? If senior officers in the Air Ministry received political orders they did not agree with, they had the option to refuse them, or to resign. Why then did they obey them? Were they afraid to confront their political masters? Or did they place their careers ahead of their convictions? These men were the high-ranking officers who formulated the policies and directed the affairs of the Royal Air Force, many of whom were still in positions of authority in the early days of the war.

The order was a political order, and a political blunder. Despite all the warnings from the experts that the R.101 was doomed to failure, Dowding did sign the airworthiness certificate that authorized the flight of the airship. And he has stated his reasons for doing so:

> I must make it quite clear that no direct pressure was ever exercised on me to sanction the departure of this new airship without extensive trials, but of course I should have been very unpopular if I had vetoed a journey on which such important hearts were set, after being in my new saddle for only a few weeks. This was the first technical job of my career ... And I was not sufficiently self-confident to set my individual opinion against that of the technical experts whose advice was available to me ... The venture seemed to me to be reasonably safe, and I shall always be glad that I myself was a passenger on the last flight of the airship before its departure for India. The flight lasted for sixteen hours and was uneventful except for a minor defect in one of the engines, which was soon remedied.

> Looking back from the standpoint of greater experience, however, I think I was wrong not to insist on much more extensive trials and tests...(since) the construction of the ship was novel and previously untried.

> ... But the greatest mistake of all, in my opinion, was to make a start in the weather actually prevailing at the time.[v]

Let us go over these statements again. Hough and Richards state that 'he [Dowding] cleared the airship R.101 for her maiden flight' – that is to say, he 'cleared the airship' as being airworthy: he did not authorize its sailing for he had no authority to do so. Secondly, 'for political reasons, the ship was ordered to start ... and the RAF had to obey orders.' Dowding himself wrote: 'the greatest mistake of all... was to make the start in the weather actually prevailing at the time.' It is clear that, whereas Dowding signed the airship's airworthiness certificate, the ultimate responsibility for ordering the ship to depart was the captain's. And if the captain deemed the sailing unsafe he should have refused to comply with the order. If Dowding's refusal to sign would have made him 'very unpopular', one can imagine how the captain of the airship would have felt, and how he would have been treated by the higher authorities in the Air Ministry and the Government if he had refused to fly that night.

Dowding is not, to my mind, 'passing the buck' when he says that 'the greatest mistake' lay with the captain of the airship, for he accepts his role in the disaster. He was to show in subsequent years the greatest qualities of leadership in assuming the most burdensome responsibilities that any man can be asked to shoulder; and he was to make himself knowingly a very unpopular officer in his subsequent relations with the senior air marshals of the Air Ministry in the execution of his duties.

This whole question of obeying orders emanating from higher authority, or of disregarding such orders, is one of the most important that can arise in matters of military discipline and, especially, in circumstances of war and military action. We present here a few general remarks on the subject, first because of its vital importance in itself, and second because it may be seen as a factor in Dowding's subsequent career as head of Fighter Command. That it is generally believed that military orders are sacrosanct, and to be obeyed without question, we have seen implicit in the passage quoted from Gray's history: 'the Air Ministry and the RAF had to obey orders.' This is just not true: we now have to state that in some situations it is imperative to disregard orders especially if carrying them out is likely to lead to disaster.

In English history some acts of refusal have become legendary: we think of Howard's refusal to disband his fleet on receiving Elizabeth's command with the Armada approaching, and Nelson's 'turning his blind eye' at the Battle of Copenhagen. At the Battle of Jutland Beatty sent a panicky signal which drew from Admiral Fisher the famous retort: 'Does he not know that the first principle of war is to disobey orders? Any fool can obey orders!'

The French historian Jean Norton Cru has written: '*Si les ordres avaient été obéis, à la lettre, on aurait massacré toute l'armée française avant août 1915.*'[vi] (If the orders [from Headquarters] had been carried out literally, the whole French Army would have been destroyed by May 1915.) He had preceded this startling judgement with a general comment about orders. 'Of all documents, orders are the least significant. An order is only an effective instrument in garrison life. In battle, it is annulled by the enemy who issues a counter-order. Moreover, an order is only an order if it is obeyed. It is in the barracks; it rarely is in war, at least in absolute terms. Too many factors intercede to change the situation between the issue and the receipt of the order.

Further, when it comes to disobeying, war teaches us there is a right way of going about things.'

There is another factor: the distance from the action of the authority issuing an order. In the First World War, the generals sending out orders were often fifty miles or more from the front and had no clue what was going on there. In the Battle of Britain the Commander-in-Chief and his immediate sub-commanders were at the cutting edge, and had the added advantage of being privy to the latest tactical intelligence daily, hourly, and even from minute to minute. The Air Ministry, for its part, had the regrettable tendency to offer advice or suggest courses of action precisely because their proximity to the front line conferred on them, as they thought, an equal prescience, though they lacked the very information which alone is the firm basis of reliable decision.[vii]

The events and experiences we have recounted here show that Dowding acquired early the custom of seeing for himself how things worked, a habit of mind that was to serve him well as he advanced within the Air Ministry and above all during his tenure at Fighter Command. His experience with the R.101 taught him to distrust politicians and their ways, and develop a scepticism toward the decisions and motives of the senior air marshals of the Air Ministry. This distrust and scepticism were unhappily to become intensified in the years following. And the more we study the decisions and directives sent out by the Air Ministry during the war, and the decisions that should have been taken and weren't, the more I am reminded of the chapter in Dowding's book, *Twelve Legions of Angels*, entitled 'Why are senior officers so stupid?'

Dowding overcame the R.101 decision and succeeded in establishing himself as one of the most forward-thinking officers of the Air Force. As Air Member for Research and Development he pushed for the improvement and production of radar and of the advanced fighters, which were to be christened the 'Hurricane' and the 'Spitfire'. He had to fight for these things, and to overcome the opposition of senior and 'responsible' officers living in the past. One such – and we are speaking of officers of very high rank and many years' experience (or, perhaps, of one or two years' experience repeated many times) — resisted the recommendation that the cockpit of a new fighter (it was the Gladiator) be closed. 'Gad! [we imagine him saying] I flew in an open cockpit, and what was good for me is good for these young fellers!'

We have no compunction in quoting Dowding again on this question:

One of the difficulties which confronts a person like myself in a position such as A.M.S.R [Air Member for Supply and Research] is to know when to override the advice given by professional technicians with whom he is surrounded as accredited advisers. It is a hard thing to do, but sometimes necessary when the collective official mind has got into a rut. Such a situation arose over the (then) vexed question of monoplane versus. biplane. I was advised that the biplane was superior because for a given wing area the biplane was light and stronger than the monoplane and the lower head-resistance of the monoplane did not compensate for its other handicaps. So I said: 'All right then, why didn't you choose biplanes for the Schneider Trophy?' And indeed if it had not been for our Schneider Trophy success we should have started the 1939 war with nothing faster than the Gladiator, from which the contemporary German Bombers could fly away in derision.[viii]

Here we have an instance of Dowding's remorseless logic and independence of mind, virtues that were to cause his later run-ins with Trenchard. For example, Dowding, when in Fighter Command, was occasionally invited to Air Ministry conferences to decide on the equipment needed for new types of aircraft. 'At one of these [Dowding has written] I asked that bullet-proof glass should be provided for the windscreens of the Hurricane and Spitfire. To my astonishment the whole table dissolved into gusts of laughter'. Dowding's retort was, 'If Chicago gangsters could have bullet-proof glass in their cars I could see no reason why our pilots should not have the same.'[ix] It is a black mark on the record of the Air Ministry that the windscreens of the Spitfires and Hurricanes were being replaced by bullet-proof glass as late as the summer of 1940.

It took the Air Ministry policy-makers and planners a long time to get over their most basic prejudices and blindness. Shortly after the fighting broke out on the Western Front in 1940, Squadron Leader Basil Embry (later Air Chief Marshal) was in the thick of it. When he was shot down, like dozens of his fellow-airmen, he was totally unequipped and unprepared for imprisonment or for evasion, let alone for escape. Earlier that year, he had actually written to Bomber Command recommending that aircrews be issued with the type of button compass that had been used by pilots and observers in the First World War. It was a regulation button with a difference: the inside of the button was a compass, which was obtained by unscrewing the top of the button. The reply he got was that the Air Ministry banned their use, since if the enemy learnt of it they would cut off all the captured airmen's buttons and 'How infra dig and embarrassing that would be.'!

One wonders how such men got to the top echelon of the pyramid of authority in the Air Force. Here is one opinion, that of Group Captain Ira Jones:

Towards the middle of September, 1919 . . . I saw the first complete list of officers who had been granted permanent and short-service commissions in the RAF's peacetime establishment. It was a real puzzler. How the Powers that Be had decided on those selected I cannot imagine. . . . One name on the list made me shudder. It was that of one of the greatest cowards I had known.

When it came to war in 1939, some of these people had risen to high rank and now occupied positions of authority in the Air Ministry. The Germans committed the same blunder when they came to create the Luftwaffe. Field Marshal Milch blamed Goering: 'Goering has put his old First World War comrades too much to the fore, and these are obviously not equal to the burdens of leadership that war places upon them.'

Similarly some measure of the blame for the débâcle that was to ensue in 1940 must rest on the shoulders of such throwbacks to 1918. Embry also writes:

[A] counter-attack was made [at Arras on May 21-22, 1940] without air support for the simple reason that no aircraft were available. Lord Dowding has told us since that pre-war planning had made no provision for fighters as part of the Expeditionary Force! I do not know the names of the high-ranking strategists of the time, but it is obvious that . . . they had not learned the lessons of World War One. My friends and I had always thought that during the period 1918-39 there were too many high-ranking officers with little practical experience of air warfare at the head of the RAF.

When Dowding went to Fighter Command he was faced with the huge task of creating a new organization from the ground up, to be constructed around the new fighters and the inchoate radar system which he was to be instrumental in bringing into being. His task would have been forbidding, even if he could count on the complete cooperation of the Air Staff from the beginning. But he knew the Air Staff and its workings. The Air Ministry at times gave the impression that the cooperation it accorded to Fighter Command was against its better judgement. But judgement is not a quality one attributes readily to the senior officers of the Air Staff at the historic period we are dealing with.[x]

Notes:

i. It was not until June 18 that the Prime Minister, Winston Churchill, made his stirring call to arms to the House of Commons: 'What General Weygand called the Battle of France is over. I expect that the battle of Britain is about to begin. Upon this battle depends the survival of Christian civilisation. Upon it depends our own British way of life, and the long continuity of our institutions and our Empire... Hitler knows that he will have to break us in this island or lose the war.'

ii. Reference lost. However he writes essentially the same thing in a letter to Trenchard quoted by H. Montgomery Hyde in *Solitary in the Ranks* (New York, Atheneum, 1978), p. 170-71.

iii. H.R. Allen, p. 32.

iv. In his reply to a paper submitted by Trenchard proposing the appointment of a military overlord in Britain, Churchill wrote, among other things : 'If I were convinced that this solution would bring about a speedy victory, I should be very glad to make way for him. Would it be too much to enquire whom you have in mind? You say there are many. I was not aware that our Services were so rich in talent as to have a number of officers who have already commanded in this war, who take your view about the Air, and who are capable of being the "one brain responsible for the purely military (in its widest sense) strategical conception of the war in Europe."' Ref. CHAR 20/54 A, dated September 4, 1942. (The Sir Winston Churchill Archive Trust, Churchill College Cambridge.)

v. 'Personal Notes', pp. 147-48.

vi. Jean Norton Cru, *Témoins* (Paris, 'Les Étincelles', MCMXXIX), p.20. The following quote is my translation. I am indebted to Dr. Peter Bradley of the Royal Military College, Kingston, Ontario, for this reference.

vii. It is likely that these experiences lay at the root of Dowding's intervention in the War Cabinet of June 3. Dowding might also have learnt this difficult lesson from the First World War, when Haig's intelligence officer shied away from incurring the Field Marshal's displeasure by conveying unwelcome intelligence to him, a cowardice that cost us tens of thousands of brave lives. The Fisher quip is quoted in Arthur Herman, *To Rule the Waves* (New York, HarperCollins, 2004), p. 502.

viii. 'Personal Notes', p. 157

ix. 'Personal Notes', p. 159. Living in the past and the refusal to accept new ideas is an infirmity of the human mind; certainly it has been endemic in military circles. For example, Norman Dixon (p. 119) quotes thus from David Divine's *The Blunted Sword*: 'Of the twenty major technological developments which lie between the first marine engine and the Polaris submarine, the Admiralty machine has discouraged, delayed, obstructed or positively rejected seventeen.' Dixon preceded this dismal recital by stating that 'even in 1938 one of the main preoccupations of the new C.I.G.S., Lord Gort, was how to get rid of Major-General Hobart, leading specialist in tank warfare.'

x. Another case in point. We quote from Dowding's *Twelve Legions* (p. 34) : 'No specific provision for field force fighters had been made, and all the fighters had to be provided at the expense of the Home Defence organization.' This blunder on the part of the Air Ministry is one of the causes of recrimination at the root of the subsequent fight he had with the War Cabinet to retain as many full, operational front-line squadrons in the UK for the battle that he foresaw would come.

CHAPTER 2

Seeds of Discord

—ɯ—

The Personal Factor

Dowding has written, albeit summarily, of the stresses that he endured while directing his slender forces during the Battle, a stress that is in its intensity almost unimaginable to most men. In 1959 he wrote these words in his Foreword to Alan Deere's book: 'Even after all these years I can scarcely bear to be brought back to the atmosphere of those days because of the almost intolerable memory of stress and sadness which it engenders.'

The years 1936 to 1940 were equally years of stress, but stress of a different kind. Throughout those years he was driven by the imperious need and task that he kept always in the clear focus of his mind : to provide an effective defence of Great Britain against a possible aerial attack.

As the weeks and months and years went by, Dowding became increasingly anxious and frustrated by the slowness of the construction of the defensive apparatus. He has expressed that anxiety in a pithy summing-up:

> 'The defence of the country had been allowed for too long to exist in a state of grave inefficiency. I was continually having to fight that situation while there was yet time.'[i]

It is impossible for us to put ourselves in Dowding's shoes and form even a remote idea of the problems he faced at the time. It goes without saying that if he had not been a perfectionist – that is, if he had not been imbued with a sense of the gravity of the task entrusted to him by the Air Ministry, and an idealist to boot – he would not have been Dowding, and the battle would have been lost.

The problems he faced at Fighter Command were unbelievably complex, and necessarily interrelated. We will draw up a list, in no sort of order here, which can be only partial:

- shortage of aircraft and related equipment
- lack of anti-aircraft armament
- training of plotters for the Operations Rooms
- selection of sites for the early warning stations
- testing of RDF equipment
- installation of RDF towers and stations around the east and south coasts from Scotland to Cornwall

• selection of Observer Corps coastal sites and the selection and training of Observers
• integration of the Observer Corps sightings at their coastal stations with the RDF reports
• installation and testing of a network of telephone landlines
• organization of a search-and-rescue service to locate and recover pilots downed in the Channel
• provision of concrete runways in the place of grass fields.[ii]

The list is interminable. The mental and physical energy expended by the Commander-in-Chief, fighting against a deadline that seemed to shrink with the deteriorating political situation in Europe from month to month, leaves one aghast merely in contemplating it.

A recent biographer, David E. Fisher, has summed up this achievement of Dowding's :

If he had been only the man who pushed through the development of the eight-gun monoplane fighters that won the battle ... If he had been only the first military man to understand the promise of radar, and who had the faith to base his defenses on it ... If he had been only the man who fought to implement the supporting facilities–the Ops Rooms, Controllers, WAAFs, and complex underground telephone system–that made it possible for the radar to work ... If he had been, finally, only the man who understood what was at stake in the battle–as his adversary, Hermann Goering, did not–- and who thus set in place the strategy that won ... If he had been any one of these men he would take his place among the heroes of the Second World War. But he did it all.[iii]

The correspondence and personal encounters between the Air Ministry and Fighter Command – who should have been working together towards a shared cause – served instead only to exacerbate their differences and to poison their relations. Both of Dowding's early biographers, Collier and Wright, have dwelt on this question. Collier, in particular, has well summarized the relations that developed between Dowding and the Air Ministry, and looked behind the façade to catch a glimpse of the personalities:

Dowding's knowledge of air defence and his understanding of its problems were unrivalled... At heart he did not dissent from the orthodox view that ultimately only offensive measures could bring success. He held merely that the strategists must be careful not to lose the war before they had a chance of winning it. But he had urged his case so vehemently and pertinaciously that his assent to orthodoxy might well be doubted. Consistent and unyielding where others at times were weak and hesitant, he seemed one who might not easily be persuaded to bow to ex cathedra rulings where the balance to be struck between offensive and defensive preoccupations was in question. He had not shown himself particularly amenable to guidance in the past, and he might not prove so in the future. Like all men, he had made mistakes, though fewer, perhaps, than most of his contemporaries. But he had been so often right in his frequent conflicts with the Air Ministry that the few occasions when he was wrong were not likely to be forgotten.[iv]

The qualities that lay behind Dowding's achievement must finally have dawned upon the governing authorities of the Air Ministry, for on September 19 Dowding received this letter signed by A.W. Street, Permanent Secretary of the Air Council:

> I am to confirm that full operational control of the active air defences of Great Britain, consisting of the Observer Corps, Fighter and Balloon units of the Royal Air Force and gun and searchlight units of the Army, is vested in yourself as A.O.C.-in-C. Fighter Command.[v]

Despite all that had been happening in the rapid expansion of the Royal Air Force, and the cataclysm that had overtaken the world with its immediate threat to this country, Dowding was still under notice, which he fully understood and accepted: he was to relinquish his command and retire from the Royal Air Force on 31 March. He had made his plans with that firmly in mind. War does worse than disrupt people's lives. Nevertheless, in view of his position, and ill-treated though he had been by the Air Ministry, he could not have expected the next letter. Only the day before he was due to go, he received a long letter from the Chief of the Air Staff that threw everything yet again into the melting pot.

> On the 20th March last year I wrote to ask you if you would defer your retirement until the end of March, 1940. [He made no mention of that date being the very next day.] Even at that time of disturbed and uneasy peace your Command was of the very greatest importance, and since then war has intervened with a consequent increase in your responsibilities. In the circumstances it has been decided to ask you to continue in your present position until July 14th of this year, on which date you will have completed four years as Air Officer Commanding-in-Chief.

With all that was staring the country in the face, this was a postponement of only three and a half months, and in its own way illustrated the unreality of the thinking of that time, especially when it came to planning for even the immediate future. Newall continued:

> I shall personally be very glad if you are willing to accept this extension as I feel it would be undesirable for a change to take place at Fighter Command at this stage when we may be on the verge of intensified air activity. Whether that be so or not, I am well aware how high the efficiency of Fighter Command stands today and I fully realise how much we owe to your personal leadership in preparing the command and bringing it so successfully into action.

Despite the upheaval that this latest notice meant for him so late in the day, Dowding felt that all that Newall was saying was pleasant enough, and obviously well-intentioned, and that after the objection he had raised a year ago, it would not be advisable to go over all that again. But there was nevertheless something of a sting in the tail of Newall's letter, which read:

> As I mentioned to you previously, I have the uncongenial task of informing the more senior officers in the Service when it becomes necessary to call upon them to make way for others in order to keep up a sufficient flow of promotions. I must now confirm the information that, so far as can at present be seen, it will be necessary for you to retire when you relinquish your Command on July 14th next. An official letter to this effect will be sent to you in due course. I know you will appreciate the difficulties involved in this decision, and believe me when I say that the Royal Air Force as a whole will greatly regret the conclusion of your active duties in the Service.[vi]

The message was clear: Dowding was to relinquish his command and retire. He had now only to make his plans with the new date in mind. In his reply, the next day, Dowding merely stated: 'I shall be glad to continue in my present Command until July 14th of this year.'

Dowding was to receive no official letter, which Newall had said would "be sent to you in due course", as was customary, confirming the extension of Dowding's last few weeks of service in the Royal Air Force until 14 July. Perhaps his tutelary deity had taken a leave of absence at this juncture, for Dowding did not get his way. It was almost as if he suspected something, for he sent a copy of this letter to the new Secretary of State for Air, Sir Archibald Sinclair. Sinclair had been appointed to the Air Ministry by his friend Churchill on May 12th, two days after Churchill became Prime Minister. It seems that some member or members of the Air Council or Air Staff were not slow in working on Sinclair, for, despite the visible evidences of Dowding's accomplishments, he (or they) took little time in convincing Sinclair that Dowding's appointment should be terminated. Sinclair mentioned this to Churchill and got the following sharp retort:

> I was very much taken aback the other night when you told me you been considering removing Sir Hugh Dowding at the expiration of his present appointment ....Personally, I think he is one of the very best men you have got, and I say this after having been in contact with him for about two years. I have greatly admired the whole of his work in the Fighter Command, and especially in resisting the clamour for numerous air raid warnings, and the immense pressure to dissipate the Fighter strength during the great French battle. In fact he has my full confidence. I think it is a pity for an officer so gifted and so trusted to be working on such a short tenure as four months, and I hope you will consider whether it is not in the public interest that his appointment should be indefinitely prolonged while the war lasts. This would not of course exclude his being moved to a higher position, if that were thought necessary.[vii]

Sinclair oscillated, this time in the right direction. On that very same day, July 10th, he wrote in reply to Dowding's letter – with a marked change of tone and attitude. It was, said Sinclair, 'my wish that you should remain in command of our Fighter Squadrons, upon whose success in defeating the German attack upon our munitions factories during the next three months will almost certainly depend the issue of this war.'

It is easy to distinguish, in this simple-seeming statement, the influence of Churchill's grasp of events and the contrasting contribution of the Air Minister. That the outcome of the war depended on Fighter Command, and that the issue would be decided in the next three months, had been the theme of one of Churchill's inspiring speeches. But to suggest that Dowding was 'in command of our Fighter Squadrons' and that the Germans would attack mainly the munitions factories reveals more than anything else that Sinclair was totally out of touch with the realities of Fighter Command and of probable German aims.

Sinclair concluded his letter thus: 'I could give you no higher proof of my confidence in you and, although it seems superfluous, let me add the assurance of my full support.' (The change that takes place in Sinclair's attitude in the next three short months, without a word of explanation, will stagger the reader and remind him of Dowding's distrust of the politician's word.) Newall wrote too, and apologized to Dowding, but he explained that among the other considerations he had to weigh when making changes in command was the need 'to maintain an adequate flow of promotions into the higher positions in the Service.' Poor Newall! The very fate of the country is to be decided by an imminent massive aerial onslaught by enemy bombers, and Newall and the Air Staff are wrestling with problems of 'an adequate flow of promotions' in the RAF! How deadening to the mind are the routines of a bureaucratic system!

Finally, Dowding also received an official letter from the Air Ministry: 'I am commanded by the Air Council to refer to personal correspondence between yourself and the Chief of the Air Staff and to enquire whether you would be good enough to accept an extension of your employment with the Royal Air Force until 31st October 1940.' The change in tone must have been gratifying. But the new date showed a certain calculation: it seemed to cover the estimated three months during which the success (or otherwise) of the German attacks and of Fighter Command's defences would be decided.

Were Sinclair's confidence and expression of support genuine? Was Newall's apology genuine? If they were extending Dowding's 'employment' by only three months, they could afford to be conciliatory and reasonable. Was the Air Ministry's new courtesy genuine? The question is important, for the Air Ministry had the means to make and break officers' careers. Up to now, the relations between Dowding and the Air Ministry had been stormy, and they were at that point deteriorating. Well, they too could afford to be courteous, since Dowding would be out of their hair for good in three months. One will never know whether their courtesy was genuine or not, for they were simply following the instructions of Newall and Sinclair.

The picture was to brighten suddenly for Dowding in an unexpected way. Three days later, on July 13th, Dowding was included among the guests who dined at Chequers with the Prime Minister. Churchill and Dowding talked about the forthcoming battle and Fighter Command. Dowding wrote to Sinclair about it the following day; the Prime Minister, he said, 'was good enough to tell me that I had secured his confidence, and that he wished me to remain on the Active List for the time being, without any date for my retirement being fixed. He told me that he had written to you on the subject.' Dowding took pains to ensure that Sinclair knew about his, Dowding's, role in this new development: 'In case you should think that his [Churchill's] intervention was something more than coincidence, I may tell you that neither he nor any other minister was made aware of my approaching retirement through any action or word of mine.'

The Luftwaffe's assault, on shipping in the Channel initially, had already begun on July 9th; and Messerschmitts had already, on the 9th, begun to look successfully for prey. With his retirement deferred, Dowding was able to turn his attentions to the battle. Yet doubts must have nagged at the back of his mind,as a whole month elapsed before Dowding received confirmation.

Finally, on August 12th, with the battle about to be joined in earnest, he received a letter from Newall. 'When I wrote to you on July 13th, I could not see any alternative to indicating the end of October as the time for your retirement. [No alternative? Newall is sparing in his explanation. How had things changed?] In the present circumstances, however, I fully realize the disadvantages involved in this decision and I am now glad to be able to say that it has been decided to cancel the time limit to the period of your appointment as C-in-C Fighter Command. I sincerely hope that this information will be agreeable to you.'

Dowding still had to wait a further ten days to receive an official letter to confirm that 'information'. He received, on August 22nd, at a stage in the battle when his vital airfields were being subjected to damaging and worrying attacks, and his losses were mounting, a letter from the Air Ministry which reverted to their customary clinical formality. 'I am commanded by the Air Council to refer to their letter dated 13th July 1940, reference 809403/38/57c and to inform you that they have decided to cancel the time limit to the period of your appointment as Air Officer Commanding-in-Chief, Fighter Command.'

With his eye and his sensitivity to nuances, Dowding noted that Newall's letter referred to both 'the period of (his) appointment' and his 'retirement'. The Air Ministry letter, on the other hand, mentioned only 'the period of (his) appointment'. He noted also that Newall had made no reference to Churchill's letter to Sinclair and to Churchill's wishes in the matter. And here, presumably, the matter stood: leaving Dowding in the dark as to when his appointment would terminate, and whether at the end of it he would be retired or offered a new appointment.

Dowding was again free to devote himself to the defence of his country, seemingly secure in his belief that in a fortnight's time he would not be receiving yet another deadline and notice of termination of employment. During that crucial time when it seemed that the German concentrated attacks against the sector stations might prevail, Fighter Command stood firm.

But other clouds were gathering on the horizon for Dowding.

Questions of Doctrine

Of all Dowding's battles with the Air Ministry none gave rise to greater resistance on the Air Ministry's part, and hence to greater persistence and dogged insistence on Dowding's part, than the fundamental task of Fighter Command. The lesson that Dowding had to teach was nothing other than the fundamental differences between strategy and tactics, and the fundamentally different aims of defence and offence.

The strategic thinking of the Air Ministry had been suggested in the doctrine expounded by the Italian Air Force's General Giulio Douhet in a series of articles which were collected in a book entitled *The Command of the Air*. But there were radical differences between Douhet's teaching and the policy that became known as the Trenchard Doctrine. This doctrine was summed up dogmatically in the course of a dispute between Lord Swinton, the then Air minister, and Sir Thomas Inskip, over strategic priorities: 'The bomber force is fundamentally the basis of all air strategy.'[viii] The crucial question was: how was this strategy to be carried out against the enemy? Malcolm Smith describes succinctly the way it was meant to work:

> They [the British airmen] claimed that the advantages open to attacking bombers were manifest, the vast cubic airspaces available, which would make it nigh impossible for defenders to guess the direction of attack or even the target; and stable gun platform available to the larger aircraft if defending fighters should find them in the first place. These advantages meant, as Stanley Baldwin later famously put it, that the bomber would always get through. This being so, there was simply no need to target the enemy air force. The implications were that close fighter defence was largely a waste of time and that its provision should be confined only to the most significant of national targets.[ix]

This doctrine was enunciated at a time when there was no difference in performance between bomber and fighter. The power of air forces was to be demonstrated convincingly by the Italians against the defenceless, people of Abyssinia in 1935, and by the Germans against some towns in the Spanish Civil War. It was to be demonstrated once more against Warsaw in 1939 and against Rotterdam in 1940. An historian of air warfare sums up the situation in this way:

> The irony of the situation was that at the very time that the RAF reemphasized its commitment in the mid-1930s to a strategic bombing force, other British airmen were at the forefront in the development of a theory of air defence. The bomber theorists of the 1920s had rested much of their case on the belief that there was little effective defence against bombing. Douhet wrote that 'the aeroplane is not adaptable to defence' and that 'nothing man can do on the surface of the earth can interfere with a plane in flight'. By the time Baldwin made his remark that 'the bomber will always get through', the disparity in performance between fighter and bomber aircraft was still so low that the prospect of a successful fighter defence seemed correspondingly unlikely.[x]

This was still the attitude and policy which prevailed in the Air Ministry when Fighter Command was created and when Dowding became its first commander. Nothing seems more likely to refute the notion that Dowding was sent to Fighter Command in the belief that the Air Ministry had finally seen the light, than the struggle that he had to wage, for four long years, from 1936 to 1940, in order to build Fighter Command into a strong defensive force capable of withstanding and repelling any assault against the home base.

The shift towards a mixed air doctrine of defence and offence was met with some reluctance by those in the RAF who favoured the bombing strategy. To admit that there was a defence against the bomber was to question the whole basis upon which an independent air force had been built.

If Dowding had been totally alone in his mission to convert Whitehall to thinking fighters, he must have failed. The fact is that in 1936 a new office was created in the Government, that of Coordinator of Defence. The first, and only, incumbent was Sir Thomas Inskip. The doctrine which bears his name, as enunciated in his Report of 1937, challenged the principles of air strategy which had been the very basis of British air policy since the early 1920s. What it did was to question, undermine, and finally to brush aside the policy of parity with the growing German air force, with its overriding emphasis on the offensive, and the bomber. The Inskip Doctrine made a clear separation between offence and defence, and laid the primary emphasis on the defence of the home base. The Cabinet accepted Inskip's recommendations on December 22nd, 1937. 'The air marshals raged, and Trenchard declared in the House of Lords that the decision "might well lose us the war".'

Inskip's iconoclastic doctrine was not inspired by strategic insight or vision. It found its origin in a Treasury report. From it Inskip realized that it was beyond Britain's economic capacity in the short term to build both defensive and offensive arms. If there had to be a choice, that choice had to fall first on defence; Britain's strength, and Germany's weakness, lay in a long term conflict. The longer and more drawn-out a war was, the greater the likelihood that Britain would outlast Germany. The time to construct a heavy, strategic bomber force would come after the security of the home base had been assured. That security could only be attempted –no talk of assured – by the creation of a fighter force. There is, however, little evidence to suggest that Inskip had any idea what would be required to bring into being a fighter force adequate to parry a determined German aerial onslaught, even without fighter escorts.

Notwithstanding the priority given to the defence of Great Britain as a strategic policy by the Government, especially from 1937, the Air Staff never let up on its insistence on the greater importance of a strong bomber force. The new CAS in 1937 was Newall. The Director of Plans had been Group Captain Arthur Harris, who was succeeded in May 1937 by Group Captain John Slessor. Both were staunch bomber men. Moreover, the Air Staff were totally unconvinced that Fighter Command could put up an adequate defence against a determined enemy onslaught by, say, 1940, no matter how great the resources devoted to its preparations. As late as 1938, the Air Ministry put forward yet another scheme, this one known as Scheme L, which called for a front line force of 1320 bombers, making allowance for only 554 fighters. 'The views of the Air Staff grew increasingly unrealistic during 1938 and 1939. . . . By this stage . . . the Air Staff arguments had all the appearance of whistling in the wind. The Munich crisis and its aftermath lent an air of unreality to the last-ditch stand of the Air Staff on the bomber deterrent.'

Long before Munich, criticism of the Air Ministry had been gathering steam. To cite an extreme example: on April 2nd 1938 the Permanent Under-Secretary of the Treasury (who was also the Head of the Civil Service), Sir Warren Fisher, sent an uncompromising report to the Prime Minister, Neville Chamberlain, scathing in its indictment of the Air Ministry, which, he said, had been dishing up nothing but 'soothing syrup and incompetence' for some years. He gave the comparative strengths of the German Air Force and the Royal Air Force and concluded that as a consequence 'for the first time in centuries our country is (and must continue to be) at the mercy of a foreign power'. Fisher repeated this condemnation after Munich. But the accusation, though no doubt motivated by deep concern for the safety of his country, harked back to the abandoned policy of parity. There was truth in it, and a woeful unfairness. It was unfair because it was the Government, the politicians, who were entirely responsible for allowing Britain's defences to have evaporated to an ineffective obsolescence. The Air Ministry's culpability lay in its over-riding faith in a bomber force as both an offensive and a defensive arm.

The Battle of Britain proved beyond all question that 'the bomber would not always get through.' Moreover, the Blitz that the German air force launched against British cities and other targets from early September 1940 to late May 1941 demonstrated a) that night attacks were not capable of hitting their supposed targets most of the time, and b) that what damage they did inflict on civilians and their houses – and they were considerable – had little effect either on war production or on the morale of the people. But the Air Staff did not learn these lessons. They were resolutely committed to the Trenchard doctrine of bombing Germany into submission by their own unaided efforts, despite the obvious fact that the British bombers, obsolete as they were, were even less capable of inflicting any real damage on the German industries and populace than the Germans had on British targets.

But the Germans learnt the lessons, and they inflicted crippling losses on our airmen. One of the chapters of Dowding's book *Twelve Legions of Angels* is entitled, 'Why are senior officers so stupid?' He includes examples of his own stupidity, but he has in mind chiefly the officers of the Air Staff; they held fixedly to a strategic doctrine of air power despite the evidence surrounding them that they had no means to carry out their policy, and despite advances in technology which suggested the opposite. Dowding makes a telling point in his dealings with the Air Ministry when trying to get them to decide on the issue of competing demands for fighters made by the Army and by Home Defence:

> I wanted to get a principle laid down before a war started rather than leave
> matters in a hopeful haze and have a bitter dispute at a critical period of the

war... I had two answers from the C.A.S. One was that Attack was the best form of Defence, and the other was that in no circumstances would any Expeditionary Force leave our Country until the safety of our Homeland was assured. I still can't make up my mind which of these answers is the sillier.[x]

In the light of the mulish persistence that prevailed in the Air Staff over these questions of strategy and tactics, we can see just how difficult Dowding's long, uphill battle to get them to understand the very first article of all strategic thinking – the security of the home base – was.

In his correspondence with the Air Staff, Dowding showed himself a master of sharp rejoinder which does little to conceal the writer's view of the mental equipment of his adversary. Sure of his ground, convinced that he was right, and confident of a favourable reception before the supreme tribunal of his conscience, he was not an easy man to argue with. An expert in air defence, for six years holder of the highest technical posts in the Royal Air Force, he had the advantage of understanding many issues better then anyone outside his own headquarters could hope to understand them. Lifted above compunction by the vision of calamity impending, the iconoclast of Bentley Priory demolished, and with what sometimes seemed unholy glee, the hierophants of Whitehall used pious evasion to cloak official reluctance to surrender to Dowding's logic.[xi]

This view is supported by Dowding's personal assistant, Flight Lieutenant Wilkinson, as reported by Robert Wright:

In what to Dowding was the Air Staff's grave lack of realism, that was one of the main reasons for the differences of opinions . . . between him and the Air Ministry. 'The fundamental stupidity of too many people on the Air Staff was almost unbelievable,' Francis Wilkinson has commented. When Francis was challenged on the reason for his feeling that way, he snapped: 'I didn't just feel it! I knew it from what Dowding was having to put up with. What used to beat me completely was how those people could sit up there in their ignorance and have the audacity to set themselves up to pass judgment on matters that they simply didn't seem to be able to understand.' The vehemence of that statement was to find some support in my own experience in serving under Dowding later in the year, and an even stronger support when, over the years since then, a closer examination was made of the treatment that was accorded Dowding.[xii]

It is hardly surprising, therefore, that when the fighting actually started, the Air Staff would manifest a woeful incomprehension in another area of Fighter Command's concerns:

In the fighting that started on May 10, the severe losses of aircraft, including fighters, suffered by the RAF caused an alarm in high quarters that was so sudden that to Dowding it approached imbecility. He was told by a Senior officer on the Air Staff of the Air Ministry, who had come to report to him, about the grave losses of Hurricanes that were being reported from France, as though such losses were a complete surprise. 'What do you expect?' Dowding snapped, finding it hard to contain himself. 'When you get into a war you have to lose things, including precious aircraft. That's exactly what I've been warning you about.'

After all the wretchedness, it affords us a pleasurable relief to turn to three eminent figures who co-operated with Dowding and gave him a measure of support and assistance without which even Dowding, as he testified later, would have had difficulty in carrying on. They were Sir Henry Tizard, Lord Beaverbrook and General Pile.

The treatment of Sir Henry Tizard by the Air Ministry and others was worse. To begin with, he was not an employee of the Air Ministry; he had no official position, but fulfilled the office of personal adviser to the Chief of the Air Staff on scientific matters. He was the Rector of Imperial College London and a renowned physicist, who gave of his time, learning and advice unstintingly, without remuneration, and with the full consent of his Board of Governors, out of a sense of duty to his country. The priceless worth of his contribution to the Royal Air Force and his country can best be grasped from this appreciation written by Sir Solly Zuckerman in his Foreword to Clark's biography:

> Tizard's single greatest achievement [he wrote] was the encouragement he gave to the development of the chain of radar stations which assured the RAF's victory in the Battle of Britain. None of the scientific ideas behind radar was his, but without his support, backed by the prestige gained through many years of intimate and successful co-operation with members of the Air Staff, it is doubtful if our defences would have held in those vital days of 1940. Tizard's own place in history is secure for this contribution alone.

Since the first meeting in January 1935, Tizard had been the energetic and forceful chairman of the Committee for the Scientific Survey of Air Defence — the Tizard Committee, as it became known. This committee, comprising a number of eminent scientists, was founded when the potential of Radio Direction Finding (RDF) was first demonstrated. However, Tizard's report to the Air Ministry that 'a practical system for detecting and locating aircraft fifty miles away could be developed' provoked a certain resistance. The reaction of one high officer is typical of many at the time. 'Why', said he, 'if that is possible the whole plan of Air Defence will be revolutionized!' Tizard's retort was to start revolutionizing it without delay. This was just a taste of the opposition to be put up by dinosaurs 'resolutely preparing for the last war.'

Tizard and Dowding not only worked together harmoniously for four years, the scientist admiring the airman for his prescience and his appreciation of scientific problems, and the airman admiring the scientist for his understanding of the air and problems of defence: their correspondence shows a relationship that was personal and warm.

Beaverbrook was the Minister for Aircraft Production. Every morning he telephoned Dowding to ask him what he could do for him. Always the same answer came back: More Spitfires! Better performance! More speed! Longer range! Heavier armament! No doubt Beaverbrook derived a double pleasure from treating Dowding with deference. He too had his difficulties with the Air Ministry and its red tape, and became a second thorn in their side. But the professional results of the relationship between the two men was what irked the Air Ministry most keenly, for it removed from their authority an important strategic role which was theirs by right, namely, the decision over the types of aircraft to be built. Beaverbrook, on Dowding's urging, gave overwhelming priority to fighters.

General Pile was the commanding general responsible for all anti-aircraft units, guns and personnel. Every morning at ten o'clock Pile would report to Dowding and they would have a free and frank discussion of Dowding's needs. Pile's daily visits, when Dowding frequently unburdened himself to him, were savoured by Dowding; and the warmth of their personal relations was a salutary counter-balance to the acrimony which so often embittered his relations with the Air Ministry. Pile reports that, on his daily visits, Dowding talked freely and volubly, to a sympathetic ear, about the problems he was having with the Air Ministry. It is a very great shame that Pile did not keep a diary of his meetings with Dowding. (In this same vein, the Queen, when she visited Fighter Command Headquarters with the King, recalled that Dowding entertained her with a continuous flow of talk about Fighter Command.)

No one has ever disputed the contention that Dowding's every act and word was motivated by the need to strengthen Fighter Command, and to protect the sanctity of the home base – to save England from invasion and defeat. No Air Ministry historian or apologist has dared to try to account for Dowding's alleged uncooperativeness, instead putting his supposed 'cussedness' down to a personality defect. But these traits were the product of his having to fight for everything that Fighter Command needed to win the battle to come, and the battle that came.

If one who, having read at least some of the correspondence which passed between Dowding and the Air Ministry, puts himself in the position of the Air Staff and tries to view Dowding from their perspective, Dowding would appear, it is true, a difficult person to deal with. He was prickly, argumentative, stubborn, strong-willed, tenacious, obstinate, unyielding. Even his friend General Pile said of him: 'A difficult man, a self-opinionated man, a most determined man, and a man who knew, more than anybody, about all aspects of aerial warfare.' But then, as he also said of him in the same appraisal: 'Of the great Service leaders, Dowding was the outstanding airman I met in the war.'

Notes:

i. 'Personal Notes', p. 180. See also Collier and Wright. Excerpts from Dowding's 'Personal Notes' – see Bibliography – have been selected and presented in Appendix 'A'.

ii. As late as 1937 not a single aerodrome of Fighter Command had a concrete runway. Grass fields are subject to inclement weather. So bad was the winter of 1936-37, Dowding's first winter with Fighter Command, that no flying was possible for three weeks at Kenley, a vital link in the system defending London. The situation was so bad that Dowding had to warn the Air Ministry that in the event of his aerodromes being out of action for only half a day, 'it might have the most serious consequences.' Collier concludes his account as follows: 'Runways were long opposed by the Air Ministry on the ground that they did not lend themselves to the accepted principles of camouflage.' But at last persistence triumphed over official obtuseness: Dowding got some of his runways. But it wasn't until March 1939 that the Air Ministry agreed to Dowding's appeal for all-weather runways and perimeter tracks to dispersals. Moreover, when war came, the Air Ministry had made no provision for the repair of bombed airfields. A conspicuous instance occurred on August 28, when Churchill visited Manston, the RAF's most forward airfield, in East Kent. He saw bomb damage unrepaired since several days earlier, and wrote angrily to Sinclair and Portal about it. Park also got into the action when he saw his airfields bombed and left with craters. He had to borrow some local Army personnel to repair the damage, and said: 'I was severely criticized by the Air Ministry for accepting Army assistance.' He added: 'Had my fighter aerodromes been put out of action, the German Air Force would have won the Battle by 15 September'.

iii. The most significant omission from this list is the decision that Dowding himself considered the most crucial decision of his entire career, namely, his confrontation with Churchill and his refusal to send any more fighters to France.

iv. Collier, pp.159-60.

v. PRO AIR 2 4195. The reader will note the emphasis on the element of personal responsibility that this injunction places on Dowding.

vi. Correspondence quoted in Wright.

vii. The idea of moving Dowding to a higher position – which could only mean the office of the Chief of the Air Staff – must have caused a panic wave in Sinclair's heart! Ref. CHAR 20/2 A, July 10, 1940.

viii. H. Montgomery Hyde, p. 409.

ix. Malcolm Smith, 'The RAF', in Addison, p.23. See Smith's *British Air Strategy Between the Wars*, especially chapter two. He writes, for example (pp. 64-65): 'the British air theory only superficially resembled that of Douhet and was a quite separate development. It can be stated quite categorically that the British air theory was entirely home-grown.' The reader is also referred, for a critique of Trenchard's theory, to 'Freeman's letter to Portal on bombing policy' in Furse, Appendix VI, pp. 312-14.

x. Smith, p. 115. Dowding's expression 'before the war started' is telling. See also his concern about preparing an adequate defence 'while there is yet time' on page 25. Throughout the period of the creation of Fighter Command's defensive system Dowding was fighting what seemed a losing battle against time. I am reminded of General Douglas Mac Arthur's statement about being 'too late': 'The history of failure in war can almost be summed up in two words: too late. Too late in comprehending the deadly purpose of a potential enemy; too late in realizing the mortal danger; too late in preparedness; too late in uniting all possible forces for resistance; too late in standing with one's friends.' The 'friends' are the British: the General's statement, brief as it is, is reproduced in Appendix 'B'.

xi. Collier, pp. 163-64.

xii. Wright, p. 79.

CHAPTER 3

Questions of Tactics

—⚍—

The historical record, and the actual results of the protracted air battles over England in August, September and October of 1940, are beyond dispute. Yet the debate about tactics lingers on. The dispute in question is called the 'wings' debate.[i] This controversy has become an inescapable feature of any study that deals with the Battle of Britain and with the fate of the Commander of Fighter Command. If we bring the matter up once again, and hopefully for the last time, it is solely because Dowding himself believed that his removal from his command in November was directly related to his handling of the battle. He based this belief on what happened at the conference at the Air Ministry in October. This conference, organized and manipulated by the D-CAS, Sholto Douglas, for the purpose of undermining Dowding's and Park's authority, had the ulterior motive of promoting Douglas's own claim to superior expertise in matters of air warfare. We will show that Dowding was mistaken in his belief, but correct in his suspicion; while we will also show that Douglas was wrong in his ideas, and dishonourable in the means he used to achieve his ends.

The 'wings' dispute refers to a disagreement between two factions within Fighter Command itself, and between Fighter Command and the Air Ministry. It centred on the question of whether single squadrons or pairs of squadrons acting independently but together, or wings of three or more squadrons under a single commander, was the more effective answer to the German daytime attacks. We do not intend to review the whole controversy and its history. We will limit ourselves to an examination of the actual results achieved by the 'wings' as they were formed, used, and led; and to an analysis of the Air Ministry conference.[ii]

For purposes of defence against aerial attack by enemy forces, the Fighter Command divided the United Kingdom into regions on geographical lines. Each region was defended by a Group, with each Group deploying a number of fighter squadrons based at certain Air Force stations. The regions closest to the enemy protected the most vital potential targets: airfields, aircraft manufacturing plants, heavy industry, ports, centres of government. The two Groups closest to the enemy were the one defending the south and south-east, including London, and the other defending the east coast and central England, including the industrial Midlands.

When Fighter Command was established in 1936, and during the following three years when Dowding was building its foundations and infrastructure, the only threat to Great Britain came from Germany, whose bombers would have had to fly across the North Sea. At that time, therefore, the brunt of the defence would have been borne by 12 Group, defending the Midlands. For that reason, it was on the east coast that the first radar early warning stations were erected. After the defeat of France in June 1940, and the subsequent occupation of French airfields by the Luftwaffe, the main thrust of the aerial assault came from the south; and the tactical centre of gravity shifted onto 11 Group.

There was an additional factor, one which ultimately made all the difference between success and failure. That was that bombers taking off from France would have fighter escorts, an impossibility for bombers starting from Germany because of the range. As the battle evolved, the German tactics, which changed constantly, were devised to entice the British fighters into the air, to be dealt with by the German fighters, while the bombers carried out their bombing.

The strategy devised by Dowding, and followed without deviation throughout the Battle, was to take such measures as were required to conserve Fighter Command as a fighting force, and ensure that there were always squadrons in the south to meet incoming attacks, while other squadrons were held in the north and west to defend their own areas. In order to understand how it was that the German Air Force, with its numerical superiority and the advantage of the initiative, failed to secure a victory by destroying Fighter Command as a prelude to establishing air supremacy and to invading England, one must study the role played in the air fighting by the system of control exercised over the RAF's fighter squadrons from the ground.

The chain of radar stations around Britain, established through the energies and genius of Watson Watt and Tizard, received signals indicating enemy aircraft or formations approaching. The information was not always accurate or complete – we are talking about the earliest, pioneering days of radar– but the interpreters did well to form an estimate of numbers, altitude, and bearing.

The masses of information were received at Fighter Command HQ, analysed and 'filtered' there, and passed on to the Groups. The Group Headquarters passed the relevant information to Sectors, who 'scrambled', or dispatched, a certain number of fighters, according to Group's instructions. The number of fighters – one or two sections, one squadron, or two squadrons or more – depended on the number available, the estimated number of enemy aircraft, and the distance between enemy and interceptors. The essence of the defensive system is summed up in the concept and the word: control. The radar receivers plotted both enemy aircraft and defending fighters. The fighters were 'controlled', that is, they were under strict orders to fly where and when they were so ordered to do in order to effect an interception. For the Group HQ and sectors alone could 'see' both; and the sector controller alone could direct his fighters to a position from which to intercept the enemy most advantageously to the defenders. It was only when the fighter leader actually sighted the enemy aircraft that he was released from control, and only then did he deploy his fighters and give instructions for engaging the enemy.[iii]

Air Vice-Marshal Keith Park, the AOC of 11 Group, whose squadrons were based close to France, and to the attackers, seldom had sufficient time to send off more than two squadrons together to meet any one raid; and because of the sheer limitations of his airfields, he did not have the resources to send more than two; most often it was a single squadron, or even half a squadron. For it was essential to keep other squadrons in a state of readiness, in anticipation of other raiders coming in. As it was, Park's resources were such that it was not unknown for some squadrons to be 'scrambled' three, four, or even five times in a single day.

To the north of 11 Group, in 12 Group, as the battle wore on, some people, honorably motivated, seeing their 11 Group comrades constantly outnumbered, believed that, because of their greater distance from the action, they had the time to assemble three, four, or even five squadrons in a wing, and thus meet the enemy on more even numerical terms and inflict heavier casualties on them. This idea of wings took such a hold in the minds of some pilots that, feeling justifiably frustrated by being left out of the action, they began muttering criticisms of Park, and even of Dowding, for not trying out a few wings of several squadrons.

Now, few men knew more about fighter tactics than Park. Numerical superiority is a principle of war as old as the hills; no commander would have seized the opportunity more keenly and promptly than Park, had he been able. In 12 Group, one pilot in particular was noted for his enthusiastic and vocal championing of the 'wings' idea. He was Squadron Leader Douglas Bader. Bader was the commanding officer of 242 (Canadian) Squadron. He had been appointed to his command – his first squadron command – by the AOC of 12 Group, Air Vice-Marshal Trafford Leigh-Mallory. He liked Bader's aggressive spirit; he seized on Bader's ideas, and gave him full authorization to put them into effect, and appointed him wing leader.

The first wing, comprising three squadrons, was first formed in early September: Bader led it on its first operational patrol on September 7th. This wing was further engaged against the enemy on September 9th. On the 11th, a wing of four squadrons, but without Bader and 242 Squadron, made a successful interception. And on the 15th, Bader led for the first time a 'big wing' of five squadrons.

Two sets of reports have been consulted in the preparation of the claims of enemy aircraft destroyed and/or damaged by Bader's wing. They are: (1) 'Reports of Wing Patrols and Fighter Tactics' submitted to Fighter Command Headquarters by Leigh-Mallory on September 17th. (2) 'The All-Canadian Squadron', a narrative of 242 Squadron's and Bader's wing actions written by Wing Commander F.H. Hitchins of the Royal Canadian Air Force.

Readers of a later time have been, and may continue to be, surprised by the extraordinary discrepancies between the claims of enemy aircraft destroyed put out by the Air Ministry, and the actual numbers destroyed. The figures, believed by historians today to be reliable, are those released after the war as a result of researches made into the records maintained by the Quartermaster-General of the Luftwaffe. An indispensable record of these events is to be found in the magnificent compilation published under the title of *The Battle of Britain: Then and Now*, edited by W.G. Ramsey, which gives precise details of each aircraft destroyed and damaged during the

Battle. If the results submitted to the Air Ministry by Fighter Command[iv] as a whole are seen to be off the mark, sometimes widely, the summing-up by Wing Commander Hitchins borders on the fantastic. He wrote:

> During 1940 No. 242 Squadron had fought three campaigns – The Battle of Dunkirk, the Battle of France and the Battle of Britain. It had lost seventeen pilots, killed or missing, in the course of the year's operations, eleven during the French Campaigns and six in the later actions over Britain. All but three of these pilots were Canadians. Against these losses it boasted a record of at least eighty-seven(?) enemy aircraft destroyed (the incomplete state of records leaves some doubt as to the precise number); sixty-two of these had been destroyed during the Battle of Britain when the squadron led the Duxford Wing. The five squadrons forming that wing had amassed a total of 158 enemy aircraft confirmed, for a loss of only nine pilots and fifteen aircraft.[v] [Read that last sentence again!]

Equally remarkable are the comparative figures put forward by Leigh-Mallory in the concluding 'Summary' of his report:

Enemy Casualties		**Wing Casualties**	
enemy a/c destroyed	105	pilots killed or missing	6
e/a 'probables'	40	pilots wounded	5
		aircraft destroyed	14
		aircraft damaged	18

These results have, of course, been contested. They seem all the more difficult to understand when considered in the light of the narrative account of each patrol in Leigh-Mallory's own report. In what follows, we either quote directly or summarize:

> First Wing Patrol. 'The three Squadrons were at a disadvantage through the loss of any element of surprise and also through the necessity of having to climb up to the enemy. There was the added disadvantage in that when attacking the bombers, the German fighters were coming down on them [our fighters] from the sun'.

> Second Wing Patrol. 'The Spitfire Squadron (19) climbed to 23,000 feet to attack the fighters whilst the Hurricanes climbed to attack the bombers. The number of escorting fighters was large enough to enable some of them to dive on our fighters as they attacked the bombers . . . .'

> Third Wing Patrol. 'As 74 Squadron went into the formation of Ju.88's they were attacked by enemy fighters (He. 113's) diving on them, but continued their attack on the main formation. AA fire which had drawn our fighters' attention to the enemy was troublesome during the engagement, and hampered the plan of attack.'

Fourth Wing Patrol. 'The leader saw Spitfires and Hurricanes, belonging to No.11 Group, engage the enemy and waited to avoid any risk of collision. As the Hurricane Squadrons went in to attack the bombers, Me.109's dived towards them out of the sun, but, as the Spitfires turned to attack them, the enemy fighters broke away . . . In the meantime the Hurricanes were able to destroy all the Dorniers that they could see and one of the Squadrons saw a further small formation of Dorniers . . . and promptly destroyed the lot.'

Fifth Wing Patrol. The leader of the Wing found that he was at a tactical disadvantage as he had not had time to reach his patrol height, with the result that this formation was attacked by Me.109's, as they were trying to get into position. Because of this, the leader of the Wing told the Spitfires to attack the bombers, and the Hurricanes to...engage the fighters. 'The results of the engagement were satisfactory so far as it went, but . . . it was impossible to break up the bomber formation and so achieve the same tactical superiority as in the Fourth patrol.'[vi]

We have presented the claims made by 12 Group for the success of its wing operations for what they are worth. It is not our intention to discuss how the pilots, the squadrons or the Group arrived at these figures. We know today that all the claims made by Fighter Command were considerably greater than the actual results. Our main purpose in presenting the foregoing figures, and those to be quoted shortly, is to discover to what degree the wing operations were successful.

The significant fact is that the numbers of enemy aircraft which Bader's wing claimed to have destroyed turned out to be wildly erratic. That is not the point; the point is that the pilots and squadrons believed them. We feel that that belief was sincerely arrived at. Whether or not Leigh-Mallory himself believed them we do not know. Dowding had something to say about it, as we shall see. Let us now look at the total picture of the wing operations.

During the period covered by the 12 Group report, the 'missing' dates – September 8, 10, 12 and 13 – saw no wing operations because of bad weather. After September 15th, however, the only days on which the Duxford wing was not 'scrambled' were the 19th, 25th, 26th, 29th and 30th. The 30th was the last great daylight battle. The German Air Force lost forty-seven aircraft against twenty RAF fighters and eight pilots killed or wounded – this without the help of 12 Group and the Duxford wing. On every other day except September 27th, Bader's wing, of three or five squadrons, was 'scrambled' eleven times on seven days and failed on every occasion to intercept plotted enemy formations. Leigh-Mallory and Bader, in particular, blamed their failures on 11 Group for calling on them too late. On many of these occasions there was in fact no request from 11 Group. The major reason for the failures is that the Duxford controller, Wing Commander A.B. Woodhall, whatever his merits as a controller, never controlled Bader; he merely 'requested' or 'suggested' where Bader might look. On some days he permitted Bader to take his wing up on a free-lance, and fruitless, hunt.

We said that Bader's wing carried out a successful interception on September 27th.

On that day the enemy raids were numerous and heavy. The Duxford wing was 'scrambled' three times. On its second patrol Bader, contrary to Woodhall's suggested vector, led his wing on a random search. He was lucky: he found 'bandits'. One writer has described the scene thus:

> It was almost exactly noon. The Wing was up-sun and higher. He [Bader] observed the Bf109s. There were about a hundred. They had no formation. They had no bombers to escort. They seemed to have no purpose. There was no logical pressure point to attack, no focus. A co-ordinated attack was pointless. He instructed the squadron leaders: 'Break up and attack.' Now, each section aimed for a point in the milling mass of fighters. It was a classic 'bounce': up sun and above the enemy.[vii]

The wing claimed thirteen enemy aircraft 'destroyed', five 'probables', and three 'damaged', for the loss of five fighters and two pilots killed. In point of fact – following Ramsey's Battle of Britain – the Germans lost to Bader's fighters only four or five of the seventeen Me109s destroyed over England that day.

We now come to the wing's record in October. From the last days of September the Germans changed their tactics yet again. Being unable to sustain the losses inflicted on their bombers throughout August and September, the Luftwaffe resorted almost exclusively to incursions by bomb-carrying Me109 and Me110 fighters flying at altitudes of 20,000 feet, 25,000 feet, and even 30,000 feet. Wood and Dempster express the new situation succinctly:

> These tactics were difficult to counter because of the height at which the German fighters flew. Above 25,000 feet the Me109 with a two-stage supercharger had a better performance than even the Mark II Hurricanes and Spitfires then coming into service. Moreover, raids approaching at 20,000 feet or more had a good chance of minimizing the effect of radar observation and were difficult for the Observer Corps to track, especially when there were clouds about. Secondly, the speed at which the formations, unencumbered by long-range bombers, flew was so great that at best the radar chain could not give much more than twenty minutes' warning before they released their bombs. Thirdly, Park had no way of telling which of the several approaching formations contained bomb-carrying aircraft and should therefore be given preference.[viii]

Despite these difficulties, 12 Group persisted in sending up wings of three, four, or five squadrons under Bader on days when the weather was suitable. Those days were: October 1, 2, 5, 7, 8, 10, 11, 13, 15, 17, 19, 25 and 29. Bader and his wing failed to make a single interception on any of those patrols.

Let us now summarize the results of all Bader's wing operations from September 7th to October 29th:

operations	37	enemy aircraft destroyed	(?)[ix]
interceptions	7	fighters/pilots lost	7/9

One of the most persistent critics of the big wings was the late Group Captain Tom Gleave, who was the official historian of the Battle of Britain Fighters Association. Gleave is quoted by Norman Gelb in his book, *Scramble*, as dismissing the results of the wings: '12 Group was supposed to cover Biggin Hill, Kenley, Northolt and the other 11 Group airfields while 11 Group squadrons were off the ground meeting the Hun coming in. It failed to do this. I know of at least one occasion when Keith Park rang up 12 Group and said, "You're supposed to be looking after my airfields." He got no change out of that.'

On June 25th, 1990, a conference was held at the RAF Staff College, Bracknell, to mark the fiftieth anniversary of the Battle of Britain. (The proceedings were published by the RAF Historical Society under the title: *The Battle Re-Thought*). Gleave repeated there the figure we have quoted above; and he was challenged by (the now late) Air Marshal Sir Denis Crowley-Milling to state his sources: 'I do not know where Tom Gleave got his figures from. Gleave informed this writer later, in reply to his query, that he did not have his papers with him and could not satisfy Crowley-Milling with any assurance.

Crowley-Milling was one of the most stalwart champions of the wings. He was a junior pilot in Bader's 242 Squadron. His case leant heavily on the 12 Group report. It was this writer who provided a copy of the report to the air marshal in 1989, and Crowley-Milling never ceased to wave it about thereafter in vindication.

When Leigh-Mallory's report was received at Fighter Command Headquarters, it was forwarded to the Air Ministry a few days later with a brief covering letter from Dowding. The key paragraphs read:

> The figures of enemy losses claimed in the table attached to the report can, in my opinion, be regarded only as approximate. It will be seen from these figures that the losses inflicted on the enemy were not increased in relation to the number of our fighters engaged on the later patrol when a large number of Squadrons took part. Nevertheless, the losses incurred by the Wing were reduced and I am, in any case, of the opinion that the AOC No. 12 Group is working on the right lines in organising his operations in strength.[x]

Crowley-Milling also quoted this document at the Staff College conference, emphasizing the last sentence. However, it is important not to rest on one's laurels. One wonders whether the air marshal ever asked himself why Leigh-Mallory never issued subsequent reports on the wings' failed operations.

On September 25th, 1940, Dowding, doubtless after having studied the report and the accompanying table more attentively, expressed his scepticism about them to Leigh-Mallory without beating about the bush: 'I read a great many combat reports, and I think I am beginning to pick out those which can be relied on and those which throw in claims at the end for good measure.' This is a most serious suspicion and charge: it comes as close to an accusation of 'cooking the books' as it can without saying it in so many words.

On October 15th, Air Vice-Marshal Park had issued new tactical instructions. He concluded by saying: 'Bitter experience has proved time and again that it is better to intercept the enemy with one squadron above him than by a whole wing crawling up below, probably after the enemy has dropped his bombs.' The 'experience' of which Park speaks is not an oblique criticism of the 12 Group wings. Far from it: Park had deployed wings of two and three squadrons since Dunkirk. His 'bitter experience' had been learnt from the lessons of his own wings in September and October. In response to the increased enemy activity from September 7 on, Park countered with wing formations. Accordingly, a wing was formed at Debden on September 11 and its two component squadrons, nos. 17 and 73, led respectively by Squadron Leader A.G. Miller and Squadron Leader M.S.W. Robinson, had a successful interception. Further wing operations were carried out with the addition of 257 Squadron, commanded by Squadron Leader R.R.S. Tuck, on four occasions. Of the eleven wing operations, only one, the first of two on September 27, was successful.

After September, 257 Squadron ceased to operate with the wing. The other two squadrons continued to operate as a wing until October 20, but had no contact with the enemy and seldom saw any enemy aircraft.

A feature of the Duxford wing on its third patrol has attracted little scholarly attention. On this occasion, on September 11th, Bader was at 12 Group Headquarters, and 242 Squadron did not take part in the wing patrol. This September 11 patrol comprised four squadrons. One of the squadrons (taking part in its first action in the wing operations) was 74 Squadron. This famous squadron had had an exceptionally busy time in 11 Group. From July 7th until the end of August it had been stationed at Hornchurch, and often deployed to Manston; and like all eleven Group squadrons it had been in the thick of the fighting for many weeks, until being withdrawn to another group for a comparative rest. It was during 74 Squadron's fighting in the south that its commander had established himself as a fighter leader *sans pareil*. He was Squadron Leader A.G. 'Sailor' Malan. In our view, Malan was the greatest fighter pilot and leader in the Battle of Britain. His fame was renowned when he went to 12 Group. Malan and his squadron moved to 12 Group on September 4th. Two days later, accompanied by Flight Lieutenant H.M. Stephen, one of his flight commanders, Malan had an interview with Leigh-Mallory, who wanted to discuss with the two pilots their views of wing formations. 'Malan was happy enough to be part of the Big Wing idea (according to Stephen's recollection), if only as a way to get back into action. The only thing he insisted upon was that he and his Tigers should be on top in the air, above everyone else.'

It is significant that in this participation in a wing operation, each squadron acted under the independent orders of its own commander; and that this action was 74 Squadron's only participation in a wing operation. In the first half of October, when Bader was putting his wings into the air, his and Malan's squadrons were the only two squadrons stationed at Duxford. Malan and 74 Squadron took no part in Bader's wings. In one biography of Malan, a slim volume inadequate to its subject, the author makes no mention of it. We turn to Bader's biographer, Laddie Lucas, and surprisingly he does not mention this joint occupation of the same base either.

On October 15th, Malan and 74 Squadron moved back to 11 Group, returning to

Biggin Hill. He, and they, must have rested up long enough. It is not difficult to envisage Malan trying to persuade Bader to move down with them. But Bader and 242 Squadron stayed put. It is probable that Malan must by then have wearied of the inaction, for the Squadron Record Book noted on the day of its return to Biggin Hill: 'Should now get back into our stride again.' And get back into their stride again they did. If we accept the account given by Group Captain Ira Jones in his history of 74 Squadron, they were successfully directed by Sector Control and intercepted numerous high-flying Me109 and 110 raiders, on some occasions even with the advantage of sun and height. Other squadrons had their successes as well. In the month of October, 379 enemy aircraft were destroyed. Of this number no fewer than 241 were fighters. On the last day of major engagements, October 29th, thirty-three German fighters were destroyed for the loss of twelve RAF fighters.

Having established, as we believe, the failure of the Duxford wings, we feel obliged to attempt to explain the failure. We are fortunate to have a detailed account in Bader's own words of how he operated his wings. Bader was interviewed by the historian Alfred Price in connection with his research, and the following account is based on these interviews.[xi]

> The five squadrons were deployed at two airfields: Duxford with three Hurricane squadrons, and Fowlmere with two Spitfire squadrons. The Hurricane squadrons took off in flights of three in formation abreast; when the lead flight was 'getting towards the far hedge the next three would be taxiing into position'; and so on until all squadrons were airborne. Bader led and climbed on the directed course at 140 mph until all flights had caught up.
>
> The Spitfire squadrons, flying faster aircraft, had to throttle back in order to stay with the Hurricanes. The Spitfires flew 5000 feet above the Hurricanes, and were under instructions to tackle the enemy fighters while the Hurricanes attacked the German bombers.
>
> The five squadrons and the ground controller did not have the same radio frequency and could not therefore keep in touch. The controller would give the wing leader instructions, and he in turn 'would have to keep changing frequency from squadron to squadron.'
>
> When it came to engaging the enemy Bader would not 'personally . . . control the Wing'. His objective was 'to get the Wing into the right position'. From that point 'my section of three would go down, followed by everyone else. As soon as we had made one pass, the formation was broken up.'

It is clear from this outline of how the Duxford wing was worked that it contains the seeds of its own failure. The wing could not climb as fast as a squadron and much crucial time was lost in the take-off and climb. In fighter interception operations during the Battle of Britain time was of the essence. Even a minute or so lost in reaching the advantageous altitude was often enough to make the difference between a successful and a failed interception. (Bader constantly blamed 11 Group for calling on them too late.)

Bader did not direct the wing in the fighting: after the initial 'pass' it was broken up and each pilot was on his own. He did not even direct or control the Spitfire squadrons since he could not see them, and in any event they knew what they had to do as the squadron commanders directed their own squadrons. So one wonders again: what was the purpose of the wings? The wing leader had only two decisions to make in the entire operation: to manoeuvre the forty to fifty-six aircraft into position, and to give the order to attack.

We have laid stress on the time factor. Bader's preoccupation was with the delay in being sent off. Why? Because he did not have the time to reach an advantageous position relative to the enemy. What was that position? Always above him: never climbing to meet him.

Bader's idea of actual air fighting is of a piece with his fascination for big wings. He constantly preached three over-riding rules:

He who has the height controls the battle.
He who has the sun achieves surprise.
He who sees them first shoots them down.

These 'rules' trip off the tongue like lines learnt by rote. Moreover they seek an ideal situation. The test of the fighter pilot is his performance in a situation not of his making. The above maxims may be the lessons of hard won experience, but of experience hard won by others – in the First World War at that. Furthermore, most successful fighter pilots considered that superior height was only a marked advantage in action against other fighters, and not an essential condition against bombers.[xii] The ideal position against bombers was either behind and slightly beneath, or, in the words of Keith Park himself– in a letter quoted by Richard Collier (p.215): 'The head-on attack from below by a squadron of Fighters was...devastating to massed Bombers.' When Jeffrey Quill, Supermarine's chief Spitfire development test pilot, arranged a posting to 65 Squadron in order to get some battle experience, he made a point of talking to the pilots, who had begun to develop definite ideas about air fighting and tactics as the result of hard experience. Among the pilots was the New Zealander Al Deere. 'I learned much,' wrote Quill, 'which I have no doubt contributed to my own subsequent survival. From this and other sources I acquired . . . many nuggets of sound advice such as "Get in as close as you can; you're usually further away than you think"; "You get shot down yourself by the man you don't see"; "If you hit a 109 don't follow him down to see him crash – another will get you"; "You need eyes in the back of your head"; "Scan the sky constantly — it's essential to see them before they see you"; "Never get separated if you can help it — and don't hang about on your own."

The failure of the big wings, and persistence of their use, calls into question the leadership of Bader, and of the motives of Leigh-Mallory, who never ceased to encourage and support him.

The sum of Bader's experience of air fighting in the Battle of Britain amounted to only eight actions in the month of September; yet this limited experience was the basis of very decided views on how to win the battle. The 'wings' concept as preached by

Bader was entirely theoretical, and not borne out by experience. It was an ad hoc innovation whose purpose seems to have been to show those fellows in 11 Group how to do it. A more experienced wing leader, 'Johnnie' Johnson, came to the conclusion later that the optimum wing formation for air fighting was two squadrons: 'My own later experience on both offensive and defensive operations confirmed that two squadrons of fighters was the ideal number to lead in the air.'

Bader's courage and will-power are justly renowned. He also had other qualities; he was a dynamic and tireless leader who was 'keen as mustard' and desperately anxious to prove himself – that is, perhaps, one key to his character: his relentless drive to excel others. That he was an inspiring leader of men who encouraged them and helped them to rise above their fear is attested to by all who served with him. But Bader was also – self-confident is too mild a word: cocksure, convinced of his own rightness, in both his ideas and his own powers. He 'knew' with complete assurance that the 'big wing' was the answer. He did not have that tincture of humility, that golden gift of detachment, which might have made him pause and stand back and seek the reasons for the repeated failure of his wings. Instead, he blamed others.

A fellow-pilot has explained this obsession with wings on Bader's part:

> Douglas Bader was completely wrong on tactics at the time. He was very brave. But he'd been out of the air force for ten years. He lagged completely behind in modern concepts. All he could think of, as far as I could see, was the old First World War flying circuses, which had nothing to do with what we were up against in the Battle of Britain.

That Bader aspired to fame and glory as a fighter pilot and destroyer of enemy aircraft is scarcely to be disputed, yet this ambition is a worrying feature of his personality. The leader may lead by example; but to seek his own glory is the last attribute of the leader. It suggests putting himself first, to the detriment of his fellows; when the desire to teach and shepherd those in his care should have been his first concern.

Another pilot has confirmed this feature of Bader's personality: 'he also had the less enviable reputation of being somewhat over-devoted to his own interests, a characteristic which did not endear him to everyone, particularly those of us who suffered as a result of his personal enthusiasms.'[xiii] What must be the ultimate condemnation of an operational pilot, and of a wing commander at that, is the commentary recorded by Kenneth 'Bing' Cross, who wrote:

> Later when some of the pilots reached us in the desert we learned of the feelings in the wings at this time. Billy Burton for example, who commanded 616 Squadron in Bader's Wing at Tangmere, maintained that by the time Bader was shot down in August 1941, the Wing was in a state of mutiny brought on by his reckless leading in an effort to increase his own score.[xiv]

Bader chafed under direction, he did not take orders easily, he resisted control. This impatience with being 'controlled' by a man sitting at a desk on the ground led him to challenge the very heart of the defensive system of Fighter Command. Bader believed that the Sector Controller should only guide and advise where the enemy might be found, and that the squadron or wing leader was the only person capable of deciding when, where and how – and indeed whether – to meet the enemy. The narrative accounts of his patrols in 12 Group's Report, together with the Price interview, show that that is how he led his wings. If he saw fit, he went charging off in any direction in pursuit of the enemy – even on occasions when he was under orders to patrol and protect 11 Group's airfields. Nothing could better illustrate this union within him of cocksureness and thirst for action; he occupied only a very small part of the sky and saw only a very small portion of the total tactical picture: yet he knew best what to do.

A further leader has pinpointed this failing of Bader's. He is Squadron Leader (later Air Chief Marshal) Harry Broadhurst. He was leading wings of two and more squadrons from Wittering, also in 12 Group, as early as June. He told 'Johnnie' Johnson:

> Sometimes in 1940 our control and reporting system was unreliable so that plotting enemy raids on the ops [operations] tables at Fighter Command and 11 Group was not always accurate. I remember at least one occasion when there were no hostile plots on the table and yet some of our chaps were shot down. It was, therefore, very important for a fighter leader to obey the controller's instructions so that, down in the hole, he would know exactly where the leader was. If, like Douglas [Bader], you went darting about all over the place, it upset the whole plotting table. So, when I led the Wittering wing, I obeyed instructions and did what I was told to do.

For the proven failure of the Bader wing operations, the ultimate blame must be laid at the door of Leigh-Mallory, who, as Air Officer Commanding the Group, not only encouraged Bader but failed to ensure that Woodhall carried out his duties in accordance with Fighter Command policy.

It would not be surprising if we learned that Bader also had an idea about the larger conduct of the Battle. We are indebted again to Price for it. Bader believed that 'the Battle should have been controlled from Fighter Command HQ, where they had a map of the whole country and knew the state of each squadron.' The author of *Big Wing* accepts Bader's view uncritically and elaborates:

> Instead of assuming control and direction of the air defence of Britain, which was the C-in-C's job, Dowding left the conduct of the battle to a subordinate commander, A V M Park of 11 Group. A map of the whole of England lay on the plotters' table at Fighter Command. It showed every Fighter airfield, with the location and state of readiness of every squadron on the board above it. The difference was paramount. A controller at the Fighter Command operations room would have seen the enemy position as it was plotted. With the whole picture spread out in front of him, he would instantly have realised the need to scramble squadrons from the further away airfields first against the enemy.[xv]

A more complete and comprehensive ignorance of the Fighter Command system cannot be conceived. It would be equally unsurprising if Bader's opinion was not shared by the real authorities. Group Captain Townsend records these opinions:

> Douglas Bader . . . wanted control by Fighter command, by Dowding himself in the last resort. But as Commander-in-Chief, Dowding was far too preoccupied with strategic problems to follow the battle blow by blow. He left that to his Group Commanders. 'Bader's suggestion beats the band,' was Park's subsequent comment. 'It would have been impossible for one controller to handle fifty squadrons.'

As many writers and commentators on the Battle of Britain have demonstrated a failure to understand the distinctions between the tactics of air battle and the techniques of air fighting, so also many have failed to understand the differences, admittedly delicate at times, between tactics and strategy. That Bader should have so signally failed to study and understand the principles underlying the entire defensive system of Fighter Command, and the specific respective roles of the Commander-in-Chief, and the Group Commanders within that system, is reprehensible to an unheard-of degree. But that Bader, a mere squadron commander, a squadron commander only newly appointed in June 1940, should presume to know better than the two men most responsible for having created Fighter Command and themselves masters, respectively, of strategic and tactical matters, is a manifestation of arrogance which boggles the mind.

An explanation of Bader's single-minded stubbornness may be found in the very chain of early-warning stations which made possible a successful defence by Fighter Command. Despite the secrecy surrounding the radar system, all squadron commanders were necessarily *au fait* with it; and hence aware of the crucial importance of obeying instructions. As we have seen, Woodhall never 'controlled' Bader. But Bader was on intimate terms with Woodhall, and had close relations with Leigh-Mallory; so it is inconceivable that Bader was not informed about it. That being the case, his contumacy becomes all the more unforgivable.

This is not quite the end of the story of air tactics and fighting. The practice of flying a squadron in three or four vics of three aircraft was being found impractical early in the battle. Some squadrons lost a number of aircraft and their pilots without ever seeing the enemy. The pilots were so intent on keeping station in the formation that they had no time or occasion to look around them. Yet here was Bader insisting on formation take-offs and landings, and on keeping his massed squadrons in formation in the air.

'Sailor' Malan was an early critic of and rebel against 'rigid "book" tactics'. To Malan a fighter aircraft was simply a 'flying gun'. In this he was following the example of his predecessor of 74 Squadron, the illustrious 'Mick' Mannock, who taught that 'Good flying never killed a Hun.'

Malan was not alone. The Polish pilots scoffed at such 'pretty flying', good only for air shows, and both ridiculous and dangerous in battle. And many of the Polish pilots had had not only more flying experience than the British, but considerably more battle experience against the Germans. One Polish pilot, Karol Pniak, of 32 Squadron, 'was appalled at the British flying formation.' Adam Zamoyski describes an incident: 'On his first sortie Pniak, who was flying in the last threesome, dropped back to cover the weaver, and was severely reprimanded by the squadron commander after landing.' Pniak based his action on his ten years' experience and thirty wartime operational sorties. 'That is why (he explained) I could in no way accept the commander's opinion, and I struggled in my poor English to explain that their way of flying was useless and dangerous.'[xvi]

The Polish fighters had, paradoxically, a further advantage. They had not had the advantage of radar and radio-telephones, and hence relied on keeping a sharp look-out; they consistently saw enemy aircraft long before their Royal Air Force comrades. Similarly, their experience had taught them to act cooperatively, to fight together as a team. Bader's formations inhibited this necessary practice; as did his corollary method of fighting. His flights of three attacked together, after which each pilot was on his own. The Poles fought together, and looked after each other, and were not often surprised. They were the bravest of the brave; their reputations spread, and every RAF squadron wanted some Poles with them. No. 303 Squadron became legendary, and was the highest scoring of all squadrons engaged in the Battle. Initially, Dowding had his concerns about how the Poles would fit in. He modified his views about them very quickly. So much so, indeed, that he paid them this ultimate tribute: 'Had it not been for the magnificent material contributed by the Polish squadrons and their unsurpassed gallantry, I hesitate to say that the outcome of the battle would have been the same.'

In concluding this section, we have to record that no other squadron commander or wing commander thought as Bader did, they merely understood the system and obeyed orders. Subsequent champions of Bader and defenders of his ideas stand on shifting sands. However Leigh-Mallory's role was quite different; in the early stages of the Battle he followed Dowding's directives and restrained Bader. But Bader pressed and persuaded, until Leigh-Mallory saw the tactical merits of his ideas.[xvii]

This is not the end of the story. The 'big wing' theory of defence as espoused by Douglas and Leigh-Mallory went so far as to permit the German bombers to reach their targets unchallenged, and even inflict heavy damage, reasoning that the defenders would take such a heavy toll of the retreating bombers that they would not want to try that tactic often.

Douglas Bader's idea was that as soon as a build-up of German formations was detected assembling over Northern France, his wing of five squadrons should be 'scrambled' and sent south to intercept them. This manoeuvre would give his wing plenty of time in which to gain the height judged essential by Bader to gain the tactical advantage; and it would also give 11 Group's squadrons time enough to gain height for the defence of their own airfields.

Both these ideas have been dismissed as either dangerous or impracticable. In particular, the Douglas/Leigh-Mallory idea is preposterous, if not lunatic. The

51

defects of Bader's idea stem from an ignorance of the very system of radar control, without which Fighter Command would have been destroyed in the first few weeks of fighting.

In the first place, there was no knowing, while Bader was leading his wing south, whether the German formation over France was going to break up into a number of feints and major attacks, all headed in different directions over England. The sober truth is that, at this stage of the war, the information from the radar chain was neither sufficiently complete nor sufficiently reliable to permit the added option of the policy with success. Although the initial build-up of a raid was quite often reported over the Pas de Calais, the strength and composition could not be accurately determined immediately.

Secondly, once the wing had penetrated well into the 11 Group area of control, there was no way in which 11 Group sector controllers could direct the Bader wing to intercept the enemy formation or formations, since they were not equipped with the same R/T apparatus. And finally, bereft of control, Bader and his wing would be 'on their own', seeking their prey wherever they could. Incredibly, as we have seen, that is exactly what Bader wanted! He wanted to escape from the control of the ground controllers and go off, as the whim took him, in pursuit of an elusive enemy. This scheme of Bader's was, in the word of Dowding, when he heard of it very much later: 'Monstrous!'.

Other questions arise. Was Bader's wing the only wing that was to be sent south? Would even Bader's sixty fighters be sufficient to oppose, say, 300 attackers? How many other wings would be ordered south? How – this is the key question — how would they be controlled? If they could not be controlled, how would they be prevented from interfering with each other's operations? And finally, if wings from 12 Group – and maybe from 10 Group as well – were sent to intercept the incoming raiders, what is the point of having an 11 Group, whose sole function, according to Bader, was to protect its own airfields? What would be the point of having airfields there at all? We have already demonstrated the failure of the Duxford wings to take toll of the enemy; that failure, allied to these objections to Bader's and Douglas's ideas, and considered in the light of Douglas's own recognition of the success of Park's handling of his resources, make nonsense of the claim that these were grounds for Dowding's removal, as we shall see in Chapter Six.

Perhaps Leigh-Mallory saw more: he saw in Bader's tactics a potential challenge to Dowding's and Park's leadership, and he had the well-placed connivance of Sholto Douglas at the Air Ministry. And, as we will see, the two ambitious men[xviii] exploited the challenge to the full.

Notes:

i. The latest book to examine this controversial question is *Honour Restored* by Squadron Leader Peter Brown AFC, a 12 Group Battle pilot himself, and the definitive study of the wings and of Bader's claims for it.

ii. This is a necessary exercise if only because Dowding himself was convinced that it was the chief factor in his removal from command. Whether it was or not we will examine in chapter six.

iii. From the very beginning of his work to create Fighter Command Dowding established the principles for what became known as the Dowding System. Among the principles was a clear distinction between strategy and tactics. In his lecture to the Royal Air Force Staff College on May 24, 1937, he made these statements: ' we must be prepared for anything, and ... our dispositions and tactical methods must be flexible and adaptable instantly to counter varitions in methods of attack;' and 'I must now say a word about my own operations table, which differ essentially from Group and Sectors in that it is strategical and not tactical in character.' In a word, Dowding had retained complete strategic control in his own hands, whereas he delegated total tactical discretion to his Group Commanders.

iv. Results that were accepted by the Air Ministry without attempts to have them verified by field researchers or any other agency or method.

v. See Bibliography. I have been informed by the University Library that this document has subsequently been lost.

vi. It is important to stress that the reader should study the comparison of the tabulated results and these narratives. It will show a marked discrepancy between them. Above all, one is struck by the remarkable results claimed, despite complaints that they were tactically disadvantaged in the air fighting.

vii. Gelb, p. 101.

viii. Wood and Dempster, p. 375.

ix. It will never be possible to calculate, from the figures and other information available, how many enemy aircraft were destroyed or damaged by pilots of Bader's wings during their operations. The facts 1) that their claims of the first five patrols have been shown to be totally unreliable, and 2) **that they only managed to make two more interceptions in the next thirty-two patrols** demonstrates as clearly as anything can how ineffective they were.

x. AIR

xi.The first observation made by Bader about the interview was this: 'You are the first author who has ever come to see me about it. Despite everything published about my Wing, you are the only one .' This statement is incomplete. Many battle pilots have written about the Battle, critical of Bader, and they knew what was going on. And Bader himself became fully aware of the dispute between 11 and 12 Groups when it broke out into the open in his presence at the Air Ministry meeting of October 17. This author met Bader on three occasions between 1976 and 1984, twice in Winnipeg and once in London, and, although I did not interrogate him, it was clear from our discussions that he was unrepentant in his views, and remained thus for the rest of his life.

xii. 'Sailor' Malan developed his ideas of air fighting from his own experiences and drew up *My Ten Rules of Air Fighting* while at Duxford. He would not have approved of one of Bader's pilots, Sergeant R.V.H. Lonsdale, who is recorded in *The Bader Wing* on at least two occasions as expending all his ammunition in prolonged bursts of 10 seconds and 15 seconds against an enemy aircraft. Malan recommended one- or two-second bursts, on the grounds that it was difficult to hold an enemy steadily and accurately in one's sights for longer, and that you left yourself vulnerable to attack by another enemy whom you would not see. We can add two comments: 1) Did Bader not teach his pilots about air fighting? 2) Prolonged firing over-heated the barrel and rendered it useless if it did not actually destroy it. Not something to endear oneself with the armourers on whom your life depended.

xiii. Arrogance is, regrettably, the word. In the Price interview we have quoted. Bader also says: 'The Battle of Britain was not won by Malan, Stanford-Tuck and myself, who got all the accolades, it was won by kids of nineteen or twenty, who maybe shot down nothing or just one before being killed themselves.' He repeats it: 'So don't think that it was Bader and Tuck who won the Battle of Britain'. Price's next question was: 'If they shot down nothing, how did they contribute?' Bader answers: 'Well, by being determined, by going off to fight and being prepared to die if necessary, that's the point.' One is not enlightened. No one ever made the mistake of thinking that Bader won the battle; one admires Bader's generosity, but battles and wars are won by killing the enemy, not by being killed oneself. (Our modem world is characterized by a fascination with celebrities, by the promotion of the individual over the prior demands of the commonweal: 'our tendency is to admire individual greatness far more than the national'). It is a hard thing to admit what all military history has to teach us withal, that there is no one so stupid as the gallant officer.

xiv. *Straight and Level*, pp. 123-24.

xv. If that was indeed Bader's idea he wouldn't have liked the result, for the AOC-in-C would have reined him in very sharply and not let him wander all over the sky at his own behest. Franks is still at it in 2008, when writing in *Flypast* magazine in April that Wg Cmdr H.S. 'George' Darley was 'a part of Leigh-Mallory's "Old Boy Network".' David Darley, his son, wrote an indignant letter of rebuttal in the June issue, and stated, among other things: 'My dad loathed L-M ... He hated self-promoters, arrogance and disloyalty to colleagues, particularly to Dowding, Park, and Quintin Brand of 10 Group ... My dad and Bader were opposites. Father rated him as ... a self-promoting, bullying, misguided acolyte of Leigh-Mallory'.

xvi. Zamoyski, p. 97. For an account of the skills, experience and tactics of the Polish pilots, see pp. 71-74 and 91-94.

xvii. It took the Air Ministry sixty years to acknowledge Bader's and Leigh-Mallory's error, if we accept the view of the current head of the Air Historical Branch as expressing the official position. In 2000 Sebastian Cox wrote that 'there can be no doubt that tactically Park was absolutely right, and had Leigh-Mallory been in command of 11 Group he would have had to modify his ideas quickly or he would have lost the Battle.' (Addison and Chang, p.65.) Our position is that their ideas were wrong for 12 Group as well. The best summary of the tactical dispute is to be found in an article by Alan Deere. It is reproduced in Appendix C.

xviii. My good friend Squadron Leader Peter Brown has explained to me his theory of ambition. He distinguishes between 'men of ambition' and 'ambitious men'. If I understand him correctly, he applies the former term to men of the stamp of Douglas and Leigh-Mallory, and the other term to men who are ambitious for achievement, not for personal gain and advancement. I would put them the other way round.

Part II

Conspiracy and Cabals

CHAPTER 4

Betrayal at the Top

We demonstrated in the last chapter that an underhanded collusion between Sholto Douglas and Leigh-Mallory led directly to a conference at the Air Ministry, arranged and chaired by Douglas, for the purpose of discrediting Dowding's and Park's leadership in the conduct of the daylight air battle.

A remarkable feature of this sad story is that Dowding's eventual removal from his command was engineered by a number of people, both in Whitehall and Westminster, acting behind the scenes to undermine Dowding's authority and to make his position untenable. We have to penetrate behind the scenes and find out who those people were and their motives. Other questions of equally significance, must be answered.

Was there complicity among Dowding's critics and enemies? Was there a conspiracy and how widespread was it? We think we can show that there is hard evidence to show connivance between some people to accomplish the same end. However, while we can prove no collusion between the cabals and the individuals who involved themselves, to their discredit, in this disreputable business, the chief actors in the drama, in their order of appearance, are these, to name only the most prominent, at this stage of our investigation:

1. Irene Ward MP, and others unknown
2. Lord Trenchard and Sir John Salmond
3. Flt. Lt. Peter Macdonald MP
4. Reginald Clarry MP and the 1922 Committee.

1. Irene Ward MP

Irene Ward was the Conservative Member of Parliament for Newcastle upon Tyne. On August 17th – this date we will show later to be of some significance — she wrote the following letter to the Prime Minister:

Dear Mr. Churchill,

I know it is nothing to do with me but I always believe in handing on information as I am sure you'll agree that there are things which shouldn't be withheld. I'm one of the members who have been kept informed about the views of many people in the Air Force who want a change in the Air Chief Marshal (sic) and have seen the confidential memorandum.[i] I am told a change may take place and I write to say that on all sides there appears to be among the service people an overwhelming desire that the Commander-in-Chief Bomber Command Air Marshal Portal should be appointed to succeed. My information is that the RAF would consider it a disaster if the Commander in Chief of Fighter Command were given the supreme office. I know you'll agree with me that one of our most attractive qualities is loyalty and that the fierce views held by many men in the RAF which they express fully realising the implications must betoken a genuine concern at the present direction. You've always been a straight speaker yourself so I know you'll forgive me. I thought with no axe to grind I perhaps was in a position to express an opinion.

Yours sincerely,
(Signed) Irene Ward

Churchill received a typed copy with the original handwritten letter, and this he forwarded to Sinclair on August 21 with the note: 'Archie. Let me have this back. WSC.'

This letter elicits a number of questions. To that end we feel that a commentary on certain statements made by Miss Ward would be instructive. As she involves herself in the matter, even though she admits to knowing nothing about it. She also hands on information without any scrutiny of its merits; in this case, not information but a speculative and defamatory document. She is one of the members ofwhich group who have been 'kept informed'? Members of Parliament? Or of the 1922 Committee? We wonder how many, and who the others were who acted on the 'information'. Those 'members' want a change in the Air Chief Marshal (sic). She means the CAS. The CAS in question is Sir Cyril Newall. The 'confidential memorandum' has been circulated widely. And many senior officers want to see Newall replaced. Is there any connection between the many who want to see Newall replaced and the many who have seen the document? She said she was 'told': this is the key to the enigma. Who told her? Did the same person also tell all 'the members who have been informed'? She goes on to say 'Portal should succeed', but no reasons are adducible except 'the overwhelming desire among the service people'.

The 'information' that the appointment of Dowding as CAS would be 'a disaster' was clearly conveyed orally by a person known to, and presumably trusted by, Irene Ward. Hence the lack of documentary evidence. The people involved in this conspiracy were careful to leave no tracks. (It is the general opinion, still today, that Dowding would not have been a good CAS. I hold the contrary view. See chapter ten and Envoi: Strategic Afterthoughts.)

The 'confidential memorandum' in question accompanying Miss Ward's letter is a three-and-a-half page, single-spaced typed document entitled: 'A Weak Link in the Nation's Defences.' This extraordinary document comprises three parts: 1) an analysis of the perceived defects and shortcomings of the Chief of the Air Staff, Air Chief Marshal Sir Cyril Newall; 2) his reluctance to remove incompetent officers; and 3) Summary.[ii]

Newall's shortcomings – which, taken with the consequences flowing from them, is the 'weak link in the nation's defences' – have no bearing on our inquiry, except to note the fourth 'weakness' listed, namely, his reluctance to remove incompetent officers. These 'incompetent officers' are identified, named and criticized. They are: the Director of Intelligence (Air Commodore Boyle); the Air Member for Supply and Organization (Air Marshal Welsh); the C-in-C Bomber Command (Air Chief Marshal Ludlow-Hewitt); the AOC Training Command (Air Marshal Pattinson); the AOC RAF Forces Ulster (Air Commodore Carr); and the Air Member for Personnel (Air Marshal Gossage). Of these officers, we will note only the criticisms made against one of them.

Ludlow-Hewitt was AOC-in-C Bomber Command from September 12th, 1937, to April 3rd, 1940, when he was replaced by Portal. The writer again declares that 'outside pressure' had to be brought to bear (on Newall) to make the change, which was 'long overdue'; and that Portal was an 'outstanding improvement'.(We shall have occasion later to review a very different appreciation of Ludlow-Hewitt; and a serious related criticism of Portal.)

What we note first in the foregoing criticisms is the sweeping nature of the deficiencies of the officers singled out for attack: there is, except in the one minor case noted, nothing concrete or specific. The judgements are notable for their subjective character. Secondly, the subjectiveness of the criticisms becomes more evident when one considers the number of times the author accuses his victims, including Newall, of lacking character and mental ability – attributes which disqualify the officers in question from holding their appointments. Finally, the judgements and criticisms are made from the perspective of the Air Ministry. Not only that: the author is seen as placing himself in an all-dominant position from which to judge; and in so doing not only loses sight of some of the realities of operational commands, but also shows himself out of touch with events and ignorant of some of the officers he casts judgment on.

The most detailed analysis of an allegedly 'incompetent' officer, after Newall, is found in a section of four paragraphs of the memorandum sub-headed 'Fighter Command.' We reproduce it here.

> Two of the three duty Senior Air Staff Officers at HQ Fighter Command, and who are liable at any time to be called upon to direct the operations of the whole of the Fighter Command in the absence of their Commander-in-Chief, are Air Commodore Webb Bowen and Air Commodore Bonham Carter. Both these officers retired from the RAF many years ago, and neither have (sic) any knowledge of modern fighters and modern air fighting. Air Vice-Marshal Nicholl has long passed his prime and is incompetent to hold his present appointment as Senior Administrative Officer at HQ Fighter Command. Indeed, HQ Fighter Command is substantially a one man show and is ruled by Air Chief Marshal Dowding who has definite personality, but unfortunately he has inadequate mental ability and a very slow brain. He is also a classic example of a complete non-co-operator either with the Air Ministry or any other

authority. His treatment of his staff is deplorable and he tolerates only 'yes' men. Air Chief Marshal Newall has not the strength of character to deal with Air Chief Marshal Dowding or to insist on having a strong and balanced staff at HQ Fighter Command.

We do not comment on the charge of incompetence levelled against Webb–Bowen and Nicholl, or on their retention in the Air Force. We need only add that, in one respect, the writer was in error, for in the absence or incapacitation of Dowding, neither Webb–Bowen nor Bonham Carter would have been 'called upon to direct the operations of the whole of the Fighter Command': that task would have fallen to Air Vice-Marshal D.C.S. Evill, an experienced and highly capable officer, who had been described as 'a tower of strength' during the final operations of the Air Force in France before the collapse.

In point of fact, in this criticism the author demonstrates his ignorance of the operational functions of Fighter Command Headquarters: the AOC-in-C of Fighter Command did not himself 'direct the operations of the whole of Fighter Command'. If by 'operations' we mean the air fighting and their direction, that work was the task of the squadrons, stations, sectors and groups. Fighter Command Headquarters played no role in them. What appears to be the key paragraph, with its denigration of Dowding, makes him out to be some kind of monster; if this thumb-nail sketch represents the view of Dowding as he was perceived by the Air Ministry, it explains, in part, the wretched relations which existed between them. In fact, of course, it is a calumny. What of his 'inadequate mental ability' and his 'very slow brain'? It is enough to point to the whole structure and operation of Fighter Command, with its unique radar control system, which was in a very real sense the creation of Dowding, to realize how ludicrous the statement is.

The author also fails signally to give any examples of Dowding's 'deplorable treatment of his staff.' It is a serious charge to make against a commander. Neither of his two personal assistants, Francis Wilkinson and Robert Wright, have ever breathed a word of recrimination; on the contrary, both have praised his qualities and leadership, in a manner which few high operational commanders have elicited from their personal assistants. To that we must add his unfailing consideration and courtesy to the young airwomen plotters at the headquarters filter room, in whose skills he frequently expressed his confidence. Dowding was one of those very rare men who was a terror to those set in authority above him if they exhibited incompetence, stupidity or duplicity, and who became an admired father figure to his junior staff.

Dowding enjoyed the support, confidence and selfless efforts of many fine and capable men and women. To say that he was 'substantially a one-man show' and tolerated only 'yes' men is not only a calumny; it is especially a slur on the integrity and courage of his headquarters staff. To say that men of the calibre of Park (who was Dowding's Senior Air Staff Officer before going to 11 Group), McEvoy, Evill, Hamilton, Gleave, and many other fine officers were yes-men deserves nothing but contempt for the writer's judgement – and calls in question his motives.

A further observation is called for. If the author is sufficiently familiar with the personnel of Fighter Command Headquarters to know of these officers' incompetence, it cannot have escaped Dowding's attention either. Did the writer seriously mean to imply that Dowding retained them precisely because they were incompetent, and hence, presumably yes-men? And he would do such a thing in the certitude that, in the event that he, Dowding, were incapacitated, either of them would step into his shoes and, by their very incompetence, contribute by default to the success of the Luftwaffe's attacks and perhaps to the defeat of Great Britain?

The date of composition of this memorandum is of considerable interest, both in itself and in relation to the date of Miss Ward's letter. It carries no name and it also carries no date; but there is internal evidence which enables us to date it with fair precision. On page two the author bases his opinion of Newall's bad judgment on 'his personal order to despatch (some aircraft) to Malta and the Middle East on 18/6/40 after France had laid down her arms.' Here we have a precise date. The memorandum opens with an allusion to forthcoming events which cannot be misinterpreted: 'Upon the achievements of the Royal Air Force in the coming weeks, and its development in the coming year will, more than upon any other factor, depend the final outcome of the present war with Germany.' This can refer only to the Battle of Britain.

These references therefore date the memorandum towards the end of June; it will be recalled that Churchill made his speech about the survival of Christian civilization on June 18th. It is important to note what the memorandum says and what it does not say. It says that, in view of the coming anticipated Battle, and the outcome of the war, the best man available should be chosen as Chief of the Air Staff, and that Newall was not the best man. The author does not suggest who the best man might be, however. There is nothing in the 'confidential memorandum' to suggest or imply that, if its author's intentions were realized and Newall were removed before his due retirement date, Portal would be his successor. On the contrary, the complaisant wording of his appointment as AOC Bomber Command intimates that he was there for the long term. And Portal's own submission of May 8th to the Air Ministry, expressing in strong terms his objections to and criticisms of the French Army's ideas about tactical strikes by his bombers against a German offensive, corroborates this conclusion.

Between the composition of the memorandum and the date on which Miss Ward sent it to Churchill, how much had changed! In a period of six to seven weeks, Miss Ward, in her covering letter, says there is to be a change of CAS, almost insists that Portal should succeed Newall, and states the view that 'the RAF would consider it a disaster if the Commander in Chief of Fighter Command were given the supreme office.'

The questions pile up; one question, however, we can answer: Where did Miss Ward get this information? Denis Richards wrote in his biography of Portal:

Miss Ward, who knew nothing of RAF politics or personalities, had recently spoken on Services welfare. Following this she had been approached in the Central Lobby at Westminster by a group of young RAF officers including some Canadians from Bomber Command. They told her that the Service had no confidence in Newall's leadership, that if he were to be replaced by Dowding it would be a disaster, and that their chief at High Wycombe [i.e. Portal] was exactly the man for the job.

This statement raises more questions than it answers. Firstly, the expression 'Following this' implies that the meeting between the officers and Miss Ward took place immediately after her talk. Yet there is little likelihood that any RAF officers, let alone Canadian bomber aircrew officers, were ever interested in hearing a talk about Services welfare. Secondly, they were far too removed from the high command of the RAF to know anything about Newall and the Chief of the Air Staff. It is true that they were closer to their own commander; but experience tells us that the bomber crews were equally remote from their commander-in-chief. Moreover, Portal had only been in his command for a month or two. Even less likely are any of these supposed RAF and Canadian officers to know anything about so remote a figure as Dowding. The whole scenario as described by Richards is somewhat more than farfetched.[iii]

We are left with the impression that, with all respect to Mr. Richards, we have a practiced politician pulling the wool over the eyes of an historian trying to get at the facts, whilst the politician is deviously throwing her questioner off the scent of the person or persons who had given her the document in the first place. If we are not surprised by Miss Ward's duplicity, we are flummoxed by the apparent readiness with which Mr Richards, a professional historian – albeit in our estimation a descriptive rather than a critical one – is led away by the false scent.

Other questions, important questions, impose themselves, to which one cannot hazard even the most tentative or speculative of answers. Where did Miss Ward get all her information? Who kept her personally informed? Why was Miss Ward selected for this role in the first place? Who selected her? Was there a third party who recommended her to her informant and mentor? And finally, seemingly closely related to them, what happened in that brief period of July and August to make Portal so favoured?

We come now to the question: what was done about this document? As we have seen, Churchill minuted it to Sinclair on August 21st: Sinclair locked it away and forgot about it. Then still other questions intrude themselves: i) what did Churchill expect Sinclair to do with or about the document?; ii) why did Churchill himself, as self-appointed Minister of Defence, not call Sinclair in and together agree on what action to take?; iii) why did Sinclair, with Churchill's inaction, not initiate an inquiry? For he receives from a fellow-MP an anonymous document full of slanderous allegations against some of his most senior officers, including the two most senior of all, Dowding and Newall, and he does nothing. The very least he should have done was to summon Miss Ward and demand to know how she obtained the document. The mere fact of his taking no action in such a case is sufficient to cast the grave suspicion that he agreed with the criticisms, and hoped that they would produce the desired result.

This same document surfaced again three weeks later. The following is a letter written by the same Irene Ward to Brendan Bracken, the Minister of Information.

Dear Mr. Bracken,

Referring to our conversation in the Lobby on Thursday I enclose herewith copy of the Memorandum to which I referred.

As from our conversation it seems unlikely that Mr Churchill will have got my letter may I briefly recapitulate what I said. In the first place that I have no personal interest in the matter at all as I do not know any of the personalities concerned but that from a great many quarters I have been told that the Air Force would welcome the appointment as CAS of Air Marshal Portal and that his appointment would give very much greater confidence to those in the Service than the appointment of C-in-C, Fighter Command... .

I always believe in handing on information which I have been given in good faith. I have tried to check up on the Memorandum and am told by those who have an intimate knowledge of the working of the Air Ministry that the Memorandum is ninety-nine per cent true.

Yours sincerely,
(Signed) Irene Ward

Bracken forwarded the memorandum to the Prime Minister with the minute: 'This stuff is being widely circulated. I think you should see it. Miss Ward, MP, is a rather ferocious female.' On September 18th, Churchill minuted it **again** to Sinclair: 'To see and return.' A full month later, Sinclair wrote to Bracken about it, and her.

My dear Brendan,

I saw and heard your virago and then, because the stuff you sent me was so secret, I locked it away and it has only just emerged from its box when I was looking for something else. I observe that Winston asked for it to be returned so here it is.

Miss Ward was fairly apologetic. She talked to me and admitted she knew nothing of the subject. On the other hand, she made it clear that she felt she ought to have had an answer and that she was not to be trifled with. I explained to her that it was my fault and that I had tried, unsuccessfully, to see her before the House rose and had then forgotten about it. At the same time, I recited to her a prose poem about the officer whom she does not like and told her that he enjoyed my complete confidence and that of the Prime Minister... .[iv]

That Sinclair regarded the contents of the memorandum as inflammatory is clear since he locked it up in a box. He did not return it to Churchill as he had requested: that he simply forgot about it stretches the credulity. If, as he states, Dowding 'enjoyed (his) complete confidence,' it is **again** reprehensible that he took no action, and failed to institute an inquiry into the sources of Miss Ward's information and the purveyor of the defamatory document. Sinclair's inaction implies once again rather that he did not want to stop the circulation of the calumnies.

2. Trenchard and Salmond

There is pleasure in seeing knaves fall out and go for each other's throats; there is none in seeing good men at odds. Among the greatest figures in the history of the Royal Air Force, outside the ranks of the men who earned renown in air warfare, are Trenchard and Dowding.

Trenchard and Salmond were deeply involved in attempts, carried on behind the scenes by Trenchard and overtly by Salmond, to have Dowding removed from his command. Although the relations that existed between Trenchard and Dowding, over the years, were very close, and although Trenchard and Salmond worked in lock-step and hand-in-glove against Dowding, we have to treat them separately.

Trenchard

Trenchard's and Dowding's careers, like those of most of the officers who rose to high rank or who became known in the Second World War, intersected in France in the First World War and ran along disparate lines until converging again in the years 1929-40.

While in France, in 1916 and 1917, Trenchard and Dowding crossed swords three times. The first occasion of dispute was over the supply and fitting of the wrong propellers to the aeroplanes of Dowding's squadron, 16 Squadron, when Trenchard commanded the Wing. When the propellers arrived and Dowding inspected them, he saw that they were meant for a different engine from the one installed in his aeroplanes. He telephoned Trenchard and told him so. Trenchard ordered him to fit them anyway.

Dowding had one modified, with great difficulty, and, because of the risks involved, test-flew the aeroplane himself. On landing he found that the hub of the propeller had cracked; he refused to fit the others and telephoned Trenchard to protest. Trenchard then had the correct propellers delivered. What incensed Dowding was that Trenchard would accept the word of the supplier in Paris, who was no more than a garage mechanic, over the expert advice of the man at the fighting end who had to use the equipment. Dowding was not going to send his men up against the enemy with questionable equipment or needlessly risk their lives. Dowding was not the first, and he would be far from the last, who felt strongly that the 'superior' officers at headquarters who sent down unconsidered commands abused their authority, and that the men at the operational level were in the best position to know their essential needs and whose advice should be sought and heeded by the 'authorities' ensconced in their offices far from the enemy.

Trenchard's second brush with Dowding occurred when Trenchard, keen on establishing air superiority over the Western Front, was urging 'maximum effort' on his squadron commanders. Many squadrons suffered heavy casualties, Dowding's among them. When he judged the losses justified his action, Dowding asked Trenchard to rest and relieve his squadron. Trenchard scorned Dowding as a 'dismal

Jimmie', feeling that the request was an implied criticism of his policy.

Were Trenchard's scorn, and his policy, justified? Here is a sympathetic writer, Trenchard's own biographer, writing of Trenchard's command in France:

> In the five months of the Somme campaign Trenchard lost five hundred aircrew casualties – well over 100 per cent of his starting figure – and this was a heavy mortgage on the Corps' future. . . . Even when, as Trenchard had feared, the German air force came back on the offensive, he went on throwing his squadrons forward against the superior new Albatross and Halberstadt fighters – if they could get across into enemy territory before being 'jumped'. The climax came in 'Bloody April' of 1917, over Arras and Vimy Ridge. The Red Baron, von Richthofen, averaged a victory a day throughout the month, and in all the Corps lost 316 aircrew, or a third of its strength – and for very little result.

In 1917, Dowding was sent home to take charge of the Southern Training Brigade. He was dismayed by what he found. In order to make up for the heavy losses suffered during the Somme fighting in the second half of 1916, and to pursue the policy of achieving air superiority, the training establishments had been bled not only of their output of pilots, inadequately trained as they were, but also of many of their instructors. Dowding foresaw the grave consequences of pursuing such a policy. He made representations to the War Office. He also wrote to Trenchard's senior staff officer, explaining the situation. This officer showed the letter to Trenchard. Trenchard regarded it as an uncalled-for meddling in his policies, which were approved by the War Office; and it had the effect of exacerbating their relations, which remained strained for several years.

In 1927 Dowding was posted to the Air Ministry where he came under the direct orders of Trenchard. There they established an unruffled working relationship which one writer has called 'almost cordial.' There can be no question that Dowding had come to know the moral integrity, high ideals, and lofty standards that were hallmarks of both the personal and the professional figure of Trenchard. Can it be doubted that Trenchard for his part recognized the same qualities in Dowding? The three years that Dowding spent as the Director of Training were uneventful; but he and Trenchard worked so well together that Trenchard made the uncharacteristic confession to Dowding one day: 'Dowding, I don't often make mistakes about people, but I made one about you.'

Indeed, Trenchard had come to appreciate Dowding's qualities to the point that, in the autumn of 1929, with trouble brewing in the Middle East and the fear of an Arab uprising that threatened the safety of Europeans, he sent Dowding out there, on twenty-four hours notice, to study the situation and 'to advise on the minimum force which would suffice to maintain order in Palestine.' Dowding's mandate was extended from two weeks to three months; he surveyed the area from the air and drove round it with escort. His frequent reports and letters stressed that the situation was almost entirely political, and that he had to be entirely impartial in his judgements; in his assessments he reported his view that the British were largely responsible for the inflammatory situation, having violated the agreements that Colonel Lawrence had made with them – in the name of the British Government – during the war. It was, he said many years later, 'a dishonesty for which we have never ceased to suffer'. Dowding drew on his experience in Iraq in earlier years, and reported that the RAF would be able to handle the situation, if backed up by a few Army elements.

What interests us in this episode is not so much the outcome of Dowding's mission as the reception of his reports and the results that he reported. In one letter Trenchard wrote to say: 'I would like to [say] how well you are doing everything I want.' On another occasion he wrote: 'Your letters certainly are very human and interesting.' In yet another letter he wrote: 'The atmosphere at home is that you are doing very well, and that you are the one cheerful spot.'ᵛ

That took place at the end of 1929. Trenchard retired in 1930. For the following five years he was the Commissioner of the London Metropolitan Police (Scotland Yard). It was from 1936, therefore, that he had the leisure to interest and involve himself increasingly in Air Force matters. One is left to wonder what happened between this date – which was the same year that Dowding became the first Commander of Fighter Command — and the summer of 1940 to again cause Trenchard to change his mind and his views. One may search the published sources, such as Boyle's biography of Trenchard, as well as the unpublished records, and end up with nothing. In the light of these blanks, we are left to speculate on the new cause or causes of the disagreement or friction that arose between them. In point of fact, to say 'between them' is misleading, for the hostility was entirely a one-way street, from Trenchard to Dowding.

Our knowledge of the integrity of these two men leads us to one possible conclusion, namely, that they locked horns over questions of doctrine. If we accept that premise, much becomes clear. For Trenchard was, as we have seen, not only a bomber man but an uncompromising, a dogmatic, bomber man. Whereas Dowding's career, as we have also seen, took him through research and development, the new fighters and radar, and the creation of Fighter Command. Dowding became the expert in defence, the champion of the security of the home base. Dowding's was the view of immediate strategic necessity: Trenchard's was the long-term strategic goal. Trenchard's goal could not have been achieved without first ensuring the security of the home base. On the other hand, Trenchard's strategic goal could not have been realized without the fighter. And that was a prospect that never crossed Trenchard's mental horizon. Peter Townsend makes the case forcefully:

> Dowding was not a man for half measures. He was resolved to get what he needed to make the 'base'– Britain – safe and secure. On one occasion a senior officer propounded to him at length, as if they were sacred words of truth, the Trenchard doctrine, 'attack is better than defence'. Stuffy disagreed vigorously: 'It's a shibboleth, a play on words with just enough truth, but not enough to make it a clear case. Why must it be accepted without question? Only

because you think that you are going to do so much damage that the enemy will be smashed right at the outset. And how are you going to do that?' Fiercely he insisted that, 'the one thing vital before going over to the offensive is security of the base. That overrides all considerations.' His unshakeable belief in the principle and his obstinate insistence that all his demands should be met did not endear him to all his brother officers. 'Always remember,' he would say later, 'that my name stank on the Air Staff.' ... As time went on Dowding was to become more and more aware that certain of the Air Staff were trying to get rid of him.[vi]

Yet Trenchard was – or had at one time been – fully aware of the needs and occasions for defence. He had himself had a first-hand experience of it in 1918. In a significant paper published in 2000, the author, Wing Commander P.J. Daybell, describes how, at the time of the great retreat of March of 1918, Trenchard was the Commander of the RFC in the field and 'prepared his own detailed plans for the RFC in defence.' He quotes the official history of the air war by H.A. Jones, who lays down the aims and requirements of defence:

> The first and most important of the duties of the Royal Flying Corps in connexion (sic) with defence is to watch for symptoms of attack, and to use the endeavours to obtain and transmit at once all information which may assist responsible commanders to determine beforehand when and where an attack is coming and by what force.

Not only did Trenchard devise the plan, it was carried out by Salmond. Daybell explains: 'Trenchard's defensive plan was skilfully and flexibly executed by Salmond, despite the unprecedented difficulties of the retreat.'[vii] Yet despite this experience, a lesson which would be applied – with outstanding success – to the defensive needs of the British Isles in 1940, Trenchard devoted himself when CAS to the implementation of his bomber doctrine.

From 1930, as a former Chief of the Air Staff and, especially, as a Marshal of the Royal Air Force, he remained, I repeat, closely in touch with Air Force matters, as he did with many of the senior officers in the Air Force, especially at the Air Ministry. 'Indeed his influence over Air Staff affairs during the ten years after his retirement was as considerable as during the ten years he spent as Chief of the Air Staff.'[viii]

As the war became increasingly grim in 1940, Trenchard and Salmond must have turned their gaze onto Dowding and the leadership of Fighter Command. They exchanged views at meetings and in correspondence, and came to a common ground in their dislike of what they saw. If this is the origin of Trenchard's renewed antipathy toward Dowding, in his letters to Salmond he was doing no less than pushing Salmond to use his influence with the Air Council to bring about Dowding's removal. Salmond for his part was urging Trenchard to involve himself more directly in their campaign. I have found nothing to show the precise reasons, or motives, that explain Trenchard's extraordinary *volte face*, but I am convinced that Trenchard became the leader in the campaign to unseat Dowding. Had it not been for Trenchard pulling strings and browbeating those in command – with the willing collaboration of Sinclair and Douglas – Churchill would not have been swayed and Portal would not have had the backing to write the terminal letter to Dowding.

We come now to the events initiated by Trenchard that led to the eventual demise of Dowding. His letter of October 4th 1940 to Salmond is revealing in this twofold respect.

Dear Salmond,

Yours of the 3rd September. I have done all I can in the last two or three days of rubbing in about Dowding, and I am going to rub in again today. At least I know some of my remarks have got to the right quarters. I fancy it is too much to ask for any conditions to be made by Portal and I feel it would be difficult for him after what has happened to sack Dowding unless we can get sufficient pressure to bear to bring it about. I fully realise with you, that my activities are so much more outside than inside, but I will see what more I can do. I feel your pressure has done as much good as anything I know from what I have heard from other sources, but I never mention that you and I are working in agreement on this matter as I feel it is more use our apparently being independent but working for the same cause.

This letter is a deeply disturbing document, on a number of counts. Firstly, there was connivance between Trenchard and Salmond over those two months of September and October to contrive Dowding's removal. Trenchard is using his prestige and influence, by taking advantage of his ready access to members of the Air Council and to others in the Air Ministry, to undermine confidence in Dowding. In this he is having some success. Yet Trenchard is keen to preserve his reputation by making it appear that he was acting, and agitating, as a lone, concerned observer rather than in cahoots with Salmond, and part of a cabal.

The expression 'rubbing in about Dowding' is particularly significant and yet difficult to read. What was he 'rubbing in' about? What were Dowding's failures or shortcomings, and how would the 'rubbing in about' produce the desired result? In chapter nine we will construct a scenario where these questions are examined.

The fourth sentence is enigmatic, unless we know of the relations between Trenchard and Portal. Portal's appointment as the next Chief of the Air Staff to succeed Newall, on October 23rd, just nineteen days after this letter, was not only obviously known to Trenchard: Trenchard had a direct hand in Portal's appointment. Portal was Trenchard's 'favourite disciple'. Yet Trenchard could not expect Portal to sack Dowding on becoming CAS 'after what has happened'; what is Trenchard referring to here? He cannot mean anything other than Dowding's handling of the daylight battle, which at this date, October 4th, was seen to be in the ascendant. And what are the 'conditions' referred to? Since this sentence runs into the next and constitutes a single line of thought, he can only have in mind the possibility – instantly to be dismissed – of asking Portal to impose conditions upon Dowding if he is to remain at Fighter Command. (He cannot conceivably mean Portal laying down conditions before accepting his appointment.)

The crux of the matter seems to lie in getting 'sufficient pressure to bear to bring it about.' Not only pressure, but sufficient pressure. That would mean pressure applied in the right place and by the right person. That place was Churchill – and other influential politicians, such as Beaverbrook. They were already applying 'sufficient pressure' to get rid of Newall; but that was to be accomplished within the Air Ministry. Dowding was altogether a tougher nut. It was Salmond who was to turn the vice that would exert the pressure. It was he who was working on the inside – of the Air Ministry, the Air Council, the Government. He was also the only one with tenacity. His biographer has described him in these terms: 'a perfect gentleman who knew how to be ruthless' and as one who was 'capable of considered ruthlessness'.

One must ask yet again in what way were Dowding's shortcomings, in Trenchard's and Salmond's eyes, so grave as to warrant, and incite, their direct and prolonged interference in Air Force matters? For Dowding was seen to be conducting a successful defence of the United Kingdom and thereby preventing invasion. The perceived shortcoming, or rather pretext, must have lain elsewhere. Already, on September 12th, Salmond had written to Trenchard to voice his concerns about the night defences. Just one week before, Salmond had concluded a report on the night defences, and was visibly dissatisfied. His concerns sharpened to the point of spurring him to strong and direct action. In a long letter to Trenchard dated September 25th, Salmond apprises Trenchard of his actions, his aims, and his views of both Dowding and Newall. The letter, dated September 25th, is worth reproducing in its entirety. (This is taken from a copy, without signature.)

Dear Trenchard,

This is in answer to your letter received today, and the following is the position. You will remember the copy of a note I sent you, the original of which went to Beaverbrook on the subject of the failure to cope with night bombing. From this it arose that I was told to enquire into the whole situation and I completed a report two days afterwards. On it I put a private note to Beaverbrook to say that I considered Dowding should go. Beaverbrook told me that he had been working so closely with Dowding that he could not take any part in it. Dowding has been seeing a great deal of Beaverbrook and Beaverbrook has formed a very high opinion of him, and had informed the Prime Minister who also, apparently, had the same opinion. I think that Beaverbrook is now a bit shaken on it. I then went to see Sinclair and told him I considered that Dowding should go. I could see that he was frightened of putting it forward, although he is aware that the CAS and the whole of the Air Staff, I believe, almost without exception, are in agreement with me. When I left him I felt he was not going to move in the matter.

Yesterday I was invited to the Air Council to discuss the report [on night bombing]. I told Newell (sic) previously that I was quite prepared to raise the matter of Dowding at the end of the discussion, when any civil member would have left. He seemed a bit rattled at the prospect and said he would think about it during the course of the meeting. Towards the end of the meeting he passed me a note asking me not to raise it. Consequently a major opportunity of getting the opinions of the Service members of the Air Council on the matter has passed by. It is really incomprehensible on the part of Newall as he had told me some days ago how extremely keen he was that Dowding should go and what enormous difficulties he and the Air Staff had had in getting him to accept new ideas regarding fighting at night. I frankly do not feel that, if he remains in his post, we shall get any move on in the matter, until things have become very much worse. Apart from this, as you and I know, he has not got the qualifications of a Commander in the Field, as he lacks humanity and imagination. He is now living on the reputation he has gained through the successes of the pilots in day fighting, a great deal of which, of course, must be due to his account. When I saw Beaverbrook he said to me, 'If Dowding is to go, why not Newall, as Newall must be responsible too'. Personally, of course, I have no objection to coupling them as I think Newall's strategic judgment is completely at fault...[A]t this moment [he] is so impressed with the possibility of invasion that he will not even tell off a couple of day fighting squadrons to be trained for the night, even though they could be at once used for day work if invasion took place. If you see Beaverbrook I would very much like you to bring up the matter of Dowding, and also Newall, because I believe that with these two in the saddle, we are not getting the best we should expect.[ix]

It is difficult to conceive of a more damning indictment of Dowding especially coming, as it does, from a former Chief of Air Staff and addressed to another former Chief of Air Staff. But the letter, for all its undoubted sincerity, is an equally damning indictment of the writer. It is firstly remarkable for its vagueness. The conspicuous absence of detail to reinforce the allegations against Dowding serves to suggest two things: first, that Trenchard knew what Salmond was talking about; second, that they had talked, and continued to meet.

The descriptions of Beaverbrook, Sinclair and Newall as being, respectively, 'shaken', 'frightened', and 'rattled' – subjective judgments of states of mind, and hence notoriously subject to error – offer, if remotely accurate observations, revealing insights into Salmond's toughness and the relations of these three men with Dowding. It was well known that Beaverbrook was one of Dowding's staunchest champions, but his aircraft factories were being bombed! While Sinclair had recently written to Dowding assuring him of his unswerving confidence, Newall was, it is true, apt to dither, and was fearful of the prospect of a showdown with that formidable character, Dowding. In the background, present but unnamed, was Churchill; Churchill was Dowding's most admiring supporter. Beaverbrook and Sinclair knew this. Therefore if they were to get rid of Dowding, they were going to have to convince Churchill. Salmond was not daunted; he saw Churchill and put his case against Dowding to him. At the top of the letter quoted above, he had written in his own hand (with an arrow pointing downwards towards the text of the letter): 'My views, which I eventually explained to the P.M. He practically blew me out of the room.'

Salmond's indictments of Dowding call for examination. They are as follows :

1) Newall and the Air Staff had 'enormous difficulties . . . in getting him to accept new ideas regarding fighting at night.' (This issue will be addressed in chapters seven and nine.)

2) Dowding 'has not got the qualifications of a Commander in the Field'. As usual, Salmond is vague and subjective in his allegation, and fails to support it with evidence. However, we note Dowding's success for 'by the end of the month, it became apparent that the Germans could no longer face the bomber wastage which they had sustained' – in other words, the daylight battle was essentially won. And have we not already seen that when Salmond saw Churchill on or about October 6th, i.e. a couple of weeks after this letter, 'he practically blew [him] out of the room.' We shall also see in chapter seven what Churchill thought of Dowding's 'ideas regarding fighting at night.'

3) Dowding 'lacks humanity and imagination.' On the question of humanity no greater error, no more scurrilous accusation, could be made. Where could Salmond have got such a notion? Dowding was renowned, above all, for his concern for the men under his command. He had demonstrated it – to Trenchard of all people, who could have set Salmond right – in the First World War. Between the wars, when Dowding was the Chief Staff Officer, HQ Iraq Command, a post he held from September 1924 to May 1926, he was under orders to carry out the policy of bombing unruly Arab tribesmen. Dowding argued that warning leaflets should be dropped first, a measure that was accepted and spared many lives. Finally, in 1939-40, his pilots, who never saw him, by some subtle and mysterious process of communication, were keenly aware of his profound solicitude. Dowding himself wrote: 'In the early stages of the fight, Mr. Winston Churchill spoke with affectionate raillery of me and my "chicks". He could have said nothing to make me more proud; every chick was needed before the end.'[x]

Salmond reiterated his denigration of Dowding's leadership and command by adding: 'He is now living on the reputation he has gained through the successes of his pilots in day fighting'. If he had said such a thing to the pilots themselves at the time, he would have felt a stronger blast than the one 'which practically blew [him] out of the room.' Salmond's resort to vituperation can have been the result not of a considered professional judgement but only of a deep personal antipathy; and the accolade, appended as an afterthought – 'a great deal of which [reputation] . . . must be due to his account' – is too grudging to conceal the bias or to attenuate the slur. In fact the whole tenor of Salmond's letters to Trenchard is of a deeply personal antipathy to

Dowding. His criticisms precede the first night attacks on Britain – and the failure to meet them convincingly – and condemn Dowding for what he perceives as a less than adequate answer to the daylight attacks.

Neither Salmond nor Trenchard ever visited Fighter Command; so it is not so much where they got their information that raises questions, but how they reached the conclusions that they did. Obviously, from people they knew in the Air Ministry – members of the Air Council and the Air Staff, who were known to be hostile to Dowding. We recall that Salmond wrote of bringing pressure to bear to effect the changes which he and Trenchard deemed necessary. Miss Ward's anonymous memorandum also mentioned 'outside pressure' which had to be brought to bear to remove Welsh and Ludlow-Hewitt from their appointments. Now we are witnessing Salmond himself exerting his influence and strong 'outside pressure' – on Trenchard, Beaverbrook, Newall and Churchill – to get rid of Dowding. One wonders whether poor Newall suspected that while Salmond was urging Newall to remove Dowding, he was simultaneously scheming to remove Newall himself.[xi]

3. Macdonald

In the summer of 1940 Peter Macdonald wore two hats: he was, as Flight Lieutenant Peter Macdonald, a reserve officer in the RAF; and, as Sir Peter Macdonald, the MP for the Isle of Wight. In the Royal Air Force officer he was the adjutant of 242 (Canadian) Squadron, whose commanding officer was Squadron Leader Douglas Bader. As we have seen, Bader was the chief proponent of the 'big wing'; in Macdonald he had a sympathetic lieutenant and a faithful servant.

Macdonald's squadron was normally stationed at Coltishall, a few miles north of Norwich. Throughout September and October, however, when Bader formed his wings, 242 Squadron moved to Duxford, a few miles south of Cambridge. This location permitted ready travel to London, a situation which Macdonald availed himself of freely.

Macdonald's doings in the cause of Bader's ideas and discontent, and in furthering Leigh-Mallory's ambitions, are dealt with fully in the next chapter, because his intervention led to an immediate reaction and unpleasant repercussions. He is introduced here in order to underscore his twofold responsibilities. As an MP he will have known Irene Ward. A measure of cooperation and an exchange of views are almost certain to have taken place; Macdonald may well have been one of the people who 'kept (Miss Ward) informed' about some Air Force matters. Macdonald and Miss Ward were also, of course, members of the 1922 Committee.

4. Sir Reginald Clarry and the 1922 Committee

In early November, when the daylight battle was manifestly won – and when the night battle was beginning to get ominous – another surreptitious broadside was fired against Dowding. This one emanated from the 1922 Committee.

The 1922 Committee, or, to give it its full name, the 1922 Conservative Private Members Committee, is composed of all Conservative Members of Parliament who are not Ministers of the Crown and who are in receipt of the Party Whip. Its function is to keep an eye on the policies of the Government and the administration of the Government departments by the Ministers. Its powers are nil, but its influence considerable. It would be a brave, and perhaps foolhardy, Minister who declined an invitation to give an exposition of his policies or practices to the Committee.

In November 1940, the Vice-Chairman of the 1922 Committee was one Sir Reginald Clarry. On November 6th, he wrote the following letter, in longhand, to Mr. Churchill:

My Dear Prime Minister,

In the chair of the 1922 Conservative Private Members Committee held today, the Executive Committee were requested to meet and hear certain criticisms of the Fighter Command (RAF) brought forward by several members.

This meeting was held and I was requested to represent to you the lack of confidence in which Sir Hugh Dowding is held in certain quarters of the personel (sic) of the Force, and the grave concern felt by my Executive. It will be my duty to report to the full Committee at their next meeting, and any reply you care to give me to this representation will be greatly appreciated.

I am, my dear Prime Minister,
Yours very sincerely
Reginald Clarry

One would like to know the nature of the criticisms made vocally of Fighter Command and of Sir Hugh Dowding in the 1922 Committee. One would like even more to know the identity of the 'several members' who brought forward the criticisms. The conspicuous features of this letter are, first, its vagueness, and, second – although there is no disclaimer – the fact that the 1922 Committee had no business sticking its nose into the affairs of Fighter Command, and that the Committee – like Miss Ward – had no knowledge of Fighter Command and its Commander. It is defamation by innuendo; this, as the Vikings would have said, is 'nerding's werk'.

Churchill's reply two days later delivered a merited rebuke:

Your Committee will I hope believe that all these questions of high appointments are continually in my mind, and that I have many sources of information and opportunities of forming a right judgment. I have not only to try to make sure that the best men are chosen, but also to make officers discharging tasks of extreme difficulty feel confidence that they will be supported and protected while they do their duty. I do not think it would be at all a good thing for the 1922 Committee to become the kind of collecting house for complaints against serving Commanders-in-Chief or other important officials. This I am sure would be a function which the Members of the Committee would be the first to repudiate.[xii]

* * * * *

The assaults on Air Chief Marshal Sir Hugh Dowding cited and discussed in these pages show some remarkable common features, and some equally remarkable timing. The first thing to note is that every criticism, explicit and implied, was addressed to Churchill. The questions impose themselves insistently: why did they involve themselves? Why did they go direct to the Prime Minister instead of through the normal channels?

The second thing is that Miss Ward and the 1922 Committee had little or no knowledge of the matters they were meddling in. They therefore received their information from another (or other). Macdonald, on the other hand, had direct access to sources of information. 'Information' is perhaps too mild and vague a word; it is necessary to visualize not just the casual passing of information, but the deliberate briefing of these people, their convincing, and the assurance that they would do something about it.

In the case of Irene Ward, she was given a document, with the agreement on her part to send it on to Churchill. The passing of the document to her can only have been in person, from someone she knew. Similarly, this same person must have convinced her, in confidential personal discussion, that the information in the document was reliable. (As we have seen, Sinclair, on receiving it from Churchill, locked it up in a box and later claimed to have forgotten about it. This action cannot have been taken to protect Dowding, for Sinclair knew that other copies were being circulated. In other words, he intended to do nothing about it, for the likely reason that he hoped something would come of it, without action on his part.)

It is equally obvious that the 'several members' of the 1922 Committee who had voiced 'certain criticisms of the Fighter Command' and who had convinced the Committee of 'the lack of confidence in which Sir Hugh Dowding is held in certain quarters of the . . . (Air) Force' must themselves have been briefed on the issues. (The 'several' may of course have only two.)

One certain conclusion we can reach is that Miss Ward and the 1922 Committee did not act on their own initiative. Despite their professed ignorance, which was real; they were 'put up to it'. We believe, on the other hand, that Macdonald, despite his Air Force position, could have taken the action that he did on his own unprompted initiative. But we also believe that Macdonald could as easily have been persuaded by Leigh-Mallory to tackle Churchill. What most probably happened is that Miss Ward and Macdonald, having themselves been successfully 'enlisted', were the members who raised the matter in the 1922 Committee.

We have finally to look at the timing of the representations made to Churchill, the specific purpose of each one, their success or otherwise, and the connection between them and the stages of Dowding's tenure and appointment.

The first document, the anonymous one that Irene Ward was circulating, was forwarded to Churchill with a covering letter dated August 17th. This letter put forward the view that it would be a disaster if Dowding succeeded Newall as Chief of the Air Staff, and that Portal was by far the best choice. Before this letter was written, Dowding's term of office, as Newall's letter to him of July 10th specified, was due to terminate on October 31st. However, on August 12th Newall wrote again to Dowding telling him that now there was to be no limit placed on his appointment as Commander-in-Chief of Fighter Command. The anonymous diatribe against Newall and Dowding had, as we have seen, been composed some weeks before; but its distribution, if any, must have been restricted to insiders or intimates of the author. Now, suddenly, it began to be circulated to a larger audience. It was circulated widely from August 17th onwards; that is to say, its larger, outward circulation began exactly five days after the indefinite extension of Dowding's tenure of office. Not only that; its circulation extended throughout September and into October. Whether or not this document, allied with who knows what other manoeuvres, achieved all its desired effects, the fact remains that some time in October the appointment of Portal to succeed Newall as CAS was made and became known.

Miss Ward's letter did not specify the shortcomings of Dowding which were serious enough to disqualify him as a candidate for the highest RAF office. However that was not the case with Salmond's letter to the Prime Minister, and his meeting with Churchill shortly after. Salmond's case was specific: Dowding had failed to meet the night attacks and prepare adequate counter-measures, and for that failure he must be removed.

The Trenchard-Salmond correspondence and campaign against Dowding – according to the documentation that is publicly available – were carried out in September and October. They seemed to bear no fruit, or no immediate fruit.

It was on October 24th that Macdonald had his meeting with Churchill. Macdonald's position as adjutant of 242 Squadron suggests that he wanted to see Churchill to apprise him of Dowding's failure to settle the discord between 12 Group and 11 Group of Fighter Command. This represented a progressive raising of the stakes against Dowding:

1) in June, the call was to find a Chief of the Air Staff who could deal with Dowding;
2) in August, it was deemed necessary to block his elevation to Chief of the Air Staff;
3) in September-October, it became urgent to remove him from Fighter Command;
4) in November, the Air Staff wanted nothing less than his definitive retirement.

It is unlikely that the increasing severity of measures to be taken against Dowding was mere coincidence. It raises the possibility of design and intent on the part of some person or persons unknown, almost certainly within the Air Ministry, who knew of, or were a party to, the criticisms being circulated against Dowding and of the agitations for his removal, and who attempted to further the cause by pulling strings and dropping words in the places that would produce the desired results. Cabals met and schemed; conspiracy was seething beneath the surface.

The final question – and this we can answer with confidence – is: why Churchill? Churchill was known to be Dowding's strongest supporter. In order to get rid of

Dowding, Churchill had to be persuaded that Dowding was no longer up to it. Churchill was so persuaded; the stream of criticisms and calumnies undoubtedly took their toll. But something more was needed to convince him of Dowding's inability to deal with the immediate, or future, operational demands required of Fighter Command.

Notes:

i. The memorandum is discussed below.

ii. Following is the text of the Summary:

The above mentioned weaknesses in the character of Air Chief Marshal Newall have their reactions on the Air Ministry and on the whole Royal Air Force. It is, therefore, not surprising that many informed officers of medium seniority in the RAF are in despair at the day to day drift, the counter-orders which follow orders, the muddles, the waste of effort and the consequent unnecessary loss of life and aircraft which result from weak higher direction within the Air Ministry. Even more serious is the loss of grip which has seemed to permeate the Air Ministry during almost every crisis which has arisen since the war began.

From the foregoing criticisms it will be obvious that there is the most urgent need to replace Air Chief Marshal Newall as Chief of the Air Staff by the best officer who can be found for the appointment. The change is necessary to repair an injustice to the magnificent personnel of the Royal Air Force units and also to the whole nation.

(If these criticisms of Newall are compared with the attacks against Dowding; and if the relative achievements of Newall and Dowding are compared; a comparison of their respective 'fates' is illuminating. Newall, when he was retired in October, was promoted to Marshal of the Royal Air Force and appointed Governor-General of New Zealand.)

This memorandum, it has recently been disclosed, was written by (then) Wing Commander Edgar James Kingston McCloughry, at the time working in the Directorate of War Organization of the Air Ministry. (See the article, 'A Political Intrigue Against the Chief of the Air Staff: The Downfall of Air Chief Marshal Sir Cyril Newall', by Sebastian Ritchie, in *'War and Society'*, vol. 16, no.1 (May 1998) published by the University of New South Wales.)

In my correspondence with Denis Richards, Mr. Richards put forward the idea in his letter to me of April 2nd, 1996, that he suspected Kingston McCloughry was the author of the document. 'I've always understood [he wrote] there were things linking him with the document'. Kingston McCloughry's judgement was warped, it seems, by his failure to be promoted. (See also Furse, p. 145.)

iii. Richards, p. 169. Mr Richards informed the author in a personal letter, in reply to a series of questions that he graciously answered in every detail, that he obtained this information in an interview he had with Miss Ward on December 6, 1973. The author hoped to question Miss Ward himself, in 1988, but learnt that she had died in 1980.

iv. This and the previous letter are in the National Archives at PREM 4/4/6.

v. Wright concludes his account of Dowding's mission in Transjordan with this quotation from Dowding's final appreciation of the situation in the Middle East. We quote it only to show the sanity and prescience of Dowding's judgement and how well Trenchard acted in choosing Dowding for the mission: 'I feel that we must not allow our sympathy to lead us into any condonation of murder and robbery by whomsoever they may be committed. If the Zionist Policy is to be imposed on the country, it can only be imposed by force; for the Arab will never believe that it has any sanction in equity. If this force is applied half-heartedly, or with insufficient means, further outbreaks are to be apprehended; and a further outbreak must not be allowed to occur. If it does occur on a considerable scale in Palestine, it is my firm belief that it will not be confined to this country, and that its eventual consequences will be incalculable.'

vi. Townsend, pp. 126-27. On the other hand, it is certain that Dowding would have concurred with this judgement by 'Johnnie' Johnson: 'The bomber is the true instrument of air power, and the fighter, when used offensively to assist the bomber, is merely a means to an end.' If Johnnie were still alive I would ask him if he would be willing to amend the phrase 'merely a means' to 'an indispensable means'.

vii. See the article 'The March Retreat of 1918. The last battle of the Royal Flying Corps' by Wg Cmdr P J Daybell, who quotes H.A. Jones, in the RAF Historical Society Journal 22 (2000), p. 112. This is as accurate a description as possible of the operation of the Dowding System when it came into effect in 1940.

viii. H.R. Allen, p.68.

ix. The Trenchard-Salmond correspondence is held in the Royal Air Force Museum.

x. The charge of inhumanity against Dowding is outrageous. Few military men can have had a greater concern for humanity and been more horrified by the destructiveness of war. How many other men of Dowding's stature have written a treatise against war? We feel that it is Dowding's very humanity that aroused Trenchard's and Salmond's distaste and enmity. Trenchard had already called Dowding a 'dismal Jimmy'. And Salmond had a ruthless streak. We will see in chapter nine a similar parting of views that separated Churchill from Dowding.

xi. Salmond's hostility towards Dowding may have had a doctrinal origin, for he, like Trenchard, was a committed bomber and 'offensive' man. Yet by 1940 he had clearly become poisoned by a deeply personal animus, the origin for which may lie in Salmond's access to Dowding's correspondence with the Air Staff in the formative years of Fighter Command and in his siding with the Air Staff in their dealings with Dowding. This suspicion is fostered by the fact that Dowding was critical of former air defence commanders, including Salmond and Joubert. Salmond's biographer and Henry Probert have nothing to say on the matter.

xii. Ref. CHAR 20/2 A.

CHAPTER 5

The Conspirators Prevail

——⚍——

High Drama – and Tragedy

The daylight attacks were contained and turned back in September. In October, as we have seen, the Luftwaffe resorted mostly to hit-and-run tactics with bomb-carrying Messerschmitt 109s and 110s. At 12 Group Bader was still massing his fighters in big wings, and still not having any success, against an enemy which was now a far swifter and more elusive prey than the bombers had been. At the same time Leigh-Mallory's voice was being heeded in the Air Ministry, where the Under-Secretary of State for Air, Harold Balfour, and the Vice-Chief of the Air Staff, Sholto Douglas, were championing the idea of superiority in numbers as promised, on paper at least, by the big wings. In this chapter we will narrate the events which followed one upon the other in remorseless sequence and which were to culminate in the removal from their commands, first, of Dowding, then of Park. The events are these:

October 24 . . . . Macdonald sees Churchill
October 27 . . . . Sinclair visits Duxford
November 2/6 . . . . Balfour visits Duxford : the 'Duxford Memorandum'
November 13/14 . . . . Dowding sees Sinclair -- and Churchill
November 15 . . . . Sinclair's telephone call
November 18 . . . . Portal writes to Dowding
November 25 . . . . The End of the line.

1. Macdonald and Churchill
In October, Flight Lieutenant Peter Macdonald went to see Harold Balfour, the Under-Secretary of State for Air, and asked him to set up a meeting for him with Churchill. Balfour, according to Balfour's own account, refused to arrange a meeting with Churchill, yet reminding Macdonald of his right as an MP to ask to see the Prime Minister. Balfour described Macdonald's request thus in *Wings over Westminster*:

Peter returned periodically to the House of Commons in the uniform of a Flight Lieutenant. The position of a serving MP is always a delicate one in relation to his service life. Peter wished to retail to me what was happening between the Groups and the failure of the C-in-C Fighter Command to rectify

77

the position. I asked Peter not to talk to me about RAF affairs, feeling that it would be wrong for me to listen to a junior officer, even though a member of Parliament. He then asked if I could arrange for him to see Churchill. I replied that I could do no such thing, but that as an MP he had a right to ask to see the Prime Minister. He saw Churchill and hence down the pipeline came the Churchill enquiries.

Macdonald had his meeting on October 24th and was closeted with Churchill for over an hour. We must ask by what right an MP, who was also a serving RAF officer, might take it upon himself to seek a meeting with the Prime Minister in order to apprise him of Air Force matters? And by what means did Macdonald presume to know that Churchill was not already 'in the know' when an officer as lowly as a squadron adjutant seemed to 'know it all'?

The propriety of this action by Macdonald has not been subjected to critical examination. The few writers who have discussed it have approved Macdonald's initiative, on the ground that it was the business of the Prime Minister, who was also Minister of Defence, to know what was going on. This is to put oneself in the shoes of the Prime Minister, and not in Macdonald's place. Macdonald, having failed to enlist the direct help of Balfour, who saw its irregularity – but still encouraged him – should have requested a meeting with Sinclair, the minister responsible for air matters. And one cannot fail to ask why Macdonald did not go through the regular air force channels. Did he write to Leigh-Mallory or telephone him, as he could well have done, without telling Bader of his action, to suggest a meeting between Leigh-Mallory and Dowding? There is no evidence that he took any such action. (On the other hand, many officers have left behind no evidence of their actions and of many events no record.)

There is a more profound reason why Macdonald took the course that he did – a course of action, let us not forget, which can only be deemed highly irregular. That reason — the need for secrecy – has nothing, and everything, to do with keeping Bader in the dark. He could not let Bader know what he intended to do, for the reason that Bader would have vetoed it, and because his interview with Churchill was all of a piece with his other activities, as we shall show. What Macdonald did was to use his position as an MP to influence Air Force policy. Nothing could be more reprehensible. As an MP, his proper activities had to be restricted to the interest and well-being of his constituents and his constituency of the Isle of Wight. As a serving officer of the RAF, his activities were necessarily bound to Air Force matters.

Macdonald wore two hats. They were different hats. And they were not interchangeable. Did Macdonald go to the Isle of Wight and inform his constituents of Air Force matters? Of course not. In point of fact, Balfour was culpable by the very fact of advising Macdonald that it was his right – and these are Balfour's own words – 'his right as an MP to ask to see the Prime Minister.' Precisely: 'his right as an MP' – that is, as a Member of Parliament. Macdonald was the member of parliament for the Isle of Wight; he was not the member of parliament for RAF Station Duxford or for

242 Squadron. But Balfour incriminates himself; for did he not also tell Macdonald: 'I asked Peter not to talk to me about RAF affairs, feeling that it would be wrong for me to listen to a junior officer, even though an MP'?

Macdonald's action smacks of as one of the gravest duplicity. His deed was an act of treachery against his Commander-in-Chief, in going behind his back to report to the highest authority in the land on issues which were the Commander-in-Chief's province. There is worse. Let us read again what Balfour had said about Macdonald's visit: 'Peter wished to retail . . . the failure of the C-in-C Fighter Command to rectify the position [between 11 and 12 Groups].' What position? Why, the antagonism between Park and Leigh-Mallory over their differing tactical ideas. And how, in Macdonald's view, was this position to be 'rectified'? How else than in favour of Leigh-Mallory and 12 Group – that is, in favour of his squadron and its commander, his CO, Douglas Bader? It sticks out a mile that if Macdonald had meant in favour of Park, and hence of Dowding, he would not have used the word 'rectify' and he would not have needed to see Balfour. He went to see Balfour precisely because he knew that Balfour, like Douglas, was on the side of Leigh-Mallory.

It is equally impossible to condone Macdonald's action on the pretext that he was intervening in the interest of England's defence, an issue paramount to all others. The fact is that, by the time he saw Churchill, in late October, the daylight aerial operations known as the Battle of Britain were essentially over, and Bader's Duxford wing had had no success for over three weeks.

What are we to say of Churchill, in agreeing to hear Macdonald? In his place, it is tempting to imagine oneself refusing, and telling Macdonald either to go through the usual channels, or to see the Minister in the first instance. Yet, knowing Churchill as we think we do, and his unquenchable thirst for information, his imperious desire to know what was going on everywhere, his life-long custom of finding out and seeing for himself – and let us not dismiss his propensity for a tincture of intrigue – it is easier to excuse Churchill than it is to condone Macdonald. The temptation we shall resist is to claim that this act of Macdonald's, and the consequences which flowed from it and from Churchill's next move, were to result, in themselves, in Dowding's removal. As we shall see, the top authorities in the Air Ministry were resolved in their determination to get rid of Dowding anyway. But Macdonald's session with Churchill did have immediate repercussions. And those repercussions were so baleful that one cannot help wondering whether some sinister agent behind the scenes had not been putting a flea in Macdonald's ear.

The first consequence of Macdonald's action was that Churchill telephoned Sinclair wanting to know what was going on in Fighter Command. A few days later Sinclair went to Duxford and asked a few questions. Suitably impressed and influenced, he then sent Balfour to Duxford to carry out a fuller inquiry.

2. Balfour at Duxford

Balfour spent the day of November 2nd at Duxford, and, ostensibly, spoke at length to (and listened to) the squadron and flight commanders and to the pilots of the squadrons stationed there. And especially he listened to Bader, and to Stan Turner, one of Bader's flight commanders. Back in London that evening, Balfour wrote his report. A copy lay on Douglas's desk the next morning, awaiting his arrival. It must have been a heaven-sent answer to his prayers. Or other activities.

An informed and objective critical faculty is one of the most vital functions of intelligence. On the other hand, an over-ready acceptance of what one hears or reads is an indication of prejudice. When such acceptance is provoked by the weight of authority, such as a known name, it may be understandable, but no less inexcusable. A case in point is the exchange of views between Balfour and Douglas, on the one hand, and, on the other, between Balfour and Dowding – the latter fully supported, let it not be forgotten, by his Air Staff at Bentley Priory. The opinions of Balfour and Douglas, at or near the pinnacle of authority within the Air Ministry, were those of authorities not to be taken lightly. The critical intelligence of Dowding, on the other hand, was a force not to be hoodwinked or trifled with. The authorities might be in the driver's seat, in a manner of speaking – they did exercise the ultimate authority in questions of careers, or in the 'fate' of all personnel of the Royal Air Force. But the Air Officer Commanding-in-Chief of Fighter Command was the ultimate authority in matters affecting operational control within his Command. Dowding never lost sight of this, his ultimate responsibility.

We have to examine three documents produced by this affair. They were written, respectively, by the Hon. Harold Balfour, Under-Secretary of State for Air; by Sholto Douglas; and by Dowding.

The 'Duxford' Memorandum

Balfour's report, in particular, gives rise to difficulties of interpretation and acceptance, precisely because of his career and authority. Balfour had served with distinction as a pilot in the Royal Flying Corps in France in World War One. He was one of the few pilots of the day who continued to fly in the post-war world, and who not only owned his own aeroplane, but maintained his licence by flying all the latest types. As Under-Secretary of State for Air, he flew the second prototype Spitfire to be built. He was a distinguished gentleman, and, as MP for the Isle of Thanet, an adornment of the Conservative Party of the 1930s and 1940s. But one must not be influenced by the reputation of the writer: one cannot but examine his words and deeds. The text of Balfour's report of his visit to Duxford on November 2nd reveals exactly what the objective researcher condemns in the reporting of one's inquiries; namely, an uncritical acceptance of what one hears. As we mentioned, an uncritical acceptance of what one hears is attributable to immaturity or lack of intelligence. Neither defect can be said of Balfour; to those two we must add a third defect, the commonest of all: a willingness to hear only what one wants to hear. Balfour visited only Duxford, and only for a few hours. Duxford was then the home of 19 and 310 (Czech) squadrons. Bader had flown down with his 242 Squadron for the day. The fact that Balfour listened predominantly to Bader, and that he visited no other squadrons in 12 Group, and none at all in 11 Group, colours his report to the extent that it stands out as one of the most partisan documents written within the Air Ministry at this time. The allegations that he relays in his report to the Secretary of State and the Deputy CAS (Sholto Douglas) the next day are unsubstantiated opinions voiced by Bader. Among them are the following:

> Some pilots of 12 Group's 'Balbo Wing Formation' are resentful against 11 Group and its AOC for letting things develop as they have.

> 11 Group [AOC or pilots?] are accused of jealousy of 12 Group's capacity to shoot down more Germans than they can.

> 11 Group pilots, in failing to repel the enemy with the forces at hand, are 'shaken in their morale'.

These allegations are pure Bader and Company – and calumny. We need only make these observations: 1) Bader's insistence on his so-called 'Balbo Wing Formation' is tantamount to their, and 12 Group's, telling 11 Group how to fight their battle in the south; 2) the admission that they, 12 Group, had 'not had contact with the enemy since the end of September' – and here we are in November – despite their having flown 'at least one sortie per day' in favourable weather, would have made any intelligent leader look to factors other than being called too late by 11 Group; 3) throughout October enemy action comprised mostly raids carried out by high-flying, bomb-carrying Me109s and 110s, and hence much too elusive for the unwieldy wings; 4) for nearly five weeks, from September 10, 74 Squadron, under the leadership of the incomparable 'Sailor' Malan—as we have already seen – was rested from 11 Group and stationed at Coltishall, where 242 Squadron was also based. (It is significant that Malan's squadron took no part in any of Bader's wings.)

The Dowding/Douglas Correspondence: November 3–6

A point-by-point refutation of the allegations and criticisms contained in Balfour's report is the substance of Dowding's response three days later. The covering letter from Sholto Douglas is another matter, and commands comment. After placing himself, again, squarely in Leigh-Mallory's camp, he reverts to the Air Ministry conference of October 17th – as Balfour had done in fact, gratuitously – to buttress this support, and quotes the three principal recommendations imposed by the Balbo champions. In so doing, Balfour and Douglas seem to turn a blind eye to the changed conditions of the battle, of the enemy's changed tactics; and above all they blithely side-stepped the pointed application of the recommendations in question. Those recommendations, favouring big wing formations, were, as we have already discussed, not intended to be put into effect at that time: they were pointers to the future. The introductory paper prepared for the conference, let us recall, conceded the success of Dowding's and Park's tactics and handling of the battle. It then went on to look ahead to a renewal of heavy daytime raids and asserted the necessity that the lessons learnt should be applied generally 'to enable the fighter defence to operate at maximum efficiency.' No one could object to that realistic aim, even if honest tacticians might disagree over the lessons; indeed, it can only be applauded. But one must speculate why the matter is raised again, by Balfour and Douglas, at this juncture, when the attacks are far from 'heavier' but conspicuously lighter.

A second issue raised by Douglas's letter is of great interest. He writes: '[the] difference of opinion [between Park and Leigh-Mallory] should be resolved as quickly as possible, . . . and I think that it is for you to put the matter right by an authoritative statement of your views. This would be far more satisfactory than for the Air Ministry to try and act as referee.' This strong invitation 'to give the Groups an authoritative statement of your views' is repeated in the final paragraph.

It is important to note that Douglas refers only to the 'difference of opinion' between Park and Leigh-Mallory, i.e. to a professional difference over tactics and cooperation between the Groups. Even so, it is a piece of gross meddling in Fighter Command's operational policies, and an impudence on Douglas's part that he should presume to tell the wiser and more experienced Commander-in-Chief how to fight the battle. Dowding issued no such statement, but had he done so he would merely have reiterated that only the Groups were in a position to assess the immediacy and the level of the danger presented by an incoming raid; and that only the sectors could decide which squadrons to scramble to meet the raiders in their region. He might also have insisted that the Groups re-examine the use of wings in their areas of responsibility while recommending that wings of more than two squadrons should not be assembled.

Dowding had delegated to his Group AOCs almost total authority in matters of tactics, so that he could no longer issue tactical directions to them. That was an essential feature of the Dowding System: the separation of the strategic and the tactical elements of the air battle. It is doubtful whether Dowding felt he could even order a Group to use no more than two squadrons in a wing formation. But let Dowding speak for himself:

> [What] so many people seemed to forget, or to overlook, was that Park's whole position during the battle had to be one of defence. All that I had planned and built up in the structure of the Command was for the defence of the country. The big wings idea was for offensive tactics, not defensive, and it failed to prove its worth in the defensive role.
>
> [The Air Staff at the Air Ministry] didn't seem to understand, or didn't want to understand, why I was allowing this great latitude to my Group Commanders. By that, I mean in (sic) how many squadrons they should send up to meet the different kinds of raids. That was the Group Commander's problem, and it would depend on how many squadrons they had in the air and how many they had left on the ground. I did not want to tie their hands in any way, and I felt that they must be flexible in their own thinking. Also, it was because of the difficulty of full discussion with headquarters in questions which demanded instant action on the part of the Groups that I left them with this free hand. On the other hand, I would not have been prepared to concede to my Group Commanders powers to go contrary to my views and wishes in important strategical issues.[i]

The sole recourse Dowding had, if a Group Commander's actions failed persistently to meet the AOC's expectations and strategic plan, was to replace him. It seems to us that that is precisely what Leigh-Mallory did, when he failed to understand that big wings had no place in a defensive battle. Moreover, when Leigh-Mallory placed a sort of *cordon sanitaire* around the squadrons that comprised Bader's wing, it was tantamount to a challenge to his Commander-in-Chief. This Dowding should not have ignored. Dowding further told his biographer that when 'the time came for me to intervene it was too late'. This is rather a startling admission, as he had clearly failed to keep his finger on the pulse.

One writer, Peter Brown, himself a Battle pilot, of 12 Group at that, has written, in defence of Dowding, that it was Evill who kept from Dowding the important exchanges relating to the dispute between 11 and 12 Groups, arguing that Evill, having served mostly in Bomber Command, was himself an enigmatic figure whose role in the matter calls for investigation. I cannot agree; as soon as Park refused to submit his requests directly to 12 Group and passed them to Fighter Command instead, Dowding should have smelt a rat and done something about both Leigh-Mallory and Bader.

Further, the counter-criticisms levelled by Dowding against Leigh-Mallory and Bader in his rebuttal of Balfour's report might have seemed serious enough to warrant their removal. We cannot know whether this radical measure occurred to Dowding, especially in Leigh-Mallory's case.

Some later writers, notably among Dowding's critics, have pointed up Dowding's failure to tackle the issue of the personal feelings harboured by Leigh-Mallory towards Park and Dowding. In the one case it was an intense jealousy that he did not have command of 11 Group in the Battle; and in the other a deep hatred of Dowding for his slights. But should Dowding really have interfered? A commander has no business allowing personal factors to affect the performance of his duties; Dowding himself had known enough hostility, unpopularity and criticism in his time, and he rose above it. For two or three years he shrugged off the ill-feeling that he knew many officers and high officials in the Air Ministry entertained toward him. He expected nothing less of any officer who rose to high levels of command: he judged himself, and he judged others, only by their professional conduct and skills. High feelings, animosity, jealousy, even hatred, are common among men in all walks of life when rivalry and ambition are the directing passions. This is even truer in war when the stakes are so much higher, when the rewards are fame and glory, or, conversely, humiliation.

We will wind up this debate by quoting the judgement of John James:

> The amount of naked ambition, self seeking, malice and intrigue within that headquarters [between Esher, Haig, French, Wilson and Robertson] makes the quarrels between Montgomery, Eisenhower and Patton look like tiffs over cups of tea at a Mothers' Union meeting.[ii]

And the Park/Leigh-Mallory dispute is as dandelion chaff in the breeze. Except, of course, for the dismal fact that Dowding's enemies, who sided with Leigh-Mallory, made the most of it - to Dowding and Park's disadvantage.

3. Dowding and Sinclair – and Churchill

Dowding was invited to see Sir Archibald Sinclair, and duly had a meeting with him in the Air Ministry on November 13. From this it seems that the Air Council must have taken the decision at some time in late October or early November on a change of command at Fighter Command. Sinclair drafted a summary of their conversation at the request of Beaverbrook and his notes are held in the Beaverbrook Library archives.[iii] According to this document, Sinclair told Dowding that the Government wished to send him, Sir Hugh, to the United States as adviser on the production of military aircraft. 'We believed [in Sinclair's words] that the Americans would be willing to accept the guidance of a man whose opinion and personality would command respect.' Sinclair expressed to Dowding his appreciation of Dowding's great services as Commander in Chief of Fighter Command, but he had come to the conclusion that 'it was right to make the change which this new project would involve.'

Dowding replied that it would be one thing if he was only being asked to undertake a temporary mission, but that he would want to return to his command at Fighter Command. The document concludes: 'I replied that I must tell him that that was not in my mind and that I was proposing to appoint Air Vice-Marshal Sholto Douglas to Fighter Command. He said that he quite understood, but that he would want a night to think it over and that he would want to see the Prime Minister. I answered that, of course, I would not press him and that he should have time to think it over. I had no doubt that the Prime Minister would be most willing to see him; at the same time it was possible that after thinking it over he might not think it necessary to see the Prime Minister. He answered that he would certainly wish to see the Prime Minister – and so we parted.'

Let us examine these statements: Sinclair, after informing Dowding that the Government wished to send him as head of a mission to the U.S., added: 'I had come to the conclusion that it was right to make the change which this new project would involve.' Orwell would have admired the double-speak: 'the change which this new project would involve.' A change of command had already been decided on, i.e. Dowding's removal, then a new assignment was thought up for Dowding. Now the logic is turned upside down, and the new project becomes the reason for the change. What must have stuck even more bitterly in Dowding's craw is the claim of the rightness of the change. A.J.P. Taylor's letter concludes: 'Lord Beaverbrook, who favoured Dowding, was himself locked in conflict with the Air Council and therefore could not support him. He proposed the mission [to the United States] as a way out.'

Beaverbrook was assuredly one of Dowding's most faithful supporters throughout the Battle, 'locked in conflict' with the Air Ministry to the same degree as Dowding. Perhaps that is one reason why Beaverbrook admired Dowding: both men were independent thinkers, decisive, unorthodox in their ways, and contemptuous of shallow minds and bureaucratic obstruction. It is therefore difficult to understand Taylor's assertion that Beaverbrook 'could not support him' because he 'was himself locked in conflict with the Air Council.' His being locked in conflict with the Air Council and the Air Staff had been a constant state of affairs from the day he had been appointed Minister of Aircraft Production, and it had never hampered him before in his relations with Dowding. What had changed now – and apparently so suddenly – as to make him unable to support Dowding? If ever Dowding needed support it was at this moment. Beaverbrook, if Taylor's account is correct, betrayed Dowding.

But let us look again at the last sentence of Taylor's letter: 'He [Beaverbrook] proposed the mission to the United States as a way out.' A 'way out' of what, and for whom? A way out of embarrassment for Dowding in the light of his removal from his command? A way out of an impasse for Churchill, now forced to acquiesce in his removal? A way out for the Air Council, in view of Dowding's accomplishments? None of these, we suggest, although the proposal certainly helped them. The idea was Beaverbrook's; if he 'could not support' Dowding, his proposal was a way out for himself, to save his own face and cover his betrayal of Dowding.[iv] Taylor prefaces his last statement with these words: 'It seems clear that the Air Council had decided to make a change at Fighter Command and that Sir Archibald Sinclair and the Prime Minister acquiesced.'

There we have the truth, albeit inadvertently: 'the Air Council had decided to make a change at Fighter Command'. But in what follows, Taylor knows not whereof he writes; Sinclair was the President of the Air Council and had wanted Dowding's removal shortly after he became Secretary of State for Air, so acquiescence is hardly the appropriate term – though it is not hard to envisage Sinclair as wanting to appear to acquiesce in Dowding's removal. But the acquiescence of Churchill was, as we have seen, a *sine qua non* of Dowding's removal, and a stumbling block to his enemies' schemes and ambitions.

Before we examine the various reasons put forward by numerous writers to explain or justify the removal of Dowding from his command, it is necessary to clear up once and for all the controversy surrounding the manner of his removal; Dowding's removal, or dismissal, from his Command has been the subject of interminable debate. The controversy centres in great part on the technicality of whether Dowding was retired or sacked, and has provoked prolonged discussion. The controversy exists, to this day, because of the hitherto unresolved debate between the champions of Dowding and the defenders of the Air Ministry, whose official, though unwritten, policy, as we have already pointed out, persists in denying recognition of Dowding's achievements.

The Air Ministry position is that Dowding was properly informed that his tenure as Commander-in-Chief of Fighter Command was being terminated, and that Dowding had no complaint about the termination and the manner of its communication to him. (It must be said, however, that the Air Ministry has never issued any statement about either the fact or the manner.) Dowding's defenders insist, on the contrary, that he was sacked abruptly and out-of-the-blue by a telephone call from Sinclair, and that Dowding harboured an ineradicable resentment over this cavalier treatment for the rest of his life. We hope to show that, unlikely though it seems, both versions have a basis in fact; and that one version is truer than the other.

We will start by quoting Harold Balfour's account of the event: 'Dowding says that in the second week of November 1940 he received a sudden phone call at his headquarters from the Secretary of State for Air. "He told me I was to relinquish my Command immediately. I asked what was meant by 'immediately' and I was told that it would take effect within the next day or so." This version of the conversation is the foundation of the allegation that Dowding was "sacked on the end of a telephone." It just does not stand up.' A few pages earlier, Balfour had written: 'sacked after the Battle of Britain at a moment's notice by the Secretary of State on the end of the telephone, he certainly was not.' Robert Wright also suggests that this is what happened in his biography of Dowding: Wright's source of information was Dowding himself. This is his account:

> He told me that I was to relinquish my Command immediately. I asked what was meant by 'immediately', and I was told that it would take effect within the next day or so. Since that was tantamount to my being given twenty-four hours' notice, and verbally at that, I pointed out that it was perfectly absurd that I should be relieved of my Command in this way unless it was thought that I had committed some major crime or something like that. But all that I could get in reply was that the decision had been reached, and that was that, with no explanation for such a precipitate step being taken.

Before we try to resolve the mystery of the telephone call and the story of Dowding's dismissal, let us look at another view. One of the accounts that deserves the closest attention is that given by Hough & Richards:

> After the three very short extensions of his tenure, the latest time–limit, fixed for 31 October, had on 21 August been completely withdrawn. Then, quite unexpectedly to him, he was required to relinquish his Command at a few days' notice. In later years he even told his biographer, Robert Wright, that in the second week of November he received 'a sudden phone-call' from Sinclair telling him he was to relinquish his Command 'immediately'. . . . Sinclair, a devoted minister and the soul of courtesy, was not a man to sack a respected commander over the telephone.

Shortly after the publication of Wright's book, there was a flurry of letters in *The Times* in January 1970 seeking to throw light on 'the mystery'. The first, on January 14, from Marshal of the Royal Air Force Sir John Slessor, gently took Dowding to task for his failure of memory. We quote almost the entire letter:

> There is one passage in Mr. Robert Wright's very interesting book, *Dowding and the Battle of Britain*, which I feel must be called in question, namely the allegation attributed to Lord Dowding that just after the real battle of Britain had been won, in the second week of November, 1940, he was summarily – and by implication unexpectedly – dismissed from his command in the course of a sudden and very brief telephone conversation by the Secretary of State for Air, Sir Archibald Sinclair (now Lord Thurso). No one who knows Lord Dowding would suggest for one moment that he is capable of deliberate

misrepresentation of facts. I am among the many who think he was shabbily treated at the end of the Battle of Britain and has behaved with great dignity ever since. But from my own experience over a number of years of writing some military history, I know how strangely easy it is to forget completely some significant details even of really important events in which one was closely involved, even relatively few years before. And I respectfully suggest that in connection with this event, it is not impossible that Lord Dowding's memory may have let him down...

The Directorate of Plans, of which I was then the head, was not directly concerned with the battle; and I had no idea of what was going on within Fighter Command until – for some unaccountable reason which I can neither remember nor imagine – I was present at the famous (or notorious, according to one's point of view) conference in the Air Council room on October 17. . . . Lord Dowding had been at Fighter Command for a long time; he had not always seen eye to eye with the Air Ministry; and, as Mr. Wright reminds us, the question of his retirement had been discussed with him on a number of occasions in 1939 and earlier in 1940...

That the final decision and notification to the C-in- C was made in the way described in this book is so much more incomprehensible as to be unbelievable. I have in recent months consulted a number of the now sadly diminished band of individuals, political, military and in civil service, who were in positions of responsibility connected with these events in 1940. For the most part they have (I think understandably) no recollection of what happened in this particular connection during that period of desperate crisis nearly thirty years ago. But all agree with me that it is incredible that Sir Archibald Sinclair can have acted in the manner alleged in Mr. Wright's book.

Both Lord Dowding and Mr. Wright on his behalf took great trouble to verify the facts as far as possible from official records and Dowding's own papers. The telephone story finds some corroboration in the fact that there is no copy in the archives of any letter, which one would have expected, on the lines of the typically generous and well-deserved tribute which Sinclair addressed to Dowding after VE day. Apart from that I am informed by the responsible historical authority that they can throw no light on the story, which they think is one of those mysteries likely to remain insoluble. There is one possible explanation – I put it no higher – as follows. One who at the time was in an exceptional position to know tells me that he has a clear recollection that Lord Dowding had one and possibly two appointments with the Secretary of State at about the relevant time. And I agree with him that it is a reasonable assumption that Sinclair then told him of the intention finally to retire him after the great strain he had undergone in his four years at Fighter Command, culminating in his victory in the Battle of Britain; and that the telephone call was merely to let him know that his retirement was to become effective in the immediate future. However all this may be, Lord Dowding earned the everlasting gratitude of all British people as the victor in one of the most decisive battles of history. And if it should turn out that, in view of the almost unbearable strain to which he was subjected at the time, and with the passage of years, certain details of what happened so many years ago had slipped his memory, no one could hold that against him.

This letter was followed, on the 19th, by a blunt rebuttal by Robert Wright:

In his letter to you of January 14, Marshal of the Royal Air Force Sir John Slessor calls in question the description given in my book, *Dowding and the Battle of Britain*, of the way in which Lord Dowding was notified that he would have to relinquish his command. The work that I did on this book called for an intense search over a long period of time in my effort to discover exactly what happened in this matter. The account given in the book of how it was actually done is as it was first told to me by Lord Dowding years ago, and which has been discussed by us in the numerous talks that we have had about it over the years since then. I questioned him rigorously about it; and in support of that I could find no evidence in his personal files that Lord Dowding was relieved of his command in any way other than that given in the book. As Sir John admits, there is no evidence whatsoever in the official files to support any other view. Sir John has offered what he describes as a possible explanation for the abrupt nature of my account of the dismissal, but he bases it largely on the memory – while at the same time questioning the memory of Lord Dowding – of someone whom he does not name. He further offers the view that the whole episode is an insoluble mystery. I do not accept it as a mystery.

Whether Lord Dowding was dismissed in an interview, or on the telephone, or through both, it was still one only by word of mouth, at a very short notice, and in a shabby manner. There is nothing in the record to prove otherwise. And that still leaves us with the inescapable fact that to treat him in this fashion, after all that he had achieved, was nothing short of disgraceful, made all the more so by the curious conduct of the Prime Minister. There is widespread agreement that a grave injustice was done to Lord Dowding in November, 1940. He is described by Sir John as 'the victor in one of the most decisive battles of history'. When in the name of pride, honesty and decency, is that injustice going to be corrected?

We now have to ask, in the light of the evidence presented: who is right in all this? Balfour and Slessor, among others, in rejecting Dowding's version of events, suggest that he must have had a lapse of memory in later years, for Sinclair was too decent and considerate a man ever to do such a thing. Yet is it possible that a man of Dowding's mental acuity, even as late as 1970, should have imagined it, or blown it up out of all proportion to its actual message? No: there was a telephone call, and for it to have had the impact that it did, it must have been very much as Dowding remembered it. Nevertheless, Wright's book shows a serious lacuna: it makes no mention of Dowding's meeting with Sinclair. That there was a meeting, and that they discussed the termination of Dowding's tenure, as Taylor writes, there can be no doubt. Balfour confirms it – though it took place on November 13th, not the 17th as he states.ᵛ

That there was a telephone call is equally no longer in doubt. Slessor's letter confirms it. And the Hough and Richards book confirms it: 'The telephone call, saying that a change at Stanmore was to take place immediately, must have come a day or two later.' No wonder that Dowding, not having been apprised of a date by Sinclair, was appalled, and shocked to the roots of his being. The account given by Dowding is therefore the more accurate of the two, and should be accepted by all future writers, unless other, documentary, evidence comes to light.

Dowding's discussion with Sinclair established four things: 1) that Dowding was to relinquish his command; 2) that he was to go to the United States 'as adviser on the production of military aircraft'; 3) that Douglas was to be his successor; and 4) that on the completion of his mission he would not be returning to his Command. What must be emphasized and re-emphasized here is, first, that Dowding had a document formally cancelling any time-limit to his tenure as AOC-in-C of Fighter Command; second, that Sinclair informed Dowding of the termination of his command by word of mouth, first in person and then by telephone; and third, that neither he nor any other authority ever followed it up in writing, as formality, custom, and simple courtesy demanded. This second point is insisted upon by Wright in his rebuke to Slessor: 'Whether Lord Dowding was dismissed in an interview or on the telephone, or through both, it was still done only by word of mouth, at very short notice.' (We see here, incidentally, for the first time, Wright's acknowledgment of Dowding's meeting with Sinclair.)

The third point is equally heinous. In all his, Dowding's, dealings with past and present Secretaries of State for Air and Chiefs of the Air Staff, a personal or telephone conversation having to do with Dowding's career was unfailingly followed by a letter to confirm the substance of their talk and the decision arrived at. This time there was no letter or other written communication. For one thing, as we shall see, events overtook such niceties, even on the part of such a gentleman as Sinclair. For another thing, no explanation was possible. The over-riding, by word of mouth, of a formal, written document cancelling Dowding's retirement date, is an act unprecedented in the annals of the Royal Air Force both for its illegality and its insensitivity. Still having no date to go on, Dowding continued, as usual, with the task at hand, namely, the night defences.

On the night of November 18-19, Dowding got home at nearly half past one in the morning, having been on yet another visit to his night fighter operational research station. He found a letter awaiting him. It was from Portal, the recently appointed Chief of the Air Staff. In the most ordinary and matter-of-fact manner, and as if nothing were amiss, the letter said:

> The Secretary of the State has asked me to consult you about the announcement and the date of Douglas's taking over from you. There has unfortunately been a slight leakage to the Press which we all much regret, and we therefore want to announce a list of appointments, of which this will be one, on Monday, 18th. Douglas cannot be made available to take over until Monday week the 25th, and what I am asking is whether you would agree to carry on in command until the later date.

In the announcement the date of the hand-over would be described as in the near future. If an almost uncontrollable indignation wells up in the mind of the reader he may well be excused. And those feelings have nothing to do with the contents of the letter, which are suspect enough. A 'slight leakage', bad enough if there had been one, smacks suspiciously like an excuse for delaying Douglas's assumption of command, lest otherwise the change-over look indecently precipitate. This callous, unreflecting inconsiderateness beggars belief. At the same time, Portal's letter states for the first time a precise date. On the very next day, November 20th, *The Daily Telegraph* carried on the front page a photograph of Sholto Douglas with the caption: 'Fighter Command New Chief.' (And one is expected to believe that the photograph was a 'slight leakage'!)[vi]

As to Douglas, he has told us of his reaction when he learnt of his new appointment. He wrote in his memoirs: 'Within the space of only a few days there was a sudden and rather breath-taking development. . . . I was to take the place of Dowding, who was to retire; and a day or so later there was an official announcement about the change.' (We will have more to say about this 'breath-taking development' in chapter ten.)

Dowding was a widower, and his domestic affairs were managed by his sister, Hilda, in the house provided for him by the RAF. Her recollection of the event is as follows:

> It was all a terrific rush. I had to make my own arrangements for where I was going to live. And I had to plan for the servants who had been working for us. We were working against time; and up to the very last moment we were still packing things up in order to get out as quickly as possible. And then, for all the rush, when the new man arrived he decided not to live there.

Of these few days, Robert Wright, who was Dowding's personal assistant at the time, wrote:

> In the face of all this, Dowding was completely withdrawn. He gave very little sign, even to those who were in closest contact with him, of what he was feeling. But to the more observant, or to those who, perhaps, knew him better than he realised, it was obvious he was unhappy and bewildered. It has always been my belief that he was in a state of shock.

It was only through Dowding's will that he was able to exercise that control of self that was the hallmark of his command in the Battle of Britain.

> What though the world be lost?
> All is not lost; th'unconquerable will, . . .
> And courage never to submit or yield:
> And what is else not to be overcome?
>
> Milton, *Paradise Lost*

Notes:

i. Wright, pp. 198-99. Sir Philip Joubert publicly criticized Park for his tactical handling of his resources and got a merited rebuttal from Park, who is quoted at length in Kaplan and Collier, pp. 218-223.

ii. *The Paladins*, p.47.

iii. What follows is taken from a letter by the historian A.J.P. Taylor, Beaverbrook's biographer and archivist, to *The Times* of January 22, 1970.

iv. Beaverbrook is nothing if not a politician. Little wonder that Dowding had scant respect for politicians – as, in fact, he told Churchill the very next day at their meeting. He would have agreed with 'Tizard's belief that politics is, in Rosebery's words, "An evil-smelling bog." Alanbrooke writes in his *War Diaries* (p.xvi): 'The more I saw of him [Beaverbrook] throughout the war, the more I disliked and mistrusted him. An evil genius who exercised the very worst influence on Winston.'

v. In the exchange of long letters between Slessor and Balfour held in the Churchill Archives Centre, in which Slessor claims to be searching only for the truth of the matter, they come to the agreement that Sinclair is fully vindicated by the evidence; and that Wright finally agrees with them. The evidence consists solely in the fact that Dowding had had an interview with Sinclair during which Sinclair informed Dowding that he was to leave his Command. In our view that changes nothing. Dowding had never complained about his being relieved of his Command. His unhappiness and resentment stemmed from the manner of its doing.

vi. After his retirement Dowding made sure that he was never in the same room as Portal. On the other hand we reproduce a post-war social photograph of Dowding and Trenchard taken together with Dowding's wife. Does this mean that Dowding never learnt of Trenchard's role in the conspiracy, not only to remove him from his command, but also to deny him the coveted promotion to Marshal of the Royal Air Force – and so put him on an equal footing with himself and Salmond?

Part III

Reasons and Motives

CHAPTER 6

The Reasons

—ɯ—

The Air Council had kept Dowding in suspense for two years, and even up to a dangerous phase of the Battle, in deciding on the date when he would be retired. Then, in mid-August, his retirement date was cancelled, so that he expected to serve indefinitely. Then, with a shocking suddenness, he was ordered to relinquish his command and vacate his official residence at a moment's notice. Dowding had a right to expect a word of explanation about being removed from his command both from the Air Minister, Sir Archibald Sinclair, and from the Chief of the Air Staff, Sir Charles Portal, but he received not a word from either.

Dowding's removal is not the only issue at stake here. Park was also removed from his command of 11 Group. In Park's case there can be no question of retirement. His removal was nothing less than a demotion. The removal of Dowding and of Park, within a month of each other, cannot therefore be considered except in conjunction with the intrigues underlying the events.

Dowding and Park were not isolated instances of removal either – albeit the most illustrious. Other officers had suffered, or were to suffer, the same fate; four other officers, distinguished in their fields, were removed from their appointments, without explanation. They are: Air Chief Marshal Sir Edgar Ludlow-Hewitt, Wing Commander Sidney Cotton, Group Captain 'Sailor' Malan, and Air Chief Marshal Sir Basil Embry.

These circumstances are recorded here in order to drive home this important principle, that it was not difficult or unusual for men who occupied high offices of State to carry out deeds of questionable honesty and motivation without being held to account for their acts. If those other four officers were removed without much of a whimper, Dowding was another matter entirely. He was the most senior officer in the Royal Air Force, senior even to the CAS. Moreover he had earned the admiration and the support of Churchill. But in the end, even Dowding's removal – with Churchill's consent – caused not the slightest ripple of inquiry from the Press. This silence bears testimony to the overriding dominance of the Prime Minister.

It is generally held that once an officer crossed Churchill, Churchill did not forgive him, and that officer's effective days were numbered. Was Dowding one such example? An examination of this question is deferred to chapter nine, where we discuss Churchill's role in the Battle of Britain and in Dowding's removal.

It is true, as some writers have pointed out, that Dowding had earned his retirement. But a man of his vigour and accomplishments still had much to offer. He was not consulted about his removal from his command, as simple courtesy required. To cast Dowding aside, at this critical juncture of Britain's destiny, is not an act showing confidence in the wealth of military talent and leadership available in Britain at the time. The war was just beginning and the British forces had suffered nothing but defeat. Dowding was the only leader who had accomplished something – and something of such valour that, even at the time, it was recognized for what it truly was. We state these things to put what follows into their historical context.[i]

The question we have to examine is how 'certain Air Staff', and the power-brokers on the Air Council, succeeded in persuading Churchill that Dowding had to go. This issue is far more complicated than the question suggests, and therefore invites different approaches, which themselves call for different methods. The methods we have adopted are: critical, analytical, and synthetic. In the first, we state and expose the 'reasons' put forward by previous writers. In the second, we subject the role of Churchill in Dowding's dismissal to a careful examination. And finally, we present our own interpretation of the events.

1. The 'Reasons': Other Writers

Many writers have speculated, *en passant*, in their account of Dowding or the Battle of Britain, on the why of Dowding's removal. Only two writers have developed speculation into a thesis. They are Group Captain E.B. Haslam, who published a twelve-page article in 1981; and John Ray, who wrote a doctoral thesis on the subject which he rewrote for publication in 1994. To their number we will add two other historians whose opinions attract attention. They are Denis Richards and Sebastian Cox. We propose to draw up a list of the reasons they severally give; then, after dismissing the irrelevant items, subject the most common explanations cited to a critcal study.

Haslam

In 1981 Group Captain Haslam was the Head of the Air Historical Branch in the Ministry of Defence. His article was a reply to a book and a series of articles by Len Deighton on the Battle of Britain in which Deighton repeated the account given by Robert Wright in his biography of Dowding, namely, that Dowding's dismissal came out of the blue via a telephone call from Sinclair. Haslam refutes Deighton's account as being 'both simplistic and inaccurate'.

The burden of Haslam's article is that Dowding's removal had nothing to do with the dispute over tactics and the 'wings' dispute, and little to do with Dowding's failure to resolve the personal hostility between Park and Leigh–Mallory. It had to do almost entirely with Dowding's failure to find counter-measures to the Luftwaffe's night attacks. 'The situation [he wrote] was desperate and desperate action was called for.' The first action was the setting up of a committee headed by MRAF Sir John Salmond, 'to undertake a **thorough** inquiry [our emphasis] . . . on the preparation of night fighters.' Haslam quotes Joubert, who wrote years later in his memoirs, *The Third Service*: Dowding 'would not listen to those who advocated an early diversion of effort to the solution of the night interception problem.' Haslam refutes this claim by recounting that Dowding sent a stream of reports on night interception to the Air Ministry. These reports showed Dowding's own dissatisfaction – reports that were 'characteristically honest, forthright and factual. But – (and what a 'but'!)– Dowding 'was not moving fast enough for the Air Staff.' Haslam sums up in these words: 'What is clear is that Salmond . . . represented Dowding as the obstacle to new thinking and progress at Fighter Command.'

Ray

In 1994 John Ray published a book entitled *The Battle of Britain: New Perspectives*. Ray acknowledges his debt to Haslam's slender article. He bases most of his case on Salmond's campaign against Dowding, and buttresses it with the findings of the separate committees on night defence set up by Churchill and the War Cabinet. In the Introduction Ray itemizes the 'reasons' for Dowding's removal and states: 'One aim of this book is to show that, in reality, there were seven reasons why Dowding was replaced in November 1940. Three existed even before the Battle of Britain started.' They are:

i) his age ('at fifty-eight he was an old man');[ii]
ii) he had been AOC-in-C of Fighter Command for four years and was tired, and the need for a change was felt;
iii) his relations with the Air Ministry had been contentious since 1937; . . . he was stubborn [and] unwilling to cooperate;
iv) he failed to resolve the controversy over the use of Big Wings;
v) he failed to appreciate the need 'for an urgent response' to the night Blitz;
vi) 'a more dynamic leader was sought for Fighter Command' by the end of the year when the RAF was moving to an aggressive role;
vii) Churchill and Beaverbrook came to appreciate that a new man was needed.

In his discussion of these reasons Ray fails to suggest a hierarchy of importance, with one significant exception. We may, however, dismiss as irrelevant and trivial the first, second and sixth reasons.

Richards

Richards published his *Jubilee History of the Battle* in 1989. In chapter twenty-two, 'Retrospect', he mentions some of the factors that led to Dowding's replacement:

– the 'big' wing' controversy played a part, though only a part, in the 'dismissal'.
– 'Both commanders had been under enormous strain, and Park was visibly tired.'
– '[Dowding] had held his post for the exceptionally long period of four years'.
– 'the urgent demand was for success in countering the night bombing . . . and [then] for offensive operations over the continent.'

Cox

On June 25, 1990, a symposium on the Battle of Britain was held under the joint auspices of the Royal Air Force Historical Society and the Royal Air Force Staff College Bracknell. The proceedings were published under the title, *The Battle Re-Thought*. In this volume the following remarks are attributed to Cox:

- 'Dowding was not a good co-operator';
- 'the problem of night defence, which he was thought not to be grasping with sufficient energy';
- 'the dangerous deterioration in relations between two Group commanders'.

Putting aside for the time being the ill feeling that existed between Park and Leigh-Mallory, we note three substantive reasons, common to all four writers, justifying the removal of Dowding from his command. They are: 1) Dowding was at loggerheads with and did not co-operate with the Air Ministry; 2) the tactical handling of the air battles left much to be desired; 3) his failure to counter the night attacks. We will examine them in that order. In view, however, of the patently spurious nature of the third charge and the length of our study of it, it will be treated separately in the next chapter.

I. Co-operation

It is difficult to know what Dowding's critics mean by the allegation that he did not co-operate; or, to extend the charge, that he was set in his views and was difficult to move; or, to go even further, that his uncooperativeness soured the relations between him and the Air Staff. His critics are invariably short on concrete examples. The criticism also suggests that if the Air Staff made a strong suggestion or recommendation to Fighter Command, and if Fighter Command rejected it, the Commander would be labelled as hostile to new ideas or a difficult man to deal with.

All writers, on both sides of the dispute, have commented on the acerbic relations that existed between Fighter Command Headquarters and the Air Ministry. We examined the causes of those poor relations in Chapter Two; but it is important to hear what Dowding had to say from his side of the controversy:

> It would have been easy enough to remain on good terms with the Air Staff if one had been content to accept every ruling without question, but the Home Defence Organisation had been allowed to lapse into a state of grave inefficiency and I was continuously fighting to remedy the situation while there was yet time.

There, as we have stressed, we have the origin of the 'awful rows' with the Air Staff. And it now becomes clear that Dowding, in having to create Fighter Command and build up its infrastructure and equipment from ground up, with all the highly technical training of personnel implied, was fighting two serious obstacles at once: one was time; the other was an Air Ministry that was so set in its ways that it was almost impossible to make the officials responsible understand the needs of Fighter Command, nevermind the urgency of those needs. We saw in Chapter One the litany of Dowding's woes; here we need only repeat the substance of the allegation made against them:

> I can say without fear of contradiction that since I have held my present post I have dealt with or am in the process of dealing with a number of vital matters which generations of Air Staff have neglected for the past fifteen years.

It is equally clear that the Air Staff took Dowding's criticisms and complaints personally; this not only coloured their views, but warped their decisions. Moreover, they tried to turn the tables and accuse Dowding of the very sins they were guilty of.

We quoted Dowding as saying that he felt he was expected to 'accept every ruling without question.' The very notion that the Air Staff, when making a 'ruling' or recommendation, should expect the Air Officer Commanding-in-Chief to accept it 'without question' belongs to an order formerly found commonly in British military circles and which has been responsible in the past for most of Britain's worst military disasters. In this case, it is a feature of authoritarian organizations which, by their very nature, see themselves as always right, and hence incapable of learning from past events, let alone from the events unfolding before their eyes.

There is worse: the Air Ministry appoints a Commander-in-Chief; this position should, supposedly, grant Dowding the authority to conduct the affairs falling within the defined areas of his command, in the manner he judges to be the most fitting to the occasion. Thus when the Air Ministry proposes a course of action, the Commander is obliged to give it serious study. Similarly, when the Commander receives a letter from the Air Staff, he does not reply offhandedly with an expression of his own views; he passes it on to his Air Staff with a request for their considered views, founded in experience and other evidence. Only then does Dowding reply with a statement of his course of action and the reasons for pursuing his own policy. Of this, of course, the Air Ministry is already fully apprised, knowing that often it is proposing measures inconsistent with those of Fighter Command and its Commander, and has no legitimate complaint if they are rejected.

In the event that there is constant disagreement between the Air Ministry and a Commander-in-Chief, the Air Ministry has no option but to remove the Commander. That was always Dowding's position. Every Commander is in the same situation, and takes up his command knowing it. Dowding told Newall that was his position; but he added the significant rider that the Air Ministry, in removing a Commander, had better be right. It is our firm contention that the Air Ministry in its disputes with Dowding was nearly always in the wrong. When it discovered how much it had been wrong, its hostility to Dowding festered and became a vindictiveness that, first, resolved on his removal, and only then stimulated a search for reasons to justify the deed. They did not issue an explanation for their actions, and have not to this day.

There is still more to this question of uncooperativeness that has not received the attention it deserves. The Air Staff's interest in Fighter Command and its operations – even when inspired by an ardour to help Fighter Command – expressed in the form of advice, suggestions, recommendations, and even, at times, of instructions, often amounted to interference in the direction of vital operational affairs. One cannot help but ask: why did they interfere, and interfere so much? (Let us recall the expressions of complete confidence in Dowding's direction of the Battle, and of his Command, uttered by both Sinclair and Newall.) Was there no communication between the Air Staff and the Air Council? Furthermore, what was Newall doing?

This interference takes on a peculiar colour when considered in the light of operations in Malta, in North Africa, in West Africa, in the Indian and Burmese theatres, and in Malaya. Was the War Office, in 1940, studying the battle in France and telling the commander-in-chief what to do? Was the Admiralty peering at the engagement of British warships with the *Graf Spee* in 1939 and issuing tactical instructions to the commander? Of course they didn't. Perhaps those operational theatres were too remote for them to know what was going on; but the Battle of Britain was taking place over their very heads. Not only that, but Fighter Command headquarters was only a few miles down the road from Whitehall.

The temptation for the mandarins was irresistible. Yet the principle remains the same, in peace and *a forteriori* in war: a commander is appointed to a command with plenary powers. If he loses the confidence of the ultimate authority, he must be removed. Otherwise he must be supported, aided and encouraged in every way possible. **Of course** the Air Staff co-operated with Fighter Command. **Of course** Dowding wrote many harsh letters to the Air Ministry. But when all is said and done, the Air Staff were signally negligent in their failure to rise above their personal prejudices and to give to Dowding and Fighter Command the full and unstinting collaboration that the situation demanded. Having neglected the air defences of Great Britain for many years, they suddenly appointed themselves experts in the field and expected their advice to be heeded. Little wonder they were invariably wrong. Still less wonder that Dowding's patience wore thin, and drove him to express his frustration in intemperate terms, especially in view of the stakes, namely, the survival or irremediable defeat of Great Britain. The charge of uncooperativeness is but one of the pretexts conjured up by Dowding's critics to undo him and belittle his achievements.

II. Conference on Tactics

This conference, which has achieved notoriety in the Air Force and among some historians, was convened by the deputy Chief of the Air Staff, Sholto Douglas, 'to discuss major day tactics in the Fighter Force.'[iii]

This stated purpose is itself misleading and will be examined shortly. Writers who have discussed this conference have themselves been misled by this statement and have gone off on a wild goose chase. The chase has led them to discuss: the pros and cons of squadrons and big wings; the tactical ideas put into practice by 11 Group and by 12 Group; whether 12 Group's ideas could work in 11 Group; the sour relations between Park and Leigh-Mallory; the contribution to the discussions, if any, made by Dowding; and, after the draft minutes were sent to the AOC-in-C and to Group Commanders, the misrepresentation of Park's views, and the refusal by Douglas to add a correcting statement of Park's to the final minutes.

All that is interesting enough, and important to our thesis. But the most heat has been generated among historians, and others, over the presence there of Squadron Leader Douglas Bader. We analysed some of Bader's ideas in chapter three; here we show that his contribution to the debate, which, ironically, was insignificant in terms of his contribution but became of some importance historically. What the commentators have failed to see is the underlying significance, the portent, of Bader's presence; a superficial explanation for this is that Leigh-Mallory was himself out of his depth in debating tactics with Dowding, Park and Brand, and leant heavily on Bader to speak for him. The real explanation is to be found in the true purpose that fermented in Douglas's mind in calling the conference, and in his conniving – perhaps 'conspiring' is not too far off the mark – with Leigh-Mallory to 'invite' Bader. Leigh-Mallory took Bader along as a challenge to Dowding, in the hope that a mere Squadron Leader would point out Dowding's shortcomings.

The notice of the meeting was sent on the 14th. Dowding and the Group Commanders were therefore given all of two days' warning of the conference. The notice was accompanied by an Introduction drafted by Douglas; a paper called 'Air Staff Notes on the Operation of Fighter Wings'; and a copy of Leigh-Mallory's 'Report on Wing Patrols Sent up by No.12 Group' of the previous month.

Douglas did not explain why he thought it necessary to discuss tactics at this particular time, since the daytime battle was essentially over. This belief is stated in the Introduction to the paper: 'At present it seems that our fighter defence has defeated the GAF [German Air Force] in their attempt this year to gain day air superiority over this country.' Note: 'this year'; and 'it seems'. There was no 'seems' about it. The note of belittlement is struck.

However, Douglas did make it clear why he wanted the conference: 'we must have regard to the possibility that more determined, better organized and heavier attacks may be made in the Spring of 1941, if not before. In consequence it is necessary that the lessons we have learnt should be applied generally to enable the fighter defence to operate at maximum efficiency.' This statement is revealing. The application in the future of 'the lessons that we have learnt' implies that those lessons have not been applied hitherto. What lessons? The statement also implies, derogatorily, that 'maximum efficiency' had not been achieved.

The papers mentioned above are equally revealing: they deal with massed wings of fighters and praise Leigh-Mallory's (and Bader's) use of wings. There were in fact two Agendas: one was a secret agenda which was not circulated but which was addressed in the subsequent Minutes sent to all participants. This Agenda contained nine items for discussion on day tactics, every one of these items directed the discussion toward approval of big wings.

The Agenda sent to the members of the conference listed three propositions which 'he [Douglas] would like the meeting to consider':

(1) We wish to outnumber the enemy formations when we meet them.

(2) We want our superior numbers to go into the attack with a coordinated plan of action.

(3) If possible we want the top layer of our fighter formation to have the advantage of height over the top layer of the enemy formation.

The eventual Minutes included answers to the first and second of these items and ignored the third.

It is impossible not to see, it is so conspicuously one-sided, that the discussions, conclusions and recommendations were a foregone conclusion: all was concocted in advance. Douglas, the Air Staff and Leigh-Mallory had connived to bring about that result, and only that result. The inclusion of Leigh-Mallory's report on wing operations was a revealing impertinence: impertinent because the figures of enemy losses claimed were wildly exaggerated, and revealing because the report was a month old. Why then was an up-to-date report not included? For the simple reason that Bader's wing had had no successes. The writing was on the wall, writ large and bold. When, and if, mass formations of German aircraft again attacked this country, they would be met by even larger mass formations of our fighters. Ah! but under whose direction? Dowding and Park were too much the loyal and dedicated Air Force officers, and hence too far removed from all notions of duplicity, to suspect the existence of the wall, let alone to see the writing. But Park had received a warning several months before, from Leigh-Mallory himself, as we will see later.

Douglas and Leigh-Mallory were of one mind in the 'wings' dispute and ranged against Dowding and Park, even though evidence provided by Douglas and Leigh-Mallory was demonstrably untenable. The conference, Leigh-Mallory's report, and Bader's presence proclaimed their fraudulence. How was 11 Group going to muster wings of fighters in the spring of 1941 when 12 Group did not have the time to do it? Such a consideration was irrelevant! It must already have been decided – no doubt between Douglas and Sinclair, with Portal's acquiescence – that Douglas and Leigh-Mallory would replace Dowding and Park.

When the minutes of the meeting were circulated to Fighter Command and the Groups, a number of objections were raised about their bias and incompleteness. Park in particular objected to the way in which his submission to the conference was reported and requested that a further statement, which he provided, be included in the final minutes in order to set the record straight. His request was rejected by Douglas, and the final minutes were approved and published as if the last word on the subject. This, relatively minor, incident is but one further piece of evidence in the case we are presenting against the conspirators.

The purpose of the conference was to undermine Dowding's authority by showing him up as not making the best uses of his limited resources, and by showing him as reluctant or unable to settle the dispute between his two chief group commanders. This has also been corroborated by an eyewitness:

In light of what happened later, Douglas succeeding Dowding and Leigh-Mallory succeeding Park, coupled with all I had heard in the various telephone conversations [between Leigh-Mallory and Douglas], I believe this meeting was just part of a move to discredit the two principal figures fighting the battle with a view to the takeover later. . . . [It] was altogether a disgraceful episode and highly discreditable to Douglas and Leigh-Mallory. Bader of course was just a pawn in the game.[iv]

Here is Dowding's version of events:

I thought [he told his biographer] that the . . . discussion [i.e., the October 17 conference] about whether we should use three, four or five squadron wings was so simple and inconsequential that it hardly deserved a long statement. . . . It became obvious after a while that several people in responsible positions did hold opinions that were contrary to mine. And since, in their eyes, I seemed to be refusing to listen to what they had to say was sentenced without trial. There's no doubt at all in my mind now that it was on that subject – the big wings – that Park and I were judged and condemned.

We must now tackle the question, related to the wings dispute, of the bitter feelings between his two Group commanders, Park and Leigh-Mallory, and Dowding's failure to resolve it for some of Dowding's critics suggest this was the reason for his dismissal. Once again we have no need to rehash the facts of the dispute, which were brought into the open by Sinclair's and Balfour's visits to Duxford. The big questions are: when did Dowding become aware of the rift and ill feeling between them? How did he assess the gravity of the situation? And what did he do about it?

Park became tired of asking 12 Group directly for support to protect his airfields when all his squadrons were airborne, and passed his requests directly to Fighter Command. The evidence supports 11 Group's contention that the situation did not improve after that. And it was not because of the time it took to transmit the request. The reason was the same as it always had been: the inability of the wings to assemble and move south in time. The nature of Park's request was sufficiently unusual to alert Dowding to the seriousness of the situation, for there can be no doubt about 11 Group's entire satisfaction with the cooperation they received from 10 Group to their west; though there is little to suggest that Dowding monitored the relations between his Groups, to ensure that his instructions were being carried out.

Although the Conference dwelt on day tactics and the usefulness of big wings, Dowding failed to see that this was the pretext for the conflict: Leigh-Mallory was going his own way, irrespective of Dowding's views or policies.[v] That he dared to do so should have sounded the alarm bells and alerted Dowding to the suspicion that Leigh-Mallory was not acting alone and had support in higher places. That is the lesson of the Conference of October 17.

Notes:

i. Richard Overy expresses a different opinion – and for the strangest of reasons– when he writes (p. 129): 'The lack of any clear sense that a great battle had been won was reflected in the treatment of those who had won it.' It was clear at the time how great the stakes were; it was equally clear by the end of September that invasion was out of the question that year. The 'treatment of those who had won it' was delayed precisely until after the victory became clear.

ii. It is worth pointing out that Air Chief Marshal Sir Robert Brooke-Popham was not only recalled to active service at the age of sixty-one—when Dowding was only fifty-eight – but was actually sent to Singapore as the Commander-in-Chief of the British land and air forces in Malay in October 1940. He would soon demonstrate how out of touch he was.

iii. The papers relevant to this Conference are in AIR 2/7281 and AIR 16/735. We give only a summary here. The fullest account is to be found in Peter Brown's book, *Honour Restored*, where he reproduces the Agendas and the Minutes.

iv. Air Chief Marshal Sir Kenneth Cross (then Squadron Leader. See *Straight and Level*, pp. 116-123) was at that time Group Controller at Leigh-Mallory's 12 Group headquarters. He also says: 'It was noticeable that the difficulties that existed between 11 and 12 Groups did not occur between 10 and 11 Groups since Brand appeared to accept his supporting role to 11 Group, even though he had a front of his own across the western end of the Channel.' Park's view of the Conference is this: 'The very Air Staff responsible for this failure [to provide for the training of fighter pilots] arranged after the Battle had been won for the Commander of Fighter Command and myself to appear ... before the full Air Council, not to be thanked, but to be questioned as to why we did not try out certain minor tactics favoured by the Commander of a Fighter Group in a back area that had little fighting experience in 1940.' (Keith Park to Richard Collier in Kaplan and Collier, p. 217.)

v. The tactics put into effect by Park in 11 Group, and the wing tactics implemented by 12 Group, must be considered in the light of Dowding's strategic plan, which all Group Commanders were familiar with. Dowding himself stated it in his Despatch and in his 'Personal Notes' : '[War] is between two forces, one is attacking while the other has the task of defending. The Germans were out to invade our country and so end the war. My job was not to win the war with Fighter Command, on the contrary, my task was to prevent the Germans in succeeding in their preparation for an invasion of England. I had to deny Germany the right to gain control of the air.' The key to success in the battle was to conserve his forces. How Park creatively adapted his tactics to the Commander's strategic plan, and how Leigh-Mallory failed to do so, is examined in a perceptive article by Alan Deere, which we reproduce in Appendix 'C'.

CHAPTER 7

Night Defences

—⁂—

The failure of Fighter Command to mount an effective defence against the night attacks on Britain's cities in the winter of 1940-41 is, in the eyes of the writers who have dealt with the issue, the paramount reason for Dowding's dismissal. The whole question calls, therefore, for a thorough investigation.

The case against Dowding is based mostly on the findings and recommendations of two separate committees on night defence, set up respectively by Beaverbrook at the Ministry of Aircraft Production, and by the War Cabinet. The former, initiated and chaired by MRAF Sir John Salmond, had three meetings, on September 16-18, and a report was completed on the 18th. A number of comments are required before we examine the report and Dowding's response.

Firstly, Beaverbrook and Salmond recognized early the serious inadequacy of the British defences against night aerial attacks, and took the initiative in seeking to remedy the deficiences. (Those deficiencies were, of course, glaring, in the light of the failure of the Air Ministry to have made any provision to meet such attacks).[i]

Second, all the nine regular members of the Committee were drawn from the Air Ministry and the Ministry of Aircraft Production, who described 'the existing night fighting organisation' ; one wonders why a Fighter Command staff officer was not called upon.

Third, a number of officers, both air force and scientific, were invited 'to give evidence' at the three meetings. Among them were the Station Commander of Drem, who was hardly engaged in the battle, and a squadron leader of a Blenheim night fighter squadron – of which more later. Dowding himself was not called until the third day; and Park did not appear at all, although A-VM Sir Quentin Brand, AOC 10 Group, did.[ii]

Fourth, it is noted that the deliberations – for that is what the meetings amounted to: they cannot be called an inquiry – occupied only two days, and that the committee did not see fit to visit any of the night fighter squadrons, or even the Night Fighter Interception Unit. Whereas the committee appreciated the virtue of haste, it lacked the greater virtue of thoroughness.

Finally, none of the members of the committee had any expertise in night aerial defence[iii] and these defects showed up in their report. For example, it is noted that two measures recommended improving the Blenheim as a night fighter, despite the evidence of two Blenheim pilots that the aircraft 'was too slow', and 'was not a good night fighter'. Another recommendation urged 'specialisation of existing 8-gun fighter squadrons in night work', in the face of evidence that 'the 8-gun fighter was worthless [without AI] unless searchlights could usefully operate.' On the other hand, some of the committee's recommendations were eminently sensible; e.g. the formation of a special Night Fighter Staff Section within Fighter Command; the transfer of experienced night flying pilots to night fighter squadrons; and the acceleration of the development of the Beaufighter and Mark IV AI.

Salmond submitted his report to the Air Council. The Air Council, in its turn, having accepted and approved it, sent it with a covering letter to Dowding on September 25th, asking for his views.

Critics of Dowding seem often to have overlooked that he had at his disposal a cadre of competent staff officers. In all such cases, Dowding would pass the report to his Senior Air Staff Officer with a request for comments grounded in experience and established facts. When he received the information he needed he would draft a reply. Dowding submitted his reply two days later, on the 27th.

Salmond's document, entitled Night Air Defence, comprises twenty-one 'conclusions' in eighteen paragraphs. In preparing his reply, Dowding marked Salmond's recommendations in the margin, in blue pencil, with a tick, a cross, or a question mark; or made no mark. Some commentators, Ray among them, have suggested that these signs meant, respectively, that he agreed or disagreed with the recommendation in question, or was undecided in his own mind. A reading of Dowding's reply to the report, and a close comparison of his comments with the recommendations, show that such an interpretation is not so simple. Dowding, on his copy, has marked a cross beside ten, a tick beside three, a question mark beside five; and three are unmarked.

Of the unmarked ones, Dowding's reply shows: one agreement, with modification; one disagreement; and one is deemed unrelated to the issue. Of the recommendations marked with a question mark, Dowding agrees with one, disagrees with two, finds one unrelated, and does not understand one. Of others with which he disagreed, three had to do with modifications to the obsolescent Blenheim and the use of single-seat eight-gun day fighters for night interception (two and one).

In general, it might be said that the other, non-technical, conclusions reached by Salmond's committee tended toward a division and dispersal of Fighter Command's responsibilities in matters of night defence. On Dowding's side, it might be concluded that he opposed recommendations which seemed to complicate his task; and 'cordially' approved those measures which promoted the Beaufighter and AI, and aircrew training and efficiency. As Dowding marked the paragraphs of his copy of the Salmond Report, so his letter of reply was glossed by someone on the Air Staff. Two comments are worth quoting.

Salmond's recommendation no. 13 reads: 'The establishment of pilots and AI operators in night fighter squadrons should be balanced so that each officer pilot has an officer AI operator and each NCO pilot an NCO AI operator. Pilots and operators should be trained together at the existing OTU.' Dowding comments thus: 'I see no point in this recommendation, which would merely add to the existing serious difficulties in the production of AI operators.' Perhaps Salmond and the Air Council were horrified at the idea of NCOs giving directions to officers. (Later, in Bomber Command, it became a matter of survival.) Dowding shows himself far more realistic and progressive-minded. But the marginal (Air Staff) comment is revealing. It says 'Obstruction(?). Why'. Dowding was often accused of being obstructive to Air Ministry recommendations, but one fails to comprehend the accusation here.

Paragraph number two recommends: 'The operation of filtering should be transferred from Fighter Command to Group Headquarters in order to reduce delay.' Dowding replied as follows:

> The question of decentralisation of filtering was raised by Air Marshal Sir Philip Joubert in a minute dated 11th January, 1940, and was finally dispose of (I had hoped) by my letters FC/S.18082 dated 17th and 31st January,1940. . . .
> At any rate my last mentioned letter terminated the correspondence. The matter has no particular connection with night interception, and the arguments which were adduced against it in January of this year still hold good. I request, therefore, that I may be spared the necessity of discussing the question afresh.

If this is an instance of Dowding's not co-operating, or of not suffering fools gladly, it is hardly surprising, perhaps, that there is no comment attached to this reply.[iv]

One of the irregular things about Salmond's committee is that the whole process occupied only two and a half days. Salmond committed the most egregious of the type of offences usually attributed to what is termed 'officialdom'. They carried out their assigned task in two days. One is tempted to ask: what could they find out in two days? They completed their so-called inquiries, and made judgments and recommendations which implied a certain muted criticism of Dowding and Fighter Command. Above all, they did not intimate whether their recommendations were meant to constitute a definitive answer to the problems of night defence, or only a provisional and stop-gap solution. Salmond's committee erred, we have suggested, in not seeking the real experts' views – those of the Air Staff of Fighter Command, of the night fighter squadrons, and above all, of the scientists. This failure, in Dowding's eyes, would have constituted the gravest offence of all. As we have stressed before with some insistence, it is the men and women engaged in actual operations against the enemy, and the scientific minds that had helped to create this highly technical arm, who are in the best position to know their strengths and weaknesses, as well perhaps as the enemy's. The principal war function of the Air Ministry is to fulfil the needs of the operational commands and their supporting organisations. In order to do that they must constantly consult and confer with the commands. That is precisely the principle that dictated Dowding's and Fighter Command Headquarters' relations with their Groups, Stations and Squadrons.

It soon became clear that Salmond's report was not going to achieve the results hoped for. It was this setback that impelled Salmond to write his demanding letter to Churchill on October 5: 'Recently on Lord Beaverbrook's instructions, I have carried out an inquiry into Night Air Defence, the result of which, together with what has since occurred, make a change, in my view, imperative.'[v]

Churchill wanted to satisfy himself and acted immediately to set up a new, and more authoritative, committee. But whereas Salmond's committee, and Fighter Command, were concerned solely with the means of winning the night battle, Churchill, as a politician, and above all as Prime Minister, was driven by concerns about the morale of the people and their ability to withstand the night bombing. He need not have worried – at least not at this stage; but the political worries seeped, or rather poured, into the Air Ministry – after all, its head was a politician – and affected their judgment. Churchill called his committee the Night Air Defence Committee, and it had its first meeting on October 7 under his chairmanship. The committee comprised seventeen members – Cabinet members, Air Council and Air Staff officers, and Government officials. Dowding was of their number and attended all the meetings.

Three other meetings were also held on October 21 and November 19 under Churchill's chairmanship, and on December 9 with Beaverbrook in the chair. These dates – two weeks, four weeks, and three weeks apart – do not exactly suggest the idea of urgency, and contrast strangely with the 'rush to judgement' of Salmond and his committee. This difference of approach – haste as opposed to thoroughness – is particularly notable in light of the heavy raids which took place on November 6 and 7: the devastation of Coventry on November 14, and the major raid on London on November 15.

The decisions and recommendations of the first three meetings completely vindicated Dowding's views. On October 10, twelve of the eighteen recommendations dealt with radar detection and interception and AI-equipped Beaufighters. On October 21, of the twenty-nine recommendations, the first seventeen dealt with and approved the same and other related measures. On November 19, it is the same story: twelve of the twenty items approved the work done and progress achieved in the use and development of radar in the detection, tracking and destruction of enemy aircraft by fighters and anti-aircraft artillery.

These deliberations produced a number of other recommendations put forward by the fertile and impractical mind of Lindemann, Churchill's personal scientific adviser, who suggested: wire-carrying shells; balloons carrying explosive charges released in the path of enemy bombers; aerial mines sown in the path of enemy bombers; airborne searchlights with attendant single-engined fighters, and searchlights in clusters to guide fighters.[vi] These recommendations Dowding pooh-poohed. Some were implemented, but without success. (When Douglas replaced Dowding he was keen to pursue these measures. Douglas reported on them in his *Despatch*. They all proved to be will-o'-the-wisps and were progressively abandoned, though Douglas never conceded that Dowding had been right all along.)

At the time, of course, Dowding's scepticism was condemned as one more instance of his uncooperativeness: of his stubborn unwillingness to consider ideas outside the sphere of his familiarity – rather than as his refusal to accept new ideas unless supported by scientific trial and error.

The meeting of the Air Defence Committee, held on October 21, was more immediately significant; the Air Ministry reported that instructions had already been issued to Fighter Command, over Dowding's objections, that, 'as an experiment, three 8-gun Fighter Squadrons should be earmarked for night fighting'. The squadrons assigned by Dowding were Hurricane squadrons. These differences of opinion between Dowding and the Air Staff and Air Council, exposed as they were personally to Churchill's view, would appear to give some substance to the Air Staff's repeated complaint about Dowding's stubbornness and unwillingness to co-operate.

The pugnacious side of Churchill revelled in a good knock-down argument between opposing views in committees he chaired. Furthermore, he actively stimulated and stoked them. He provoked and welcomed opposition, but there was more to his interrogations and hectoring. He used such means as a weapon to cut through waffle and to expose unpreparedness in order to get at the facts. He surely subscribed to the French dictum: *Du choc des opinions jaillit la lumière* (From the clash of opinion springs the truth). If he was not familiar with the French proverb itself he was assuredly a friend to the idea. He was open to the free play of criticism and discussion, and may indeed have known the view of Lord Palmerston on the question, which amounts to an exposition of the proverb:

> It is by comparing opinions – by a collision of opinions – by rubbing one man's opinions against those of another and seeing which are the hardest and will bear the friction best– that men, in or out of office, can most justly arrive at the knowledge of what is most advantageous to the interests of the whole community.[vii]

There is no point in examining these committees further, for no matter what they recommended the decision had already been taken by the Air Council before this date to get rid of Dowding. Instead we will look at the results achieved by both the Hurricane night fighters and the AI-equipped Beaufighters. We will also present the views of several night fighter aircrews, and a number of works on radio counter-measures.

Two of the aircrews are a fighter pilot on one of the Hurricane squadrons, and the AI operator of a Beaufighter. One of the three designated Hurricane squadrons was 85 Squadron. It became a night fighter squadron, in 12 Group, on October 23rd. Its commanding officer was Squadron Leader Peter Townsend, one of the most skilled pilots in Fighter Command at the time. Of the Hurricane itself, as a night fighter, he has this to say:

> About the Hurricane there was practically nothing that could remotely qualify it as a specialized night fighter. . . .While the Hurricane was a formidable day fighter . . . it was not designed as a specialized night fighter and would never

properly perform as one. What the Hurricane did not possess told even more heavily against its suitability as a night fighter. First, it was not fitted with a radar set. Had it been possible to install one, there would be need as well for a radar operator. But the Hurricane was a single-seater. Single-engined too, which put it at high risk in case of engine failure at night.

After several months as leader of his squadron on night interceptions, Townsend himself shot down, on February 25th, 1941, the one and only enemy aircraft destroyed by 85 Squadron. A few weeks later, in April, his squadron was converted to and became operational on Havocs, a twin-engined aircraft which, like the Beaufighter, had a radar operator/navigator, was equipped with AI radar, and armed with four 20mm cannon. Townsend destroyed an enemy bomber two days after becoming operational. After a month he sums up the situation in these terms:

> Since October 1940 we had spent six months groping blindly for the enemy in the dark. . . In the past four weeks, with Havocs, AI and GCI, we had downed two of the enemy with four 'probables' and six damaged. . . .[We] felt certain at last that we were on our way to attaining the standard set by our onetime commander in chief Dowding, who on the very eve of 85's conversion from day to night fighters, had vowed that Fighter Command would never rest 'until we can locate, pursue, and shoot down the enemy by day and by night.'

The implied criticism of those responsible, muted though it is, comes through clearly: 'at last we were on our way to attaining the standard set by .. . Dowding.' Townsend refers to the events of early May 1941 here; Dowding had pinned his entire faith, founded as it was on the best scientific evidence and operational research available then, on the twin-engined fighter equipped with AI, armed with cannons, and guided by GCI. Despite Townsend's optimism, the actual results seemed poor. He reported that the 'two horrible massacres [of April 16 and 19, 1941] were a measure of the continuing failure of the British night defence . . . to protect the civilian population.' This acknowledged failure becomes dramatic, and tragic, when we learn the result of the defences on the night of May 10/11. After seven hours of bombardment, by a force of over 500 bombers against London alone, 'The Luftwaffe lost only eight aircraft that night.'

Some writers have blamed the failure on the defects of the Beaufighter itself. This aircraft had the teething troubles often associated with a new design. Then again, the Night Air Defence Committee heard at its meeting of October 7 that the 'production of Beaufighters has been completely stopped by enemy action'. But production was resumed and four or five Beaufighters were expected that same week. The problems were overcome, so that by April 1941 there were six Beaufighter night squadrons in action, in addition to Townsend's Havoc squadron.

The reasons for the failure of the defence, on the technical side, are made clear by C.F. Rawnsley. Rawnsley was the radar operator of a Beaufighter of 604 Squadron, whose pilot was the celebrated John Cunningham. As early as September 1940 Rawnsley wrote: 'I could not help feeling that . . . the future belonged to the man who could make the new radar sets function as they were supposed to.' (The reader is invited to read that opinion again, very carefully.) In early 1941 Rawnsley was bemoaning the fact that there were still plenty of problems with the airborne radar. Indeed, his book constitutes a record of the failure both of the AI to work as it should, from one mark to the next, and of the operators to use it to the best possible advantage. So ineffective or unreliable were the early marks of airborne radar, and so untrained the operators, that it was almost two months, from the end of September to November 20th, before Cunningham and Rawnsley had their first successful night interception. Dowding was toiling against insuperable odds. The continued failure of the night defences under Sholto Douglas, from December to April, cannot be attributed to the Beaufighters or to the aircrews themselves whose efforts were exemplary. It can be laid to the charge only of the AI equipment, and beyond that to the inadequate training of the operators – and that implies lack of leadership at the top.

Historians such as Denis Richards are emphatic in their insistence that this was the sole visible answer to the problem: 'Though the Air Ministry rightly neglected no field of experiment, the real hope for the future depended, as Dowding and Pile constantly stressed, on perfecting and producing certain radar apparatus.' Richards continues: 'In essence, our chances of success now rested on the speed with which the new radar apparatus and the Beaufighters could be brought into service.'

The designers and manufacturers of the AI sets devoted all their skills and energies into improving the equipment. From September to November and December respectively, Dowding and Park submitted to the Air Ministry a stream of reports devoted to their efforts to combat the night raids. (Douglas and Leigh-Mallory, during the worst six months of the Blitz, submitted none that we have been able to discover.)

In his *Despatch* on Fighter Command's night operations during the time when he was the AOC-in-C Fighter Command — written in 1948 – Douglas acknowledges that the AI-equipped night fighter had the major role in meeting the enemy threat to British cities. On the other hand he is at pains to claim 'success' for his idea of using Hurricanes – while conceding that their only successes were obtained on moonlight nights.

What were the actual results? The figures given by Douglas in his *Despatch* are these:

Sept. - Dec.:	4 e/a destroyed by fighters (1 by AI)
March:	11 e/a destroyed by s/e fighters
	11 e/a destroyed by AI fighters
	21 e/a destroyed by guns & balloons
May :	19 e/a destroyed by s/e fighters
	4 e/a destroyed by AI fighters
	4 e/a destroyed by guns.

We recall that Townsend claimed that on this night of May 10/11, only eight enemy aircraft were destroyed *in toto*. Who was correct? Robert Watson Watt, who had no axe to grind – except perhaps to put the successes of radar-equipped fighters in a good light – gives these figures, inadequately broken down (H = Hurricane, S = Spitfire, B = Beaufighter):

	Fighters (H/S – B)	Guns	Balloons	Other
Sept.7 – Nov. 13	8	54	4	–
March	22	17		
April	48	39		
May	96	31		10

These figures are confirmed by Denis Richards in his official history, *Royal Air Force 1939-1945*, whose work preceded that of Watson Watt by four years. What were the real losses by the Luftwaffe? How many of their aircraft were actually destroyed by the defences? We have studied the day-by-day accounts given in *The Blitz: Then and Now* (vol. 2), and arrived at the following figures (S/E= single-engined):[viii]

	Total	Beaufighters	S/E fighters	Defiants
March	20	8	2	–
April	47	15	5	9
May	73	22	2	13

These figures correspond closely to those given by Richards and Watson Watt. But they do not correspond closely to Douglas's figures. Indeed, Douglas's figures, especially those of enemy aircraft destroyed by single-engined fighters, and the figures for the disastrous raid of May 10th, bear no resemblance to the facts. And let us not forget that Douglas wrote his account in 1946.[ix]

Douglas would further have the reader believe that he, Douglas, was the architect of the successes achieved by Fighter Command in the night battle; for he manages to write his report without discussing tactics, without touching on the obstacles facing the aircrews, without dealing with the development and production difficulties experienced by the designers of the Beaufighter and AI radar, and without seemingly being aware of the training problems of AI operators.

The key to success in night interceptions, given the equipment at the disposal of the aircrews, lay in the intelligence of the AI operators. Three unchallengeable witnesses to this contention are an operational research scientist and two pilots. The scientist is Sir Henry Tizard, who testified: 'When the Service AI's were properly tested in the air, under scientifically controlled conditions, it was found that the real trouble was that they squinted, and that an aircraft which was believed, by the indications of the instruments, to be straight ahead, was in fact on the beam.'

One of the pilots is Basil Embry. When he was appointed Station Commander of

RAF Wittering in early 1941, one of his squadrons was 25 Squadron, a Beaufighter night fighter squadron. He knew its potential and he 'took an immediate interest in its training and preparation for intensive night operations'. His first discovery was 'a lack of ability in certain navigators to operate the AI sets efficiently.' The second was his conclusion that 'more than half the success in night fighting lay in the intelligent use of the AI.' This view was clinched when Embry had the inimitable Squadron Leader David Atcherley posted in as the 25 Squadron commander. David Atcherley, with the Group AI technical officer, Flight Lieutenant J.H. Hunter-Tod as his set operator, 'a man of exceptional intelligence and technical ability', intercepted and shot down an enemy bomber on their first or second patrol. What followed is pure Embry; he and Atcherley 'raided' nearby Cambridge University one Sunday afternoon and 'conscripted' a small number of science undergraduates. 'We worked hard at their training, and the very first time one of them went on a night patrol, it ended with the interception and shooting down of an enemy bomber.'

The second pilot, another witness to the slapdash attitude toward the training of aircrews, and especially to the attitude of some RAF station commanders, is Roderick Chisholm, a successful night fighter pilot. He wrote in *Cover of Darkness*:

> I visited fighter-training stations, and I learnt that there was another aspect of staff work. Stations had been left much to themselves to train night-fighter crews as they thought fit, and in consequence the headquarters assumption of authority to direct policy and methods was unpopular. Enthusiasts – many of them in those days inexperienced in operations – had worked out their own plans, and they did not like changing them. But some had to be changed. There was a limit to the flying hours which could be devoted to the training of each crew, and into this time had to be packed as many as possible of the lessons learnt, in this new realm, since the war began. This work was as interesting as it was at times frustrating. One station commander would listen politely and act, another would only listen, and one, I recall, would hardly deign even to listen.

This account speaks volumes about the non–existent leadership at the top, at the time of Douglas's command. It was Tizard's role, however, that was the decisive one. 'The successful defence of airborne radar through a long period of disappointment was an almost personal achievement of Tizard alone.' And Watson Watt's second-in-command at Bawdsey, Dr. Edward G. Bowen, has said: 'He [Tizard] was always keenly aware of the problems and clearly indicated the need for adequate training of personnel . . . However, the business was plagued with a headquarters staff which was largely ignorant of the problems and requirements, and Tizard's clear view of the problem did not get across to the people concerned. This was largely the reason why the successful use of airborne radar was delayed until 1941 and 1942.'

Douglas makes the assertion in his *Despatch* that 'if the enemy had not chosen to pull out [in May], we should soon have been inflicting such casualties on his night bombers that the continuance of his night offensive would have been impossible' (para. 51)and despite the disastrous failure of the defences on the night of May 10/11 – the last major raid of the Blitz and one of the worst raids of all on London – the successes of the AI fighters in this month went a good part of the way to justifying Douglas's opinion, even if we cannot but regard it as unwholesomely subjective.

But if subjectivity is to attain to a degree of offensiveness, in the place of the objectivity and detachment which Douglas's position called for, it is in his failure to give credit to all to whom it was due. If the figures we have culled from *The Blitz: Then and Now* (p. 249) are correct, the credit for them, the figures and the claims alike, belongs overwhelmingly to Tizard, Watson Watt and Dowding. Yet Douglas does not give them so much as a passing mention.

These results vindicate Dowding's early work and insistence on the AI night interceptor to the exclusion of the other defences, with the sole exception of anti-aircraft artillery. Dowding was convinced that he had found the answer to the problem. He wrote in his *Despatch*: 'I had to leave the development of night interception at a very interesting stage; but it is perhaps not too much to say that, although much remained to be done, the back of the problem had been broken.'

Dowding is his usual modest self; but 'the back of the problem' had indeed been broken thanks to the unremitting efforts of a relative handful of brilliant scientists and dedicated airmen, who actively engaged in operational research – an avenue of research which seeks precise answers to specific problems that can only be arrived at by practical, scientific experimentation. Dowding – like Tizard, and contrary to Lindemann – insisted on seeing things for himself before taking important decisions or considering the next step. He involved himself in the research by observing the practical results achieved by AI in the only way possible–by flying with the crews. This he did in the back of a cramped Fairey 'Battle' in 1938 at Martlesham. E.G. Bowen has given us a vivid account of both the problem and the breaking of its back. He wrote:

> Before the flight, the Commander-in-Chief had emphasised that he was particularly interested in the minimum range performance. As we made the last interception, he said: 'When we get to minimum range, tell the pilot to hold the position so that I can see how close we are.' This we did. When we had settled down at minimum range, Stuffy said: 'Now let's take a look.' For the previous 30 or 40 minutes our heads had been under the black cloth shielding the cathode-ray tubes. The cloth off and Stuffy looked straight ahead. He said: 'Where is it? I can't see it.' I pointed straight up; we were flying almost directly underneath the target. ... The Commander-in-Chief was clearly pleased with what he had seen.[x]

Following this flight Dowding took Bowen aside and discussed night defences with him for a good two hours, during the course of which 'Stuffy gave me a long dissertation about the problems of night fighting as he saw them.' In what follows we give a résumé of the talk as reported by Bowen.

(1) The night problem was so entirely different from day fighting that both the aircrews and those in command of night operations would have to come to

terms with the differences. One difference, for example, was that the night fighter's task would be a long drawn-out cat-and-mouse affair; consequently the aircraft would have to be of high endurance.

(2) The pilot would be completely occupied with flying his aircraft and could not hope to handle the radar as well. This meant a two-man aircraft. Moreover the pilot would have to be dark-adapted; hence, even in the best flying conditions, it would be difficult for the pilot to see another aircraft at night if he was also staring at a bright cathode-ray tube.

(3) Navigation was also a problem. During a protracted interception the night fighter could stray far from its base, and the pilot, intent on his prey, could not keep track of his position as well. Time would tell whether the radar operator could be navigator as well. If experience showed otherwise the night fighter might have to carry a third crew member. These requirements pointed to the need for a multi-seat, twin-engined aircraft.[xi]

(4) The pilot would have to make a definite visual identification of his target before opening fire, for if he shot down our own aircraft instead the effect on morale would be devastating – both for other aircrews and for the attacking crew.

(5) The fire power of the night fighter was of even greater importance than that of the day fighter, for, once he opened fire, and missed, he would not have another chance, his target, alerted, would take evasive action and not be found again. Therefore the night fighter would have to be very heavily armed with 20 millimetre cannon, which again argues for a twin-engined fighter.

Bowen concludes his summary by stating: 'I had never heard such a clear and definite analysis of the fundamentals of night fighting.'

A little later that year a demonstration was given to Winston Churchill in the same 'Battle'. Bowen writes of it: 'The target aircraft roared around the field and the radar display showed the changes of range and bearing as it did so. It was as good a demonstration of air-to-air radar as was possible from an aircraft sitting on the ground and the great man seemed well satisfied.'

A few weeks later again Lindemann called to have his own demonstration; it was arranged on July 10, 1939. Bowen wrote of it : 'We expected Lindemann to be impressed, at least with the technical part of the demonstration, but ... [he] seemed to be in his usual mood of finding fault with everything and did not have a single positive suggestion to make ... When he got back to London he gave us a poor report. Of all the distinguished people to whom we demonstrated airborne radar, Lindemann was the only one who was unimpressed. For reasons best known to himself, he continued to depreciate British radar, at least in its defensive role, for most of the war.'[xii]

We have touched on some of the operational and technical problems which had to be solved in order to mount an effective defence, a recent study shows the mark of its indebtedness to Bowen:

The technical complexity of providing for the night defences dwarfed those of daylight operations. Three additional weapon and detection systems were required. First, it was critical to have a night fighter with a two–man crew, capable of carrying a powerful armament. . . . Second, to guide the fighter to within 3 to 4 miles of its prey, there had to be an entirely different type of ground based radar, GCI or Ground Controlled Interception. Finally, it was imperative that the night fighter be equipped with an airborne aircraft Interception (AI) radar, capable of taking up where the GCI left off, steering the interceptor from 20,000 to just under 500 feet from the target...Of these three systems, the most vital was AI radar; without it few night interceptions were possible.[xiii]

We have had occasion to quote Haslam who wrote – and we repeat it: 'there was no dramatic improvement in the performance of our night fighters when Sholto Douglas took over from Dowding.' However, Haslam introduces this opinion by stating: '**As might have been expected** there was no dramatic improvement.' [Our emphasis.] Haslam fails to explain why no improvement was expected, if that was, in his view, one of the compelling reasons why Douglas was chosen to replace Dowding. And yet, as Haslam had written earlier, Dowding 'was not moving fast enough for the Air Staff', and 'the results were not coming fast enough to satisfy either the Air Staff or the politicians'. Haslam, intent on indicting Dowding for his failure to counter the night attacks, is unaware of this contradiction.

The claims made by Haslam, Ray, Richards and Cox, writing long after the events we are examining, are attempts either to explain the failure of the night defences or to posit a pretext for the removal of Dowding. In the case of Salmond, his report might now be seen, together with Douglas's hearing of October 17 into the use of big wings, as inquiries, justifiable in some respects, but in other respects conceived in order to put Dowding in the wrong and to discredit his leadership.[xiv]

It is abundantly clear: the testing and production of the Beaufighter and its armament, of GCI, and of AI were the responsibility of the Air Ministry. Only the training of the AI operators fell within the jurisdiction of Fighter Command–and then only in part, for again it was up to the Air Ministry and Training Command respectively to recruit the airmen and to provide the basic training for them before sending them out to an operational unit.

The historical record confirms this assessment of the problem of night defence. From 1936 on it had been the concerted policy agreed by the Air Ministry and the Air Officer Commanding-in-Chief of Fighter Command to give almost absolute priority to the day defensive system. The decision and the policy were, indeed, more or less dictated by technical and by strategic factors. Another view is worth reporting. One historian, in recounting the fruits of a meeting called by Trenchard in 1923, (whose decisions, in his view, 'would set the seal on the design of the RAF for certainly the next ten years and probably into the future'), wrote: 'There was not much discussion on the need for night fighters presumably because an enemy was supposed not to have any night flying ability. This left the way for the Luftwaffe to drop 10,000 tons of bombs on London in 1940... and suffer precious few casualties in the process.'[xv]

Technically, before 1936, there were no means of early warning, so the case for interception did not exist. As for AI, the first successfully condensed and compacted set — what Watson Watt called 'tabloid radar'– was constructed and flown only in mid-1939. 'It was on 1 June 1939 that a complete AI set, with all the elements substantially embodied in AI Marks I to IV, flew in a Battle aircraft.' Although the potential threat of night attack was recognized, and though Watson Watt and his teams at Bawdsey Manor and elsewhere toiled to perfect and improve the equipment, they could not overcome the immense difficulties involved in view of the lateness of the hour and the shortness of time.[xvi]

Strategically, it was recognized by the most enlightened and objective thinkers – and they include Tizard and Dowding — that Britain could be defeated by the Luftwaffe in a daylight air war, but not by night assaults, however bad the damage might be. 'Failure to win the battle against the night bomber might prolong a war; failure to win the Battle of Britain would probably have lost one.'

Night fighting received less attention in pre-war years than any other phase of aerial warfare development. This was true not only in Germany, but also in the Allied nations. This omission was to handicap both Germany and Britain in defending themselves; night fighting techniques were largely developed from 1940 onward, and the full significance of the night fighter force was not appreciated by the German High Command until it was almost too late.

One historian, in a recent study, has itemized the causes of the failure to mount an effective defence against the night attacks as follows:

In large measure, the delay in developing a successful AI was the direct result of the shortage of personnel and time. With much of Bawdsey's staff devoted to completing the chain in the last eighteen months of peace, Bowen's group suffered. Nor was any outside assistance sought until it was too late to influence the course of events during the Blitz. The Air Ministry was equally ignorant [of the complexities of the development phase of the AI programme]. No one, not even Watson Watt or Rowe, objected to turning Bowen's research team into what amounted to a small-scale manufacturer. [By] December 1938 it was accepted that radar research would have to be moved from Bawdsey . . . Ironically, Bawdsey did not experience a single major attack during the war. Yet, what Watson Watt did instead was perhaps as destructive as the most devastating air attack. Watson Watt decided that . . . the radar researchers should move to Dundee and use the existing university college facilities. . . . The move from Bawdsey crippled AI research at a critical moment and ended any chance that an effective night defence system would be in operation during 1940. On 10 November [1940] Tizard met with Rowe and Watson Watt at Dundee and suggested that they enlist the aid of GEC Research Laboratories, and perhaps some other industrial research laboratories. Watson Watt disparaged the capabilities of the private companies [to conduct primary research] and Tizard did not disagree. But he later told Dowding, in his report of the meeting: 'You may have guessed rightly that one of my objectives in suggesting this plan is to provide some much needed competition to DCD [i.e. Watson Watt] and his staff.' Dowding concurred with Tizard's recommendation because he saw his chief trouble at that time as being the complete stagnation in the fitting of AI, and added EMI to Tizard's list of manufacturers to be brought into the AI picture. This exchange of correspondence marks the turning point in AI research; for it would be EMI that would eventually make the improvements that would turn the radar device into an effective weapon system.[xvii]

In summing up, we cannot but conclude that the Air Ministry had no policy relating to night defence, and hence had provided for no means of aerial defence against night attacks, beyond a few antiquated anti-aircraft guns. In its failure to give to Dowding the backing and support that he needed in this crisis, the Air Ministry betrayed its country's, and the Royal Air Force's, most devoted servants, and condemned itself to its own woeful insufficiency, a failure that can be laid at the door of none other than Trenchard himself – plus, of course, the generations of subservient acolytes on the Air Staff.

The betrayal adds to the Air Ministry's tarnished reputation, and reinforces the suspicion that they were ready to go to almost any lengths to get rid of Dowding. Months after Dowding's and Park's departure, while the Blitz was still raging, it is difficult to form an idea of what Sholto Douglas and Leigh-Mallory were doing, i.e. how they actually spent their days and hours. Douglas's *Despatch* gives few clues to what occupied him; and his autobiography is no more helpful. And yet, not a word of reproach is levelled by Portal at Douglas's inertia, from December to May and far beyond, which makes Dowding's work a shining example of energy and rightness.

Notes:

i. At the second War Cabinet meeting of May 28, 1940, the 'various possibilities now under development of countering night-bombing were referred to', but it seems the matter was not followed up. (See Lukacs, *Five Days in London May 1940*, p. 181.)

ii. Brand's presence is interesting. Michael Bragg reports (R D F 1, p. 226) : 'On 14 September, Dowding received a letter from the Air Council inviting him to nominate a representative to be associated with a committee, with Marshal of the Royal Air Force Sir John Salmond as chairman, that the Minister of Aircraft Production, Lord Beaverbrook, was setting up to undertake a thorough inquiry into the equipment and operation of night fighters. They had suggested that AVM Sir C.J.Q. Brand would be particularly suitable and on the 17th, Dowding's short reply was that he understood that Brand had already been summoned and given evidence. Bragg continues: 'There is an indication that Dowding was not at all pleased as this letter was the second one he had written; the first one was not sent and is missing from the file. His suspicions were no doubt confirmed when he received a copy of the committee's report..., that had, no doubt to Dowding's astonishment, been completed by the 17th.'

One wonders why Beaverbrook took it upon himself to set up such an inquiry – and not exactly 'a thorough inquiry' – when he had no jurisdiction in the matter. He must surely have known that, with the relations between Salmond and Dowding being what they were, no good case could come for Dowding in Salmond's report. What was Beaverbrook up to? We are tempted to say, in view of Beaverbrook's insalubrious reputation–and despite his championing of Dowding during the Battle–what 'dirty little game'?

iii. No one had, for that matter. One feature of Dowding's reply is that, whereas the Salmond paper addresses problems of air defence, broadly speaking, Dowding refers more specifically, and technically, to night interception and night operations.

iv. The arguments against the transfer of filtering were again dealt with by Dowding in his Despatch, and explain his irritation. He wrote, in particular: 'In order to avoid waste of flying effort and false Air Raid Warnings it was obviously very necessary to differentiate between friendly and enemy formations, and this was the most difficult, as well as the most important, task of my Filter Room.' He goes on to explain the essential functions of Command, Group and Sector, which required that filtering be done at Command. Incredibly, the Draft Conclusions of the Air Council meeting of October 2nd contain the assertion that the Air Officer Commanding-in-Chief of Fighter Command and MRAF Sir John Salmond had reached agreement 'on all the points which were in issue following the Council's letter dated 25th September, 1940, to AOC-in-C, Fighter Command'. Of those points, the first reads as follows: '(a) the decentralisation of filtering to Group Headquarters: this arrangement would not come into operation until IFF equipment had been fitted into all fighter aircraft.' This paragraph has been heavily scored through with three lines of black pencil. Dowding's views are corroborated, and justified, seventeen years later, by Basil Collier, when he wrote (p. 256): 'As for devolution of the filtering and air-raid systems, they would take some time to put into effect, and in any case had little bearing on the immediate issue.' This is far from the end of the dispute. On October 1st, Sinclair called a meeting to thrash the problem out. Joubert and Dowding were again at loggerheads. We are jumping ahead in our story, but this is the place to continue and end it. At the War Cabinet meeting of October 7th, where the controversy was raised again, Churchill instructed Dowding to submit a statement of his views of the matters at issue. When Churchill approved the Salmond Report, with the omission of the filtering recommendation, the Air Council objected. Churchill then wrote to Dowding, on a personal level, and asked him to state his case again. Dowding replied the following day, on October 24th, as follows: 'The Secretary of State's minutes contain a few inaccuracies, only one of which is important and that is the statement that it is really an undoubted fact that time is saved in getting squadrons into the air by filtering at Group HQ - it is substantially untrue. Plots are told to Group HQ from my table without delay, with the average lag in transmission of a plot less than 15 seconds. The metaphorical edifice which you have seen in my Filter and Operations Room has been built up brick by brick under my own eye during the last four years. My predecessor, Joubert, had left the Fighter Area as it was, without having made the slightest effort to tackle what had been in fact one of the gravest problems of the defence, by the differentiation between friendly and enemy aircraft .... The system that I have devised might not be perfect but it cannot be improved by the disruptive criticism on the part of people who do not understand it as a whole. I started with the idea of decentralisation of filtration and abandoned it in favour of centralisation. My greatest grievance, however, is the matter of expenditure of my time in arguing with the Air Staff of every intimate detail of my organisation. Surely the C-in-C should be left to manage his own affairs if the general result is satisfactory. As the Secretary of State says, I agreed to decentralise under strong pressure because it is not a matter that is going to lose the war and I have to fight the Air Staff over so many important issues .... I feel that we shall pay £100,000 in material and labour in order to secure a slight reduction in efficiency.'

In the end the issue of decentralization was taken out of everyone's hands by the inexorable march of events. The Filter Room at Fighter Command HQ was simply swamped by the mass of information coming in from the CH stations and the lack of physical space to handle more people round the plotting table. I quote Bragg (p. 236): 'Centralised filtering that had appeared to Dowding in 1938 as the most effective and economical way to conduct air operations had been rendered almost unworkable by the sheer quantity of information coming in from the chains which had doubled in size in less than a year and were continuing to increase.'

v. This letter of Salmond's is one of the most crucial, and revealing, in the whole campaign of vituperation against Dowding, and in the drama of his removal from his command. The date of the letter tells all: it is October 5th, that is to say, a mere eight days following Dowding's reply to the Air Council. Salmond was obviously wasting no time. He, and Trenchard, had made up their minds, and were going to pull every string possible to get rid of Dowding. The true aim of Salmond's committee must now be seen for what it was: a device calculated to elicit from their victim the replies that Salmond knew he would receive, and show Dowding in the light that would enable his enemies to 'hang' him. What is also equally clear is that Salmond must have known in advance that he was going to get all the support he needed from the key members of the Air Council. That seems to have been Trenchard's role in the drama.

vi. The first three of these measures were dreamt up by Frederick Lindemann, Churchill's personal scientific adviser, a position he held throughout the war. The Air Ministry Scientific Committee's 'all-important preoccupation with radar meant nothing to him .... Sometimes he argued that the parachute mine deserved higher priority than radar.' Joubert wrote: 'It is sad to have to record it, but there is no single authenticated instance of any of these methods having brought about the destruction of the enemy, although the mine field laid by one aircraft may have been successful. What did happen was that the entire countryside became littered with wires to which bombs were still attached, and all these had to be cleared up laboriously by the Bomb Disposal Squads.' (*The Fated Sky*, p.187) Lindemann's views on the area bombing of German cities, the use of 'windows' to throw off German radar, and the use of anti-submarine aircraft in the Battle of the Atlantic, were equally wrong-headed and dangerous, and cost thousands of Allied lives. And Churchill kept him on throughout the war.

vii. Quoted by David Thomson in *England in the Nineteenth Century 1815-1914* (London, Penguin Books, 1963), p. 226.

viii. The differences between the totals for each month and the aggregate of the other three columns – respectively 10, 18 and 36 enemy aircraft destroyed – are accounted for by anti-aircraft artillery, balloons, engine failure, and unknown causes. In some cases the agency is stated as 'shot down by night fighter' without specifying. These latter cases have not been counted. The results for January and February are, respectively, 8 e/a destroyed (two by fighters) in a month of fourteen major or heavy attacks; and 5 e/a destroyed (six by fighters) in a month of eleven attacks. The devastating raid on London on the night of May 10-11, the last night attack against the capital, is revealing about the defences, and disheartening for the citizenry. 'During the night 571 sorties were flown by German long-range bombers over Britain, together with 24 by long-range fighters' over the period 2250-0515 hours. Fighter Command sent up 325 fighters, and claimed twenty-eight enemy aircraft destroyed. The Germans lost, in fact, eleven aircraft, five of which fell to Beaufighters.

ix. The true figures could not have been known at the time, or even by 1946, because it was impossible to know how many enemy aircraft crashed in the sea or on return to Occupied Europe after combat over Britain. On the other hand it was possible to know precisely how many were destroyed over Britain. The following figures are reproduced, by permission of the author, from Michael Bragg's RDF1 (p.259):

November 1940	NIL planes destroyed	NIL damaged
(Coventry raid over 400 aircraft)		
December 1940	2 planes destroyed	6 damaged
March 1941	24 planes destroyed	50 damaged
April 1941	52 planes destroyed	88 damaged
May 1941	88 planes destroyed	172 damaged

These figures tell everything when comparing claims with the actual numbers of German aircraft shot down over this period, as shown above. Bragg introduces his table with these words: 'The great success of GCI is best shown by the statistics of night fighting, all the more remarkable as only five night-fighter squadrons were equipped with AI, plus a further eight squadrons known as 'cat's eye' fighters, which were directed by GCI but had to continue their search visually: they were very successful especially during moonlit nights.'

x. Bowen, p. 70.

xi. At this point Bowen comments: 'This was the first time I had heard the argument for a two-engined, two-man aircraft advanced with such certainty and with such authority; in all previous discussions, at the Air Ministry and at Fighter Command, for every advocate of a two-engined aircraft as night fighter, there was at least one vehement advocate of the single-seat, single-engined machine.' We know of no one at Fighter Command who argued in favour of the single-seater for night fighting; at the Air Ministry the prime advocate was Sholto Douglas – because advocated by Salmond.

xii. When Dowding submitted a report on night defence, which was acclaimed as 'brilliant' by Churchill, Lindemann scoffed at it as mere undergraduate stuff. The explanation lies in the fact that Lindemann opposed Dowding's ideas because a) he had demonstrated previously that he had no faith in the promise of what radar would do, and b) he had not thought of it himself. I quote a long section of a recent book, by a scientist himself, that goes all the way to justify Dowding's ideas of night defence, based, as they were, on operational methods. The author's summary, quoted here at length, is based on Dowding's own report:

> The basic concept of radar-controlled night fighters was quite different from the day fighting scheme ... By day the bombers came over in large formations, all too visible, surrounded by a shield of fighters. Ground-based radar brought the fighters into visual contact, and then they were on their own. By night, the bombers slunk in one by one, invisible and alone. To combat them was a totally different proposition, and one more difficult to implement. The idea was to have night fighters patrolling a specified area rather than waiting to be scrambled. When a bomber intruded into his airspace, the pilot would be directed by ground radar to fly

as near to the bomber as could be accomplished, at which point the fighter's own radar would take over and guide him in close. Finally, visual contact would be made and the bomber shot down. Easy enough to say, but infinitely hard to accomplish. The problems were many:

1. Producing a radar set small enough to be carried aloft. Remember, the Chain Home radars used transmitters on towers hundreds of feet high.
2. Directing the night fighter from the ground in close to the bomber. Any bomber pilot worth his salt would not be flying straight and level...
3. Operating airborne radar and flying the plane so as to get close enough for visual contact.
4. Finally, actually shooting down the bomber.

In the spring of 1940 a young Welshman named Taffy Bowen had produced a radar set that was sort of workable, and he prepared to demonstrate it to Dowding. The aircraft he had been working with was a Fairey Battle, a single-engine and two-seater originally designed as a light bomber ... To fit both himself and Stuffy into the backseat, they had to dispense with parachutes, but they did manage, and the demonstration was a success – as far as it went. Another Battle flew straight ahead while Bowen, his head under a black hood along with Dowding, directed their plane to intercept successfully.

This was progress, but it was a far cry from having mass-produced sets that worked consistently and were simple enough to be operated by RAF crew, rather than by an expert like Taffy Bowen. The test was also a far cry from intercepting a bomber that was taking evasive action along a prearranged and steady course. When they landed, Dowding took Bowen aside for a two-hour detailed discussion of the problems.

Bowen was impressed: 'I had never heard such a clear and definite analysis of the fundamentals of night fighting.' He was not as impressed with Professor Lindemann, who also received a demonstration of the system, but who was quite worried about a dinner appointment in London that evening which he did not want to miss and seemed to be in his usual mood of finding fault with everything and did not have a single positive suggestion to make....When he got back to London he gave us a poor report. Of all the distinguished people to whom we demonstrated airborne radar, Lindemann was the only one who was unimpressed. The reason was that Lindemann had his own ideas and couldn't bear the thought that anyone else's might work. After his infrared scheme he came up with another disaster, code-named 'Mutton', that involved dropping bombs in front of oncoming bombers. (Fisher, pp. 241-44.)

Fisher goes on to explain and demolish gleefully that and others of Lindemann's ideas. Bragg tells us in his masterly work on radar (p. 140) that according to Dowding, 'the eventual solution of night fighting would be found in air to air RDF and that a specialised type of night fighter would be required for that purpose.' That was as early as August 1939. Dowding remained convinced, stubborn, and inflexible. And right. A terrible combination of qualities for a commander!

xiii. Bragg, pp. 232-33.

xiv. Henry Probert, in his book on the high commanders of the RAF, says of Salmond: 'One of his most significant tasks was to chair in 1940 the committee which investigated the performance of the night air defences.' This statement appears to us as a classic example of damning with faint praise.

xv. See H.R. Allen, p. 51-52.

xvi. The official, unpublished, Air Ministry account entitled *Air Defence of Great Britain*. Vol. iii, Night Air Defence, entirely supports this view. (See AIR 41/17, I-E.)

xvii. See Zimmerman, *Britain's Shield*, pp. 214-226.

CHAPTER 8

The Motives

—⚂—

In our preceding examination of the factors that lay behind the removal of Dowding from his command, we have demonstrated that the explanation is not to be found in a simplistic statement of 'reasons'; Indeed there was something more behind the decision than shortcomings of a technical nature. The criticism of the day tactics became a questionable device used to justify Leigh-Mallory's wings: they relied on an outdated report filled with exaggerated claims of enemy aircraft destroyed. The charge of failing to counter the night Blitz was also a classic case of fingering a scapegoat for the Air Ministry's own neglect.

The previous chapter addressed the question: what reasons did the Air Council and Air Staff have to replace Dowding? – or rather, what reasons did later writers claim they had, as no contemporary authority put pen to paper. The second section answered the question: how did those involved convince Churchill that Dowding must go? In this final section we pose the only remaining questions: who were the people who wanted to get rid of Dowding, and what were their motives? In the absence of evidence to justify Dowding's removal, we have no recourse but to seek the answer to the riddle in the one area generally avoided by historians: the personal factor. We start by harking back to Haslam's article, from which we cull these observations:

> He [Dowding] was not one of the intimate circle to whom Trenchard turned for advice. Trenchard suspected Dowding of being 'a dismal Jimmy' and obsessed by fear of casualties.
>
> He was a known 'stuffy' character, difficult to work with and often at loggerheads with the Air Ministry. Neither Salmond nor Freeman were (sic) friendly towards or admirers of Dowding's.

These opinions point the way towards the missing pieces in the puzzle: that is, they are of a personal nature. Dowding himself would have concurred; in his typescript *Personal Notes for a Biographer*, he conceded that he was not popular within Air Ministry circles, and that, as we have just seen, 'the Air Council had been anxious to be rid of me before the start of the war'. We also saw, in chapter two, that he had furious arguments with officers on the Air Staff. Now, his unpopularity had become such that, at the height of his powers and triumphs, his greatest achievement was swept aside by others who exposed themselves as being incapable of rising above their personal aversion, even in their country's interest, and even when the prospect of

120

defeat had not been entirely vanquished. They regarded Dowding as a constant thorn in their collective and individual sides, with his incessant demands and complaints. Notably in the case of Trenchard, differences of opinion over strategy also played a decisive role.

We will attempt to demonstrate that the critics and enemies of Dowding were spurred by powerful emotions, such as dislike, fear, jealousy, ambition, spite, hatred, and inferiority. We will consider the principal agents and their likely motives.

A Weak Link

This document is conspicuous for the defective judgement shown by its author, despite his claims otherwise. Nowhere is this lack more in evidence than when he claims that the replacement of Air Chief Marshal Ludlow-Hewitt by Air Marshal Portal as C-in-C Bomber Command was 'an outstanding improvement'. This assessment is made without evidence, i.e. it is a personal opinion. All competent opinion sides with Ludlow-Hewitt, and would only prefer Portal because he was 'cooperative', whereas Ludlow-Hewitt was, like Dowding, a thorn in the Air Ministry's side – and for the right reasons. The writer's assessment of Fighter Command is wildly biased and erratic, and his opinion of Dowding is distorted by a palpable antipathy. He must have felt that he would benefit from Newall's removal, having been passed over for promotion; and that Dowding's elevation to CAS would not be to his advantage. How easy it is to find arguments to conceal one's true motives!

Ward and Clarry

These bit-players in a dark drama, who involved themselves while acknowledging that they knew nothing about the issues and that it was no business of theirs anyway, are deserving only of scorn and contempt. Whether they had hoped to benefit from their meddling is impossible to judge.

Macdonald

Macdonald's offence, and it was egregious, was to put loyalty to his squadron commander, and perhaps to his group commander as well, above that to his commander-in-chief. Loyalty of a personal nature is a bond stronger than a loyalty to a remote and unknown authority. And Macdonald's loyalty to and admiration of Douglas Bader knew no bounds.

Leigh-Mallory and Macdonald came to know each other well, given their respective positions. It is conceivable that Leigh-Mallory urged the action on him. It is, we believe, the sort of thing of which he was capable.

Macdonald's political interests would induce him to put personal loyalty above 'party' loyalty, as he demonstrated when lobbying Churchill. In politics, one furthers one's career and fortunes by building networks of personal relations.

In an earlier and less squeamish age Macdonald's treachery to his Commander-in-Chief would have been met with condign punishment.

Salmond and Trenchard

It is impossible to separate these two officers: they formed what is commonly called a 'cabal', and operated in cahoots with each other from September onwards until their campaign bore fruit.

They saw eye to eye with each other in every respect. They both harboured a personal dislike of Dowding, and their views departed radically from his on how to conduct the war.

Salmond took the aggressive role in the case, and Trenchard was happy to play second fiddle. The reason for this reversion of roles is simply explained: Trenchard had far more to lose than Salmond in either case.

Salmond and Trenchard plotted with the single aim of getting rid of Dowding. They were in constant touch with each other: they met frequently, and when they didn't meet, they wrote. Their letters form the basis of the conclusions we reach here; they not only conferred and intrigued together: they had the ear of people in the highest positions in the land and knew that their views would be listened to.

If the scheming and plotting that this cabal engaged in does not come under the heading of **conspiracy**, then the word has lost its meaning. The possibility of a conspiracy to oust Dowding was officially denied by the Air Ministry for over fifty years.

Salmond was a high ranking and prestigious officer who carried great weight in the councils of the Air Ministry. In early September he authored a report on night defences which was clearly flawed, and showed so little understanding of the real problems of successful defence against night bombing, that one cannot but conclude that his report was motivated by keenness to undermine Dowding's position. Salmond had nothing to gain personally from Dowding's going, except the intense satisfaction of helping to remove from a position of authority someone you dislike, and, even more, of finding oneself able to assert influence even when no longer in an official position of authority. He had already met with success in his intrigue against Newall: this success encouraged him. That he was motivated by a visceral dislike of Dowding is beyond dispute.

Another factor is worth considering. Salmond was a former Air Officer Commanding-in-Chief of what was then called Air Defence of Great Britain. He may have thought he had a sort of proprietorial right to judge and criticize the successors of this command, even though all its methods and equipment had long since left the ADGB far behind.

Trenchard's hostility to Dowding was of very long date. His animosity was based, at least at first, on a fundamental difference of values. It may be summed up in the word 'humanity'; Trenchard, like other First World War commanders, sacrificed the lives of the soldiers and airmen under his command with gross unfeeling, while accusing men like Dowding of being 'dismal Jimmies', and, later, of lacking humanity.[i] These personal slurs suggest a difficulty in accepting contrary views with good grace. That was enough to unite the two men in their hostility to Dowding. There was more, and it added fuel to the fire: doctrinal difference.

We have seen that, from 1937 onwards, a possible strategic defence of the British Isles became a distinct possibility. The victory of Fighter Command in the Battle of Britain demonstrated that the Trenchard doctrine was founded on false premises; Trenchard's independent air force was created on that sole belief, and continued to exist for the sole purpose of carrying the attack against any enemy and of bombing it into surrender. In that summer of 1940 they saw the entire justification of their independent Royal Air Force shattered before their eyes. Defence was not only a possibility: it was victorious. With the result that Trenchard saw a major part of his life's work and credo demolished before his eyes.

And yet we see in this great victory a crowning irony, for if Trenchard had not prevailed in his aim to create an independent air force, Britain would surely have been defeated in 1940. If, therefore, the Royal Air Force had not existed, the pre-existing situation would have prevailed; that is to say, there would have been two air forces, component elements of the Army and the Navy, as they had existed until 1918. If the RFC had still existed in 1940, the Army commander would have been able to call on all the resources of his air arm– until it had been destroyed. It would not have been able to stem the German advance, and the United Kingdom would have been denuded of its air defence.

Salmond was not a great man; the record of his actions suggests he resented Dowding's triumph.[ii] Trenchard was a great man. It is all the more regrettable, therefore, that he was blinkered in his vision of air power to the extent that he was unable to see one of the very greatest virtues of his own creation of an independent air force.

Sinclair and Portal

We now turn to a consideration of the highly placed officials who were personally, by direct or indirect means, interested in and working for Dowding's removal.

The very question, and the idea of the need for it, introduces a disturbing note. If senior officers and politicians determine to get rid of those who have accomplished prodigious tasks, and then observe a total silence in explaining their decision and action, eventually there will appear visible and ever-growing discrepancies between the silence and the explanations. When the discrepancies are subjected to literary and psychological analysis, the perpetrators of the dismissal will be found to be involved in intrigue and deceit.

We begin our inquiry with the question: who was the authority with the ultimate decision to get rid of Dowding? There are only two candidates: Sinclair and Portal. If there had been disagreement between them, Portal's view would have prevailed. However, both men were so indisputably in the anti-Dowding camp that disagreement was not at issue. Moreover, if we enter the Trenchard and Salmond factor into the equation, it is equally clear that Portal's efforts would not have prevailed without support – and perhaps encouragement – from the Air Council. Indeed, Portal's – and Sholto Douglas's – antagonism towards Dowding may well have been one of the key factors in Portal's appointment by Sinclair as Chief of the Air Staff.

First, do we know anything of Portal's hostility to Dowding? Portal was a cagey man: he gave nothing away. But it is possible to glean a clue from Dowding's fate. The crucial decision was whether to offer Dowding another appointment or to retire him. Dowding's outstanding qualities and his great achievements demanded a position in which he could put these qualities to good use; Portal's 'decision' to retire him, despite the official cancellation of his retirement date, was tantamount to declaring that he wanted no part of him in his Air Force.

Britain was still alone, and only at the beginning of a war which was going to be long and hard. Another CAS might have put his country's need ahead of his personal antipathies, or even their doctrinal differences, and invited Dowding to meet him, alone, the two of them, in a series of conferences in order to reach a *modus vivendi*. No such initiative was taken. This silence is eloquently suggestive. But it is clear that it was not Portal's decision alone: it was Portal's connivance in the decision arrived at jointly by Sinclair in cahoots with, and prodded insistently by, Trenchard.

Portal was a protégé of Trenchard's, an unquestioning disciple of his bomber doctrine. That is one of the main reasons why he was sent to head Bomber Command in early 1940. He would have been there for the normal three to four year tenure had circumstances not intervened. The most pressing circumstance was a replacement for Newall. Trenchard was determined that a) one of his bomber faithful should be appointed in order to bring the Royal Air Force back to its primary mission and purpose, that of re-instating the Trenchard doctrine and of creating a large and impressive heavy bomber force; and b) Dowding should be prevented at all costs from being appointed as Chief of the Air Staff.

Trenchard's leading role in what we have called this 'dark side of the Battle of Britain' has not received adequate academic attention. There is little documentary evidence to sustain the suspicion, and all official writing (and most unofficial writing) dealing with this period since the war has been sympathetic to or dictated by the Air Ministry position on controversial issues.

Trenchard's influence throughout the Air Force loomed large throughout his life, and at no time greater than during the war. He had ready entry to all offices and constant access to all the important people in the Air Ministry, on the Air Council, and on the Air Staff. His resentment of the emphasis placed on defence from 1938, at the expense of the forces of offensive action, was deep and bitter. This alone, together with Portal's appointment as CAS, is enough to explain the complete absence of any policy respecting the meaningful use or development of Fighter Command after the Battle of Britain.

We come now to a grievous injustice, of which Portal was the principal agent. We have insisted that Dowding's dismissal cannot be considered in isolation from other events. Air Vice-Marshal Keith Park, the Air Officer Commanding 11 Group, was also removed from his command. All the 'reasoned' explanations of Dowding's removal break down further when Park's demotion is factored into the complex equation we have been constructing. They are inseparable. If Park had been promoted, and then moved to a less demanding appointment, one's suspicions might not have been aroused. But his removal by Portal, without promotion, after his role in the daylight battle, raises a red flag of alarm.

Park was posted to an appointment in Training Command on December 23, one month after Dowding's departure, having occupied his command for only seven months. No writer has gone so far as to suggest that he was removed for technical or professional reasons. Park himself was not consulted about it.

When Dowding went, Park, his loyal lieutenant who not only shared Dowding's ideas but ensured that his tactics fitted in with mathematical precision with his strategy, also had to go. Their joint dismissal would seem to give point to the contention that they were removed for 'professional' reasons, that is, their mismanagement of the battle.[iii] Though the true explanation becomes clear when his and Dowding's replacements are known; they were, respectively, Leigh–Mallory and Douglas.

Leigh–Mallory and Douglas

Leigh–Mallory's hostility to both Dowding and Park has been documented by Park's biographer.

> One day in February 1940, while Park was still at Bentley Priory, Leigh-Mallory 'came out of Dowding's office, paused in mine and said in my presence that he would move heaven and earth to get Dowding removed from Fighter Command.' Dowding only learnt of this episode many years later, and it came as a shock that Leigh-Mallory had harboured such bitterness toward him – an enmity provoked, no doubt, by Dowding's having rebuked Leigh-Mallory for professional lapses. Later in that year Leigh-Mallory 'made it quite clear to me [Park] that he was very jealous of my group, which was in the front line [after Dunkirk].'[iv]

Leigh–Mallory would not, of course, have been successful without substantial help and cooperation from others well situated to give it. The chief of them was Douglas. One writer, who witnessed what Douglas wrote, informs us that Leigh–Mallory and Douglas were in frequent contact by telephone. The fact of their conferring together – 'conspiring' is a more accurate word – behind Dowding's back, shows a deceit common enough in political circles but rare in the higher reaches of the Royal Air Force. Park summed up his feelings in later years: 'To my dying day [he told his biographer] I shall feel bitter at the base intrigue which was used to remove Dowding and myself as soon as we had won the battle.' And he was not shy in revealing the names of the plotters when declining an offer to write his biography: 'No doubt the intriguing that Joubert and Douglas did at the Air Ministry in collaboration with Leigh–Mallory would make exciting reading, but it would not enhance the reputation of the Royal Air Force.'[v]

Douglas was in cahoots with Sinclair from the beginning of the latter's appointment as Air Minister: Sinclair, as we have seen, sounded Churchill out in July about getting rid of Dowding. What did Sinclair know so soon about Dowding? The answer appears to be nothing. What he heard in the Air Council Meetings was a factor, ut the selected information Douglas fed him appears to have been more powerful.

Sinclair and Douglas

Sinclair's treatment of Dowding in November when informing him he was to leave Fighter Command 'immediately' was a gross violation of every form of decency. Dowding's view of his removal distinguish between 'reasons' and 'manner'; he informed his biographer that if the Air Ministry had decided that he and Park were wrong in their handling of the battle and Leigh-Mallory and Douglas were right in their views, 'they were right to get rid of me.' But in all the important matters they were demonstrably wrong. The manner of Dowding's dismissal by Sinclair was also particularly offensive; it was almost as if Sinclair was settling a score.

The relations between Douglas and Sinclair were decisive in Dowding's fate. And here we have a spark of evidence which we can fan into an illuminating flame. When Sinclair retired from his ministerial post on May 28th, 1945, shortly after the end of the war, Douglas wrote to him. In his reply Sinclair said, among other things: 'Many charming letters softened the blow of my departure from the Air Ministry but none which I shall treasure more than the one which you sent me. You were my first friend at the Air Ministry. . . You helped me enormously in those early days. . . I felt as though I had won a battle when I got Fighter Command into your hands – and, looking back, how right I was!' How much a simple-seeming statement can reveal! Douglas occupied a high position on the Air Ministry totem pole, and exercised both authority and influence. Hence Sinclair's naïve, and heartfelt, tribute lends itself to some interesting deductions: i) Douglas went out of his way to ingratiate himself with the new Air Minister while helping him into his job; ii) Sinclair, accepting Douglas as a friend, and relying on him for advice in a job which he never mastered, came under Douglas's influence; iii) Douglas exploited this influence to his own ends; iv) two of those 'ends' were to aid and abet Sinclair in dethroning Dowding, and, crucially, v) Sinclair got Fighter Command into Douglas's hands as a reward for a friend.

Douglas was not a discreet man; he confided in Wing Commander Sidney Cotton, the pioneer of photographic reconnaissance, who was harried and persecuted by the Air Ministry in 1940-41 until unceremoniously discharged. When Cotton first met Douglas, in March 1940, Cotton was having his usual difficulties in getting authorization for his actions. Cotton wrote of that confused time:

> It was consoling to know that I wasn't the only one who was fighting on two
> fronts – the Germans and the Air Ministry. Another man – Air Commodore
> Douglas Colyer, then the British Air Attaché in Paris – advised me to handle
> the Air Force machine much as a good mechanic would handle a troublesome
> motor-car engine; keep tickling the carburettor, and if one spanner didn't fit,
> try another. Sholto Douglas, whom I met about this time, told me much the
> same thing. The RAF, he said, was full of regulations which had been thought
> up over the years by people with nothing better to do, and which gave those

who studied them the chance to delay and sabotage anything they could get their hands on. 'But take my advice, Sidney,' he added, 'learn how the machine works and you can beat them. You can rise to any heights if you study the machine and use it properly.' [Cotton adds sardonically] It seems he knew what he was talking about, for he subsequently became C-in-C Fighter Command, C-in-C Coastal Command, and C-in-C British Forces in Germany.

The key to the enigma of Dowding's sacking was his unpopularity with the Air Council and the Air Staff – though 'unpopularity' is a mild word, to say the least – and Dowding's unpopularity boiled down inevitably to personalities, that is to personal feelings and conflicting aims and ambitions. No man has ever acted on pure reason. He is not an *animal rational*; he is an animal *rationis capax* – only endowed with reason. He may be a creator of ideas; but he needs something more: he needs a stimulus. An idea is of no account unless it moves to action. A man is always moved to act; he is motivated, that is, swayed by emotional forces. The factors that motivate him are personal, either existing already within the person, like a seed awaiting germination – and it may be a poisonous or a beneficent seed – or existing in the incompatible chemistry of two beings.

Now in regard to the well-springs of human conduct, Dowding and his enemies constitute an instructive study in contrasts. His stepson, David Whiting, who knew Dowding well, has said that he was a man to weigh evidence, never to be swayed by his emotions. 'I never saw him make an error of judgment or a bad decision. He had the ability to brush away surface things and see even beyond the solution. He had an orderly mind – essentially he was a mathematician.'

Dowding came to his overall strategic ideas by study and thought, that is by the light of reason; and thereafter, moved by the conviction of their soundness, sought to realize them with a passionate intensity, directed and controlled by a steely will. The *idée maîtresse* that was the foundation of all his thinking was the imperious need to protect and defend his country.

Those who opposed Dowding reached their ideas by the murky and erratic path of passion and wishful thinking; and readily found plausible arguments and 'reasons' in which to cloak them. A classic case is Trenchard's strategic view of the power of the bomber to smash an enemy into submission. This view was dictated by an aggressive personality which simple-mindedly espoused, and subsequently promoted, the dogma that offence is the best defence–or rather, the only defence. But it was a view devoid of evidence and unknown to experience; and yet in spite of this it became entrenched Air Force policy, a policy followed slavishly by succeeding generations of air marshals who had neither the intelligence to question nor the courage to oppose him. To the penetrating logic of Dowding – 'How do you prevent the enemy from destroying your cities while you are bombing theirs?'– Trenchard had no answer. His mind was so rigid that he was incapable of looking at the question. Instead he sought to get rid of the questioner, and he was not content to charge Dowding just with professional shortcomings. Trenchard and his allies resorted to personal vituperation, accusing

Dowding of defects which would have a professional impact: a stubborn attachment to his ideas and rightness; a refusal to try out new ideas; a slow brain; a persistent refusal to cooperate with higher authorities; unimaginativeness; and even – heaven forfend! – a lack of humanity. We know, from Shakespeare and the Old Testament, that it is possible that air marshals and others, men who had reached the top of their professional ladder, could be swayed by emotions like jealousy and ambition – 'green-eyed jealousy' and 'tyrant ambition, the tyrant of the mind'.

The suggestion that some air marshals might actually have been motivated by fear of Dowding is also plausible. It was said, for example, that Newall was intimidated by Dowding. But the fear went beyond the personal. Some were very afraid of what would almost certainly happen, to themselves and to their policies, in the event that Dowding were appointed to replace Newall as Chief of the Air Staff. They were not sure what his policies would be, but they were sure that he was not a disciple of Trenchard and an out-and-out bomber man; and that if he became Chief of the Air Staff there would be an unprecedented shake-up and weeding-out of the Air Staff. In a word, heads would roll. His appointment had to be prevented at all costs – and by any means. We have seen how shabby and underhanded those means were. And we have seen how, progressively, from June to November, the stakes were raised bit by bit against Dowding. We will see, in chapter eleven, the measure of their vindictiveness, when we discuss Dowding's claim to promotion to Marshal of the Royal Air Force.

An occurrence of far-reaching significance was the appointment, in 1937, of Sir Thomas Inskip as Minister for Coordinator of Defence. It will be recalled that the Government of the day accepted, as national defence policy, his urgent recommendation that the Royal Air Force turn away from its insistence on bombers and plan more energetically for an effective defence and the production of fighters. Many years of planning overturned in a trice! Someone would pay! Inskip and his colleagues were out of reach, but there was a target for their anger nearby.

We must also recall other events, closely inter-related, which may well have struck deep at the heart of the powers-that-be in the Air Ministry. When the German Blitzkrieg met with such bewildering success and shattered the Allied armies; when the humiliating Dunkirk evacuation took place; and above all when France collapsed, and Britain, without a single ally and close to bankruptcy, faced the prospect of imminent invasion, a wave of panic ran through Whitehall and swept the nation's leaders into a paralysis of indecision. Even Churchill was not unaffected. There was one man, however, who never wavered.

As early as May 16, 1940, Dowding wrote to the Government that historic letter in which he laid it down that, in the event of the defeat of the Allied armies in France, 'there is no one who will deny that England should fight on, even though the remainder of the Continent of Europe is dominated by the Germans.' (Many did deny it, high in Government circles, and favoured seeking terms with Hitler.) Dowding, with his Fighter Command, was the immovable obstacle against which the irresistible force of the Luftwaffe was broken. How would the men of Whitehall feel now? More to the point, how would they feel when Dowding prevailed against the enemy? The

Critics

Air Vice-Marshal William Sholto Douglas, Vice-Chief of Air Staff, whose treacherous scheming against Dowding served only his own ambition.

MRAF Lord Trenchard, 'Father' of the RAF and first CAS, who became Dowding's arch enemy. E18087

Harold Balfour MP, Under-Secretary of State; Sir Archibald Sinclair, Secretary of State for Air; Air Chief Marshal Sir Charles Portal, Chief of the Air Staff. Balfour should have known better and tried to modify Sinclair's and Portal's hostility. CH2329

Irene Ward MP, the prototype of the critic whose criticism became shriller with ignorance.

ACM Sir Wilfred Freeman, Portal's right-hand man throughout the war. A very fine officer, a critic of Portal's bomber policy, and who saw too late the injustice done to Dowding. CH2351

MRAF Sir Geoffrey Salmond, with Dowding at RAF Hendon in 1932, in happier days. It was Salmond who, with Trenchard's urgings, lobbied Churchill with poisonous effect.

Flight Lieutenant Sir Peter Macdonald MP, Adjutant of 242 Squadron, who, as a devotee of Bader, lobbied Churchill to undermine Dowding's authority.

Squadron Leader Douglas Bader, OC 242 Squadron. In terms of leadership and air fighting, Bader remains the epitome of bravery usurping intelligence.

—⚡— Three officers who betrayed their duty of loyalty to their Commander-in-Chief by criticizing his direction of the Battle behind his back. —⚡—

Air Vice-Marshal Trafford Leigh-Mallory, AOC 12 Group, whose disloyalty to his Commander was rewarded by his alliance with Sholto Douglas.

Wing Commander E.J. Kingston-McCloughry, whose scurrilous anonymous document was circulated throughout Government by Irene Ward, among others. (AHB)

Partners

Lord Beaverbrook and son Max Aitken.

Reginald Mitchell, designer of the Spitfire.

Keith Park, AOC 11 Group.

Richard Saul, AOC 13 Group.

Robert Wright, Dowding's PA.

Sir Quentin Brand, AOC 10
Group.

Sir Henry Tizard.
HU42365

Robert Watson Watt.
CH13862

Winston Churchill.

Dowding

—ɯɯ—

Among these characters, plucked, as it were, from the pages of war histories and battle archives, it was inevitable that Dowding should be given the major attention. Here truly was a man of heroic and yet tragic proportion; the architect of victory in the Battle of Britain who, even in the midst of it, as the object of a mean-minded intrigue; whose reward for having beaten back the German attack and forced Hitler into abandoning the invasion of Britain was to be summarily retired at the end of it. He still [1969] remains the only active British commander of the air forces during World War Two who was overlooked when the monarch* appointed the rest to be Marshals of the Royal Air Force. (Leonard Mosley, *The Battle of Britain – the making of a film*, p.59)

* The monarch was following the advice of the Government, or rather the Air Ministry, which was the guilty agency. (JD)

The Commander-in-Chief escorting the King and Queen on a visit to Fighter Command HQ, RAF Bentley Priory, in September 1940. CH001233

LORD DOWDING / HURRICANE

Royal Mail stamp commemorating the 40th anniversary of the Battle of Britain.

With Muriel, Lady Dowding and Trenchard at the Royal Air Force Club in 1946. Dowding could not have known of Trenchard's role in the conspiracy.

HM The Queen Mother unveiling the statue of Lord Dowding outside St Clement Danes, the Royal Air Force Church, The Strand, on 30 October 1988. The officer on the left is Air Chief Marshal Sir Christopher Foxley-Norris, who was the Chairman of the Battle of Britain Fighters Association.

A characteristic pose in 1940.

At Westminster Abbey, September 1946

Official portrait in full ceremonial uniform by Faith Kenworthy-Brown. This portrait hung in the entrance hall of Bentley Priory until the whole estate, including the building housing the Heaquarters of Fighter Command during the Battle of Britain, was sold by the Government in 2008 in order to eradicate a part of Great Britain's military heritage.

At Duxford, near Cambridge, in 1968, for the shooting of the film of the Battle, with some of his pilots. Far left is Tom Gleave; then Bob Stanford Tuck. Leaning on Dowding's chair is Alan Deere. Johnny Kent is behind Deere on the left.

With 'Sailor' Malan (centre) at a reception in September 1945. (Who is the gentleman on the left?)

At Duxford with the actor Trevor Howard, who played the role of Keith Park in the film.

One of the few smiling pictures: giving a speech at the Royal Air Force Club, 1952.

Sir Hugh Dowding

WHOSE SIGNATURE AND PHOTOGRAPH
APPEAR HEREON IS EMPLOYED BY THE

BRITISH AIR COMMISSION
WASHINGTON, D. C.

DIRECTOR GENERAL

SIGNATURE OF HOLDER

NOT VALID UNLESS COUNTERSIGNED BY
J. E. KEEL, DIRECTOR OF FINANCE AND
ADMINISTRATION.

Dowding's Identity Card during his
visit to the United States in 1940-41.

Cover portrait,
12 June 1943.

THE ILLUSTRATED
LONDON NEWS

SATURDAY, JUNE 12, 1943

The sage of
Oakgates,
Tunbridge Wells.

Being greeted by Her Majesty the Queen at the premiere of the Battle film, the Odeon cinema, London, 15 September, 1969.

Pilots

They mourned each other so simply and with no fuss and went rushing off into the air and throwing their glorious young lives away to safeguard us all... And now we began to know and understand a little, and now we knew war. We were uplifted. We trudged on through dust and bombs and discomfort. We lay in ditches and watched the dogfights and cheered on our warriors and laughed and danced and sang with them in the evenings, and saw them off the next day with the tight fist of fear knotted deep in our insides – and more and more fell. The one we called 'The Noble Badger', a Squadron Leader from Northern Ireland – well-named noble; the gay and gallant American Bobby Fiske; the two Wood-Scawens, inseparable brothers, devout catholics, charmers both – and all of them so young and so well endowed, and such a wicked, wicked waste. I mourned them then, now and forever. They held our lives, our happiness and our heritage in their strong young hands and they never flinched. I wish I could write music, and I would create one great triumphant shout of a hymn, praising and honouring them and telling them of our love and gratitude to them for ever and ever, Amen. (Anne Turley-George, *ICARE* 1980.)

Desmond Sheen, 72 Sqdn.

Henry Lafont, 615 Sqdn.

René Mouchotte,
615 Sqdn.

Michael Robinson,
73 Sqdn.

J.E.L. Zumbach, 303 Sqdn.

Gene Tobin, Vernon Keough and Andrew Mamedoff, 609 Sqdn.

Stanislas Skalski,
303 Sqdn.

HM Stephen, 74 Sqdn.

Peter Brothers,
32, 257 Sqdn.

Alan Deere, 54 Sqdn.

David Scott-Malden, 611 Sqdn.

Peter Townsend, 85 Sqdn and Caesar Hull, 43 Sqdn. CH 000089

J.H. 'Ginger' Lacey, 501 Sqdn. CH 002793

A.G. 'Sailor' Malan, 74 Sqdn and Alan Deere, 74 Sqdn. CH 009994

GEOFFREY PAGE
D.S.O., D.F.C.

T.P. (Tom) Gleave, 253 Sqdn.

Geoffrey Page, 56 Sqdn.

Dowding at Duxford with some of his pilots, Deere, Gleave, Bob Tuck, ?, Bader, ?, Kent, Townsend.

Richard Hillary, 603 Sqdn.

Jan Frantisek, 303 Sqdn.

Jeffrey Quill, 65 Sqdn.

Mike Cooper-Slipper, 605 Sqdn.

Paddy Bathropp, 602 Sqdn.

Roly Beamont, 609 Sqdn.

Paul Tomlinson, 29 Sqdn.

good men, the fair men, the strong men, would rally to his side. The weak and fearful, consumed with envy and hatred and ambition, would seek his removal. And, sad to say, the latter were not only more numerous but, with the one notable exception, held all the places of power.

We have referred to the removal of Ludlow-Hewitt, Cotton, Embry, Malan and Park from their commands. They were men of intelligence and initiative who fretted at apathy and obstructionism, and, impatient about red tape and lesser minds, had a marked proclivity for getting things done in their own way. Unorthodoxy is a 'crime' which the entrenched bureaucratic mind cannot understand, and even less tolerate. It thrives on red tape, chains of command, and conformity, as weeds thrive on dung-heaps: it finds comfort and security in the tortuous corridors wherein it has its being; and in constituted authority, howsoever modest, it finds a necessary protection. Nothing so alarms and activates the vindictive juices of the bureaucratic mind as the spurning, the violation, or the by-passing of its authority.

Bureaucratic authority not only jealously safeguards its rights and prerogatives; it is also maniacally sensitive to criticism or to any challenge to its plans, policies and decisions. Bluntness and outspokenness in expressing views, and, worse, decisiveness in taking actions without consulting the 'mandarins', is suicide. The fate of the officers we have illustrated, and, signally, of Dowding, gives point to the contention that, no matter how brilliant, successful and high-ranking an officer is, he will become *persona non grata* if he doesn't play according to the unwritten rules laid down by those who wield the power; just as the 'triumph' of Douglas and Leigh-Mallory makes it clear that inferior people, if possessed of ambition, wiles and malice, will prevail if they know how to turn the rules to their advantage and to ingratiate themselves with the power-brokers. The case of Dowding and Park sadly illustrates the truth of Voltaire's observation: 'It is dangerous to be right when the powers are wrong.'

The Role of Churchill
We will be devoting the next chapter to a detailed study of the role of Churchill in Dowding's removal from office, and in Dowding's subsequent career, but a few preliminary comments may be made here.

Dowding's biographer, Robert Wright, refers in his account to the Prime Minister's 'curious behaviour'. For the fact is that Churchill went from being Dowding's most stalwart champion in October, to allowing Dowding to be removed from his command a few weeks later. Did the Prime Minister have to be persuaded? Yes, and no. No, in the sense that the Secretary of State for Air and the Air Council had the constitutional authority to promote, move, retire any officer they chose, without consulting the Prime Minister. However, the Prime Minister had also appointed himself Minister for Defence, albeit he was 'careful not to define [his] rights and duties.' Churchill was known to be a strong supporter of Dowding's; and it would have been a very brave or desperate Minister and CAS who risked the explosion sure to come if they retired Dowding without Churchill's consent. It was for that reason that all the criticisms of Dowding, both in writing or in person, were addressed to

Churchill. That fact alone suggests a certain collusion between at least some of Dowding's critics.

The question we must now answer is, what had happened of sufficient gravity to implant in Churchill's mind the persuasion that Dowding had to be replaced? Or rather, what arguments did the Secretary of State for Air and the Chief of the Air Staff muster – for it must have devolved upon those two men – to persuade Churchill that Dowding had to go? The early campaign against Dowding had had no effect. It was the accumulation of attacks on Dowding by Macdonald, Balfour and especially by Salmond that took their toll and weakened Churchill's confidence and judgment to the point that one last volley was enough to push him over. We have no doubt that it was Portal's appointment as Chief of the Air Staff on October 25 that brought matters to a head and precipitated events. Sinclair, we have seen, had wanted to get rid of Dowding as early as July. It was therefore Sinclair who made sure that he appointed as Newall's successor not only an anti-Dowding man, but an anti-Dowding man who would act.

It is clear that there must have been an agreement between Sinclair and Portal to confront Churchill. It is not difficult to imagine the arguments they must have put forward forcefully enough to persuade Churchill, perhaps *à contrecoeur*, that Dowding had to go. We are fortunate to have Dowding's own reaction to his fate. He reports on his meeting with the Prime Minister on the day following his interview with Sinclair.

> Churchill told me that I was to be replaced as C-in-C Fighter Command. He told me of his surprise that this recommendation should have been made 'in the moment of victory', but did not indicate any personal opposition. It seemed natural enough to me: the Air Council had been anxious to be rid of me since before the start of the war, and this seemed to be an appropriate moment.

We need not speculate on Dowding's grievous disappointment and sense of having been let down by the Prime Minister. We permit ourselves to wonder why Churchill did not offer Dowding the chance to hear the allegations made against him by Salmond, Trenchard, Sinclair and Portal. It is likely that Dowding would not have been in a mood to defend himself, feeling, perhaps, that his exemplary record was his defence. Salmond met Churchill shortly after Dowding had gone, and wrote: '[Churchill] said I was right – D. had gone, "but it nearly broke his heart".'

There is further, and later, testimony in favour of Dowding. In 1944, Air Chief Marshal Sir Wilfred Freeman, who served throughout most of the war as Portal's right-hand man, wrote to Portal: 'Why did we get rid of Dowding, who did something, and retain a number of inefficients a little junior to him who have nothing whatsoever to their credit?' In his book, *Right of the Line*, John Terraine quotes this query, and asks: 'The phrase "we get rid of Dowding" is interesting: who are "we"? The great collective Air Ministry "we" – or is the meaning rather more personal?' Terraine almost answers his own question by adding that Freeman 'went on to suggest that it might be time to "get rid of Sinclair".'

Freeman's question is assuredly rhetorical: it is clear he was revolving the question in his mind, and the answer – which he knew well enough – now, some years later, seemed to have bothered him. But Terraine's response to the question is beside the point. It is the phrase 'get rid of' that is important. For, sure as God made little apples, 'get rid of' Dowding they did. Summarily and rudely. And now, as we have said, some years later, Freeman looks back, and finds only a suspicious question mark hanging over what they had done to Dowding – 'they' being himself, Portal and the others – notably, Sinclair and Douglas. Freeman, who in 1940 was an anti-Dowding man, looks back with the benefit of hindsight, which has a way of dissipating the fog of the passions felt then, and sees events and personalities more clearly.

Notes:

i. Moreover Trenchard knew it was not true. When he, with Churchill and T.E. Lawrence, devised the policy of passing the responsibility for the control and policing of the desert tribes of Arabia to the RAF in the 1920s, this was done successfully, and very economically, by dropping a few bombs on the villages of offending tribesmen. 'This policy was adopted but later modified due to pressures applied by Lord Dowding', who insisted that the villages be warned in advance by the dropping of leaflets. This humane measure was found to be equally effective.

ii. Just three years later Salmond was to write this in the 'Daily Dispatch' on September 25, 1943: 'Fortunate too, we were in having as Supreme Commander of the Fighting Squadrons a man who knew the job in all its technical and operational detail and had been in the saddle during the three years before the war, Air Chief Marshal Sir Hugh, now Lord Dowding.' How much can be revealed in so few words! This acknowledgement of Dowding's **professional** mastery of the forces he commanded, and of his strategic thinking, cuts the ground from under the critics who claimed there were 'reasons' for his dismissal. Time tempers passions, and enables one to look more objectively, hence fairly, on events and people one had formerly condemned.

iii. Park's subsequent career belies this interpretation. He was appointed A-O-C Malta in July 1942 and immediately instituted the radar-controlled forward interception tactics that had been successful in the Battle of Britain.

iv. Orange, p. 120.

v. Orange, p. 145.

Part IV
Interlude

CHAPTER 9

Churchill, War, and the Battle of Britain

—❦—

A very recent book entitled *Churchill and War* has not a single word about the Battle of Britain. Yet we find this statement: 'Wars determined the course of history, and battles determined the outcomes of wars. Churchill wrote exceedingly well about battles, and not just because they absorbed and thrilled him. They settled the fate of nations.' On an earlier page, recounting Churchill's first days as prime minister in May 1940, we read this : 'Being the leader at the time and persuading the Cabinet to support him – another momentous act of leadership ... – Churchill was able to swing the people his way, and by so doing to change the course of history.'[i]

The air was **the** decisive strategic military arm of the Second World War, yet it seems that Churchill had not studied it as he had military history. We make this claim in the face of what Churchill himself had written much earlier:

> Except for the year 1916, I was continually in control of one or the other branch of the Air Service during the first eleven years of its existence. From 1911 to 1915 I was responsible at the Admiralty for the creation and development of the Royal Naval Air Service; from July, 1917, to the end of the War I was in charge of the design, manufacture and supply of all kinds of aircraft and air material needed for the War; and from 1919 to 1921 I was Air Minister as well as Secretary of State for War. Thus it happens to have fallen to my lot to have witnessed, and to some extent shaped in its initial phases, the whole of this tremendous new arm, undoubtedly destined to revolutionize war by land and sea, and possibly in the end to dominate or supersede armies and navies as we have known them... From the outset I was deeply interested in the air and vividly conscious of the changes which it must bring to every form of war.[ii]

His record throughout the war does not bear out this interest or the predicted impact of the air on 'every form of war.' Yet in the popular imagination the Battle of Britain and the name of Churchill are inseparable. The explanation for this is threefold: Churchill's was the commanding public presence from May 1940 to the end of the war; this presence, and his leadership, were projected largely by his speeches; and

Dowding, who might have become a public figure, was far too preoccupied with the war, and was equally far too private a person to seek the limelight.

Militarily speaking, as we have insisted, Churchill had nothing to do with the conduct of the Battle, though he watched it with, at times, almost hypnotic fascination, and with intense admiration. Churchill's life and experience were intimately involved in war. At times he seemed to revel in war; he described his early experiences in writings which he hoped would bring him fame and fortune. On leaving school he joined the Army, being accepted as an officer cadet at the Royal Military College, Sandhurst. The regiment he joined on passing out, the 4th Queen's Own Hussars, gave him leave to report on the civil war in Cuba for the *Daily Graphic* newspaper. There he came under fire for the first time in his life, and wrote glowingly of the experience both to his newspaper and to his mother.

In 1897 Churchill was on the North-West Frontier between India and Afghanistan as a correspondent for *The Daily Telegraph* in the months of October to December, where he witnessed military action involving gruesome slaughter. The following year, recalled to his regiment, he was involved in the war against the Mahdi in Sudan. He also took part in the last genuine cavalry charge in the history of warfare at the battle of Omdurman, which destroyed the Dervishes and their control of the Sudan. It was, however, in South Africa that he made a name for himself when, as both a lieutenant in the South African Light Horse and a correspondent for *The Morning Post*, he was captured by the Boers and effected a daring escape. General Botha put out a proclamation offering a big reward for Churchill, either dead or alive.

All these experiences and escapades were exploited to the hilt by his publishing his accounts of them. Some were collections of his dispatches; others were of an autobiographical nature; one was a genuine history. They poured off the presses and earned their author some of the renown he craved. They were *The Story of the Malakand Field Force, The River War, London to Ladysmith, Ian Hamilton's March.*

In 1900 Churchill arrived at the conviction that the sphere of life that offered the most challenging prospect of fame, and the greatest opportunity to exercise an influence over world events, was political. He had already written much. During his Army years he read voluminously: not only history but also literature. And he was to devote much time and effort to the acquisition of that skill without which no politician will ever achieve fame or statesmanship, as his heroes of the Victorian age had demonstrated, namely, that of oratory.

His first important Cabinet post was that of First Lord of the Admiralty in 1911. To his credit, Churchill was alive to the role of technology in war, and in 1912, without authorization by the Government, he ordered the conversion of the Navy's capital ships from coal to oil-burning furnaces. In 1915 blame for the failure of the Dardanelles campaign, although not strictly his, was accepted by Churchill to honour the political ethos of the time; he resigned his position and re-joined the Army. He went to the Western Front as officer commanding the 6th Battalion, Royal Scots Fusiliers. As it happens, his second-in-command was one Archibald Sinclair. They formed a close friendship. Later, Sinclair became the leader of the Liberal Party. In

1940 Churchill was to reward his friendship, and acquit a political debt, by appointing him to a position which was to have baleful consequences for both Dowding and the rational prosecution of the air war.

In 1917 Churchill returned to Government and for several years held a number of important portfolios with direct connection with war and defence. At that time he took flying lessons and barely succeeded in making one solo flight, after which he abandoned flying. It is possible that this experience, and his unfitness for flying, soured him to the air, for he was to develop little appreciation of air power. He was above all an Army man, and attuned to land warfare. Perhaps he had also made his name with the Navy and felt more at home at sea than in the air.

He was Home Secretary in 1926 when the general strike threatened to bring all industry to a halt. Churchill organized military and citizen forces to combat the militancy of the union leaders, and published a daily bulletin to bring news to the people while the daily presses were shut down by the strikers. He incurred some disfavour for praising Mussolini, who, in his words, 'rendered a service to the world' by showing the way 'to combat subversive forces.' Then, for ten years, Churchill was relegated to the back benches of Parliament, a period he called his 'wilderness years'. He came into his own again, and he found his true voice, in the 1930s, when he was the most prominent of a small number of people warning Britain of the dangers that Hitler posed to European peace. Churchill fiercely opposed Chamberlain's policy of appeasement and called for Britain to rearm. He became a thorn in the side of the Government; he aroused considerable distaste for his belligerent attitude in a country that was sunk in a grievous recession, and whose people, still suffering from the appalling slaughter of the Great War, were in no mood to risk another conflict, the limits of which were unknowable, and potentially horrendous. The terrors of war, especially of a war which rained destruction on the people, were made vivid by prophetic writers such as H.G. Wells, whose 1936 movie, *The War of the Worlds*, inspired fear in people because it showed there was no defence against bombardment from the air.

War was thrust upon the British people, and eventually the whole world because of the French and British Governments' failure to challenge Hitler at the time of Czechoslovakia in 1938. In that year France and Britain, by resolute action, could have saved the Czech people and stopped Hitler. Indeed, Britain failed to support Czechoslovakia even when France and Russia were keen to challenge Hitler. Instead Chamberlain, acting alone, negotiated with Hitler and, on returning home, waved a pitiful piece of paper in the air, proclaimed 'Peace for our time.' By 1939 it was too late: France and Britain gave a worthless guarantee to Poland, knowing they could do nothing to help them if Germany attacked them, as they did. Tyrants cannot be appeased.

With all of Eastern Europe overrun and the Battle of France about to be launched, with the British Government in disarray and Chamberlain harried out of office, the whines of appeasement and a negotiated peace clashed head on with the trumpets of resistance. It was only by a slim margin that the struggle for power was won by

Churchill; that it was a struggle testifies to the strong suspicions held by leading Conservatives, and much of the country, and by the King himself, as to Churchill's reliability, for he had proved himself in the past an erratic and volatile character. On the other hand, the fact that the struggle was conducted on both sides by the arts of persuasion, according almost to the rules of parliamentary debate, was a stark demonstration of the solid foundations of parliamentary democracy in the United Kingdom. But a large doubt lingered in the background. What powers would a wartime prime minister have, or would arrogate to himself, especially a prime minister of the stamp of Churchill? As things turned out, Churchill proved himself among the greatest of respecters of parliamentary traditions.

Churchill immediately appointed himself the Minister of Defence, a new portfolio. But he did not specify his responsibilities. He took an intimate interest in the appointment of some senior officers, but he was inconsistent; he showed a marked preference for senior, operational Army appointments, and seemed to leave the Navy and Air Force much to themselves. This preference shows the bias to be expected of his own war experience.

There seems little doubt that it was his intimate experience of war, especially of successful war on the ground, that coloured his subsequent ideas. As a First Lord of the Admiralty he might have been expected to have studied the history of the Royal Navy, and observe how the Navy had not only provided the impenetrable defence of the British Isles for hundreds of years, but also, notably, had guaranteed the Pax Britannica and the safety of the seven seas for all legitimate traffic throughout the nineteenth century. Similarly, as Secretary of State for Air, albeit briefly – and especially in the light of his declaration quoted above – he might have been expected to study, and to think occasionally about, the role of the air in future wars. The evidence shows that he failed to acquire a grasp of the role likely to be played by air power.

There is, however, evidence that he was not altogether oblivious to the problems of defence against air attack. H. Montgomery Hyde, in his book about T.E. Lawrence the airman, recounts a visit that his subject made to Churchill:

> On Sunday, 25 February 1934, he visited Chartwell, Churchill's country home in Kent, where one of the guests, a cousin of Mrs Churchill's, Sylvia Henley, afterwards recalled Churchill putting a question 'rather out of the blue' to Lawrence. 'In the event of an air attack what would be the best defence?' Lawrence immediately replied: 'Multiple air force stations to intercept.'[iii]

The author concludes the episode with the laconic note: 'Churchill,' she added, 'seemed satisfied with the reply.' A politician who had once been Secretary of State for Air and who had a interest in air matters and defence, and furthermore who hoped to play further important roles in government, would not have been satisfied with the reply. He would have pursued the problem with probing questions: how many stations? How many fighters? Where to locate them? How to identify attacking enemy aircraft? Who is the enemy, and from which direction would they come? Do our fighters have a performance superior to the enemy's bombers?

Yet, two years later, when unveiling a plaque to Lawrence's memory at the Oxford High School for Boys, Churchill said: 'He saw as clearly as anyone the vision of Air power and all that it would mean in traffic and war.'[iv] But even then, Churchill did not take up the study of air power, and did not acquire the vision that could be translated into wise decisions. He remained essentially an Army man, and saw war largely through the optics of Army men.

Another episode is equally telling. In another chapter we recount a scene in which Churchill visits Park's headquarters and sees for himself how the early warning system works. When all 11 Group's squadrons are airborne Churchill asks about reserves. This question shows his preoccupations to be those of Army men: that is to say, with back-up forces. A month earlier he had delivered his famous speech about 'the Few'. Here again is the Army man seeing the action in terms of the individual soldier – or, in this context, the fighter pilot, who glowed in Churchill's eyes as the epitome of chivalry, the worthy successor of the cavalryman.

Churchill's appointment of his old Liberal Party friend and Army colleague to the vital portfolio of the Air Ministry was not wise. Sinclair knew less about the air than Churchill, and never mastered his job. Sinclair's biographer has claimed that Churchill's appointment of Anthony Eden as Secretary of State for War, and of Sinclair to the Air Ministry, was tantamount to announcing that he intended to make all the strategic decisions affecting the war himself – secure in the conviction that they would not dispute or contest him. And Churchill's 'direction' of the war was far from rational. 'Churchill's haphazard leadership was made all the more anarchic by his mercurial nature. Ad hoc advisers like "Prof" Lindemann competed with ministers and civil servants for his attention. "Insiders" clashed violently with "outsiders" [to whom we may add the name of Beaverbrook], clashes which Churchill frequently encouraged ... Suspicion, animosity and intrigue were rife, and petty jealousy came to affect grand policy.'[v]

Sinclair was out of his depth with Dowding, even more than Newall was. The Air Ministry was a hotbed of intrigue and Sinclair did not come to grips with the problems his appointment caused, he may not even have been aware of the problems. He depended entirely on his Air Council colleagues, and some senior officers on the Air Staff, for advice and decisions. Hence he came under the influence of determined and ambitious men, men who knew how to work the system.

Chief among them, we have asserted, was Sholto Douglas. If Newall vented his frustrations to Sinclair in his dealings with Dowding, it was Douglas who provided the constant goad. When Sinclair assumed his office as Air Minister on May 12, Dowding's tenure as AOC-in-C of Fighter Command was due to terminate on July 14 and Sinclair wished to hold Dowding to this date. Sinclair mentioned this casually to Churchill one evening in early July, and – as we saw earlier – Churchill wrote angrily to Sinclair to state his opposition and to declare his complete support for Dowding, who ' has [his] complete confidence.' However, a later, crucial, remark in Churchill's letter must have made Sinclair's head spin. Churchill concluded by saying that 'his appointment should be indefinitely prolonged while the war lasts', which measure 'would not of course exclude his being moved to a higher position, if that were thought necessary.' This seemingly innocuous suggestion by Churchill set the tocsins clanging alarmingly in the ears of the higher establishment of the Air Force. Sinclair mentioned it to his colleagues of the Air Council, by whom the word passed to Trenchard and Salmond. Their immediate joint reaction was: 'He must be stopped!'

The very notion of Dowding becoming Chief of the Air Staff induced nightmares in the opposition's camp. The entire independent existence of the Royal Air Force, of which Trenchard was the architect and builder, was based on the conviction that the Air would become a decisive strategic arm in its own right and determine the outcome of future wars. Salmond was both Trenchard's disciple and successor. This strategic role of the bomber was the very *raison d'être* of the Air Force, the ruling doctrine that guided and determined every aspect of the Air Force's policies: to it all else was secondary and subservient. Suddenly, it seemed, there was an event that threatened to turn upside down and negate that doctrine, their life's work. If Fighter Command was successful in defeating the Luftwaffe, it meant that defence checkmated offence, and that any future strategy that preached that the bombing of Germany could end, or even shorten, the war would come to nought.

It was precisely at this time that the German attacks against Britain intensified, and Fighter Command began to prove that it could effectively counter them. Trenchard and Salmond were obliged to bide their time; this would come in early September but they were not inactive in the interim. Newall's tenure as Chief of the Air Staff was due to terminate in October, so they bent their energies to finding a suitable successor. Their eye fell on Portal who, as a protégé of Trenchard's, was a bomber man; and not only that, but a man with the backbone to support Sinclair in the threefold task of resisting Churchill's hope of promoting Dowding: bearding Churchill in his den when it came to persuading him that Dowding had to go, and delivering the *coup de grâce* to Dowding at a time of their choosing.

Despite Sinclair's relative deference to Churchill throughout the war, on this one issue, the removal of Dowding, they were at loggerheads throughout the summer and remained so until its resolution and dénouement when, for once, Sinclair prevailed and succeeded in his objective. (We state that it was 'his' objective but Sinclair was noticeably in thrall to determined men, particularly to Sholto Douglas).

Next we turn to Salmond, and of the purpose of his intervention with Churchill there can be no doubt. Salmond, whatever his personal feelings, had a weapon readily to hand : the night defences. We have seen that, on his first intervention, Churchill 'almost blew [him] out of the room.' There was no such explosion the second time; Churchill had begun to listen, and to doubt.

Churchill was more concerned with the devastation being visited on Britain's cities and factories and ports – with the concomitant alarm over the Londoners' morale – than on any other worry that pre-occupied him during the early winter of 1940-41. Salmond's report had been highly critical of Dowding's efforts; Churchill had witnessed for himself, in the Committee on Night Defence which he himself chaired, that Dowding had no answer to the problem. Dowding did have the honesty to see, and the courage to say to the Prime Minister, that he had no immediate answer, though, given time, he would. But Churchill the politician – and the leader of the people – needed to give the people some reason to hope.

Churchill remembered with much misgiving the raids on London by German Gotha bombers on June 13, 1917, when a bomb landed on an infant's school at Poplar, killing 162 and wounding 432 children and adults; and on July 7 when the bulk of the bombs fell on the East End. 'The East End of London was ... in a very ugly mood, the result of a massive wave of sympathy for the infants killed in Poplar ... There was arson, rioting and strikes in abundance. In any case, the morale of the British working-class was at a low ebb consequent on the carnage being suffered in France, which struck the poor more than the rich as the ordinary soldiers were being used as cannon fodder. The bombing brought it [morale] to its nadir. The Prime Minister of the day, David Lloyd George, no doubt saw the possibility of a revolution against his government.'[vi] Churchill remembered this only too well, for he was both Minister for War Munitions and Minister for Air at the time. Churchill, like the British Government as a whole, was thoroughly alarmed about the morale of the people of the East End. (As it turned out, the politicians were running more scared than the workers.)

Salmond, for his part, was only too ready to point out that others were putting forward various defensive ideas which, together or separately, might well either actually destroy enemy aircraft, or at least have the effect of deflecting them from their course and so spare British cities and save lives. It was easy for Salmond, and other critics, to point out that Dowding did nothing but pooh-pooh all ideas other than his own. In war one must be flexible; one must be ready to consider all possibilities in such extreme circumstances, when the defence of the realm was paramount.

It will be remembered that Salmond wrote his report on night defence on September 18. It was brought up for discussion in the War Cabinet on October 7. Because of Dowding's opposition to a number of its recommendations Churchill asked him to submit a counter-report to state his case. Dowding singled out filtering which 'had been disinterred by the Salmond committee' despite its 'having little specific connection with night interception.' Following this, in the meeting of the Night Defence Committee of October 10, Churchill approved the Salmond report, but after the removal of the filtering item. Salmond and Joubert objected, and tried to insist that it be retained. Two weeks later, Churchill, impressed by Dowding's obvious frustration in his dealings with people who tried to impose their views without having the responsibility for carrying out the measures they involved, wrote a personal note to Dowding asking him to state his case once more. Dowding's reply has already been quoted in full. (See note iv, p.117.)

Despite his energetic appeal to Churchill – in which Dowding showed a clear grasp of what was essential and what was not – the Prime Minister eventually sided with Sinclair and all the other critics.

There is one person who, in all this debate, has not received the attention he deserves and that is Frederick Lindemann; Lindemann was Churchill's personal scientific adviser throughout the war. In appointing a scientific adviser, Churchill needed advice on scientific matters as they related to the war. But Lindemann was as ill equipped for this role as Sinclair was for the position of Air Minister. (Churchill insisted on appointing people to vital positions on the grounds of friendship or political debts). Most of the advice Lindemann gave to Churchill, and to the committees he served on, turned out to be wrong-headed. It was, for example, Lindemann's perfervid anti-German animus that stoked Churchill's natural aggressiveness, with the result that Churchill put his full weight behind the indiscriminate bombing of German populations.

The story of the clash between Lindemann and Tizard is well known. Tizard and Dowding were allies in the scientific war against the Luftwaffe. Together they had created the early warning system of Fighter Command. This alliance put Lindemann's nose out of joint; his opposition to Dowding was as much of a personal thing as a genuine disagreement over the scientific war. If Churchill had appointed Tizard instead of Lindemann to be his scientific adviser the war would have taken a different course.

Finally we come to a scene which must have taken place: the confrontation between Sinclair and Portal on the one hand, and Churchill on the other.

The dénouement took place in Churchill's office. It is, we would suggest, not hard to figure out what was said to so persuade Churchill, Dowding's chief admirer and champion, that Dowding's time was up.

One wonders how much Sinclair and Portal knew of the efforts to dethrone Dowding. The question is important because the answer affects the tactics and arguments they employed. It is probable that they knew a great deal. We need not go into a detailed analysis : it is sufficient to say they knew – as indeed they must have done – that Churchill's championing of Dowding had been materially weakened, perhaps even fatally undermined already, especially by Salmond's second intervention. Now, if the Air Minister and the Chief of the Air Staff together insisted on his removal, even Churchill, even as the (undefined) Minister of Defence, would be hard put to it to defend him. Why, even Beaverbrook had abandoned him!

Nevertheless, for the sake of the record, we must attempt to reconstruct the scene. And by 'scene' I mean it literally. It is unusual, perhaps inadmissible, in a work of purported history to resort to dramatic composition to convey one's sense of an event, but that is what I am going to attempt.

NOVEMBER 15

In the Prime Minister's office, with the Prime Minister, are Sinclair and Portal. Churchill is standing at the window with his back to them. Suddenly he whirls round:

CHURCHILL: So it has come to that! And you want to involve me in the malodorous aftermath?

SINCLAIR: That is not fair, Winston. How can we in the Air Ministry make such important changes without your approval as Minister of Defence?

CHURCHILL: But Dowding! After all he has done! He and Park with their valiant pilots have saved our Island race! And perhaps all of Europe and her ancient civilization as well, who knows! And now simply to be retired, to be put on the shelf with a 'Thank you'! Or perhaps without even a 'Thank you'.

SINCLAIR: We recognize his great service, but there comes a time, as you must know, . . .

CHURCHILL: I seem to recall, Archie, that you were anxious to get rid of Dowding last July, when you had only been in your Ministry for a couple of months, and . . .

SINCLAIR: That was a mistake, I concede. I was new to my department, and the advice I received . . .

CHURCHILL: . . . the advice you received then is exactly the same advice that you are receiving now. You came round to being – or at least to saying you were one of Dowding's most faithful supporters. Now you have changed your tune again. I see I am now beset by his detractors and that I am his sole remaining defender. Some people say that once I am crossed I do not forgive. That is not true. What is true is that Air Marshal Dowding opposed me on the issue of sending more fighters to France in June and carried the day with the War Cabinet. I admired him. The stand he took then was the right stand – for him. My position and the stand I took were the right ones for me to take. Did I bear him a grudge, try to knock him down? On the contrary. Throughout the Battle of Britain he had my constant, unwavering and wholehearted support. And I made sure that he knew it. And when I went down to 11 Group last September I knew that Dowding had been right.

SINCLAIR: I have never been one of his detractors and I am not now-

CHURCHILL: . . . I haven't finished. Let me speak – while I still have the opportunity. Has the Air Marshal seen that scurrilous diatribe that has been circulating in Whitehall? I suspect not. Two or three weeks ago I received from Brendan Bracken a malicious document defaming both Newall and Dowding. He had received it from Miss Irene Ward, a ferocious virago, it seems, who I regret to say is a member of the Conservative Party. Of course I discounted it entirely and took no action on it. I cannot express adequately how pained I am that such poisonous stuff should be written, and circulated, against one of our most brilliant and successful air marshals. If half our air marshals were half as trustworthy as Dowding I would have no qualms or doubts about the effective and disinterested conduct of policy and operations by the Air Ministry. That this scheme to remove Dowding from his Command should come on top of Miss Ward's unseemly intervention in matters of which she avows her own total

141

ignorance fills me with dismay and concern. I smell a rat! The Air Force is going to play the decisive role in this war, and I want it to be directed with the same courage and devotion to duty that our fighting airmen display. As it is, the Air Ministry is rife with jealousies and intrigue, and I mean to have them extirpated root and branch. You have just taken over as Chief of the Air Staff, Portal. None of this falls on you, so I wish you particularly to concern yourself with the moral and mental health and fitness of the most senior and responsible officers. And I expect you to report to me on it periodically, Archie.

SINCLAIR: Very well, Winston. I will take a personal hand in it. Now, if there are jealousies and intrigue, as you put it, going on in my Department, I have seen nothing of them. And if you have, you should have warned me of it and I would have done something about it. But that is not what we are discussing.

CHURCHILL: No, that can wait. What you came here to discuss was your intention to remove Air Chief Marshal Sir Hugh Dowding from his Command just after he had won one of the most decisive battles in Western Civilization. I warn you – I warn you both – that if Dowding goes you will have to answer to History for your deed.

SINCLAIR: Winston, I tell you in all confidentiality that if you had been in my place, and in Sir Cyril Newall's place, for several years – or in my case for only several months – you would see things in the same light. The simple fact is that Dowding is quite impossible to deal with. In his letters to the Air Staff he borders on a rudeness that is quite unbecoming...

CHURCHILL: (*growling*) In war you don't have to be polite, you have to be right!

SINCLAIR: He wasn't always right ...

CHURCHILL: He was in the essentials.

SINCLAIR: There is worse. He is intransigent, inflexible, immovable. Once he has an idea in his head he will not listen to any other. You have seen him and heard him in the Night Defence Committee meetings. He has one fixed idea and that idea is the only one.

CHURCHILL: But supposing it is the right idea, and the only right idea?

PORTAL: Allow me, Prime Minister, if I may. I believe the Minister is right, Sir. We can put up with incivility in correspondence, with aspersions cast on the intelligence and expertise of my Staff officers – (*Churchill allows himself another sideways grin*) – but we have difficulty in accepting the attitude of a High Commander who refuses to consider any other possible defences against the night attackers than his own. Why, just the other evening, Professor Lindemann advanced a number of very original ideas, and all Dowding did was to scoff at them. (*Churchill scowls, and nods, albeit reluctantly.*)

142

SINCLAIR: I'm rather afraid that that is the sort of thing the Air Council and the Air Staff have had to put up with for years. The Commander-in-Chief is inflexible. He knows the right way of doing things, and the only right way.

PORTAL: We must also look ahead – to next spring, especially, when we can expect massive onslaughts by a more powerful enemy. We shall have to employ different tactics. Dowding and Park still believe in forward defence, even if it means in smaller formations than is possible.

CHURCHILL: Have you discussed these matters with them and discovered their views?

PORTAL: No, Prime Minister. I know they have not altered their views. And my judgement tells me that new men are needed for the task, with new ideas. They are as single-minded in their tactical ideas about fighting the day battle, as in they are in their approach to our night defences.

CHURCHILL: Yes, we must look forward to the next stage. But what precisely do you have in mind? What kind of tactics?

PORTAL: We need to counter the much stronger attacks we expect next Spring with greater forces than we did last summer. Park did what he could with his slender forces. And both he and Dowding still believe that those tactics will be sufficient the next time. They won't be. The minister and I believe that Douglas and Leigh-Mallory in 12 Group have the answer in sending up larger wings to intercept the raiders, as they did last September.

SINCLAIR: I second the Chief of the Air Staff's summary completely. However, I agree with you also, Winston, in your appreciation of Sir Hugh's accomplishments as the leader of Fighter Command. But the Chief of the Air Staff and I have come to the firm conclusion that the Commander-in-Chief has reached the end of his useful service with the Battle now over and won.

PORTAL: I agree. Now Dowding is a master of defence. We must go on to the offensive.

SINCLAIR: On the other hand I do not intend that the Air Chief Marshal should be merely retired. I propose to ask you to consider a suitable and worthy task or assignment to offer him when he relinquishes his Command, and which will make a valuable contribution to the war effort in another sphere.

CHURCHILL: That will be very advisable. Let me know what you have in mind. But let me warn you: Air Chief Marshal Dowding is to be properly treated, as befits an outstanding officer who has shown a rare genius in the art of war.

PORTAL: May we then take it, Prime Minister, that we have your approval of the measures and changes we have proposed?

CHURCHILL: My approval you most emphatically do not have. Whether or not you have my consent is another matter. I will need a couple of days to reflect on it.

Churchill (we can imagine) listened carefully and critically. He nodded here, he shook his head there; he frowned, he growled, he quizzed, he questioned. At the end he would weigh everything in the balance and deliver his verdict in a day or two. The following day Sinclair telephoned him, and Churchill, like Beaverbrook, abandoned Dowding. At least he was confident in his own mind that, in forsaking Dowding, he had given him his full support throughout the battle and made it possible for him to achieve the fame that, as the victor of the Battle of Britain, he was due.

Some writers, notable among them Len Deighton, have claimed that Churchill threw Dowding to the wolves because Dowding had opposed him over sending more fighters to France, and furthermore that Churchill did not forgive a slight or opposition which made Churchill look wrong or forced him to give way before his colleagues.[vii] None of those writers have produced any evidence or a written source to substantiate their suspicion. I believe, on the contrary, that if the opposition turned out to be right, Churchill generously conceded. But if they were wrong, heads would roll! In the matter of the night battle, Churchill might well have felt that in this case Dowding might not be right: or at least that Dowding was too dogmatic in his insistence that there was only one way to counter the night bombers and was unwilling to try other methods. In the end, Churchill was swayed by Lindemann.

Portal's argument too might well have touched a nerve on Churchill's part. It was certainly true that Dowding was superb, unmatched, in defence. Was he an equally effective leader in attack? The question bore on their respective philosophies of war; Churchill, was never happy in defence, in countering the enemy's aggression, in trying to anticipate his next move, in having to cede the initiative, and surprise, to the enemy. In a word, on being on the defensive. He had an 'instinctive lust for action', so he revelled in aggression, in going on to the attack, in trying on his side to out-smart the enemy, to put him at the disadvantage. But there was something more to it, as he had learnt from his experience in his imperial wars. In Churchill's view, the Germans had descended into barbarism and were no different from the tribal savages of Afghanistan and the dervishes of the Sudan that he had carried war to. It was a matter of bringing civilization to the darker places of the world. This, for example, is how he concluded his last despatch from the North-West Frontier in 1897:

These tribesmen are among the most miserable and brutal creatures of the earth. Their intelligence only enables them to be more cruel, more dangerous, more destructive that the wild beasts. Their religion – fanatic though they are – is only respected when it incites to bloodshed and murder. Their habits are filthy; their morals cannot be alluded to. With every feeling of respect for that wide sentiment of human sympathy which characterises a Christian civilization, I find it impossible to come to any other conclusion than that, in proportion as these valleys are purged from the pernicious vermin that infest them, so will the happiness of humanity be increased, and the progress of mankind accelerated.[viii]

There is a final factor to be taken into account. Although his ideas about war and its pros and cons underwent change over the years – especially with the advent of atomic weapons – Churchill thought throughout most of his life that war was 'a good thing' in the sense that it brought out the best in men.

Dowding seems a more complex figure when it comes to war and his attitude to it. On the one hand he rose to the highest rank in the Royal Air Force, but he was essentially a humanitarian, a commander who was reluctant to take any more lives (even those of relative barbarians) than the situation demanded. His career shows that he was an intensely proud and patriotic Englishman who took part in military actions in the name of the Empire. It may be that after having suffered the loss of so many of his pilots in the Battle of Britain, pilots with whom he had established, even if only in his own mind, a sort of chivalric relationship; and after he had seen the horrible results of the bombing of open cities and their defenceless civilians, he was moved to consider, and to write about, ways of preventing wars in the future. It is possible that Portal had been right in telling Churchill that Dowding was not an offensive war-maker.If we are to sum up Dowding's feelings about war, we could not do better than to quote a passage from *St. Augustine's City of God*:

> Wars are waged with peace as their object, even when they are waged by those who are concerned to exercise their warlike prowess, either in command or in the actual fighting. Hence it is an established fact that peace is the desired end of war. For every man is in quest of peace even when waging war, whereas none is in quest of war when making peace. In fact, even when men wish a state of peace to be disturbed, they do so not because they hate peace, but because they desire the present peace to be exchanged for one on their terms. Thus their desire is not that there should not be peace, but that the peace must meet their terms.[ix]

We are far from the end of the story of Dowding's retirement, and of his relations with the Air Ministry and with Churchill.

We saw earlier, on Dowding's being informed by Sinclair that he was being replaced by Sholto Douglas, that he was being recommended to undertake a technical mission to the United States. When he met with Churchill to discuss the mission, which was the brainchild of Beaverbrook, Dowding countered with the objection that he 'did not wish to accept such an appointment under the Air Ministry, about which I said some rather rude things.' Churchill insisted, and Dowding felt bound to cede. His mission consisted of only one specific task, that of trying 'to persuade the Americans to build the (Napier) "Sabre" engine.' The Americans were reluctant to do so: Dowding asked for an interview with the President. A few days later he was informed that the President had agreed; but just before Dowding was to return to England he was told that the President had reconsidered his decision. Dowding tells us that the one thing that sticks out among the memories of that visit was his intervention in a fund-raising campaign for the Royal Air Force Benevolent Fund launched by the British Embassy in Washington. Dowding brought the matter up at a public luncheon because he found it to be 'wrong and humiliating' when it was a matter for the British public to support it. His remarks caused 'an unexpected commotion' and he was summoned to the Embassy to explain; Dowding expressed no regret and pointed out that, by virtue of his position on the Committee, he had cause to object to what he called this 'barefaced panhandling.' When he returned to London Churchill sent for him and 'appeared to be very angry about something. I had no idea what he was angry about... and did not inquire, but... I supposed it was over the incident of the Benevolent Fund contributions.'[x]

It was precisely at this time that the Air Ministry issued a slim pamphlet of thirty-two pages entitled, The Battle of Britain August – October 1940, entitled: *An Air Ministry Account of the Great Days from 8th August – 31st October 1940.* The most remarkable thing about this pamphlet was that there was no mention of Dowding in it. Not only was his name not mentioned, but there was no allusion to the organizing genius who had created Fighter Command from the ground up, and not the least passing reference to the existence of a mastermind behind the strategic direction of the battle on the British side. Churchill read it, and was furious with indignation. On April 12th he wrote to Sinclair in these strong terms:

> The jealousies and cliquism which have led to the committing of this offence are a discredit to the Air Ministry, and I do not think any other Service Department would have been guilty of such a piece of work.
> What would have been said if the War Office had produced the story of the Battle of Libya and had managed to exclude General Wavell's name, or if the Admiralty had told the tale of Trafalgar and left Lord Nelson out of it! ... It grieves me very much that you should associate yourself with such behaviour. I am sure you were not consulted beforehand on the point, and your natural loyalty to everything done in your department can alone have led you to condone what nine out of ten men would unhesitatingly condemn.[xi]

Let us review the war situation as it was now. We were in the seventh month of the Blitz, and there was no let-up in the destruction being inflicted on British cities and their civilian people. It was clear to see that Douglas, the new commander of Fighter Command, was having no success in the air war against the night raiders. Churchill also saw that Lindemann's ideas for bringing down the bombers – which had been supported by Sholto Douglas – had proved useless. He also saw that the forays over France, from January 1941 on, were incurring greater and greater losses of precious fighters and fighter pilots, so it was legitimate to wonder whether Fighter Command would be strong enough, and well enough trained, to meet the expected assaulted to be renewed in a month of so. Churchill must have felt that, in concurring with the reasons for replacing Dowding, he had been conned into agreeing to his removal. Churchill began to agitate for Dowding's recall to active duty.

Churchill, War, and the Battle of Britain

Martin Gilbert, Churchill's biographer, has recorded the efforts that the Prime Minister made at the time to appoint Dowding to an operational command. In March 1941, when Churchill was preoccupied with Anglo-American relations and, especially, with obtaining the greatest possible measure of aid and cooperation from the Americans in what was already being called the Battle of the Atlantic, Churchill gave to Beaverbrook control of the Atlantic Service, which was the agency charged with setting up and overseeing the newly formed Atlantic Ferry Operation. An Air Vice-Marshal Dawson was put in charge of this Service. Gilbert continues: 'Churchill subsequently hoped to use the changes involved in Dawson's appointment to give Dowding command of Army Cooperation Command in Britain. "I hope you will be able to do this," he minuted to Sinclair, "as I am sure nothing but good will come of it [in as much as it would] give confidence to the Army". But Sinclair declined to re-employ Dowding in an operational command.'[xii]

The next attempt he made was in the aftermath of the disaster of Crete – for which Churchill must be held largely accountable. (The Crete débâcle was May 20 – 30, 1941.) Gilbert writes: 'Churchill made a single change in command in the Middle East, replacing Air Chief Marshal Longmore ... by Air Vice-Marshal Tedder.' To this Gilbert adds the footnote : 'Churchill's first thought was to recall Sir Hugh Dowding to active service as Commander-in-Chief of the Middle East Air Forces. This, however, was resisted by Sinclair and the Chief of the Air Staff.' He continues without a break, although there appears to be a gap of almost five months between the events: 'On October 23 Churchill wrote in the third person ... that "the Prime Minister told the Secretary of State and the Chief of the Air Staff only six weeks ago (sic) that he thought it would be well that Sir Hugh Dowding should replace Vice Air Marshal (sic) Longmore in the Middle East. However the Prime Minister deferred to the representations then made to him by the Secretary of State and the CAS".'[xiii]

Following this refusal by Sinclair, in the same month of June the Air Council invited Dowding to write a Despatch on the Battle of Britain. This he did during the summer; and when he had finished it his retirement was gazetted on October 1st. Churchill learnt immediately what had happened and sent for him again. This time he wanted Dowding to carry out an inquiry into ways and means of effecting economies in the Air Force. Once again Dowding was hostile to the idea. The Prime Minister told him that, according to Portal, no 'further' economies were possible. Portal's motives were transparent: either he feared the unearthing of possible economies, or, more probably, he didn't want Dowding of all people snooping around in his department. Dowding's motive was equally transparent, and more honest; he told Churchill that to accept the appointment 'was certain to revive all the smouldering animosity which had existed between the Ministry and myself for the past five years.'

Dowding had another reason. He had just completed the writing of a slim volume, subsequently to be published under the title of *Twelve Legions of Angels*, and which he was anxious to publish as soon as possible, discussing as he did a number of issues related directly to air matters. He analysed the strategic, tactical, material and logistic requirements for the successful prosecution of the war: it also speculated on the ways and means whereby statesmanship might prevent wars in the future. He examined the causes of war, and, horrified by its cost in human lives, misery and in material destruction, proposed a number of measures designed to prevent it, so far as possible, in the future. Dowding gave Churchill a copy of the text and asked him to read and approve its publication before he took on his new task. He added that now he was retired there was no reason why the book should not be published. Churchill expressed his surprise that Dowding had been placed on the retired list. At which Dowding asked him pointedly whether he had not been informed or consulted about it. Churchill replied that he had not: 'I knew nothing about it until I saw it in the papers.' Dowding's retirement was gazetted on October 1st, and was probably noted in the papers a day or two later. Clearly Churchill wasted no time in seeing Dowding, for Wright records this meeting as taking place at 5pm on October 5th in the Cabinet Room.[xiv]

Churchill read some parts of the book himself, and passed it to Brendan Bracken, his Minister of Information – and one of his closest friends – who read it all. At their next meeting Churchill raised an objection to Dowding's criticism of the traditional British foreign policy in Europe of always striving to maintain 'a balance of power' between the most powerful European states, a policy which, according to Dowding, achieved the very opposite of its aim. Churchill objected on the ground that he, Dowding, would most probably be quoted favourably by the enemy. A few days later Dowding was invited to have dinner and to stay the night at Chequers. It was late at night before Churchill got round to discussing Dowding's book – or rather, to talking desultorily about it, between interruptions by the playing of gramophone records. Among other things, Churchill did not agree with Dowding's quest for 'world harmony' after the war. He was not interested in the remote future. Churchill, in Dowding's view, seemed uninterested 'in working for world peace': he believed that 'an atmosphere of struggle [was] necessary to avoid decadence.'

This difference between the two men is of vital importance. It is clear that Churchill did not like Dowding's views at all. Churchill considered that war was a necessary process in the development of the vigorous and manly qualities in a race: stalwart defence of one's homeland cannot be achieved at too high a price. If one is attacked, energetic and ruthless counter-attack is the only answer. Sport is all very well, even relatively dangerous sports, but they are no substitute for war. War alone can bring out the best in a race. Without it, a nation's youth degenerates into slothful habits, indolence and effeteness, and ends up good for nothing – good not even for sport, daring enterprise, and business adventurism.

Dowding returned to his theme in an article published in the 'Sunday Chronicle' of December 13, 1942 (and which was appended to the book in question when it was published in 1946.) 'Is war a Good Thing, or not?' he wrote. 'This is not a purely rhetorical question, because there are those who think that war and training for war are necessary for the virility of the race, and that periods of continuous peace lead to softness, luxury and decadence.'[xv]

Dowding's work on finding economies in the Air Force began to run aground, but not before it resulted in his making 'a number of proposals'. Most of them were 'hotly opposed by the Air Ministry'. He plodded on in 'an extremely unpleasant ' climate until after six months he could find no reason to tolerate it further. So, when he read an offensive note about him in a minute written by a Member of the Air Council, he used it as a pretext 'to be placed on the retired list at my own request.' He concluded this account in his 'Personal Notes' with the laconic comment, which does not conceal the tinge of bitterness he must have felt: 'so ended my forty-two years of Service.'

There is no question that Churchill and Dowding had a profound respect and admiration for each other, but in temperament and in ideas they were so far apart as to preclude any closeness of personal relations, let alone intimacy. Especially in matters military, and in the role of war in a people's moral energy, they were at opposite poles. Churchill, as soldier and politician – and this is not to diminish his protean personality – was a pragmatist who looked at what had to be done, and at the most effective means of getting it done. Dowding, for his part, was an idealist and a perfectionist. In no theatre of war would they have clashed more violently, if, say, Dowding had become Chief of the Air Staff in 1940, than over the question of the strategic bombing of Germany. I dare say that Dowding, had he had his way, would have agreed with (and worked more closely with) the Americans in the perfection of their policy of accurate daylight bombing of military and industrial targets. But there was one position that, in 1940, that was crying aloud for dynamic leadership : Coastal Command.

Churchill had already formed a Battle of the Atlantic Committee. He was so aware of the danger that at a meeting of the War Cabinet of March 20 he told them: 'I'm not afraid of the Air. I'm not afraid of invasion, I'm less afraid of the Balkans – but – I'm anxious about the Atlantic.'[xvi] Yet the Navy chiefs had not prepared the Navy for such a wartime role, and did not appear to have the political influence to ensure that the Government took the necessary action to provide for the safety of the Atlantic convoys. As we shall see in our *Envoi*, this was not achieved until May 1943.

We sum up by concluding that Churchill's view of Dowding was ambivalent, but essentially in agreement with the arguments put forward by Sinclair and Portal. We believe that the key words were 'forward' and 'attack'. Dowding had achieved prodigious deeds but defensive battles do not win wars. The Battle of Britain was over. There was a new war to be fought and won, and the distance between the two men over the question of war itself (as Churchill saw in Dowding's book) was enough to cast doubt in Churchill's mind about Dowding's aggressive spirit. The war now needed an aggressive spirit.

Churchill associated Dowding with the Battle of Britain but that was now over. The night battle caused massive amounts of damage, but it could have no bearing on the outcome of the war, so it no longer mattered who was in charge of the defences. Sad to say, by November 1940 Churchill had simply lost interest in Dowding.

To my mind the most telling factor lies in Churchill's and Dowding's opposing views about war. Churchill was a man of aggression; a man of instinct rather than of reason. He and Trenchard saw eye to eye on the question of taking the war to

Germany, even to the extent of devastating their cities and destroying the morale of the people: of destroying their very nation and race. Churchill, to his credit, was torn in two: on the one hand he admired Dowding immensely for his role in the saving of Western Civilization; on the other he knew that Dowding was not the man to carry out his policy of bombing Germany to smithereens.

Perhaps there was even a personal factor. Churchill was set on dominating the scene. He had met with resistance over sending more fighters to France, and lost. He was not going to risk further clashes, and the possibility of butting heads with a man with an equally steely will, or of facing the prospect of real rivalry for leadership in the conduct of the war.

It is a pity that Churchill did not read the whole of Dowding's book himself. He would have seen that Dowding advocated that the Battle of the Atlantic had to be won before the Battle of Germany was launched; and that in that enterprise the two men would have marched in lock-step together, for at least the next two years.

Notes:

i. Geoffrey Best, *Churchill and War* (London, Hambledon and London, 2005), p. 261-62, p. 115.

ii. Winston S. Churchill, *Amid These Storms. Thoughts and Adventures* (New York, Charles Scribner's Sons, 1932), p. 181.

iii. H. Montgomery Hyde, *Solitary in the Ranks* (New York, Atheneum, 1978), p. 224.

iv. Ib. p. 257.

v. De Groot, p.157.

vi. Allen, *The Trenchard Legacy*, p. 17.

vii. See, for example, Deighton p. 43. See also Wright, p. 108

viii. Frederick Woods, ed., *Young Winston's Wars* (London, Leo Cooper, 1972), p. 38-39. Lest the reader shudder on reading this jingoistic prose, he should reflect on the major reason why American and European armies and air forces under NATO are waging war in Afghanistan today. As recently as April 2007 I listened to a speech by Lt. General Steve Lucas, the Chief of the Air Staff of the Canadian Air Force, in which he said essentially the same thing, though in more politically delicate language.

ix. I am indebted to my late friend Bill Stiles for this quotation. The diametrically opposite view as expounded by the German Treitsche – 'The hope of expunging war from the world is not only senseless, it is also deeply immoral.' (Quoted by Geoffrey Best, p. 259) – would have been equally repugnant to both Dowding and Churchill.

x. 'Personal Notes', p. 233.

xi. Martin Gilbert, *Finest Hour*, pp. 1060-61. Quoted by Hough and Richards, p. 324.

xii. Martin Gilbert, *Winston S. Churchill, vol. VI: Finest Hour, 1939-1941*, p. 1040.

xiii. Martin Gilbert, op. cit., p. 1101. The reader will be struck by the success Churchill has in his appointment of all officers except in that of Dowding. Gilbert uses expressions such as: 'Dawson was put in charge of the Service' by Beaverbrook and Churchill. And: 'Churchill made a single change in command in the Middle East ... Longmore, whom he appointed'. On the other hand, Sinclair declined to re-employ Dowding. Again: 'This... was resisted by Sinclair', and 'the Prime Minister deferred to ... the Secretary of State and the CAS.' Churchill grounded his 'authority' in matters of appointments on his assumption of the title of Minister of Defence. For example, Kershaw states: 'Churchill himself took on responsibility for the Ministry of Defence.' (p. 24.) And: 'he controlled the Defence Ministry' (p. 479). Boyle states: 'As Minister of Defence ... Churchill was rightly determined to exercise full control over the Chiefs of Staff as well as the Cabinet' (p. 720). The fact is there was no Ministry of Defence. Churchill had no authority, no responsibility, no control. All he had was influence, since the title he gave himself had no constitutional grounding. It will be of interest to readers to know that in September 1986, on the occasion of the anniversary of the Battle of Britain, a number of letters appeared in *The Times* deploring the inadequacy of the recognition accorded to Dowding for his great services to the nation. On October 13th, Gilbert wrote to *The Times* to say that a number of people had asked him whether it was not Churchill's hostility to Dowding 'that was responsible for Dowding's eclipse.' He gave the following account of Churchill's efforts to have him brought back:

> In November, 1940, when both Sinclair and the Air Staff unanimously urged Dowding's removal, Churchill had no alternative but to accept their advice. In doing so, he stressed to Sinclair his admiration for Dowding's qualities and achievements, and seven months later urged Sinclair to bring Dowding back to an operational command. This proposal was rejected by Sinclair and the Air Staff. In June, 1941, immediately after the fall of Crete, Churchill urged that Dowding should be recalled to active service as Commander-in-Chief of the Middle East Air Services. This too was rejected. In September 1941 Churchill wished Dowding to replace Air Marshal Tedder in the Middle East. He was confronted once more by the total refusal of Sinclair and the Chief of the Air Staff to give Dowding any active command.

It is intriguing to speculate on the reasons for Churchill's insistence on appointing certain officers to certain commands, and on both his readiness to accept Sinclair's appointment of Portal as CAS without Churchill's consent, and Sinclair's and Portal's blanket refusal to countenance the appointment of Dowding to any operational command at all. What was a Minister of Defence for? How much good would have ensued from Dowding's sacking of Leigh-Mallory in September and from Churchill's replacement of Sinclair in October! Sir Martin has been good enough to corroborate these actions by Churchill to reinstate Dowding in personal letters of 27 February 2007 and 12 January 2008, in reply to my inquiries. Nevertheless, I have one reservation. Churchill was a man inspired by history and enamoured with history. Much of what he did was done with an eye to history. In trying to bring back Dowding – in seeking to redeem his earlier error – he was intent on clearing his name before posterity.

xiv. Are we bound to believe everything that Churchill said, in either spoken or written form? In the letter of November 27, 1978, that we have already quoted, from Derek Amory to Harold Balfour, we read this: 'I refuse to believe that Churchill did not know of the intention to retire Dowding.'

xv. Perhaps both Churchill and Dowding were in error. Consider this judgement by a professional soldier, Sir John Hackett, who wrote: 'Mussolini said in the early 1930s: "War alone brings all human energies to their highest tension, and sets a seal of nobility on the peoples who have the virtue to face it." This is rubbish, and dangerous rubbish at that. War does not ennoble... But the interesting thing is that although war almost certainly does not ennoble, the preparation of men to fight in it almost certainly can and very often does.' (*Profession of Arms*, p. 141.) We would agree with this, and with Churchill, to the extent that the preparation for war is limited to war of defence of one's homeland. (Best points out that Churchill often used the term 'race' when meaning 'people' or 'nations'.) Indeed, the man who will not rise to the defence of family and country is without soul or backbone.

xvi. Martin Gilbert, op. cit., p. 1040. Yet Churchill devoted too few of his enormous energies to the Atlantic.

Part V

The Fallout

CHAPTER 10

Schemers Rewarded

—⚊—

After Dowding and Park were removed from their Commands and replaced, respectively, by Sholto Douglas and Leigh-Mallory, we must now ask: what were Douglas's and Leigh-Mallory's qualifications and competence for their new appointments? Douglas was appointed as the Air Officer Commanding-in-Chief of Fighter Command by the Secretary of State for Air, Sir Archibald Sinclair. Was it also the recommendation of the new Chief of the Air Staff?

We have already seen that Sinclair was a Douglas man. One would like to know what Portal thought of Douglas, and whether he deemed him fit for this vital command. The official biography of Portal, despite the author's evident sympathy and admiration for his subject, is a fine, albeit regrettably uncritical, account; but it accords not a word to what is, in 1940, a crucial strategic appointment. One of the latest and, by virtue of the authors' reputation, most authoritative judgements is that offered by Hough and Richards in their *Battle of Britain*:

> Sholto Douglas and the Air Tactics directorate were keen to experiment with the 'big wings', and if these were to be tried there was much to be said for having an enthusiast, Leigh-Mallory, directing the Group which would put most of them into the air. As the senior Group commander, in charge of 12 Group since its inception, Leigh-Mallory had excellent qualifications for the post.

That is all: Douglas was 'keen to experiment'; Leigh-Mallory was 'an enthusiast', and one who had 'excellent qualifications'. Let us look at these 'qualifications'. First: experiment. Had there not been enough experimentation? And had it not failed? 'Keenness' and 'enthusiasm': not exactly the most inspiring recommendations for commanders in whose hands rested 'the fate of the British people'. And what exactly were Leigh-Mallory's 'qualifications'?

I. Sholto Douglas

We begin by quoting Hough and Richards again:

> Now that the daylight battle was dying down the urgent demand was for success in countering the night bombing and then, looking further ahead, for offensive operations over the continent. Dowding seemed to the Air Staff, at

this juncture, the wrong man for either task. He was having no obvious success against the night blitz, and he would certainly resist the use of his fighters over France.

The fact that the attempted night interception of German bombers was carried out by single machines, not even squadrons or flights let alone wings, and the new commanders had absolutely no experience whatsoever in night fighting, seem not to occur to the authors. Who had already decreed that Fighter Command was to be used for 'offensive operations over the continent', for sending 'fighters offensively over France'? Nowhere in Hough and Richards' book is there any discussion of it. Is that what the 'big wings' were to be used for? But the only discussion of big wings – as opposed, for example, to smaller wings – had been in the context of the Battle of Britain. This battle had been entirely a **defensive** battle.

When the changes in command were effected in late 1940, the greatest dangers lay in the continuing of the night attacks against British cities, and the renewal, in the spring of 1941, of daylight assaults against Fighter Command in preparation for more determined plans for invasion. These were the two compelling menaces which occupied all informed and responsible minds in the winter of 1940-41. Douglas knew that. He wrote of his appointment:

> I was naturally pleased and proud that I should have been selected for such a responsible post, and I had sufficient confidence in my own ability to believe that I could make a good job of it. But at the same time I could not help feeling a little overawed by the importance of such high command. To a large extent the fate of the British people would be resting in my hands.

Douglas may have had a basic grasp of the nature of his responsibility. Whether he had the ability equal to his task – to make a good job of it (!) – is another matter. In 1938, when he was Assistant Chief of the Air Staff, he tried to defend the order by the Air Ministry for 450 Bolton-Paul Defiants and to foist them onto Dowding. Dowding protested both against this aircraft, and against the decision taken to order them without consulting him. Douglas's defence was that this kind of air fighting had been very successful in the First World War. Dowding reserved their use in the Battle to the fewest occasions possible. And when the Germans cottoned on to this new type, the poor Defiant crews suffered terrible casualties. Their unexpected success at night was materially better, on moonlit nights.

A measure of Douglas's intelligence and grasp of things as they were was made manifest on September 7, 1940. On that Saturday – the most fateful day of the Battle as it turned out – Dowding had called a conference at Fighter Command HQ for the purpose of deciding on the best ways of preserving his fighter strength in view of the grave losses being suffered, especially by 11 Group, and of rebuilding his strength when the opportunity presented itself. Dowding, supported by Park, used the expression 'going downhill'. Douglas questioned the pessimism of this view; and he was rebutted by Dowding, Park and Evill. Discussion turned on the losses, and on the training of fighter pilots. Douglas tried to insist that Fighter Command had far more pilots than they did; and he bewildered Dowding and Park when he showed a lack of understanding of the differences between a pilot who had normal flying abilities and a 'blooded pilot', with actual experience of air fighting. Further ideas and problems were aired, each seeming to reveal yet again Douglas's failure to understand both the situation as it existed and the necessary, minimum remedies.

On the 9th, Evill sent Douglas a copy of the draft minutes of the conference. Douglas replied on the 14th in these terms. They reminded him, he said, of a music-hall act involving two knock-about comedians, Mutt and Jeff, one of whom was cast in the role of the 'patsy who asked foolish questions.' Douglas protested that the minutes portrayed him in that role and as such misrepresented him. 'However, life is too strenuous . . . to bother about the wording of minutes.' Evill, in his reply of the same day, rejected Douglas's implied suggestion that the minutes had been faked. They reproduced, he said, almost verbatim the remarks made by the participants.

It is strange how writers allow themselves to be seduced by the temptation to denigrate one man in the belief – hope? – that such belittling will enhance the stature of their subject. Bill Newton Dunn's biography of Leigh-Mallory indulges in that vice – perhaps in retaliation against Vincent Orange's hatchet-job against Leigh-Mallory. Writing of this conference, Dunn says: 'he [Dowding] was tired after the strain of the Battle and his readiness to admit defeat, expressed at the conference on 7 September, could have been interpreted as a lack of will to win.' Interpreted by whom? By Douglas? Or by Dunn?

This writer's interpretation of the situation and of Dowding's attitude is that Dowding had the intellectual integrity and the courage both to see the situation as it truly was and to make preparations to meet it, without for one second attempting to gloss it over or to escape the fact of his ultimate responsibility. No one who has read Dowding's letter of May 16th, 1940, could conceivably entertain the notion of his ever being ready 'to admit defeat'.

We have no intention of rehashing the tactics of the day battles of 1940. However, the thinking of Douglas about the interception of enemy bombers is worth looking at one last time.

Collier quotes Douglas as holding the view that 'it does not matter where the enemy is shot down, as long as he is shot down in large numbers'. Collier continues:

> Soon after assuming his new post [as AOC-in-C of Fighter Command] he made his attitude still clearer by announcing that he had never been very much in favour of trying to interpose 'fighter squadrons between enemy bombers and their objective'.

The origin of this thinking is significant. Before the advent of the early warning system there was no way of detecting bombers at night or above cloud, nor in daylight if they flew at high altitude. Air Exercises carried out in 1933, including fighter versus. bomber interception, proved – at least to the satisfaction of the referees, who rode in the bombers – that the bomber always got through. The post-mortem concluded that the only chance of interception was after the bombs had been dropped; for then it was possible to calculate the probable course of the bombers as they headed for their home bases, and fighters could be sent up for visual interception. In this instance Douglas, in common with so many senior officers on the Air Staff, was backward-thinking and reactionary. He was among the conspicuous dinosaurs of the inter-war years who had so deadening an influence on air war doctrine.

One wonders, finally, whose hand may be seen in the notorious Air Ministry pamphlet of 1941 which made the preposterous claim that Fighter Command was stronger at the end of the Battle than at the beginning. When Dowding and Park rebutted this nonsense, Douglas 'corrected' the misinformation in his *Despatch*, published on September 16, 1948:

> At the beginning of November 1940, the first-line strength of Fighter Command stood nominally at sixty-seven squadrons. Outwardly, therefore, the Command was stronger than at the beginning of the Battle of Britain, when fifty-eight squadrons were available. In reality it was weaker. After several months of intensive fighting some of the squadrons had only a few pilots fully up to operational standards, and the first-line strength was backed by insufficient depth. At the height of the battle the supply of new pilots had failed to keep pace with losses and it had been necessary to improvise measures to avert a crisis.

Most of what Douglas learnt after he assumed his new command he pretended he'd known all along! And, as in the excerpt reproduced here, without giving credit to the officer principally responsible for 'the necessary . . . measures' to produce more pilots, which he mentions in the following paragraph. Douglas's Despatch on '*Air Operations by Fighter Command in 1941*', published as a supplement to *The London Gazette* in September 1948, devotes six pages, of a total of twenty-one, to defensive night operations, even though claiming that the defeat of the night bomber was his 'main task'. Apart from the sections dealing with abortive measures, which we mentioned in Chapter Eight, the report deals with the most effective measures: anti-aircraft guns and fighters.

The account of the results achieved by fighters makes dismal reading. In the seven-month period December to July, only sixty-six enemy bombers were destroyed by fighters. (We will have more to say about this.) Though a reading of Douglas's *Despatch* reveals no energy or ardour on his part. Despite Dowding's efforts and real achievements in laying the foundations essential to combating the danger, Douglas, who knew the record, gave the credit to some others – as was of course their due – while denying to Dowding his. In his autobiography, *Years of Command*, he wrote:

> I had known from the outset, and from the experience that I had gained while I was at the Air Ministry, that Fighter Command in particular was going to have to make the greatest possible use of radar. But the details of its technical development so far as the night fighters were concerned were dealt with

directly by the specialist officers on the Headquarters staff at Bentley Priory, and to them and to the scientists with whom they were associated must go a great deal of the credit for what was achieved. Two of those who had been on the Headquarters staff for a long time and who were directly and intimately concerned with the use of radar in Fighter Command were Wing Commander R.G. Hart and Squadron Leader W.P.G. Pretty. . . .They had both become specialists in radar, and they were to continue to exert a great influence in developing still further the refinements in its use.

About the fighters themselves, and the arguments for and against the single-seat fighter and the radar-equipped Beaufighter, Douglas tergiversates and tries to make himself out to be at one and the same time the champion and the critic of both fighters.

> Some answer to this night bombing had to be found, and it had to be found quickly. . . . [A special committee] had decided on a number of urgent measures, . . . one of them being the recommendation that all possible use should be made of the single-engined fighters. So strongly had Dowding come to believe in his radar-equipped fighters that he had become a little blinded, I felt, to the more simple hit or miss, trial and error, use of the single-engined fighters. I agreed that it was a primitive effort to throw what were really day fighters into the darkness of the night skies in the hope that they would be able to see something. But I felt, and in this I was supported by the other members of the committee and the Chief of the Air Staff, that the effort had to be made, and despite his strenuous protest Dowding was given instructions to make more use of his Hurricanes and Defiants at night.

It is typical of Douglas that, though junior in rank and position to all the other members of this committee, he does his best to make it appear that the idea was his and that his superiors fell in with him. Of course, that the very idea was 'primitive' and 'hit and miss' meant it would be dismissed by the precise and scientific mind of Dowding. Douglas continues:

> I could never agree with Collier's statement in his official history of *The Air Defence of the United Kingdom*: . . . the prevailing opinion was that the slender chance of intercepting bombers in the dark with ordinary day-fighters scarcely justified their diversion from normal duties unless conditions were exceptional. That is being wise after the event, and as was shown by the findings of the Salmond Committee, "the prevailing opinion" at the time was just the opposite.

Douglas cannot have it all ways and hope to come up smelling roses. Collier's statement about 'the prevailing opinion' referred to opinion – that is, to informed and expert opinion – in Fighter Command. And in that he is correct. The 'prevailing opinion' which Douglas finds to be 'just the opposite' was the opinion of Salmond's committee. (And no reader will fail to notice how Douglas, after having intimated that the idea of the single-engined fighters was his, now leans heavily on 'the findings of the Salmond Committee' to support him.) This clear statement of views was far from 'being wise after the event'. It was Dowding's view at the time. Once again, as in nearly every occasion of differing of views, Dowding was right and Douglas, and the Air Staff, were wrong.

What of the Beaufighter? After stating that 'Dowding had made it clearly understood that he much preferred the idea of a more powerful radar-equipped twin-engined night fighter with a pilot and a navigator', Douglas switches sides and now wants to be seen aligned with those who were right. 'The idea of this special night-fighter and crew [he says] had appealed to me from the beginning.' But there is not the slightest scrap of evidence to support this statement. During 1940 Douglas sat on the fence until he saw which side the Air Ministry top brass would come down on, then he hastened to declare himself. Later, when it became obvious that the pundits were wrong, he discovered the benefits of hindsight wisdom – and incorporated it into his memoirs.

Of the three tasks assumed by Douglas as head of Fighter Command, that of countering the night bombing of British cities, ports and factories was the most exigent and the most crucial because of all the death and destruction it was causing. This Blitz was expected to persist throughout the winter: in fact the last raid was carried out on May 27th.

The second most important task was the preparation and training of the Groups and their fighter squadrons to meet the renewal of the daylight battle in the spring of 1941, and possibly a second invasion threat. For, as Douglas acknowledged himself, 'the fate of the British people would be resting in [his] hands.' Despite that, Douglas sums up his preparations in this field in a mere sixteen paragraphs, **at the end of his Despatch**. In these paragraphs there is not a word to suggest that the Groups carried out any training in: air firing and air fighting; in tactical exercises; in sector control; in cooperation between the Groups; or in exercises with Bomber Command. Instead Douglas's interests and energies were directed elsewhere. That 'elsewhere' was the campaign, the series of operations, that was subsumed under the general, and vague, policy called 'Leaning forward into France.' The idea of it, strangely, was Trenchard's, so Douglas must have felt the weight of his authority on his back. And since he had come to know Trenchard well while in the Air Ministry – and had learnt about his role in unseating Dowding – he was no doubt imbued with the desire to earn the great man's approbation. The operations themselves were fighter sweeps over France, called either 'Rhubarbs' or 'Circuses', depending on their aim; and they are discussed by Douglas in five pages of the twenty-one comprising his *Despatch*.

It is instructive to note in the first place that neither Richards, in the first volume of the official history of the Royal Air Force during the war, nor Cajus Bekker in his *Luftwaffe Diaries*, has a single word to say about these operations. For our discussion we have had recourse to Douglas's own report, and to Peter Wykeham's *Fighter Command*, in which he devotes two chapters to them. Here, Douglas justifies these sweeps on the grounds of i) 'wresting the initiative from the Germans'; ii) providing 'valuable experience for pilots, operational commands and the staffs of the formations concerned', and, after June, iii) of inducing the enemy 'to bring back fighters from the Eastern Front' so as to alleviate some of the pressure on the Russian defences following Germany's attack against the Soviet Union. Almost as an afterthought was added 'the primary object' of these fighter incursions as 'the destruction of enemy aircraft.'

Douglas claims that the first and second objectives were achieved – though he fails to elaborate on what advantage, if any, was taken of 'wresting the initiative from the Germans'. The third objective failed. As to losses, the RAF's were serious: from January to July they amounted to 226 fighters and pilots: of these no fewer than 184 were lost in June and July. Douglas is careful to begin by saying: 'It would be unwise to attach too much importance to statistics showing the claims made and the losses suffered by our fighters month-by-month throughout the offensive.' Very unwise–and downright embarrassing. We will show that these offensive sweeps did not achieve the results or the success that Douglas saw fit to claim.

The difference between 'Rhubarbs' and 'Circuses' is that the former were incursions of wings of fighters bent on looking for trouble and beating up any suitable target they chanced upon. 'Circuses' on the other hand comprised formations of light bombers escorted by fighters. Since the 'Rhubarbs' were of no significance in terms of waging war we will comment only on the 'Circuses', because they had the potential of causing appreciable damage if the right targets were selected. Of these operations Wykeham points out the failures and their causes; the second 'Circus', carried out on February 5, 1941, 'could hardly be called a success.' It transpired that Bomber and Fighter Commands 'had different ideas' about the purpose of the operations. Bomber Command intended this one as a means 'to deny the enemy the use of the nearer ports as invasion bases.' For Fighter Command its purpose was: 'To bomb selected targets, and to take advantage of the enemy's reaction to shoot down his fighters under conditions favourable to our fighters.' Wykeham goes on to observe that 'Neither [purpose] was quite compatible with that of the Air Ministry, which was that bombers were only needed to make an enemy come up and fight.' Somewhat naturally, Bomber Command 'did not take kindly to the idea' of their squadrons being used as bait for the pleasure of Fighter Command.

A post-mortem resulted in an agreement between the two operational commands, which read as follows (we quote Wykeham again):

> The object of these attacks is to force the enemy to give battle under conditions tactically favourable to our fighters. In order to compel him to do so, the bombers must cause sufficient damage to make it impossible for him to ignore them and refuse to fight on our terms.

The 'Circuses' continued into the spring and early summer, some successful, in the eyes of the commanders, some not so. Following another failure – Wykeham does not give the date – a further post-mortem concluded on a note of doubt as to whether the objectives were being met, and whether or not persistence in the offensive 'might tend to our disadvantage.'

It is clear from Douglas's and Wykeham's accounts that the policy of 'leaning forward into France' and the resulting offensive sweeps were viewed and undertaken as mere tactical operations. The tasks of Fighter Command were conceived as distinct and separate operational functions with an inter-relationship existing only in thought – and then not consistently. That this was so is confirmed by Richards, who wrote: 'the urgent demand [in 1941] was for success in countering the night bombing and **then, looking further ahead,** for offensive operations over the continent.' [Our emphasis.]

These incursions into enemy territory inflicted mere pin-pricks and had no lessons to impart, hence their neglect by historians of the air war. The planners do not seem to have realized that if the bombers did no real damage – and they didn't – what could the fighters do? If the leaders had stepped back and taken a larger, strategic, view of the potential of the resources they disposed of, they might have reached a very different conclusion about their use. They saw, for example, that the fighter sweeps gave the pilots a valuable experience in air fighting, which was itself a preparation for meeting the resumption of the daylight battle expected in the spring. What they failed to see was a possible relationship between the 'Circuses' and the night Blitz ravaging British cities that winter. 'Successful operations stem from clear directives,' wrote Wykeham about the failures. Similarly, successful strategies stem from clear thinking. This is not the place to present a detailed plan of action, but only to suggest a concerted line of action.

Bomber Command was the only arm of the Royal Air Force that could carry the war and do damage to the enemy. A tactical thinker might have seen the opportunity to launch an unrelenting attack against the airfields in France and Belgium, which were the home bases of the German night bombers, with all the resources the Command could muster. The bombers would strike in daylight to ensure accuracy of navigation to locate their targets and of hitting them. They would be escorted by the squadrons of Fighter Command, who would quickly learn the optimum tactics of the offensive escort, both from trial and error and from the mistakes made by the Luftwaffe in the Battle of Britain, where the Germans' major handicap was the lack of range of their fighters (from whence arose the order to remain close to the bombers they were escorting). If the planners in the Air Ministry, or the commanders within Fighter Command at headquarters, or the Groups, had learnt this lesson they might have been emboldened to carry the policy one step further, and to examine the possibility of extending the bomber strikes into Germany, for the first four-engined bomber was then coming into squadron service.

To realise this prospect would have necessitated the development of a long-range fighter; this would not have taken much genius to achieve, for the Spitfire was adaptable to many variations and modifications. On the other hand a twin-engined fighter armed with four 20 mm cannons, the Whirlwind, was already in service and could have been adapted for the role. The RAF would have had a two-year lead on the United States Air Force in perfecting the techniques of long-range daylight attacks against enemy targets; and one is readily persuaded that the war could have been shortened appreciably.

Douglas's report on his two-year stewardship as Commander-in-Chief of Fighter Command does not indicate a single idea or initiative originating with him. All the measures tried for combating the night attacks had been proposed before he took over. The idea of fighter sweeps, according to Douglas, had been suggested by Trenchard to the Air Ministry, who instructed Douglas to confer with his Group Commanders about it. As for preparations for invasion, or liaison with and between his Groups, nothing. On the other hand, his *Despatch* is larded with expressions such as the following:'I was instructed by the Air Ministry'; 'I received a letter from the secretary of State'; 'on receipt of the Air Ministry's letter'; 'a formal directive required me to'; 'obtain from the Air Ministry a clear statement'. There were no fewer than twelve such directives in the first thirteen months of his command.

The second volume of Douglas's autobiography is entitled *Years of Command*. This volume, and his *Despatch*, together suggest that he would not move without prior, and specific, orders from the Air Staff, and that he **commanded** not at all.[ii] But there is something more to Douglas's two volumes of autobiography that calls for comment. The reader is disagreeably struck by the author's constant practice not only of repeating his own rank and position at every opportunity as if to impress, but, worse, of giving thumbnail sketches of every person he mentions, with particular emphasis on how high they rose and how important they were. One such example will suffice:

Of an even closer link with those days of 1917 ... is the well-known political figure Harold Balfour, then a Captain, who came to join me in No.43 Squadron as one of my Flight Commanders. During the second war, Balfour was Under-Secretary of State for Air. Today, an old friend of long standing, he is better known as Lord Balfour of Inchrye; and he is a member of the Board of British European Airways.

Such boastful asides interrupt the narrative many dozens of times. Yet in the preface he had asserted: 'I shall do my best not to incur in the telling of my story the charge of "shooting a line".' This is far from a negligible objection. That this man, who had reached almost the pinnacle of the Air Force, should feel the need to indulge in multifarious name-dropping throughout his memoirs is telling.

We will conclude by quoting, and analysing, an episode recounted by Douglas in the second volume of his memoirs. In early 1941 Douglas wrote to the Air Ministry complaining that the Spitfire II was inferior in performance to the improved Messerschmitt Bf 109f and asked that something be done about it. A few days later he was asked to go and see Lord Beaverbrook. As Douglas was ushered into Beaverbrook's office, the latter shoved a copy of Douglas's letter across the desk at him, asking whether Douglas had written it. Douglas's avowal that he had written it sent Beaverbrook into a frenzy of anger – whether real or feigned, it is impossible to say. 'The little man started to roar and shout and wave his fists in the air, and for several minutes he set about roundly abusing me, Fighter Command, and everything to do with us.' This is very interesting and informative – especially about Beaverbrook's attitude toward Douglas. However, the telling thing is Douglas's reaction to this tirade. Douglas took it in silence for a time; but then he began to feel that Beaverbrook was going too far. 'All said and done, I reminded myself, I was the Commander-in-Chief of Fighter Command and a high-ranking officer in the Royal Air Force.' He also reminded himself that his letter had been perfectly justified, and one simple question came to him: 'Why the hell should I take this outburst lying down?' With that I promptly lost my temper. . . and started thumping Beaverbrook's desk with my fist and shouting back at him.'

We will not dwell on the contrast between the way Beaverbrook treated Douglas and the way he had treated Dowding; nor on Douglas's outburst. What is particularly telling is that Douglas had to remind himself that he was the Commander-in-Chief of Fighter Command and a high-ranking officer. In other words, he was utterly lacking in that personal authority a commander must have. He was no Trenchard or Tedder: he was above all no Dowding. He was playing a role, a role for which he portrays himself as being singularly unfitted and unqualified.

II. Leigh-Mallory

The appointment of Leigh-Mallory to command 11 Group is, in itself, a curious and contradictory posting. After all, he wanted the opportunity to muster big wings of fighters. But Park's experience with 11 Group had proved conclusively that there was simply not enough time in which to assemble a wing of three or more squadrons. The Air Ministry conference of October 17 had confirmed the rightness of Park's tactics and leadership. Moreover, the claims of enemy RAF destroyed put forward by Leigh-Mallory, even in the more favourable conditions prevailing for 12 Group's squadrons, we have shown to be wild exaggerations. How then was he going to succeed in 11 Group when he had failed in 12 Group? – that is to say, how could he assemble wings of five squadrons in time to 'see off' the much larger attacks expected in the spring of 1941? In a word, what were his 'qualifications' for the position which Richards referred to?

Leigh-Mallory was appointed AOC of 11 Group a full month after Douglas had been installed as AOC-in-C of Fighter Command, and of his new lieutenant's appointment Douglas has this to say: 'At the time when I was appointed C-in-C of Fighter Command it was decided that there should be some changes in the Group Commanders. Since I was such a new boy I had nothing to do with these decisions.'

This statement reveals three interesting things. First, since some changes in the Group Commanders were being considered while Douglas was still the V-CAS, and knowing of his imminent appointment to Fighter Command, he did and said nothing to ensure that Park stayed where he was or was even moved to a more responsible position; and therefore he acquiesced in his removal and demotion. Second, he most certainly did know about the decisions; and the Chief of the Air Staff (Portal) would most assuredly have consulted him about them. Third, by his use of the term 'a new boy', he tries to 'act the innocent' and to suggest that he was not important enough to be consulted on the matter. We might add that, in saying that he had nothing to do with these decisions he tries to suggest that he had no direct and official hand in them. That may be technically correct; but the statement is dishonest because he was one of the chief instigators in Dowding's removal and in the changes which he both engineered and approved of. Confirmation of Douglas's knowing of Leigh-Mallory's new command – and hence of his mendacity – and indeed of Leigh-Mallory knowing of it himself even before Douglas's new appointment, is provided by (then Sqn. Ldr.) Kenneth Cross, who was serving at 12 Group Headquarters at the time: 'The telephone conversations between Sholto Douglas and Leigh-Mallory continued until one evening Sholto Douglas confirmed that he was to replace Dowding as C-in-C of Fighter Command. Leigh-Mallory congratulated him and said, "I am glad that I am to be closely associated with you in my next appointment".' Note: 'in my next appointment.'

We have had occasion to review some of Leigh-Mallory's defects as a tactical commander and as a man. The following episode, recounted by Park's biographer, and which did not come to light until 1968, buttresses that judgment; an alarming instance of Leigh-Mallory's unfitness was seen on 29 January 1941 when he decided to conduct a paper exercise using the circumstances of an actual attack on Kenley, Biggin Hill and Hornchurch on 6 September 1940. His intention was to prove correct his opinion on the use of large formations. The exercise was carefully set up and Leigh-Mallory totally mismanaged it. The raid was not intercepted inbound and both Kenley and Biggin Hill were bombed while their RAF were still on the ground. When Lang[iii] explained Leigh-Mallory's several mistakes to him, Leigh-Mallory replied that next time he would do better. In fact, there was no next time. He later told Lang that 'if there are any more major battles over England I shall control all of them' and went on to declare, echoing Douglas, that if a large-scale raid approached, he would permit it to bomb its target and intercept it in force on the way back to France. The enemy, he believed, would be so badly mauled that there would be no more raids.

Leigh-Mallory's deficiencies were well known long before this. In discussing tactics we mentioned 12 Group's failure to defend its own region against a heavy attack on August 15th. This attack, by fifty unescorted Ju88s across the North Sea, was precisely the kind of attack for which 12 Group had been created. What happened? On that day Leigh-Mallory was absent from his Headquarters on a visit to Wittering. His place as controller was taken by a wing commander who, when the raiders were plotted, took the unusual step of sending most of the fighters to protect the major industrial cities instead of on a direct interception vector over the sea. As a result the fighters made no contact and two RAF aerodromes, Driffield and Leaconfield, were heavily damaged.

We do not know what Leigh-Mallory would have done. The point is that he had put a controller in charge who he must have known was inexperienced. Leigh-Mallory was the longest-serving Group Commander in Fighter Command, having been in his command since 1937; but he had not seen to the efficiency and training of a deputy Group Controller.

A direct cause of Leigh-Mallory's failure as a fighter commander operating within the Dowding system may be found precisely in the manner he had of directing operations. His biographer, Bill Newton Dunn, writes: 'During the battles, L-M sat "in the chair" in his Group's Operations Room and conducted the battle himself.

Having carried out the most pre-war practices, Cross [Squadron Leader Kenneth Cross] considers that L-M had become the best Group commander.' [Dunn means: L-M having carried out the most exercises, not Cross.]ⁱᵛ Of Park's direction Dunn says, amusingly, though without amusing intent: 'By contrast, Park at 11 Group walked up and down his Operations Room, giving advice to other people who were sitting in the chairs and having to take the responsibility.'

Churchill visited 11 Group Headquarters on September 15th. In his war memoirs he wrote a graphic and dramatic account of what he witnessed:

> The Group Operations Room was like a small theatre, about sixty feet across, and with two storeys. We took our seats in the Dress Circle. . . Presently the red bulbs showed that the majority of our squadrons were engaged. A subdued hum arose from the floor, where the busy plotters pushed their discs to and fro in accordance with the swiftly-changing situation. Air Vice-Marshal Park gave general directions for the disposition of his fighter force, which were translated into detailed orders to each fighter station by a youngish officer in the centre of the Dress Circle, at whose side I sat. Some years after I asked his name. He was Lord Willoughby de Broke.(I met him next in 1947, when the Jockey Club, of which he was a Steward, invited me to see the Derby. He was surprised that I remembered the occasion.) He now gave the orders for the individual squadrons to ascend and patrol as the result of the final information which appeared on the map table. The Air Marshal himself walked up and down behind, watching with a vigilant eye every move in the game, supervising his junior executive's hand, only intervening with some decisive order, usually to reinforce a threatened area. In a little while all our squadrons were fighting, and some had already begun to return for fuel. All were in the air. The lower line of bulbs was out. There was not one squadron left in reserve.
>
> At this moment Park spoke to Dowding at Stanmore, asking for three squadrons from No.12 Group to be put at his disposal in case of another major attack while his squadrons were rearming and refuelling. This was done. They were specially needed to cover London and our fighter aerodromes, because No. 11 Group had already shot their bolt. The young officer, to whom this seemed a matter of routine, continued to give his orders, in accordance with the general directions of his Group Commander, in a calm, low monotone, and the three reinforcing squadrons were soon absorbed. I became conscious of the anxiety of the Commander, who now stood still behind his subordinate's chair. Hitherto I had watched in silence. I now asked: 'What other reserves have we?' 'There are none,' said Air Vice-Marshal Park. In an account which he wrote about it afterwards he said that at this I 'looked grave'. Well I might. What losses should we not suffer if our refuelling planes were caught on the ground by further raids of 'forty plus or fifty plus'! The odds were great; our margins small; the stakes infinite.

This description underscores two of the magisterial features of the Dowding system.

Firstly, the important role played by every individual, who was well trained and given the responsibility and authority necessary to his task. Secondly, the system of reserves; the remark of Park's: 'There are none', has been misunderstood. He was referring to his own group. But the squadrons of 10 Group, 12 Group, and 13 Group were, in a very real strategic sense, reserve squadrons ready and waiting to be called to the scenes of action and to replace tired squadrons in 11 Group. This feature is demonstrated by Park's call to Dowding. All that has been said of Fighter Command's task in the year 1941 in discussing Douglas's role is equally relevant to Leigh-Mallory, for this officer was the commander of the group which provided all the squadrons used for the sweeps.

Peter Wykeham, in his *Fighter Command*, devotes the better part of two chapters to the tactics of 'leaning forward into France'. On the other hand, *The Luftwaffe War Diaries*, and Air Vice-Marshal J.E. 'Johnnie' Johnson in his authoritative *The Story of Air Fighting*, give them not a single line, obviously considering them as inconsequential and militarily insignificant.

But what of the wings themselves, which Leigh-Mallory championed so enthusiastically? Johnnie Johnson, who flew Spitfires in the European theatre throughout the War and took part in these sweeps, wrote in his *Wing Leader* that the wings 'were difficult to control in action because the pilots got in each other's way.' He learned from his experience that 'Park had been right: three squadrons could be worked together, more could not, and a pair was the ideal formation.'

Leigh-Mallory's opportunity for fame presented itself on August 19th 1942 when he was instructed to provide fighter cover for the Dieppe raid. It turned out to be the greatest one day air battle of the war. Portal, who had been stung by American criticism of Fighter Command's idleness, 'was only too keen to demonstrate the power of his vastly expanded fighter force .. And bring the Luftwaffe to action in the hope of inflicting a crushing defeat on the Germans.'[v]

> Control of this air operation was entrusted to Air Vice-Marshal Leigh-Mallory, and a force of fifty-six fighter squadrons – Hurricanes, Spitfires and Typhoons – was placed at his disposal. . . Caught by surprise, the German Air Force could at first challenge us only with fighters; but these appeared in growing numbers – twenty-five, fifty, a hundred. Then, at 1000 hours, the enemy's bombers came on the scene. Under strong escort they repeatedly strove to pierce the protective canopy of our fighters. As repeatedly they were driven off. . . . On the more general issues, it was realised at the time that the close support provided by Leigh-Mallory's squadrons was not entirely effective. . . . On the other hand, the all-important task of protecting the raiding troops and the vessels off shore was performed with outstanding success. Our soldiers fought completely unmolested from the air.

What successes the British fighters enjoyed was largely the work of Harry Broadhurst (now Group Captain) who observed the battle from 11 Group HQ. The losses began to mount, and he flew over to see what was going on. He saw the RAF's fighters going over in massed wings. Five times he flew over Dieppe that day, and persuaded Leigh-Mallory that the squadrons should take off independently and under the command of their own officer commanding.[vi] This operation merits a comment in *The Luftwaffe Diaries* – a succinct two lines : 'The British and Canadian landing attempt at Dieppe, bloodily repulsed and with the loss of 106 British bombers and fighters. The Germans lost forty-eight fighters.'

Another major episode in this period is recorded by the same German writer : 'The successful break through the Channel, aided by strong air cover, of the battleships, *Scharnhorst* and *Gneisenau*, and the cruiser *Prinz Eugen* on February 12, 1942.' Wykeham describes the scene thus from the British side:

> Fighter Command was caught off guard, more than at any time in the war. No. 11 Group radar began plotting the German fighter umbrella from 8:30 a.m. onwards, but for some reason decided that it was an enemy air/sea rescue operation, and it was not until 10:20 a.m, when the plot was seen to be moving at 25 to 30 knots, that Leigh-Mallory's controller concluded that it might be a convoy. Leigh-Mallory himself was taking part in a parade at Northolt. The weather was bad and a pair of Spitfires sent to investigate saw only the E-Boats on the fringe of the fleet. While the pilots were making their report, the radar stations on the south coast informed No. 11 Group that attempts were being made to jam them, and shortly afterwards they actually detected ships off Le Touquet. Yet with all these indications the first sighting report came from the merest chance.
>
> Group Captain Beamish, Station Commander at Kenley, had decided that the weather was ideal for a 'Rhubarb', and had obtained permission to fly one in company with his Wing Leader, Wing Commander Boyd. They hoped to pick up a stray Messerschmitt over the French coast, and in this they were eminently successful, for at 10:30 a.m. they bumped full tilt into the fighter escort of the German naval force. Unable to dogfight owing to the low cloud they speedily quitted the scene, only pausing to rake with their cannons an E-boat which appeared in the mist and rain below. As they turned away from it they saw the screen of German destroyers creaming along on a north-easterly course, and behind them the looming bulks of capital ships, forging through the sea in line ahead.

Churchill was furious: it was a black eye for Fighter Command. The offensive sweeps, night fighting failures, Dieppe, the *Scharnhorst* and *Gneisenau*, are the consequences of Leigh-Mallory's qualifications for his command. He sought to entice the enemy into the air and engage them in battle; and he succeeded, to our cost. Fighter Command was on the offensive; the defending Germans inflicted heavy losses on our pilots. That should have told a great deal to Leigh-Mallory and Douglas about either the relative odds, or the relative standards of training, or the calibre of leadership. The results indicate that Leigh-Mallory and Douglas had neglected the advanced fighter training of their pilots to a degree that should have set off alarm signals in the Air

Ministry. But the Air Ministry seemed to give Fighter Command the licence to do what they liked.

But what of renewed assaults against Fighter Command and invasion in 1941? Douglas opined in his Despatch: "I believe that if the Germans had delivered a second daylight offensive in 1941 . . . Fighter Command would have given as good an account of itself as in the previous Summer.' It is a cautiously hesitant and tentative opinion, but the opinion of most experts is *not* at all hesitant. Neither is it in the least complimentary to Douglas and Leigh-Mallory as neither officer had produced a single idea by himself. Every idea ever put forward by Leigh-Mallory – such as the 'big wing' idea – originated with someone else, and was appropriated by Leigh-Mallory and advanced as his own. The policy of 'leaning forward into France' was Trenchard's idea, and was costly and achieved little: Dowding 'would certainly resist the use of his fighters offensively over France'. And with good reason!

We have an eye-witness account of the futility of these incursions into France, in particular those requiring close fighter escort to bombers. In them, the new leaders of Fighter Command show they had learnt nothing from the Germans' mistakes of 1940. Leigh-Mallory used to hold regular conferences at Northolt, attended by the leaders of the fighter wings and the bomber leaders. At one such conference the fighter leader Johnnie Kent, who was commanding officer of 303 (Polish) Squadron, questioned the purpose of these operations. He first stated that using the small bombers in such small numbers had no visible effect on the enemy industry. He then continued:

> If the bombers were merely there as bait to bring up the fighters so that they could be destroyed then we should restrict our radius of activity to that which would permit us to fight without the nagging fear of running out of fuel. This mental obstacle seriously interfered with a pilot's fighting spirit and it was my opinion that we had already lost far too many first class men because these factors were not receiving sufficient consideration.

Kent goes on to say that at this challenging of policy, Leigh-Mallory looked taken aback, and turned to his Group Operations Officer for reply. This was Group Captain Victor Beamish, an experienced and successful fighter leader. To Leigh-Mallory's bewilderment, Beamish agreed with Kent. Leigh-Mallory then turned to another of his staff officers, one who had had no operational experience in this war, and presumably got an answer, fatuous though it was, that satisfied him: 'My answer to Kent is – we've done it!' Kent got angry and flung back some 'rude remarks'. 'The AOC,' concludes Kent, ' preferred the second opinion and we continued to go to Lille and lose good men, all to little purpose.'[vii] 'Worse even than the fact that these operations were virtually useless from a military point of view was the fact that they dominated all thinking about fighters.' This stultifying effect on progressive thought at the highest levels can be seen in its woeful influence on the subsequent conduct of the air war, both at home and overseas.

We have given Leigh-Mallory a 'bad press'. But he is not without his defenders: '[If] in 1940 Leigh-Mallory had walked past wearing a white coat, he would have been taken for a house-painter, whereas Park would have been taken for a brain-surgeon' (Orange). '[Orange was] a little unkind to Leigh-Mallory... Leigh-Mallory took over 12 Group from nothing and built it up... he knew the overall system better than Park' (Cross). 'Leigh-Mallory could run rings round Park intellectually' (Slessor). 'I served with both Park and Leigh-Mallory. At first I thought Leigh-Mallory was useless, but he learnt very quickly' (Porter). '[Leigh-Mallory] shows a misconception of the basic ideas of fighter defence' (Park). 'Leigh-Mallory did not understand the system at all' (Porter). 'I had the misfortune to meet Leigh-Mallory on one occasion, and the way he harangued the pilots of 266 before we went to France [in 1939] was most unpleasant' (Hancock). 'As late as May 1944 Tedder would speak of educating Leigh-Mallory up to school certificate level' (Orange). 'Leigh-Mallory was not of the same calibre [as Dowding or Park], and had he occupied either of the other two positions serious problems would have resulted' (Kingcombe). 'Leigh-Mallory was a very nice man, but he relied heavily on advice... Leigh-Mallory was much senior [to Park] and got on well with people, including the Americans. He was not as pompous as some people thought' (Porter). '[Leigh-Mallory] had the unfortunate tendency to be somewhat pompous, and the Americans did not take to that. He did not have the happy faculty, possessed by Tedder and others, for getting on well with the Americans' (Cox). 'Leigh-Mallory was not a team player; he was keen to make an impact in his own way' (Probert). 'Leigh-Mallory appeared insecure and hesitant, and the influence of Bader, who was older than most [pilots], was not surprising' (Lyne). 'Sir Denis Crowley-Milling took up the cudgels on behalf of Leigh Mallory... "I thought that Leigh-Mallory was seriously maligned this morning".'[viii]

We give the last word on the matter to Max Hastings, who presents a historical view:

> The burly Leigh-Mallory had achieved his eminence, and aroused considerable personal animosity, by intriguing successfully in .. the Battle of Britain to supplant its victors, Air Marshals Dowding and Park. He had directed Fighter Command ... ever since, and retained that post while he acted as Air Commander-in-Chief for OVERLORD. His appointment was clearly an error of judgement by Portal, Chief of the Air Staff. To his peers he seemed gloomy and hesitant. Most of the Americans admired Tedder... But they were irked by Leigh-Mallory's pessimism and indecision. 'He didn't seem to know what he wanted,' said Quesada. 'He couldn't get along with people. He seemed more concerned with preserving his forces than with committing them.' The post-OVERLORD report from Montgomery's headquarters declared: 'The most difficult single factor during the period of planning ... was the delay in deciding and setting up the higher headquarters organization of the Allied air force matter.' To the dismay and near despair of 21st Army Group, the D-Day Air Plan was finally settled only thirty-six hours before the landings took place.[ix]

Before we leave our analysis of the record of command of these two officers, one further matter requires examination. It is what has been called the Baedeker Raids.

The Baedeker Raids is the name given to a brief bombing campaign launched against a number of famous and ancient English cities in 1942 in retaliation against the RAF bombing of the Hanseatic towns of Rostock and Lubeck.[x] The principal cities bombed were Exeter, Bath, Norwich, York, Canterbury, Ipswich and Southampton, and the raids spanned the period April 23 to June 21. The following table gives the results of the raids on both sides.

Date		City	Sorties	E/A Destroyed
April	23	Exeter	40+	1
	24	Exeter	50	3
	25	Bath	163	12
	26	Bath	83	3
	27	Norwich	71	0
	28	York	74	3
	29	Norwich	70	1
May	3	Exeter	90	?
	8	Norwich	76	1
	31	Canterbury	?	?
June	1	Ipswich	11	0
	2	Canterbury	58	4
	6	Canterbury	52	6
	21	Southampton	44	4

The totals add up to thirty-eight enemy aircraft destroyed of 932 sorties carried out. And the damage done, in terms of people alone, is reported by one writer thus: 'During the course of 1942, 3236 people were killed and 4148 suffered serious injuries as a result of bombing attacks on Britain.'[xi]

The point of giving these figures is to establish a comparison with the results achieved against the bombers of the Blitz of 1940-41. The results in 1942 show some improvement, but an improvement that borders on the lamentable. Fighter Command had had a full eighteen months to perfect the system of night defence laid down by Dowding. And if this was the best that Douglas and his Group Commanders could do, one wonders what they had been doing all that time.

Another historian writes, in dealing with this period: 'The air defences, after their triumph in the summer of 1940, had suffered the frustrations of the following winter before achieving some degree of control over the night-bomber.... By the closing months of 1943 air supremacy over the United Kingdom seemed clearly within reach.' Only 'within reach'. Yet no heads rolled.

Douglas lasted for two years as chief of Fighter Command, and one wonders why. Leigh-Mallory, for his part, succeeded Douglas as Air Officer Commanding-in-Chief of Fighter Command, and the same question cries aloud for an answer; is it really possible for a man to rise so high, without the personal and professional qualifications necessary for the job? The public are accustomed to seeing this scandal take place around them all the time in the domain of politics. But even in spheres of life where applicants and incumbents are appraised constantly – in the armed services, in universities, in the civil service, in industry, for example – it happens even there all too frequently. Men are poor judges of others. Those that are a good judge of character and hidden motives are rare. But men are not what they seem. It is the first lesson – and a lesson which nearly drove him out of his mind – that we see Hamlet learn : 'Seems, madam!' he replies to the Queen. 'Nay, it is; I know not 'seems'. And three scenes later, in referring to the King, the perfidious Claudius: 'villain, villain, smiling, damned villain! . . . That one may smile, and smile, and be a villain.'

Unmerited advancement is accomplished by means of a diverse armoury of attributes and wiles, including flattery, bluff, charm, glibness, dissimulation, mock indignation, off-loading work to subordinates, taking the credit for other's work, falsification. In a word, appearance versus reality, a popular theatrical trope. Ambitious men will do anything to reach the top. But can others be readily misled and duped? Portal once said: 'I reaffirm my impression that U.J. is the goods – sincere, simple and big.' (U.J., or Uncle Joe, is Stalin.) And of Portal his biographer wrote : 'In small things as in great, Portal had a habit of being right.' Did Portal not know the horrendous record of Stalin as a mass murderer? Surely Stalin was, and was known to be, a psychopath; but Portal, who thought him 'sincere, simple and big', was not the only man-at-the-top who was taken in.

This entire question of appearances and ambition, aims and achievement, is a variation on the theme of justice itself. The moral problem of justice analyses the relationship between good and evil, and reward and punishment, and wrestles with the notion that the virtuous will be rewarded and the wicked punished. Men feel intuitively that it is only right that such a moral order should exist. Religions teach the inexorable workings of the moral law. But then they spoil things by adding the rider: 'Well, if not in this world, in the next.' Rationalists posit a natural law which also promises a universe governed by an immutable moral law (discoverable by reason alone); but the rationalists do not have the comfort of being able to fall back on an afterlife if things don't turn out according to one's hopes; or when they discover time and again that 'good things happen to bad guys'; that crime can pay; and that 'good guys come last'.

Eighteenth century France was entertained or shocked by certain philosophical novels whose central theme was an extended elaboration of the thesis that 'no act of kindness goes unpunished.' Conversely, being bad can be a good career move. Discarded principles can hasten a climber's ascent. The most popular people may be skilled deceivers or flatterers. A ruthless competitor may be safer from retribution than one encumbered by principles and pity. Ambition, jealousy, malice, revenge: these sins compound the equation. Sholto Douglas is characterized by Hough and Richards as being 'cleverer and more worldly' than Dowding. A comparison of the two men's achievements and character suggests that 'cleverer' means 'more calculating', and 'more worldly' means 'ready to put ends before means'. Such a man would know the art of dissimulation.

Douglas accomplished nothing that might be called memorable. His autobiography confirms this assessment. The style is a measure of the man. The methods of literary analysis reveal his writing to be ordinary, featureless, unoriginal, and pedestrian. To compensate, he is given to boasting, to fudging, to name-dropping, and at times to outright mendacity.

Leigh-Mallory, similarly, accomplished little in 11 Group or Fighter Command. He was out of his depth and knew nothing of fighters or their potential. After Leigh-Mallory's death in a flying accident, 'Johnnie' Johnson wrote an appreciation of him, in which he said: 'L–M was very much a "fatherly" figure and at his best when he held conferences with his young "wing leaders", because he did not pretend to know about fighter tactics and relied on us to keep him up to date.' The statement beggars belief! This was 1944. Leigh-Mallory had been in Fighter Command since 1937 – that is, for seven continuous years, five of them in war – yet 'he did not . . . know about fighter tactics' ! Johnson is altogether too kind.

In the summer of 1942, the Chief of the Imperial General Staff, General Sir Alan Brooke, had the invidious task of going to Egypt to tell General Auchinleck that he was being relieved of his command. The Prime Minister wanted Brooke to take over; Brooke, despite his burning desire to have an Army command at the fighting front again, had a number of reasons for declining. The clinching reason, as he explained in his diary, was: 'I could not bear the thought that Auchinleck might think that I had come out here on purpose to work myself into his shoes.' It is a great shame that Sholto Douglas and Leigh-Mallory had no such scruples.[xii]

We are not quite finished; Leigh-Mallory, together with his wife and the whole crew, was killed when the aircraft he was travelling in – to take up his appointment as Supreme Air Commander Far East – crashed into a peak of the Alps.[xiii] In King Henry's Chapel at Westminster Abbey a number of names of high ranking Royal Air Force officers are painted on the wall beneath the Battle of Britain window. Among them is the name of William Sholto Douglas: 'Marshal of the Royal Air Force William Sholto Douglas, 1st Baron of Kirtleside' at that. His name should be removed.

Notes:

i. The crest of Fighter Command bears the motto: Offence – Defence. One wonders where in the Air Ministry this devise was dreamt up. To place 'Offence' before 'Defence' is to put the cart before the horse; and Fighter Command could never become an offensive arm in any event.

ii. Douglas's career shows us that he took over Fighter Command after all the real work had been done; that he then went to the Middle East Command after the battle had been won; and that he then became AOC-in-C of Coastal Command after the U-Boat had been mastered in the Battle of the Atlantic. Nothing in the chapter on Douglas in Henry Probert's book, *High Commanders of the Royal Air Force*, justifies any change in this section of chapter ten. Robert Wright, who wrote much of Douglas's memoirs, complained later, regretting that he had been hoodwinked into the job of co-author, because he found that he had written accounts of events (given to him by Douglas) that were demonstrably, and knowingly, false.

iii. Wing Commander Thomas Lang, one of the senior controllers of 11 Group.

iv. A careful reading and search of the relevant chapters and sections of Cross's autobiography discloses no such opinion on the author's part. It is wishful thinking by Dunn. But then, Dunn was Leigh-Mallory's nephew.

v. Hughes-Wilson, p. 139. The author's thesis in his study of the blunder that was Dieppe targets Mountbatten in particular, on the grounds that he organized and planned the raid, after it had been cancelled, without authority.

vi. A letter of February 2005 to the author from a former Spitfire pilot, Ian Krohn, states briefly: 'I flew on a couple of big wing sweeps and I was also on the Dieppe thing. I think flying a big wing was as dangerous as anything I experienced during the war.'

vii. J.A. Kent, pp. 165-166.

viii. All quotes are taken from *The Battle Re-Thought*, pp. 69-79, except the Slessor quote, which is from a private letter to Alan Deere, already referred to.

ix. Max Hastings, *Overlord* (London, Michael Joseph, 1984) pp. 44-45.

x. They were called 'Baedeker Raids' because the cities targeted featured prominently in the German Baedeker tourist guides to British cultural centres.

xi. The figures of British casualties are in Alfred Price, *Blitz on Britain 1939-45* (London: Ian Allan, 1977), p. 143. Price gives the figures for the whole of 1942, it will be noted, not just for the raids listed here. The list of cities bombed and the dates are from Collier, *The Defence of the United Kingdom*, Appendix XXXVII, pp. 513-14. For the figures of German raids and losses I am indebted to Dr. Horst Boog, who sent me the relevant pages from *Ulf Balke, Der Luftkrieg in Europa. Die operativen Einsiitze des Kampfgeschwaders 2 in Zweirtzen Weltkrieg* (Koblenz: Berard & Graefe, 1990), pp. 102-121. I am most grateful to Ian White, the author of *AI and the Night Fighter in the Royal Air Force 1935-1969*, for sending me photocopies of thirty-one pages by various authors from *The Blitz. Then and Now*, vol. III, ed. Winston G. Ramsey (1990), and answers to questions I put to him about the raids, an edited summary of which I reproduce below.

a) The only way you can ascertain the number of night-fighter engagements per Baedeker raid is to check the operational record books (ORB) of each of the participating squadrons.

(b) The number of aircraft claimed as 'destroyed' : Volume Three of '*The Blitz, Then & Now*', published by Battle of Britain Prints Ltd in 1992 and on which Appendix four of my book is based.

(c) The vast majority of the Baedeker raiders were shot down by night-fighters, however, '*The Blitz, Then & Now*' Volume Two gives an account of each raid and any enemy aircraft that were shot down by anti-aircraft fire. In respect of your statement concerning the development of the night air defences during the tenure of Sholto Douglas and Leigh Mallory, your assertion is broadly correct. The mechanism of the night air defences: (i) A good night-fighter – the Beaufighter. (ii) A practical AI radar [AI Mk.IV]. (iii) The design and introduction of ground control of interception (GCI) radars for fighter direction. (iv) The introduction of the night-fighter operational training units [OTU], that were put in place in 1940, and began to deliver competent crews early in 1941. (v) Similarly, the establishment of Radio Schools to teach radar servicing, these too came on-stream in 1941. (vi) The expansion of the number of night-fighter squadrons [these it should be noted were dependent on the supply of Beaufighters, AI Mk.IV radar and trained air and ground crews]. (vii) The supply of experienced ex-fighter pilots who were re-trained as GCI controllers. (viii) The allocation of Defiant night-fighters operating in the 'cats-eyes' role, also did good work. This is often not recognised by historians.

All of this was put in hand by Dowding before his departure from Fighter Command in November 1940 and for which Douglas reaped the rewards, if not the credit. (My emphasis.)

I would broadly agree with your proposition that under Douglas and Mallory the night-defences were not greatly improved. However, I would rather say they were not greatly 'altered or amended' until 1943 when squadrons were drafted into the 2nd Tactical Air Force (2TAF) in preparation for D-Day.

xii. Anthony Furse recounts that when Portal sent Freeman out to North Africa to report on the situation, and then offered him the command to replace Tedder, he replied: 'The role of Judas is one I cannot fill.' (p.13.)

xiii. The lady Ironia decreed yet another surprise when she oversaw the choice of none other than Air Chief Marshal Sir Keith Park to be sent out in Leigh-Mallory's stead, in which command he distinguished himself again.

CHAPTER 11

Sinclair Snubs the King

—ɷ—

We suggested at the beginning of our investigations that the achievements of Dowding were of such magnitude and far-reaching consequences that his name should be as illustrious as any other great commander of the twentieth century. We have to ask ourselves why it is not.

In our Introduction we stated our conviction that the Battle of Britain could have been won without Churchill: it could not have been won without Dowding. Yet, ironically, it was Churchill, despite his admiration of Dowding, who was partly to blame for denying to Dowding the historical fame that was rightly his. Though we have no need to add our mite to the universal recognition of Churchill's leadership in galvanizing British resistance to Hitler's tyranny: in defending their ancient liberties and in appealing to their love of country and their illustrious past. His was the dominating presence, not only in Britain but, thanks to radio, throughout the free world – and parts of the world that were less than free – that focused attention on the Battle.

General Montgomery, later, had all the time in the world to exploit his situation and court public fame. Dowding, after his retirement in 1942, was in no comparable situation to capitalize on his achievements, for the reason that the war was still far from won, and men's minds were turned inexorably to the future. By the time the war *was* won, Dowding had been virtually forgotten. But Montgomery was still very much a public figure because of his victories from 1942 until the end of the war. Then again, in 1940 the interests of security were paramount, whereas four years later there was greater scope for personal publicity.

Could Dowding have publicized his achievements after the war in order to gain public recognition? We believe that he could have done so, and by the same means as those exploited by others, namely, by encouraging the organization of rallies and reunions of Battle of Britain veterans – both aircrews and all other personnel involved. But there lies the difference between the two men. Montgomery courted and enjoyed the public acclaim that greeted the annual reunions of his 'Desert Rats': Dowding was not a public figure. He was, strange though it may seem, a retiring man. When confronted by the needs of the nation, he fought as no one else fought. But that was behind the scenes. And yet, I for one have no doubt that, had he been called upon to do so, he would have stepped into the full glare of the public light to rally the nation or the Royal Air Force. But the call was not needed. And when the time came for him to retire he was content to withdraw into an almost total obscurity. The Air Ministry was also, not only content, but relieved, that he should do so. And therein lies the gravest obloquy attached to its name; when the Air Ministry was under the most solemn obligation to make known the accomplishments of one of its two greatest air marshals, and of its greatest operational air commander, it embarked on a policy of denial.

It was thought throughout the land at the time that invasion was only weeks, or days, or even hours away. And, after Dunkirk, Britain had precious few land defences with which to resist an assault such as the German Army was deemed capable of launching. But intelligence of the enemy's capabilities was little and poor: a true knowledge would have shown that a seaborne invasion was out of the question. A full-scale airborne invasion, if carried out in August, might well have succeeded. It was the German High Command, however, that was persuaded by Admiral Raeder that once the British Fleet was neutralized by the German air force, a blockade of Britain by submarines and the German capital ships was bound to bring about a British surrender. That accomplished, Hitler would then have embarked on his invasion of the Soviet Union. With no aid possible from or via Britain, as was in fact provided throughout the war, the Soviet Union might well have been defeated.

Similarly, with no reinforcements reaching North Africa or the Middle East from Britain, as took place throughout 1940 and 1941, those regions would also have been overrun. A link-up of the German armies from north and south on the east side of the Mediterranean basin would have given Germany all the oil of the Middle East, and would have isolated India, Burma and China, and eventually, Australia and New Zealand. Imagine, in this global situation, the position of the United States. Would Japan have still attacked Pearl Harbor, or taken some other action? Would the strategic and political decisions of the U.S. have been the same? (Let us remember that, in this hypothetical global chessboard, many South American states were very unhypothetically pro-Nazi.) Or would the U.S. have retreated into a Fortress America – either until Germany and Japan, each dominating half of the world, went to war against each other, or until the U.S. was able to develop and produce atomic weapons with their delivery systems before their enemies?

The Battle, seen from the American perspective, was fraught with soul-searching. If Britain prevailed, President Roosevelt's hand would have been strengthened in his fight with the isolationists, and in his undeclared policy to enter the war as soon as possible, and to gear up American industry on a war footing. On the other hand:

> A Nazi victory over the RAF...followed by the almost certain collapse of British resistance, would seriously have compounded Roosevelt's problems and perhaps led to an even earlier outbreak of the Japanese-American Pacific war. That this did not happen must also be counted a part of the victory of the RAF.[i]

Churchill did not exaggerate when he proclaimed, and warned, on June 18th: 'What General Weygand called the Battle of France is over. I expect that the Battle of Britain is about to begin. Upon this battle depends the survival of Christian civilization.' It is true that in this speech Churchill was appealing to the United States, with an implied threat, to enter the war, or at least to provide Britain with the weapons and armaments she needed in order to resist Nazi Germany. But the speech was also that of a statesman with olympian vision: Dowding agreed with Churchill's evaluation of the situation.

The victory in the Battle of Britain meant that the British Isles became the unsinkable platform and armed camp from which was launched the eventual onslaught against Germany: by air from 1941 and by land in 1944. In comparison Marathon, Trafalgar and the Marne were indeed just as decisive – though it is not too far-fetched to suggest that two other battles, whose outcome was of equal, and perhaps of profounder import for England and Europe, are notable for their omission from this booklet: Hastings, and the Armada. But it is not possible to conceive of an account of Marathon, however brief, without mention of Callimachus? Of Trafalgar without mention of Nelson? Of the Marne without mention of Joffre?

The booklet, which was anonymous, was an official publication of the Air Ministry. The omission of Dowding's name must therefore have been deliberate and not a mere oversight on the part of the authors. Nowhere in the pamphlet is the reason for the omission given, nor the name of the writer. It can only be assumed that he was following specific instructions, and not acting in his own name. That is why we have said not only 'authors', but also 'writer'.[ii]

We shall have to seek elsewhere for the answers to these questions. It appears that the matter was allowed to disappear from the public awareness after its publication. This twofold issue was raised again in works published to observe the fiftieth anniversary of the Battle in 1990. We will quote from two of them. In *The Battle of Britain: The Jubilee History*, by Richard Hough and Denis Richards, we read: 'The pamphlet, which cost the Air Ministry £50 in fees to the author and sold six million copies, mentioned no names at all on the British side except that of Churchill, and only two on the German – Goering and Goebbels. The Air Ministry's Department of Public Relations at the time was trying to discourage the press from building up fighter 'aces'. This was because adulatory reports about certain individual pilots or squadrons in the early days of the war had tended to create ill-feeling among others equally valorous but less well publicised.'

On June 25th, 1990, a conference was organized at the RAF Staff College, Bracknell, by the Staff College in conjunction with the RAF Historical Society. In the course of open discussions following the invited papers, this matter was raised:

'Dr Orange had said that the Air Ministry had suppressed the name of Dowding in the first accounts. It was not suppressed [said Richards]. The story was written up on the basis of blanket instructions from the Department of Public Relations, which was determined not to create personal heroes. In World War One a lot of ill-feeling had been caused by blowing up the reputations of certain 'aces', when these chaps had done no more than others in their squadrons, so when World War Two started the view was that we shouldn't personalize. There was trouble in France with a New Zealander named Cobber Kane, because the press [Noel Knights, of the *Daily Mail*] got hold of his story and blew it up. This caused some ill-feeling amongst the rest, so they decided to operate under this limitation. In that pamphlet, therefore, no individual was mentioned on the British side, and only Goering, he thought, on the German. There was no desire to do down Dowding, but the man who wrote it was told to leave out personalities.'[iii]

These explanations invite comment.

Denis Richards implies that the question of anonymity was a decision taken by the Air Ministry's department of public relations. This department was not autonomous; it acted as an agency of the Air Ministry, and necessarily followed policies laid down by the Air Ministry. The pamphlet is in fact 'an Air Ministry account.' It was therefore the Air Ministry itself – or rather, a highly-placed authority in the Air Ministry – who instructed the writer of it 'to avoid the personality cult' and to avoid 'building up fighter 'aces'.[iv] Dowding, as Commander-in-Chief, was not in the latter class. And by no stretch of imagination could it have been construed that a mention of Dowding, that giving even passing credit to the Commander-in-Chief for this famous victory, amounted to a 'personality cult'.

Even if we accept this explanation, how do the authors of the Air Ministry booklet, or Denis Richards, account for the many mentions of Goering? (One entire section is entitled: 'London versus Goering'.) To answer this we must question another statement made by Richards. We have quoted him as saying that the creation of 'aces' caused 'ill-feeling among the rest, so they decided to operate under this limitation.' If the Air Ministry and its air marshals allowed Air Force policy to be dictated by the supposed discontent of a few junior officers and NCOs, the occasion would have set a record unique in Air Force annals both for the influencing of policy and for solicitude for juniors' sensibilities on the part of the Air Ministry.

Does the claim made here by Hough and Richards hold water? It is true that, in quoting pilots' combat reports, the author of the pamphlet omits their names. But there is one conspicuous exception; he quotes at length one combat report by a Squadron Leader who makes references to his 'Wing' and his 'two other squadrons.' The writer is readily identifiable: the report in question can have been written only by Douglas Bader, whose exploits as the leader of a wing of three, four or five squadrons were being reported at that time. This contradicts Richards' claim that the air ministry wanted to avoid 'building up fighter 'aces': in fact the public demanded 'aces'. The people needed heroes; especially in that perilous time. Consider again: the booklet came out in the spring of 1941. The Battle of Britain had been over for six months. The names of several fighter pilots were already household names. And the Air Ministry itself was compiling the 'scores' of individual fighter pilots. More than that: the Air Ministry was actually issuing periodical lists of the top fighter 'aces'. The list of the end of March, 1941, put Sergeant 'Ginger' Lacey in the top place with twenty-three, Tuck fourth with twenty-two, and Malan sixth with twenty. (In the June 30 list, the rankings were: Malan, first, twenty-nine; Tuck, second, twenty-six; Lacey, third, twenty-third. It is hard to resist the suspicion that the Air Ministry, having once embarked on this course, continued it to ensure that a mere sergeant no longer occupied the top place.)

There is more. The Air Ministry maintained the long-accepted practice of singling out aircrews for decorations. Nearly every day *The Times* carried announcements such as: 'The King has approved the following awards in recognition of gallantry in flying operations against the enemy.' In that same spring of 1941 the people of Britain were fully expecting a renewal of the air battle and were bracing themselves to face again the threat of invasion. In the face of this, the Air Ministry were appointing official war artists. The eminent names of Eric Kennington and William Rothenstein come to mind, men who were commissioned to paint the portraits of pilots who were acknowledged air aces. Kennington made notes about his sitters. The note he made about Flight Lieutenant R.A.B. Learoyd VC is the following: 'This portrait was drawn in the gallery at the top of the Air Ministry in September 1940. Learoyd knew better than I that Hitler was going all out for a quick breaking of Great Britain. Distant bombing grew so close and intense that I asked him if it was not unusual. He took one stride and threw open the door. There were about 120 bombers, almost above. He only made one remark, "What rotten formation." The docks were a furnace, and I asked if we should go to the dug-out or continue the drawing as watching helped no one. He strode back and sat. I found his courage contagious.' Note: 'in the Air Ministry', in September 1940.[v]

In his *Jubilee History* Richards had the grace to concede the blunder. 'This curious omission quickly evoked the ire of the Prime Minister... On 12 April 1941 Churchill wrote to Sinclair: "The jealousies and cliquism which have led to the committing of this offence are a discredit to the Air Ministry, and I do not think any other Service Department would have been guilty of such a piece of work".'

In concluding his account of this episode, Richards notes: 'In applying a policy of anonymity in *The Battle of Britain* pamphlet ...the Department had clearly taken leave of its senses.' But in the RAF Staff College conference held in the same year as the publication of his book, Richards made no such concession, and repeated the same untenable explanation.

If it were only a matter of the suppression of all mention of Dowding's name or allusion to him, the offence would be serious enough. There is worse. *The Battle of Britain* pamphlet narrative is totally lacking in any suggestion of the existence, in Fighter Command, of overall leadership, of a directing strategic mind, of a central authority controlling the defensive forces and of thinking ahead to anticipate changes in the disposition of his forces to meet various contingencies on this chessboard of destiny. The nearest the pamphlet comes to any such notion is in saying: 'The Sectors are grouped together under a . . .Group Headquarters which in its turn comes under the general control of Headquarters, Fighter Command.' No suggestion here of one man exercising this general control: on the contrary, 'Headquarters' suggests many people, all apparently working together on their own initiative and without need of direction. Meanwhile Goering's aims, plans and changing tactics are discussed repeatedly; but never a word or allusion to indicate the presence in Fighter Command of a commander countering Goering's moves. The omission of Dowding's name, we have seen, was deliberate. The failure by the writer – and by the authors – to include a mention of Hastings and the Armada was, I would suggest, also equally conscious. Hastings and the Armada took place on or close to our shores; they were not only close in geography: they are still close in the collective national memory. Everyone knows what happened in 1066 and 1588. How many can say where Marathon, Trafalgar and the Marne are, and describe the issues or the outcome or name the commanders? (Well, Trafalgar, perhaps: at least the victor, if not the location and the issues.) The omission, especially, of the Armada, and the suppression of any mention of Dowding's role in the Battle seem to be of a piece: to deny to Dowding all recognition of his part in this heroic victory.[vi]

There is more to the story of suppression. In 1946 Dowding published a book entitled *Twelve Legions of Angels*. Written in 1941, it analysed the strategic, tactical, material and logistic requirements for the successful prosecution of the war. But it also speculated on the ways and means whereby statesmanship might prevent wars in the future. When it was published in 1946 Dowding added a foreword, which begins thus:

> This book was written more than four years ago...The fact is that when the book was submitted for censorship in due course, the powers that be (or rather the powers that were) refused to pass it for publication. When you have finished the book you may wonder what it contains which could not have been given to the world at the time it was written. It contains no military secret and...as a matter of fact, the veto was not imposed on account of anything in Part I of the book. I do not feel at liberty now to disclose the reason given for the suppression of the book, but it is one which I think few people would guess if they did not know it.

The word used by Dowding in this context is 'suppression'. Whether it is in the same class of 'suppression' as the Air Ministry booklet, we leave it to the reader to judge. The facts are that Dowding met with Churchill on several occasions in 1941, to urge him to read his book and give his approval for its publication. Churchill had Brendan Bracken read it and report to him on it, as a result Churchill refused to give his consent to its publication.

In 1969, Robert Wright published his biography of Dowding. In chapter fifteen he gives a full account of this suppression. The reasons for it can be summarized in the following terms:

> In Part II of his book, Dowding examined the causes of war, and, horrified by its cost in human lives and misery and in material destruction, proposed a number of measures designed to prevent it, so far as possible, in the future. Churchill did not like it at all. He considered that war was a necessary process

in the development of the vigorous and manly qualities in a race. Stalwart defence of one's homeland cannot be achieved at too high a price. If one is attacked, energetic and ruthless counter-attack is the only answer. Sport is all very well, even relatively dangerous sports. But they are no substitute for war. War alone can bring out the best in a race. Without it, a nation's youth degenerates into slothful habits, indolence and effeteness, and ends up good for nothing – good not even for sport, daring enterprise, and business adventurism.

In an article which Dowding published in the '*Sunday Chronicle*' of December 13, 1942 (and which is appended to the text of the book in question), he returns to this theme. 'Is war a Good Thing, or not?' He preceded this with the statement: 'This is not a purely rhetorical question, because there are those who think that war and training for war are necessary for the virility of the race, and that periods of continuous peace lead to softness, luxury and decadence.'

Following this, on Dowding's return to Britain from his mission to the United States and Canada in 1941, he was asked to write a Despatch on the Battle of Britain. When, in June that year, Germany invaded the Soviet Union, all threat of a renewed assault on Britain by the Luftwaffe vanished. There was, therefore, no obstacle, by reason of national security, to the publication of Dowding's *Despatch*. Its publication was, however, also withheld or delayed until 1946. Justification there may have been for this deferral: it appears that all such operational reports were published only in 1946.[vii] However, Dowding had a genuine grievance when he learnt that his Despatch was not even circulated to the parties within the Air Ministry and Fighter Command who would have benefited from its study.

We have seen that the writer of the Air Ministry pamphlet was instructed to suppress all mention of Dowding and his leadership. We have demonstrated that the 'reason' given for this, by someone obviously in the know, is scarcely credible. We are, perhaps, permitted to wonder who precisely in the Air Ministry gave such instructions. Of this there can be no question or doubt: it was Sinclair's. Hence Churchill's angry and indignant reaction. But could a pamphlet about the Battle of Britain have been written and published without Portal's knowledge? Absolutely not! Could such a pamphlet have been produced without Freeman's knowledge and approval? No! On the other hand, could it have been done without Sinclair's knowledge? Possibly; but not likely; and in any event, this would have been most unwise. Portal's and Sinclair's joint responsibility in the matter is clear. The next question that imposes itself is: why should Portal want to deny to Dowding the recognition that was due to him for his accomplishments?

This question of denial of recognition has been the subject of commentary and discussion for over fifty years, from the time of Dowding's removal to the recent past. Ever since Dowding's victory, certain admirers of Dowding's achievements have promoted the idea that Dowding should have been elevated to the highest rank, that of Marshal of the Royal Air Force. The Air Ministry apologists have argued that it would have created a precedent. In the past, they explained, only those officers whose careers had culminated as Chief of the Air Staff had been promoted to the highest rank. But if ever a custom or tradition called for breaking, and a precedent to be set, it was now, for Dowding's over-arching heroism. And yet this did not happen. We would suggest that there exists a final explanation as to why Dowding was denied his coveted promotion. What follows is of the nature of speculation. Perforce: for no authority implicated in this denial would have dared to commit to paper so much as a word that risked revealing the truth.

The rank of Marshal of the Royal Air Force carried with it a prestige, a cachet, which conferred upon its holder certain prerogatives. Among them was the privilege of giving advice, and of offering the fruits of mature reflection, on any weighty matter affecting policy – and indeed on any Air Force issue – to the Air Council, whether invited or not. Indeed, the dignity of Marshal of the RAF gave to its holder a permanent *ex officio* membership of the Air Council. One can visualize the situation: Dowding henceforth an uninvited member of the Air Council – of the Air Council which had sacked him! The Air Council had no fear that Dowding would abuse his new position to the end of justifying his direction of Fighter Command and demolishing his critics; they knew Dowding too well. What they did fear was his command of facts, his remorseless logic, his unparalleled knowledge of air fighting, his unequalled experience, his sharp tongue and keen intelligence.

Had the members of the Air Council been honest with themselves, they could not fail to have conceded that Dowding had much sage counsel to offer on the equipment and training of the Royal Air Force and the strategic direction of the air arm. But, sad to say, they permitted their personal antipathies to cauterize their reason and judgment.

It also appears that Denis Richards had forgotten that the 'precedent' he uses to explain away Dowding's promotion had, in fact, already been broken even at the time of his writing; on January 1st 1946, Air Chief Marshal Sir Arthur Harris was promoted to Marshal of the Royal Air Force without having been Chief of the Air Staff. This was a propitious moment and an unequalled opportunity to make amends to Dowding and to promote him at the same time. Portal and the Air Council pointedly let the moment pass.

This same date was marked by the recognition of another air marshal who had not been Chief of the Air Staff. No less an unworthy figure than Sholto Douglas was promoted to Marshal of the Royal Air Force with Harris. Who dares compare Douglas's achievements with those of Dowding ! Douglas' elevation can be regarded as nothing other than a conscious and wilful insult to Dowding on the part of Portal and the Air Council.[viii]

Dowding was honoured, however, when he retired definitively from the Royal Air Force in 1942. With no thanks to the Air Ministry, he was created a baron, and took the suitable title of Lord Dowding of Bentley Priory. A gratifying irony is attached to this honour. In his copy of the correspondence between Salmond and Trenchard which we have quoted at length, Salmond wrote this personal note, as if to himself: 'Had the PM not agreed [to Dowding's removal], I had decided to appeal to HM [the King].' In fact it was the King himself, aggrieved at the lack of recognition accorded to Dowding, who initiated an inquiry which culminated in Dowding receiving his title.

On October 13, 1987, Edward Bishop ran a letter in *The Daily Telegraph* on the subject of the statue of Lord Dowding which was to be erected in London – again with no contribution from the Air Ministry. We reproduce two paragraphs from it:

> It is sad that the official diminution of Dowding should persist at a time when commemoration of the fiftieth anniversary of the Battle of Britain is being prepared for 1990. As far back as 1942, King George VI was deeply concerned about Dowding's treatment. The monarch's view was made clear in a letter from his private secretary, Sir Alexander Hardinge, to Sir Archibald Sinclair, Secretary of State for Air, to 'raise with you the question of [Dowding] being promoted to Marshal of the Royal Air Force on retirement.'
>
> In 1942 the King, being obliged to accept Sir Archibald Sinclair's assurance that Dowding would be rewarded at the end of the war, replied through his private secretary that he was 'quite satisfied to know that his services will come up for consideration of one kind or another at the end of the war.'

Although Dowding received a barony, he was denied the marshal's baton which he so richly deserved. Sinclair's assurance of reward turned out to be fraudulent. The fraud was compounded at the end of the war. On May 8th 1945 he wrote to Dowding this letter:

> On this historic day, I send you on behalf of the Air Council a message of cordial greeting.
>
> It was under your inspiring leadership that the Battle of Britain was won and our island citadel saved. The whole nation, indeed freedom-loving men and women the world over, will always gratefully remember you and the gallant 'few' who flew and fought under your command.

Sinclair's biographer quotes this letter and adds the comment, in total oblivion of the cruel irony it contains: 'The former head of Fighter Command, bitter to the end, could not bring himself to return the compliment by acknowledging Sinclair's contribution.' No doubt Sinclair meant what he said, within his mind; but his heart was not in it. For his words were not proven by deeds. Perhaps Sinclair was trying to put himself on the right side of history. How easy to write a letter! How difficult to rise above vindictiveness and confer the only reward that mattered. His bad feelings towards Dowding were such as to induce him to betray even the assurance he had given to the King.

The official history of the Royal Air Force during the Second World War concludes with a chapter entitled, 'The Balance Sheet.' In it four air marshals are distinguished as leaders whom the 'Royal Air Force was singularly fortunate in possessing. They are Portal, Tedder, Dowding, and Harris.' All were honoured with the rank of Marshal of the RAF - all, that is, except Dowding, the one whose claim to it outweighed all the others.

There can be little doubt that had Dowding been an Army or Navy man, he would have been so honoured. If he had been a Navy man, there would be a second monumental column in Trafalgar Square, and his name, like Nelson's, would reverberate down the halls of history's noblest pantheons.

Notes:

i. See '*The American Perspective*' by Richard P. Hallion in Addison and Chang, p. 82 et seq.

ii. It was written by Hilary St. George Saunders. See *The Battle of Britain* (London: Wingate-Baker, 1969) which reprinted the Air Ministry pamphlet. St. George Saunders was, of course, the co-author with Denis Richards of *The Official History of the Royal Air Force in the Second World War*. St. George Saunders was the writer of the pamphlet, whereas the authors were those others, of the Air Ministry, responsible for some of its contents and for its omissions.

iii. *The Battle Re-Thought*, pp.78-79.

iv. Strangely, Richard Overy himself falls for this myth – or thin pretext – in his book which is sub-titled *The Myth and the Reality*, in writing: 'The fighter aces for the most part remained anonymous because the RAF wanted to avoid the pitfalls of glamorizing a few heroes at the expense of the rest of the force.' (p. 129)

v. Private publication (np, nd) presented to the author by Eric Kennington in 1948. I suspect that the judgement about the 'rotten formation' was bravado on Learoyd's part, to encourage Kennington.

vi. The Air Ministry issued a second booklet in August 1943, Air Ministry Pamphlet 156, entitled also *The Battle of Britain*. It is a fuller story, and in many ways superior to the 1941 pamphlet, and it does mention Dowding. On the other hand it falls as short as the earlier one in not doing justice to the two chief victors of the Battle. Not only in the text, but conspicuously in the illustrations. There are full page or half page photographs of Portal, Bradley, Pattinson and Bowhill, of whom only the last had even the remotest role in the Battle; and of Dowding that faintly ridiculous one, with his bowler hat, dark suit and furled umbrella, on the occasion of the second anniversary reunion with eleven of his pilots. And the list of names beneath contains no fewer than eight errors.

vii. An exception was the publication of Lord Ramsay's report on Operation DYNAMO, the account of the naval evacuation of the British and French armies from Dunkirk. Why one and not the other?

viii. On September 20, 1986, *The Times* published a letter from the (now late) son of Lord Dowding in response to a proposal to give belated recognition to his father by the creation of a statue. He wrote:

'I read with great interest and welcome, of course, today's letters from Dr Brian Porter and Air Commodore Chisholm, and have some grounds for hope that a suitable permanent memorial will one day soon be forthcoming. I write to protest mildly against the evident English belief that recognition, sixteen years after death, in some way compensates the individual concerned for the ingratitude shown to him during life. I think that my father, Air Chief Marshal Lord Dowding (1882-1970), would like to have been promoted 'Marshal of the Royal Air Force', and this indeed would have carried concomitant financial advantage. But in the event this considerable public figure was retired on a pension not far exceeding £1,500 pa, and this in days preceding indexation. His later years were clouded by financial insufficiency ... Indeed this country, 140 years previously, had granted the family of Lord Nelson £5,000 pa in perpetuity. This only came to an end in 1951. As a nation we cannot really expect people of the right calibre to come forward for public service if this is the treatment they can expect. Things are better arranged now, I know, but this particular piece of bureaucratic meanness should not go unrecorded and unpublished.'

Long before this letter, others in high places had also expressed their surprise that Dowding had not been so promoted. For example, Derek Amory wrote to Harold Balfour on November 27, 1978: 'As he [Dowding] had been C-in-C while the Fighter Command organisation was built up and the Battle (of all battles) was won, he should surely have been made Marshal of the RAF on retirement.' And Jock Colville, Churchill's Personal Private Secretary during most of the war, wrote on April 16, 1981, also to Harold Balfour: 'I still cannot understand why Dowding was not made a Marshal of the Royal Air Force'. (Both refs. BLFR 1/1 in the Churchill Archives Centre.) It is almost as if both writers were intimating to Balfour that he, as Under-Secretary of State for Air, should have exercised greater influence on Sinclair in the matter to overcome Sinclair's manifest hostility. That Churchill also, when he became Prime Minister again in 1952, failed Dowding in this matter, serves only to reinforce the suspicion of vindictiveness. See pp.150-51, note xv.

CHAPTER 12

Dowding on War

—∿∿—

Strategist and Visionary

Little has been written, here or elsewhere, about Dowding's qualities as a commander. Equally surprising, in view of his notable victory in 1940, little has been written about Dowding in terms of what Clausewitz called 'the conduct of war'.

Tribute has been paid to Dowding's 'genius for organization' in the creation of Fighter Command. This genius has been scrupulously detailed by Hough and Richards in their *Jubilee History*.[i] Tribute has also been paid, by no less a person than Churchill, to Dowding's 'genius in the art of war.' Tribute has been paid in handsome measure, by every perceptive writer who has commented on Dowding's personality, to his luminous integrity, his questioning mind, and his moral courage.

Here we begin by putting the case forward for Dowding as a visionary. In the second part we examine Dowding's dominant strategic idea. And we conclude with a study of Dowding's conduct of the battle in terms of the art of war, under the twofold rubric: 1) The Principles of War, and 2) The Qualities of the Commander. We will thereby arrive at a fuller appreciation of this 'thin inscrutable figure... the prophetic strategist who, as Chief of Fighter Command before the war, shaped the invincible lines of Britain's air defence.'[ii]

I. The Visionary

It is by no means far-fetched to consider Dowding a 'prophetic strategist', his strategical intelligence stemmed from his capacity to see ahead. I have called him a visionary. It will be useful if I define the term as I understand it; a visionary, in the everyday real world of power, politics and history, is a man who knows the past and who sees the significance of events as they take place; who grasps the consequences of those events if nothing is done to counter them; and who sees what must be done in order to halt their fateful evolution.

However, the term 'visionary' carries other connotations, and may, especially in the minds of those who know Dowding well, conjure up the image of the spiritualist, the man who not only believed in the afterlife but who conversed with the spirits of the dead. Dowding was himself well aware of this dichotomy within his personality and did not fail to address it. For example, he wrote: '[Unless] I can give you a frame in which you can see the pictures, the stories which I have to relate, graphic and vivid as they are, may seem so divorced from what we are pleased to consider the Laws of Nature, as to lay me open to the suspicion of being a victim of hallucination or worse.' And: 'I wish to retain my reputation for sanity and common sense... because the effect of my work will suffer if I am considered a wild and woolly visionary. Visionary, yes; but wild and woolly, no.' Dowding uses the term 'visionary' here in the sense of 'spiritualist': one who has visions of the future life and of the spirits who have passed beyond their physical existence to a permanent and ethereal life.

I am sure that Dowding would reject the label of 'dichotomy' and all that is implied by it. I am equally sure that it would be difficult to find any man whose personality was so completely unified as Dowding's; there was no split, no dualism: there was but oneness. I for one do not understand the spiritual dimension of Dowding's mind, and cannot therefore comment, let alone criticize, challenge or condemn.

Dowding himself understood others' scepticism. All belief must be based solely on personal experience: he insisted time and again on this *desideratum*. I quote again from the same book: 'We ... must keep an open mind, and we must not be discouraged in our search for Truth even though our most cherished idols are demolished in the process.' Again: 'Have faith in your innermost convictions: accept the words of no man: let your heart be your guide in truth and sincerity.' Finally: 'No thinking man or woman should accept the beliefs of another uncritically and without examining, to the best of his ability, the evidence on which such beliefs are based.'

In this credo we see, I think, the same man who, as a squadron commander in France in 1916 and as the chief of Fighter Command in 1936-1940, opposed dangerous instructions from higher authority, contested the facile arguments and flawed policies of the Trenchard school, and stood up against all the powers intent on denuding his fighter strength to aid a helpless France.

I will add one further note, one that links his military service, the over-riding theme of his anti-war book *Twelve Legions of Angels*, and his spiritual beliefs and work, in an unbroken chain of unity of thought and action: humanity. He wrote: 'all our work, every communication, and every action arising therefrom is directed towards the giving of help or strength or comfort to others.'

If his spiritual beliefs gave to Dowding the strength he needed to bear the unimaginable stresses that he was subjected to for four months, from July to November of 1940, we must be thankful that, whatever we may think of those beliefs, he was there when his country needed him and he was the only man who could have done what he did.

We now return to 'Dowding the Visionary' in the real and material sense of the term, and discuss his work in four sections: Radar, the Historic Letter, the Turning Point, and the Prophet.

RADAR

The first undoubted manifestation of Dowding's visionary gift of which we are aware took place on February 26th, 1935, at Weedon, a few miles west of Northampton; since September 1st 1930, Dowding had been the Air Member for Supply and

Research. (This position became Air Member for Research and Development on January 14th, 1935.) At night, on the date mentioned, it had been arranged for a Heyford bomber of the Royal Aircraft Establishment, Farnborough, to fly on a regular course between Daventry and Wolverton, back and forth, whilst a team of scientists were 'bouncing' radio waves off it. Their echoes were received, and visually recorded, on a cathode-ray oscillograph. This experimental demonstration was conducted by H.E. Wimperis, the Director of Scientific Research in the Air Ministry. Wimperis had asked his chief, Dowding, to procure funds for the development of his project.

Dowding, self-instructed as he was in scientific matters related to defence, but also heavily committed for funds for the development of the Spitfire and Hurricane at this time, had asked for a practical demonstration so that he could see for himself what he would be requesting funds for.

It is useful to understand the situation of Great Britain in military terms at this time; Britain had for centuries been protected by her Navy and had enjoyed virtual impregnability against invasion. But in 1917 and 1918 all changed overnight when London was bombed by German airships and aircraft, and hundreds of civilians were killed and maimed. The Navy was no longer the defensive shield that it had been for over eight hundred years. Beneath the bombers the Navy was powerless: not only powerless to protect, but itself vulnerable to attack. It was as if the Channel and the North Sea had dried up and ceased to provide an impassable barrier. The ringing words of Shakespeare now rang hollow. No longer was England:

> This happy breed of men, this little world,
> This precious stone set in the silver sea,
> Which serves it in the office of a wall,
> Or as a moat defensive to a house ...

During the twenties and thirties the people became increasingly alarmed by the prospect of indiscriminate attack from the air. Their fears were exacerbated by the production of a film based on the novel of H.G. Wells, *Shape of Things to Come*. A happy consequence of this growing concern was that it forced the hand of the Air Ministry, who established a committee, under the leadership of Professor Henry Tizard, 'to study all ideas which could provide a more effective defence system.' Wimperis had asked Robert Watson Watt whether he had any ideas about the use of death-rays against bombers. In reply Watson Watt suggested, rather, that radio waves might be used to detect approaching aircraft. It was decided to carry out a test. Hence, on that night of February 26th, 1935, Dowding, with a few others, watched the cathode-ray tube with expectant fascination, not unleavened by a healthy scepticism. What he saw was beyond dispute.

The small group of men, gazing into the oscillograph, saw the radiation from Daventry depicted as a straight line. But as the aircraft entered the path of the beam, they saw the line oscillate until when it was most nearly overhead a deviation of over an inch was observed. Without specially designed equipment, without control of wave-length, and without any great transmission power, it had been demonstrated that electromagnetic energy was reflected from an aircraft, and that these reflections could be depicted visually by the cathode-ray apparatus. We can only surmise what went on in Dowding's mind. But the feeble little lights on the screen before him must have been, as it were, an illumination. It was clear to Dowding what must be done, as Wimperis was to write to him a week later:

> We now have, in embryo, a new potent means of detecting the approach of hostile aircraft, one which will be independent of mist, cloud, fog or night-fall, and at the same time be vastly more accurate than present methods in the information provided and in the distances covered.

Already, in his mind's eye, Dowding was envisaging a series of such detecting stations positioned at intervals round the coast of Britain, so that approaching hostile aircraft could be tracked and followed and, if need be, intercepted before reaching their targets. Perhaps he saw much more in the future. What he did know was the historical and immemorial position of Britain as an island. He knew also that on July 24th, 1924, the then Prime Minister, Stanley Baldwin, speaking in the House of Commons, had said:

> It is easy to say, as many people do, that England should isolate herself from Europe, but we have to remember that the history of our insularity has ended, because with the advent of the aeroplane we are no longer an island.

From 1918, with the air raids on London, until this moment, February 26th, 1935, in a field at Weedon, England was in fact 'no longer an island'. But the experiment which Dowding witnessed illuminated the future, and he was heard to murmur: 'We are an island again!'[iii]

THE HISTORIC LETTER

On May 15th – five days after the opening of the Blitzkrieg, the German 'lightning war' against Holland, Belgium and France – Dowding attended a meeting of the Chiefs of Staff presided over by Churchill. The principal item on the agenda was the French appeal for more fighters to be sent to France to oppose the attacks by the Luftwaffe on forward elements of the Allied armies and on their airfields and supply lines. Dowding resisted the appeal, supported though it was by Churchill. In Dowding's view, a certain minimum number of front line squadrons, including all his Spitfire squadrons, had to be kept in England for the defence of the homeland, in the event that the worst should befall. Already, the day before, he had written to the Air Staff to apprise them of the desperateness of the situation:

> The Hurricane tap is now turned full on and you will not be able to resist the pressure[iv] to send Hurricanes to France until I have been bled white and am in no condition to withstand the bombing attack which will inevitably be made on this country as soon as our powers of resistance fall below a level to which we are already perilously close.

At this meeting it appeared to Dowding that he made little headway in overcoming Churchill's loyalty to an old friend in danger and in convincing him both of the seriousness of the drain on Fighter Command's resources and of the ultimate futility of sending more fighters to France. The following day, in an attempt to make his point as forcefully as possible, he composed this letter which he sent directly to Harold Balfour, the Under-Secretary of State for Air. It is reproduced here in full, a letter which can only be called prophetic:

Sir,

1. I have the honour to refer to the very serious calls which have recently been made upon the Home Defence Fighter Units in a attempt to stem the German invasion on the Continent.

2. I hope and believe that our Armies may yet be victorious in France and Belgium, but we have to face the possibility that they may be defeated.

3. In this case I presume that there is no-one who will deny that England should fight on, even though the remainder of the continent of Europe is dominated by the Germans.

4. For this purpose it is necessary to retain some minimum fighter strength in this country and I must request that the Air Council will inform me what they consider this minimum strength to be, in order that I may make my dispositions accordingly.

5. I would remind the Air Council that the last estimate which they made as to the force necessary to defend this country was fifty-two Squadrons, and my strength has now been reduced to the equivalent of thirty-six Squadrons.

6. Once a decision has been reached as to the limit on which the Air Council and the Cabinet are prepared to stake the existence of the country, it should be made clear to the Allied Commanders on the Continent that not a single aeroplane from Fighter Command beyond the limit will be sent across the Channel, no matter how desperate the situation may become.

7. It will, of course, be remembered that the estimate of fifty-two Squadrons was based on the assumption that the attack would come from the eastwards except in so far as the defences might be outflanked in fight. We have now to face the possibility that attacks may come from Spain or even from the North coast of France. The result is that our line is very much extended at the same time as our resources are reduced.

8. I must point out that within the last few days the equivalent of ten Squadrons have been sent to France, that the Hurricane Squadrons remaining in this country are seriously depleted, and that the more Squadrons which are sent to France the higher will be the wastage and the more insistent the demands for reinforcements.

9. I must therefore request that as a matter of paramount urgency the Air Ministry will consider and decide what level of strength is to be left to the Fighter Command for the defences of this country, and will assure me that when this level has been reached, not one fighter will be sent across the

Channel however urgent and insistent the appeals for help may be.

10. I believe that, if an adequate fighter force is kept in this country, if the Fleet remains in being, and if Home Forces are suitably organised to resist invasion, we should be able to carry on the war single-handed for some time, if not indefinitely. But, if the Home Defence Force is drained away in desperate attempts to remedy the situation in France, defeat in France will involve the final, complete and irremediable defeat of this country.[v]

Contrary to Dowding's view of the situation, who is to say whether, at that crucial moment in the history of the world, the tide of battle might not have been turned if every available aircraft in the RAF had been thrown into the fray? Perhaps if the Poles at Warsaw and, yes, the Spanish defenders of Guernica, had had the resources of Fighter Command at their disposal, their cities might not have been destroyed.

There was something to be said for the position of those who argued for sending more help to France. After all, it was only May 16th, and the war was only six days old. But Churchill was a romantic, and at times impossibly quixotic. He allowed ancient loyalties and affections to sway his judgment, and he argued vigorously in the War Cabinet for more fighters for France.

It may seem strange that in these historical and biographical contexts, and in an essay purporting to show Dowding as a visionary, the author, suddenly as it were, switches registers and tries to show that Dowding was also a hard-headed realist. But that is nothing less than the truth. They are, after all, but two facets of the same personality, as I hope to show in the Envoi.

We have already seen that Dowding always insisted on the facts, wanted to see things for himself, would not make do with less than eye-witness accounts of events. To find out what was really going on in France, he sent a scout, carefully selected:

At this bleak juncture, as the French armies were falling back in the face of the German onslaught, Hugh Dowding . . . sent a personal emissary to France to report directly on the worsening situation. . . .The officer assigned to the task was Wing Commander The Duke of Hamilton. . . . Hamilton flew this three-day mission (17-20 May) to the battle area in a tiny Miles Magister, a light, single-engined aircraft with a top speed which would have compared unfavourably with a modern small motor car...The report which Hamilton brought back convinced the C-in-C that, with the French crumbling, no further fighter squadrons should in any circumstances be sent to France.[vi]

The sequence of dates will be noted:

May 15 - Dowding's appearance before the War Cabinet;

May 16 - Dowding's letter;

May 17-20 - Dowding sends an emissary to France.

Most writers have claimed that Dowding's decisive intervention in the War Cabinet deliberations was on May 15th. If that were so, what was the purpose of his sending Hamilton to France to find out what the situation was? No, Dowding had not convinced the Cabinet, and especially he had not convinced Churchill. What he wrote in his *Despatch* after the Battle – 'I was responsible for the Air Defence of Great Britain, and I saw my resources slipping away like sand in an hour-glass. The pressure for more and more assistance to France was relentless and inexorable' – referred to the desperate days in late May. Dowding had not given up the fight to save his irreplaceable resources before they were all squandered in what he saw as a futile battle. His decisive intervention occurred on June 3rd, which was also the last full day of the evacuation from Dunkirk, when the French were still fighting and pleading for help.[vii]

Balfour testifies in his autobiography that 'Dowding had insisted on personal intervention with the War Cabinet to stop any further of his meagre force leaving these shores to prop up the failing French'; and 'he came to my room to appeal as an old friend that I should use any influence I had with my Air Council colleagues to this end.' There is no need to repeat the events of that tension-filled encounter in the War Cabinet meeting, when Dowding, with his graph of losses thrust before Churchill's eyes and the sharp crack of his pencil as he laid it dramatically (amid the tense, foreboding silence) on the table beside the graph, won the day.[viii]

THE TURNING POINT

Between August 15 and September 6, Fighter Command's aerodromes and, especially, the important bases with sector control stations, came under increasingly heavy assault by the Luftwaffe. The Germans did not know how serious their attacks were, since they knew nothing of the crucial function of these stations.

They knew about radar for they had operational radar stations themselvesv – after all, their radar had detected the RAF's bomber attacks on units of the German Fleet in September 1939 early enough to 'scramble' their fighters with disastrous results for the RAF's bombers. But their intelligence was so weak that they had little inkling of the Dowding system of radar control of the fighter squadrons. The Luftwaffe had earlier bombed the very visible radar receiving towers on the South coast. They had put a few out of action. But they had not succeeded in destroying any of the towers; and nearly all the radar stations which had been knocked out were back in action within hours, either through repair or by replacement by emergency mobile equipment.

The airfields attacked by the Luftwaffe were targeted with the twofold aim of destroying and damaging as many fighters as possible on the ground, and of inflicting the maximum damage on the infra-structure of Fighter Command's forward bases – hangars, with their repair and servicing facilities; fuel storage tanks; communications lines; ammunition dumps and administrative centres. If they had concentrated their attacks on the sector control stations, and succeeded in putting them all out of action within the space of a week or so, Park's greatest fear would have been realised and he would have been left controlling 'nothing but his desk.'

Even so the German bomber attacks inflicted more and more damage on 11 Group's important airfields, until, on September 6th, in Dowding's eyes, the situation was verging on the desperate. The front line defensive forces of Fighter Command were reeling, and the final attacks, if delivered within the next few days with sufficient concentration, seemed certain to carry the decisive blows which would – as it was thought at the time – prepare the ground for airborne invasion in the south-east. They would at the same time force Dowding to set in motion his emergency plan, which entailed the withdrawal of all 11 Group's squadrons to stations north of the Thames, and beyond the effective range of the Messerschmitt 109 escort fighters.

In the early evening of Saturday, September 7th, Dowding was in Fighter Command Headquarters Operations Room, watching with intense concentration the status of developing raids, indicated by the build-up of enemy formations over Northern France, as they were plotted on the table beneath him. The fate of England hung in the balance; the enemy formations increased, gained height, assembled – and began their relentless progression across the Channel. But, as Dowding watched, it became clear that there was something different about this raid. In previous raids the enemy formations had come in at different heights; and they had split up, and headed in different directions, making it difficult for the defenders to know where the main attack was destined for, and hence where, and in what strength, to direct the defence efforts. Now they came on, steadily, in a single stream, without varying their course, without a feint or diversion, all seemingly headed for a single objective.

At Fighter Command HQ, Dowding watched, and wondered. Even before this huge, single bomber force had begun to reach the outskirts of London, he was no longer in doubt: the target was London. The Luftwaffe had let up from its concentrated assault on the RAF's fighter squadrons and their installations. The German High Command calculated that nothing would draw up the RAF's few remaining fighters, to their intended destruction, so surely as the bombardment of England's capital city. With the RAF's defensive forces thus destroyed, southern England lay exposed, and open to invasion. This shift in tactics, an abandonment of the doctrine of maintenance of the aim, was a fatal miscalculation. It was a blessed reprieve for Fighter Command's aerodromes. London could absorb all the bombing the Luftwaffe launched against the sprawling agglomeration.

Dowding understood this, and the implications for the immediate and the distant future of this German miscalculation. If the Luftwaffe were only to persist in its attacks on London for a week, most of the damage done to his fighter installations could be made good and the personnel of the damaged stations would get a rest. As for the future, Dowding had seen eye to eye with Churchill when he had proclaimed on June 18th: 'Hitler knows that he will have to break us in this Island or lose the war.' Dowding knew, throughout the Battle, how close they were to losing and was now the first to appreciate this new situation as it unfolded. His mind went back to a comparable phase in the First World War, to an early battle which became a reprieve and a deliverance, and he summed it up, this assault against London, in the prescient words: 'It is the Battle of the Marne again!'[ix]

THE PROPHET

Anecdotes and sketches of a personal nature which might throw an unexpected light on his personality, as opposed to the stern, dour, 'stuffy' figure which legend has passed down to us, are all too infrequent.[x] It was therefore with a sense of serendipity that we came across the following description of an incident recorded by Sir Maurice Dean, who must have witnessed it himself. His description provides a fitting conclusion to this section:

> We have left to last an account of Dowding's greatest service. He was always a modest man. For all his professional skills, his ability to achieve a political judgement was inconspicuous. In fact, despite everything, it fell to him to arrive at such a judgement. In the dark days of 1940 he decided that France would collapse, that our destiny depended on the survival of Fighter Command, and that if Fighter Command survived, Britain would survive. Many arguments could have been adduced against such a view. All the same, it was Dowding's view. Around the time of the fall of France he walked into the office of the Head of the Air Staff Secretariat in Whitehall and said: 'Now we cannot lose'. His face was shining. His words and demeanour would have become a major prophet... that for practical purposes was what he was at that moment.[xi]

II. The Strategist

Dowding's vision was preeminently strategic. Yet let this reservation be added: he was pre-eminently a defensive strategist. He had no ideas, and he advanced no ideas, about how the war was to be won.[xi] On the other hand, no one in Britain had the slightest idea either, given the aftermath of the débâcle of France and the deliverance of Dunkirk. One of the final ironies of the saga we have recounted is that the German Air Force came within a hair's breadth of realizing the Trenchard doctrine of air power, whilst Trenchard's own air arm was impotent to carry the lesson to the enemy.

Even before Dowding became the first AOC-in-C of the Fighter Command in 1936, while still at the Air Ministry, he foresaw that the new Bomber Command, formed at the same time, would not be able to realize its *raison d'être* in the foreseeable future. And, though not knowing the strength of the German air force, he welcomed the opportunity to head this new defensive arm of the Air Force, and set about creating a force whose aim was essentially to interdict the success of the Trenchard strategy.

From the beginning it was a fight against time. By 1939 the basic structure of Fighter Command was in place and operating with relative efficiency. When he appointed his Senior Air Staff Officer, Keith Park, to head 11 Group he knew that they would be acting as a team: that Park's tactical handling of his resources would accord with Dowding's over-all strategic aim of conserving his forces. That principle can be summed up as 'conserving one's force in being.' It is the expression used by Dowding in his prophetic letter to the government of May 16th: 'if the Fleet remains in being'. Had Dowding read his naval history? That very expression is the one used by Lord Torrington in his defence, at his court-martial, for his loss to the French at the Battle of Beachy Head in 1689. Arthur Herman sums it up thus:

> He would claim that he had avoided an all-or-nothing battle at Beachy Head in order to make sure the fleet remained intact. 'Whilst we had a fleet in being,'

he said, he was sure 'they [the French] would not make the attempt' to invade England. Torrington was acquitted and a new concept in naval strategy was born, that of a 'fleet in being' whose simple existence would be enough to deter an opponent from acting offensively. It would become a hallmark of the British navy for more than two hundred years, and the justification for maintaining a large and powerful battle fleet in peacetime as well as at war.[xii]

This aim had been the guiding principle of the Royal Navy from the days of Henry VIII.

Dowding's pre-eminent achievement, and his great gift to civilization, was to conserve the home force in being, and thus to prevent the losing of the war at the outset. He never lost sight of this principle, and he followed and preached it with a single-minded tenacity of purpose. This was the vision which oversaw the building of Fighter Command's defensive organization and structure; which obliged him to oppose the fatal weakening of his fighter resources for France; and which inspired his conduct of the battle itself.

III. Dowding and the Principles of War

The Battle of Britain was a battle unique in the history of war. It was, as has often been remarked, exclusively an aerial battle, fought out by two air forces while navies and armies looked on idly, powerless to intervene and affect the outcome. It was, moreover, as most battles are, an aggressive action on the one side, countered by defensive forces on the other.

The air was a new medium in war; one wonders whether the air had anything to learn from past wars. T.E. Lawrence, writing to his biographer, Liddell Hart, in June 1933, said: 'With 2,000 years of examples behind us we have no excuse, when fighting, for not fighting well.' But Lawrence fought a guerilla war on the ground. Could he have had the air in mind as well? Just six months later he was writing to the same military historian: 'I think the general opinion is that they have greatly improved the RAF ship-bombing practice. In a few years aircraft will deal infallibly with ships.'[xiii]

Only in four previous wars had the air played a role of any significance: in the First World War, in the Italian aggression against Abyssinia, in the Japanese invasion of China, and in the Spanish Civil War. In the Abyssinian, Chinese and Spanish conflicts, the air action, while both strategic and tactical in its operations, was totally or largely unopposed by the defenders. In the First World War the air played no strategic role as the aircraft were of primitive design and performance, and served a limited purpose in support of the land and sea forces. When air battles took place – and there were many, involving large numbers of aircraft – they had no bearing on the decisive events taking place below.

The Battle of Britain was a very different conflict. It was a strategic action in the strictest sense of the term. For our purposes, we accept the definition of strategy elaborated by Clausewitz when he wrote: 'According to our classification . . . tactics is the theory of the use of military forces in combat. Strategy is the theory of the use of combats for the object of the war.' Or, in our case, of the Battle. He enlarged on this when he described 'the totally different activities . . . of the formation and the conduct of these single combats in themselves, and the combination of them with one another. The first is called tactics, the other strategy.' This distinction is important, for, as we have seen, Dowding delegated to his Group commanders the authority for day-to-day and hour-to-hour decisions within the parameters of his policy, whereas he retained in his own hands complete strategic control.

Clausewitz makes a further distinction between 'preparations for war' and 'the War itself'. Our study here is concerned solely with 'the War itself'. The 'preparations for War' – that is the creation of Fighter Command from the ground up– has been discussed in Chapters one - three, to the extent relevant to this narrative.

Strategically, the Battle of Britain meant in all likelihood for the defenders either total defeat or survival: for the aggressor sought to destroy the enemy's defensive forces and thereby prepare the ground for the launching of invasion forces. Any attempted invasion would be considered and planned for by the German High Command subject only to the destruction of the defenders.[xiv]

The defenders had, according to some writers, little to guide them by way of past lessons of war. A.J.P. Taylor, for example, in his introduction to Len Deighton's book on the Battle, writes: 'The key to the story is that the air commanders before the Second World War had very little experience to draw on.' Is that true? In any event is 'previous experience' the only factor? What of this opinion? Having stated the 'five fundamental factors' in war, Sun Tzu concludes: 'I will be able to forecast which side will be victorious and which defeated.' Is it conceivable that an air force commander in the twentieth century AD could benefit from a study of a Chinese genius of war of 500 BC?[xv]

Let us first consider whether a contemporary air commander could gain any help from a study of previous aerial actions. In Abyssinia, the Italian bombing of the defenceless and naked people induced panic, and a swift surrender. In Spain, the bombing of undefended towns, especially of Guernica (1937), elicited a general outrage and horror, and revived in people's minds the scenes of carnage depicted in H.G. Wells' film. The German bombing of Warsaw, which accelerated that unhappy country's surrender, brought much closer to home the potential devastation promised by the Douhet doctrine. (When it came to London's turn in 1940, the near panic reaction it provoked in some government circles, when faced with uncertainty over the British people's ability to 'take it', is equally understandable.)

It would be surprising if Dowding, along with other forward-looking airmen, scientists and politicians, was not stimulated by those events to accelerate his search for an effective defence.

What of fighter operations in Spain? The most effective action was that taken by formations of Messerschmitt 109s of the German Air Force. It was there that Werner Molders developed the basic finger-four formation: two Rotten of two fighters each comprising a Schwarm. The Royal Air Force continued to deploy its fighters in squadrons of twelve fighters, made up of four flights of three throughout 1940. A few squadrons led by innovative leaders adopted the German practice independently in late 1940, but this method did not come into general use until 1941. No one in the Air

Ministry, or Fighter Command for that matter, was apparently paying attention.

We have few means of knowing to what extent Dowding made a study of the art of war.[xvi] Yet this whole question: whether or not Dowding had studied war, as other commanders had studied, and were to study, war, is of considerable interest. It could be shown that many great commanders of the past had not studied war, in the sense that they had read widely on what others had written about it.[xvii] But they assuredly studied it in the important, and vital, sense that they devoted much thought to the military situation in which they found themselves, and to the battles or engagements to which they were sure they would be committed. And it is to their greater credit that they succeeded without having had predecessors to learn from. Dowding was pre-eminently one of them. That Dowding thought about war constantly, and thought about the role of Fighter Command in a war he was preparing it for, can be deduced from what he wrote and how he conducted the battle.

In May 1937, as we have shown, he gave the same lecture, slightly modified, to the RAF Staff College and to the Imperial College of Defence. In it he outlined Fighter Command's role, and his own, in the event of war. Among other things he stated that one of his major preoccupations was the defence of London as the seat of Government. But he had an open mind, and learnt from experience. Less than four years later he would be welcoming the Luftwaffe's diversion of its attacks away from his sector airfields onto London. He knew that a London destroyed would have no military bearing on the outcome of the war provided that Fighter Command remained undefeated.

Whilst, as we have insisted, Dowding and Fighter Command faced a totally new situation in war, it is true, and demonstrably so, that certain principles apply to all war; and that every great commander is possessed of certain essential qualities. These principles and qualities, which have been culled from some of the most illustrious writers on war of the past, form the subject of the following section, in the belief that they are fully applicable to the Battle of Britain and to the Commander of Fighter Command. Whether or not Dowding had read Napoleon, his strategic and tactical ideas and plans bear out the wisdom of this advice: 'A plan of campaign should anticipate everything an enemy can do, and contain within itself the means of thwarting him. Plans of campaign may be indefinitely modified according to the circumstances, the genius of the commander, the quality of the troops, and the topography of the theatre of war.'

In the light of these principles, it would be impossible not to subscribe to this pronouncement by General Burnod, the editor of Napoleon's Military Maxims: 'The art of war is susceptible [to] being considered under two titles: the one, which rests entirely on the knowledge and genius of the commander; the other, on matters of detail. The first is the same for all time, for all peoples, whatever the arms with which they fight. From this it follows that the same principles have directed the great captains of all centuries. The matters of detail, on the contrary, are subject to the influence of time, to the spirit of the people and the character of armaments.' General Burnod, whether he had read Sun Tzu or not, never knew how wise and prescient was this statement.

194

PRINCIPLES OF WAR

The major principles of war that form the substance of this study, as they apply to the Battle of Britain, are the following: 1) Security of the base; 2) Unity of Command; 3) Maintenance of the Aim; 4) Intelligence; 5) Surprise; 6) Reserves; and 7) Morale.

1. Security of the Base

The term 'security of the base' can encompass anything from a single individual to a whole nation. At Hastings the battle was essentially lost when Harold was killed, because of the custom of feudal allegiance. At Waterloo the killing of Napoleon, if it had happened, would have removed the directing intelligence from the scene and doubtless induced a serious demoralization in the French forces. On the other hand the death of Nelson at Trafalgar did not affect the outcome of the battle, for, as one admiring French admiral said: 'All the English captains were Nelsons.'

In the Battle of Britain the stakes were considerably higher as the base was the whole of the British Isles. Indeed, from time immemorial this had been the compass of the term. And from time immemorial the security of England, or of Britain, had been the especial concern and charge of the Royal Navy. So it was that the Navy, Britain's 'wooden wall', had come to be regarded by Britons with a unique admiration and affection. This role that the Navy played in Britain's history and destiny was ingrained in the hearts and minds of everyone. It has been expressed well by Sir Edward Creasy:

> In Raleigh's great work on the 'History of the World', he takes occasion ... to give his reasonings on the proper policy of England when menaced with invasion. Without doubt, we have there the substance of the advice which he gave to Elizabeth's council; and the remarks of such a man on such a subject, have a general and enduring interest, beyond the immediate peril which called them forth. Raleigh says: 'Surely I hold that the best way is to keep our enemies from treading upon our ground: wherein if we fail, then must we seek to make him wish that he had stayed at his own home... But making the question general, the positive, whether England, without the help of her fleet, be able to debar an enemy from landing; I hold that it is unable to do; and therefore I think it most dangerous to make the adventure. For the encouragement of a first victory to an enemy, and the discouragement of being beaten, to the invaded, may draw after it a most perilous consequence.[xviii]

By the early 1930s it had become clear to some few students of war that the British Fleet would soon no longer be able to guarantee Britain's security alone, in the face of the rise of air power; and in fact that became the whole crux of the Battle of Britain. But most people had a fateful, and possibly fatal, misunderstanding of air power. Among them was Lord Trenchard. The Royal Air Force had been formed from the amalgamation of the Royal Flying Corps and the Royal Naval Air Service. It is possibly a misfortune that about eighty-five percent of the officer corps that comprised the new Royal Air Force were RFC men, that is to say, soldiers. The soldier's mind – and this is certainly true of Trenchard and his disciples – is bent on attack and aggression; whereas the Navy mind, as we have seen, thinks first and foremost of defence and the security of the realm, before it takes upon itself the defence of its far-flung possessions.

This security is the first essential consideration, without which nothing can be planned. Indeed, it is true of all military planning, whether concerned with attack or defence. Dowding's sole and exclusive responsibility was the air defence of the United Kingdom. This responsibility exercised his mind, engaged his powers, and directed his energies for the full four-and-a-half years he was the Commander-in-Chief of Fighter Command. His remit was local and limited; yet his resources were huge; and he perceived his task with a global vision. For if he wavered or failed, all was lost. He realized that the Air Force could not alone prevent invasion, and that the security of the base could be realized only by a partnership of the Navy and the Air Force.

This over-riding principle did not seem to enter into the policies, estimates and calculations of the Air Staff during the 1930s, when they persisted in giving priority to the production of bombers – of obsolete bombers at that – well into 1938, and thereby risked losing the war before having the opportunity to strike offensively.[xix]

2. Unity of Command

All the great generals, commentators and historians of war are agreed on this principle, from Sun Tzu to Shaka-Zulu, to Napoleon and beyond, to Eisenhower in the Second World War. Sun Tzu wrote : 'He whose generals are able and not interfered with by the sovereign will be victorious.' To this principle his commentator glossed: 'Therefore Master Wang said: "To make appointments is the province of the sovereign; to decide on battle, that of the general".'[xx]

Napoleon gave the same advice, albeit in very different form. Fuller quotes Napoleon as insisting repeatedly in his correspondence, on this paradoxical axiom: '*Un mauvais général vaut mieux que deux bons.*'(One bad general is worth more than two good ones.)[xxi] Fuller explains this principle as being the 'fulcrum of all principles'. The implications are obvious. But there is a malign or arrogant spirit inherent in some people who, finding themselves in a position of higher authority than that of commander they have themselves appointed, cannot resist the temptation to oversee, to direct, and even to meddle. The principle states that a Sovereign appoints a general to command his army. In order to command an army, the general is endowed with plenary powers; no general appointed to a command with strings attached would accept the command for one moment. He would regard such an appointment as unworthy of his time.

Dowding understood this principle and acted on it. He was adamant in his repeated insistence to both Sinclair and Newall that if they did not like what he was doing, they should get rid of him. He applied this principle to his group commanders to whom he delegated certain limited authority: he did not vary from it, and he did not interfere. However the Air Staff did not understand this principle. Indeed, it is likely that they had never heard of it, so little had anyone in the Air Ministry studied the principles governing the waging of war. Hence, inferior people set in authority over commanders whom they looked down upon (for the simple reason that they were 'higher' on the 'organization chart') fell prey to the base impulse to 'lord it over' officers who were in every way superior to them.

The violation of this principle is part of the story of the Battle of Britain and the removal of its victors. The Air Staff, being as they were officers imbued with the 'bomber' spirit, could not resist the temptation to repeatedly interfere in the operations and methods of Fighter Command. Oh, yes, the Air Ministry represented all the recommendations and advice and even instructions it gave to Fighter Command as 'cooperation' and 'helpfulness', whereas frequently it was more ignorant meddling than anything else. If the Air Staff had been truly keen to cooperate, they would have telephoned Fighter Command every day, as Beaverbrook telephoned both Dowding and Park every day, to ask what they could do to help. The Air Staff did nothing of the sort.

The record of interference by Staff officers, and by government leaders who rate themselves as military experts – and here, sadly, we count both Churchill and Hitler – in the conduct of war is a chapter inscribed in the annals of human stupidity or quixotism or vanity. The Norway venture 'ordered' by Churchill was a costly folly. In the Mediterranean theatre, North Africa would have been cleared of the enemy in 1940 if Churchill had not ordered Wavell's troops to Greece in a disastrous attempt to shore up the Greek forces against the Italian and German invaders. The direct consequence was the loss of Greece, and then of Crete, and two unnecessary years of war and bloodshed in North Africa against Rommel's Afrika Korps, which would otherwise not have been able to effect a landing in North Africa.

There are military situations where a 'wider strategic view' is required to establish priorities, and where help is urgently called for. There is no more telling, and tragic, instance of failure by the British Government in this respect than the loss of Malaya and Singapore, the gravest defeat suffered by British arms in their thousand-year history. It was a disaster not only militarily, but for its ineffaceable political and economic ramifications. The causes of the defeat in this instance were many and varied – arrogance, incompetence, ignorance, racism, lack of cooperation between local civil and military authorities, compromise to accommodate Allied differences. For once the military strategists in London had it right : the defence of Singapore depended on the defence of Malaya and the two were inseparably linked. The plan was called 'Operation MATADOR', and involved the landing of troops in Siam to guard the northern route into Malaya. Trenchard had early lost the argument to have an adequate air force in Malaya equipped with torpedo-bombers.

In the autumn of 1940 Air Chief Marshal Sir Robert Brooke-Popham was recalled from retirement at the age of sixty-one and appointed Commander-in-Chief Far East of the air and land forces. His appointment specified that his task was to unify his ground and air forces, since the army needed air support, and the air bases needed defence on the ground. (The Navy went their own way and as a result lost two capital ships to Japanese bombers.)

Brooke-Popham was complacent, and not up-to-date in air force matters. In one despatch to the Air Ministry detailing the situation he wrote, : 'Let England have the super-Spitfires... Buffaloes are quite good enough for Malaya.' But Brooke-Popham was soon to change his mind. No sooner had he suffered his early reverses from the Japanese attacks than he sent an urgent request to London for large air reinforcements, including long-range bombers. 'One of the early responses he received from an uncomprehending Whitehall was the priceless advice, "All war experience shows the uselessness and wastefulness of attempting to gain air superiority by bombing aerodromes at long range." This is precisely what the Japanese had just tried with exemplary results!' It was also, let it be added, at the very core of the Air Ministry's strategic doctrine! And it was a result that the German Air Force nearly accomplished in the Battle of Britain.

Whether or not this advice was a true reflection of the Air Ministry views at the time is difficult to say. The fact of the matter is that in mid-1941 both the North African theatre and the Russians were clamouring for supplies. The War Cabinet appreciated the strategic need of Malaya as a greater priority than the Soviet Union's. But Churchill bore down on his colleagues and they gave in to this Churchill who hated communism and who loved the Empire. The Hurricanes and the tanks that were sent to Russia for one month might well have saved Malaya. At a very late date London approved MATADOR – but left it up to the commander on the spot whether and when to implement it: in a word, the decision to declare war on Japan was the local commander's to make!

The Japanese launched their invasion of Malaya on December 8, 1941. At this crucial time, Brooke-Popham was relieved by Lt. General A.E. Percival, but remained for several weeks – apparently to give advice. At the same time, to further muddy the waters, General Sir Archibald Wavell, whose General O'Connor had routed the Italians in North Africa, was sent in as Supreme Commander South-East Asia. Unity of Command was shattered, if it ever existed. As one historian noted: 'The fact that Brooke-Popham was not a Supreme Commander meant that he was simply an addition to an already cumbersome command structure.' If he had been, would it have made any difference? We will quote Percival's biographer to provide a summing-up of sorts:

> There was not merely delay; there seems to have been muddle. As late as 10.40am on 8 December Percival's headquarters was still being warned by Brooke-Popham's that 'We may still have to do MATADOR. But Brooke-Popham was not the sole decision-maker: the responsibility was shared with [Admiral] Phillips. This must have made it even more difficult for Percival's advice to have carried the day.[xxii]

Norway, Greece, North Africa, even the Battle of the Atlantic, and above all Singapore: these set-backs and disasters can be laid directly and personally at the door of Churchill, who had appointed himself Minister of Defence. Had the Chiefs of Staff learnt nothing from Dowding's intervention with the War Cabinet on June 3rd? Did they not know when Churchill's military ideas were incapable of success? Did they not have a sure grasp of strategic realities? Did they, above all, not have the moral courage and the conviction to confront Churchill and to face him down over those impossible ventures?[xxiii]

3. Maintenance of the Aim

We have seen that the major factor in the loss of the battle by the Germans was their failure to maintain their strategic aim. That aim was the destruction of Fighter Command. Once Britain's fighter force was destroyed, nothing could prevent the success of the German Air Force from either bombing or starving Britain into submission, or from carrying out an airborne invasion. It was the decision to switch the attacks from Fighter Command's airfields to London, in the mistaken idea that, by forcing the RAF's fighters into the air to defend the capital they would destroy what remained of them, that doomed the offensive effort.

Dowding made no such error. His every thought and deed were centred on the over-riding imperative of preserving the strength of his combat forces. Park and Dowding thought and acted as one, the daily and hourly tactical operations stemmed like manifold branches from one great central strategic trunk. The trunk remained firm, constant, and inflexible. The branches were designed freely to move, waver, change, like the tentacles of an octopus, in search of its prey. In an extremity, even the trunk could be moved, to a location farther from danger, with its branches moving intact with it.

The entire system comprised an intricately meshed organization of brain, eyes and arms. The brain, at Fighter Command Headquarters, was invulnerable. The arms were the fighter squadrons and their pilots, who were equally safe from annihilation, when they were scattered throughout the realm, and while some were in the air and some were on the ground. It was only the eyes, the radar eyes, that ensured that the other two components survived to perform their tasks.

4. Intelligence

Intelligence has two branches, an active and a passive: the one seeks to acquire information of the enemy's plans and intentions, as well as to learn the effectiveness of one's counter-intelligence; the other takes measures to prevent the enemy from learning yours. The side which neglects or fails in either branch is the more likely to lose the war.

The case can be put even more bluntly: 'In the great majority of cases, defeat can usually be traced to a lack of knowledge of the enemy. Whether from over-confidence, ignorance, gullibility or .. a failure to comprehend the facts, military defeat is almost invariably associated with an intelligence defeat.'

The German Air Force possessed very scanty and imperfect intelligence of Fighter Command's infrastructure and resources in 1940. They were even ignorant of their enemy's radar system of aircraft location and reporting, and although they took frequent aerial photographs of the Royal Air Force's stations and airfields, they failed to interpret the information in their hands.

The RAF, for its part, did not have precise strategic intelligence of the German capabilities. The assault on Britain which began in July 1940 was an impromptu affair; the chaos following the French military defeat militated against the setting up of an espionage network; and photographic reconnaissance of the German airfields proved woefully inadequate.[xxiv] Moreover, the breaking of the German High Command code, known as Enigma, came too late to be of use. On the other hand, there were two sources of information of priceless value, the one of a strategic, the other of a tactical nature.[xxv]

The strategic information was to be deduced simply from the time of year. The French surrender occurred at the end of June. German preparations for an invasion would have to be completed by early or mid-September at the latest before autumn weather prevented the supplying of the invasion forces across the Channel. If the expected preliminary attacks could be met successfully for three months by the scrupulous husbandry of existing resources, Fighter Command – and hence Great Britain – would survive and be able to build up her strength during the ensuing six months and so confidently face the heavier, renewed assaults in the spring of 1941.

By far the most continuous and reliable source of intelligence for the defence was that supplied by the British radar location and reporting system. The information received, after filtering at Fighter Command Headquarters, was passed to the Groups, who in turn transmitted to each Sector Station what was relevant to their regions. The Sectors, finally, acted on the information received and 'scrambled' the number of fighters available to meet the incoming raiders. Had it not been for this radar early warning system, the RAF would have had only two recourses: i) to mount permanent standing fighter patrols; or ii) to 'scramble' interceptors only when raiders were sighted visually or heard overhead. The fatal defects of these alternatives were that i) the RAF disposed of inadequate resources for this scale of operations, and ii) the attempt to intercept at the last moment would have invited destruction by the escorting enemy fighters as the defenders climbed towards the higher enemy.

As the Battle unfolded throughout July, August and September, 11 Group sent to Command HQ a steady stream of reports of the enemy raids, their changing tactics, and the Group's counter-tactics. These reports permitted an evaluation of the enemy's apparent aims. Dowding and Park did not waver: together they out-thought and out-fought the enemy.

5. Surprise

To take the enemy by surprise is one of the oldest stratagems of war, and one of the most coveted by military commanders to spring on the enemy. It is a measure advocated by all writers on war, from Sun Tzu to the Doctor Strangeloves of the nuclear age. Surprise is, however, in its essence an admirable enterprise, when successful, as a strategic manoeuvre. It is of limited tactical value – and in tactics its usefulness is most evident in defence.

When surprise is accompanied by a powerful offensive thrust launched in the right place, the effect produced on the mind of the defenders can be catatonic, as General Guderian demonstrated: in May 1940 his tank columns broke the French defenders by thrusting through the Ardennes Forest, and achieved a success far more decisive than even the German general had expected. The Battle of Britain, being a defensive battle – albeit one characterized by aggressive rather than a merely passive defence – presented no opportunity for strategic surprise. It was therefore on the tactical level, in the actual interception of enemy attackers, that the element of surprise was feasible. And one manner in which the enemy might most readily be surprised was to be 'bounced' from above.

The intent is full of merit, and the defenders were right to attempt this tactical surprise whenever they could. Its success was confirmed by no less an authority than Adolf Galland, who wrote that they, the attackers, were repeatedly bewildered by the sudden, and unexpected, appearance of defending fighters. There could be no greater tribute to the success of the tactics of Park's 11 Group.

When carried out under intelligent leadership, tactical surprise will result in appreciably greater losses by the enemy attackers. However, an equally important impact – one which did not enter into the calculations of the 12 Group enthusiasts and which 11 and 10 Groups were not able to realize for various technical reasons – would have been inflicted on the enemy morale. It is not difficult to imagine the state of mind of the hostile aircrews if experience led them to expect to be, seven or eight times out of ten, at a tactical disadvantage when they crossed into enemy territory.

6. Reserves

In war the provision and deployment of reserve forces are an indispensable component of fighting. Churchill was rightly obsessed with them. We will give two examples. In May 1940, after the Germans had broken through the Allied lines and threatened Paris, he flew to France to confer with the Prime Minister. In discussing the critical military situation he demanded to know where was the reserve (*masse de manoeuvre*). Came the devastating reply: 'There is no *masse de manoeuvre!*'

Later that summer, on September 15, Churchill was visiting 11 Group HQ, as we have seen. When all their squadrons had been scrambled he turned to Park and asked: 'What reserves do you have?' Park replied: 'There are none.'

In the first instance we are talking about a strategic reserve; in the second it is a case of a tactical reserve. If Park needed reinforcements to buttress his defences in a specific engagement he called on the resources of his neighbours, 10 and 12 Groups, for support. Churchill was to learn soon enough that Park was not at the end of his tether.

We have had occasion to point out that Fighter Command had divided the United Kingdom into four geographical regions, and that for the purposes of its defence, each region was entrusted to a Group organization. So it was that each Group, in the event of the destruction or exhaustion of the forces of one Group, became, in a very real sense, a strategic reserve. The defensive functions of the incapacitated Group were supplied by components made available by the other Groups. It was largely this interdependence of the Groups, and the moving around of the squadrons from Group to Group, and the intimate relationship between strategy and tactics as integral components of the Dowding System, which later so impressed Churchill that he extolled the Commander's 'genius in the art of war.'

7. Morale

The morale of a fighting force is so vast and complex a matter that it can only be touched upon in some of its salient aspects. To discuss it thoroughly, it would be necessary to study not only the individuals who fought the Battle, and their ground crews, but also the spirit of leadership filtering down from the Command: the national feeling among the people at the time, and, above all, the moral qualities of the commander.

Let us, at the outset, define morale. We perceive it to be the fighting spirit, the will to do battle and to win, sustained by a confidence in one's superiority to the enemy shared totally by one's comrades, and by a singleness of purpose felt intensely and intuitively rather than arrived at by analysis. Morale is a moral force with roots drawing sustenance from the deepest regions of the emotive soil.

A battle pilot experiences only a narrow field of conflict, and cannot know the larger picture, or even where in it his piece of the action fits. On the other hand, he is keenly sensible of the moral support and encouragement flooding in like a wave to encompass him and the whole Air Force from an unseen and unheard source. What could be the source of that tide of sympathy and benevolence? When the French army and government surrendered, and Britain found herself alone, without allies, to face the coming storm, the British people let out a collective sigh of relief, as if disencumbered of a great burden. Overnight the people found themselves blessed not only with a rare freedom of action, but with a stark simplicity of action. They had but one thing to do, and that one thing was a matter of life and death which concentrated their minds and energies into a unified spiritual force. The people felt as one: its power and influence were almost palpable, and imbued the people with a conviction of invincibility. This force communicated itself to the pilots; and they in their turn, by their exploits recounted hourly and daily to the people, fuelled their admiration and enthusiasm.

The unqualified support of the people was one thing, but it was not enough in itself. It would have availed nothing had the commander not radiated that power of example and decision which is the hallmark of leadership at its highest. By way of introducing our next section, dealing with the qualities of Dowding as a war commander, we quote the accolade of one of his pilots:

> Dowding's qualities of leadership produced high morale throughout Fighter Command, which, in my view was the most important single factor in the winning of the Battle of Britain.

Five years later the same author penned this greater tribute:

> Few men in our long history have shouldered such a burden, and Dowding was one of the great commanders of all time. During the contest the strands of leadership in Fighter Command flowed down from the Commander-in-Chief

through the simple chain of command – groups, stations and squadrons – to a thousand fighter pilots and their ground crews, and produced that priceless pearl, high morale, which made men bigger than their normal selves.[xxvi]

THE COMMANDER

A purely defensive battle, even though fought with the maximum freedom of action and aggressiveness, cannot fail to induce in the Commander the possibility of defeat. In Britain's case, in 1940, the consequences were so grave that possibility constrained the Commander to ponder the measures necessary, if not to win the battle, at least not to lose it; and to weigh solemnly the role to be played in it by his own conduct.[xxvii] Dowding must know, down to the last nut and bolt, the extent and the limits of his resources; he will keep a close eye on them daily, and constantly assess gains and losses.[xxviii]

The corollaries of these requirements are that, at one and the same time, Dowding pays meticulous attention to detail and has a firm grasp of the overall situation. That these essentials call for an almost limitless capacity for unremitting work goes without saying.

> The first principle of a general-in-chief is to calculate what he must do, to see if he has the means to surmount the obstacles with which the enemy can oppose him and, when he has made his decision, to do everything to overcome them. (Napoleon)

In order to carry out his campaign, the commander depends greatly on his staffs and subordinates for their reliability and skills in the performance of their duties; but in many cases, where he is faced with unknown factors, the Commander will have no other recourse than to find out or verify for himself what he needs to know. The Commander also has a clear understanding of the intimate relationship between his material resources and his human resources. He neglects no measure, he misses no chance, he overlooks no opportunity: to weed out incompetents; to promote solely on the basis of merit; to encourage improvement; to foster enterprise and inventiveness. Above all, he harbours an unfailing concern for his people, especially for those who face danger, and seeks ways to communicate his concern to them.

Having schooled himself to face the possibility of defeat, the Commander must equally be prepared to face setbacks and reverses, and to know in advance how he will conduct himself in a severely deteriorating situation. All along he has shown control of his resources: now he must strengthen his resolve and control, and at the same time exhibit to all a calmness and confidence which belie the severity of the situation, whilst guarding against the accident that his subordinate commanders and immediate staff mistake his calmness – what the Greeks called *ataraxia* – for an unawareness of the danger.

Dowding possessed and manifested all the powers and virtues we have outlined above. If it is agreed that the most powerful force exerted by a leader is the power of example, Dowding was the very exemplar of the highest moral strength. His luminous integrity is common knowledge. He wrote and spoke lucidly what was on his mind – his needs, his policies, his fears, his contempt for incompetents, slackers and self-seekers – and no one, from the highest to the humblest, was ever in doubt as to where he stood on any matter touching his professional life and responsibilities.

Dowding also demonstrated courage of a high moral order whenever he had an imperious cause to defend, or promote, and never more ardently than when Air Ministry officials should have done so (thus proving themselves deficient). Above all – and all his powers came to be concentrated on this over-arching demand – he showed an unwavering singleness of purpose and a constancy of aim which are among the hallmarks of genius. That singularity and that constancy were dedicated, first, to the creation of a Fighter Command which would not be found wanting when the clash of arms came, as he felt sure it would; and second, to the proper conduct of war when it was thrust upon him.

We have said little of the distinction between offensive and defensive battle. On defensive actions, Clausewitz has written: 'If in military history we rarely find such great victories resulting from the defensive battle as from the offensive, that proves nothing against our assertion that the one is as well suited to produce victory as the other; the real cause is in the very different relations of the defender.' It was probably Frederick the Great that Clausewitz had in mind when writing those lines, of whom it has also been written: 'Single-handed he fought all the great powers of Europe in the Seven Years' War and successfully defended the national territory.' In the statement quoted above, it is clear that Clausewitz was writing as the military tactician; and equally clear that he seemed to know little of the history of warfare. For the fact is that most of the greatest military actions recorded in human history have been defensive battles which have resulted in the defeat of the aggressor. Here the names of Alexander, Darius, Caesar, Hannibal, Attila and Napoleon ring down the ages and seem to incite the admiration of men; but they were aggressors, conquerors and butchers all, who have no claim on the respect and admiration of right-thinking people. Except, of course, for their super-human qualities which, alas, were directed to evil ends – glorifying the exploits of war as a fitting occupation for men.

A study of the history of warfare shows that the vast majority of famous battles, from Marathon, Salamis and Plataea to the Second World War, were battles of defence against aggression. The names that *should* resound in the halls of fame and the memories of men are those of the defenders of hearth and home, and of the integrity of one's native land: Callimachus, Themistocles, Scipio, Arminius, Charles Martel, Sobieski, Drake, Nelson, and Wellington. And to this catalogue of victors we add the name of Dowding.

While the Battle of Britain did not last seven years, there is no question that Dowding could have defended England successfully for that period. And he knew it; for had he not written in the prophetic letter already reproduced: 'I believe that, if an adequate fighter force is kept in this country, if the Fleet remains in being, and if Home Forces are suitably organised to resist invasion, we should be able to carry on the war singlehanded for some time, if not indefinitely.'?

In this conclusion I have attached perhaps inadequate importance to that mysterious and unquantifiable quality called morale. What was the Commander's role in the generation of that spirit, and how was it communicated from him throughout Fighter Command? The answer is to be found, I think, in both direct and indirect channels. Indirectly, and by deduction or intuition, the men and women at the fighting end of the chains of communication, far though they were from the top, knew, or presumed, that the Commander was the architect of Fighter Command as well as its chief. This knowledge gave them a high confidence in their equipment and matériel, and in the organizing intelligence behind it. This confidence was enhanced by the very excellence of their fighting machines, the Hurricane and the Spitfire, which they saw as a match for anything the enemy could throw at them; and multiplied by their intimate association with their comrades, both aircrews and ground crews.

It has often been remarked of Dowding – by some in a critical spirit – that he seldom visited the squadrons, and so on the personal level was an unknown quantity. He was, in the words of one contemporary pilot, 'an invisible figure,' and adds: 'at the time we all felt he was rather a remote figure.' He goes on to say, however: 'at the time we all felt that he was fighting a notable battle on our behalf and had implicit trust in him, but he did not come 'down amongst the people' and was rarely seen. What we had in him was total faith he would do his best for us, but this was not attained by personal contact in the great majority of cases.'[xxix]

In some cases, however, there was personal contact, and the testimony of one of their number enlarges on the above assessment. He is Robert Wright, who was Dowding's personal assistant throughout the Battle. In a personal letter to Tom Gleave written on July 28, 1967, he wrote this considered tribute:

Of all the men whom I have known in my own varied and very extensive experiences, I say without hesitation that the one who has the highest integrity, who is of the greatest strength of character, whose loyalty and fortitude are unequalled, and whose friendship I value the most is unquestionably Stuffy Dowding. You of all people will appreciate that it is for those reasons that I have for him a feeling of affection that is unique in my own personal feeling.

His courage and fearlessness have always been...an inspiration. I say that with a full realization that such a sentiment on my part is likely to be viewed in some quarters with cynicism; but those who are unable to feel that way and who would jeer at it are the poorer for not being able to understand, or know, what this great man can inspire in one through direct personal contact over a long period of time. I say with every appreciation of what that implies that he is a truly great man, one of the greatest men of our times.

205

Notes:

i. See also Peter Flint, *Dowding and Headquarters Fighter Command*, especially chapters one-three.

ii. 'Invincible'? – hardly the word at the time. The battle was as hard run a thing as Wellington's victory at Waterloo. Of this Fuller (vol. 3, p. 540) has this to say: 'Wellington was never under any illusion how close defeat had been, and in spite of Ney's inept tactics.' For Wellington, read Dowding; for Ney, read Leigh-Mallory.

iii. This makes a good story, but it appears to be a myth. The first writer to state that he was there was Basil Collier, who wrote in his 1957 biography of Dowding (p.37): 'After his visit to Weedon, Dowding took steps whose consequences were perhaps as decisive as any event recorded in British history.' However, Michael Bragg, in his *The Location of Aircraft by Radio Methods 1935-1945*, states in the course of his description of the experiment (pp.30-32) that only Watson Watt and Rowe were present. In a personal letter to me of February 9th, 2003, Mr. Bragg wrote – and I quote with his permission: 'There are two (sic) reasons for thinking that Dowding was not there. The first one is the account of the experiment in Watson Watt's book *Three Steps to Victory*. If Dowding was there, it is certain that Watson Watt would have mentioned it. Secondly, an Air Ministry official in the shape of A.P. Rowe was there as the official observer and, in his report to his superior, H.E. Wimperis, he makes no mention of Dowding, which I thought he would have done if Dowding was there. Thirdly, in the AM correspondence file there is a memo dated 4 March 1935 from Wimperis to Dowding that advises him of the result of the experiment and enclosing Rowe's report. So I came to the conclusion that Dowding was not at Weedon.' (Zimmerman also states that only Watson Watt and Rowe witnessed the result of the test in their little van.) The outcome was, however, the same. A recent book, *A Radar History of World War Two: Technical and Military Imperatives* by Louis Brown (2000, Institute of Physics Publishing), shows, according to a review by Robert Hanbury Brown, 'that the early British experiments at Orfordness . . . were turned with remarkable speed into a highly effective defence system in time for the outbreak of the war by the combined efforts of Watson Watt, Tizard and Dowding' – at the head, let us add, of a brilliant team of engineers and physicists.

iv. Note this significant accusation: 'you will not be able to resist the pressure.' That should put an end to the claim by Air Ministry apologists that the CAS and the Air Staff fully supported Dowding in his efforts to block Churchill's commitment to keep supporting the French.

v. The original of this letter hangs, suitably framed, on the front wall in the imposing entrance of Bentley Priory, still a part of Royal Air Force Station Stanmore, in recognition of its historic significance. Late Note: the Government has sold Bentley Priory to developers. A Trust has been established to preserve at least the main floor of Bentley Priory as a museum. [August 20, 2008.]

vi. Lucas, *Wings of War*, p. 50.

vii. See Bell, pp. 24-25. This was the burden of an article by Lt. Col. Rogé entitled 'Les Aviations allemande, française et anglaise du 10 mai au 25 juin 1940' published in *Revue de Défense nationale*, Ottawa, février 1951. Trenchard also thought so. Boyle writes (pp. 715-16): 'These dissensions [between both Fighter and Bomber Commands on the one hand and the Air Ministry on the other] sapped Trenchard's dwindling faith in Newall and impelled him to propagate his own uninformed views of what should be done. First, he insisted, British bombers should concentrate on military targets in Germany; second, all available fighters should be disgorged at once 'to help maintain the battle in France and Belgium.' 'Uninformed' is right: the exact opposite policies were, fortunately, the correct ones, even though only one of them prevailed. We also quote Joubert on Dowding's side: 'To his everlasting credit Sir Hugh Dowding, commanding the fighters in England, successfully resisted the policy which, as was subsequently clearly shown, would have been ineffectual and might well have turned the Battle of Britain from a success to a disaster.' (*The Fated Sky*, p. 174.) – This might be the appropriate place to record a certain inaction by Portal at the time. Wing Commander Cotton obtained photographic evidence of massed German armour in the Ardennes on May 7, 1940. He took the photos to Air Marshal Sir Arthur Barratt, the AOC of the British Air Forces in France. Barratt was disturbed: it was evidence 'of vital importance, because an attack from that quarter was totally unprepared for'. Barratt informed the Air Ministry, where the news was pooh-poohed. On the 9th Barratt sent Cotton to put the evidence personally before Portal at Bomber Command. Portal did nothing, objecting that he only took orders about which targets to attack from the War Cabinet. The photographs sent a day earlier to the Air Staff elicited an equal inertia: instead of rushing them before the War Cabinet they just sat on them.

viii. See introduction, note three.

ix. This change of tactic by Goering must rank as one of the most fateful decisions of the war. Its consequences though obviously not imagined at the time, were incalculable. It meant that Fighter Command would survive, that the Luftwaffe would fail in its strategic objective, and that the war would become a long drawn-out war of attrition which Germany could not win.

x. Sir Philip Joubert recounts in one of those delightful surprises that biography often affords, that Dowding could be an agreeable companion: 'Dowding was, in appearance, a very quiet and reserved man, lacking in a sense of humour. In fact, out of office hours he could be an extremely entertaining companion, having a fund of good stories and a quick wit with which to tell them.' He goes on: 'This sense of humour did not, as a rule, extend into his work, and he could be extremely exacting and tiresome to his subordinates. He had, however, a great sense of justice which earned him the respect of all who worked with him.' (*The Third Service*, p. 129.)

xi. In a lecture that Dowding gave to the Imperial Defence College on May 14, 1937, and delivered in modified form to the R.A.F. Staff College on May 24th, Dowding made it clear that he made provision for strategic and tactical demands. He says at one point: 'my own operations table ... differs essentially from Group and Sector tables in that it is strategical and not tactical in character.' (RAF Staff College Reference: HCTD/S/214.)

xii. Arthur Herman: *To Rule the Waves. How the British Navy Shaped the Modern World* (New York: HarperCollins, 2004), p. 220. This was also the reason why the German Grand Fleet refused all further engagements with the Royal Navy despite their victory over Jellicoe and Beatty at Jutland.

xiii. The quotes are from *T.E. Lawrence to his Biographer Liddell Hart* (London: Faber and Faber, 1938), p.75, p.200. It is a pity that the Air Ministry staff officers were not heeding the prescient views of one of their own aircraftmen! The 'general opinion' does not seem to have penetrated their 'towers of ivory'.

xiv. Whether or not the Germans could have launched an invasion of England after the elimination of the Fighter Command of the Royal Air Force is immaterial to our theme in this chapter. The essential thing is that the British thought so at the time, and took all necessary steps to repel one. One may share Grinnell-Milne's thesis, as elaborated in *The Silent Victory*, that any attempt by the Germans to carry out a sea-borne invasion in 1940 would have met with a complete defeat and disaster for the Germans, even if the Fighter Command had been destroyed. The one pre-condition of invasion was the elimination of Fighter Command. On the other hand, the Germans, had they defeated Fighter Command, did not need to invade, except for purposes of prestige. All they had to do was to cut off Britain's oil or to starve Britain into submission by mounting a blockade of the British Isles, and destroy the British Fleet from the air. The outcome of the Battle of Britain was, therefore, of quite decisive importance. It is interesting to note that J.F.C. Fuller, in volume three of his *The Decisive Battles of the Western World*, devotes all of two pages to the Battle of Britain. He bases his belief that the defeat of Britain was 'out of the question' according to Kesselring whom he quotes: 'It was clear to every discerning person, including Hitler, that England could not be brought to her knees by the Luftwaffe alone. The Luftwaffe by itself could not deal with the British Fleet.' Yet already, in September 1939 the RAF had sunk a German battleship, the *Karlsruhe*, at Kiel.

xv. The five 'circumstances in which victory may be predicted' are these:

'He will be victorious:
who knows when he can fight and when he cannot;
who understands how to use both large and small forces;
whose ranks are united in purpose;
who is prudent and lies in wait for an enemy who is not; and
whose generals are able and not interfered with by the sovereign.'

The last article is particularly significant: for 'sovereign' read 'Air Ministry'. See below: Unity of Command.

xvi. His two biographers were negligent in not having interrogated their subject on this matter. We know that Dowding attended and passed the Army Staff College course at Camberley in 1912-14 when a junior lieutenant. He was labelled one of the 'bad boys', being a non-conformist, and decried the lip-service paid to freedom of thought, which contrasted with an actual tendency to repress all but conventional ideas. On the other hand, Dowding praised the course for 'the facility of marshalling one's ideas, and setting them forth logically and consecutively with a minimum of words'. ('Personal Notes', p. 59.)

xvii. Napoleon exhorted his generals: 'Read over and over again the campaigns of Alexander, Hannibal, Caesar, Gustavus, Turenne, Eugene, and Frederic. Make them your models. This is the only way to become a great general and to master the secrets of the art of war. With your own genius enlightened by this study, you will reject all maxims opposed to those of these great commanders.'

xviii. Creasy, p. 245.

xix. As late as 1938 the Air Ministry was ordering more obsolete light and medium bombers. A few examples: a total of 1000 Battles were constructed, 5,421 Blenheims, and 1,812 Whitleys. And none of them remotely close to being a war-winning bomber. Moreover the ratio was still four bombers to every one fighter. We have stated before that the Trenchard Doctrine aimed at both destroying German industry and German morale. One historian quotes Trenchard to the effect that 'the moral effect of bombing stands undoubtedly to the material effect in a proportion of twenty to one.' The writer then comments: 'The declaration was made on singularly little evidence.' Later the same writer makes the following astounding statement: 'The failures of judgement in the Air Establishment before the war, at its outbreak, and through the early years, are to be numbered among the great misjudgements of military history.' (Divine, p. 162, p. 265.)

xx. Sun Tzu, *The Art of War*, p. 83.

xxi.Fuller, *The Second World War*, p. 220.

xxii. Kinvig, p. 144.

xxiii. Hughes-Wilson, p. 3.

xxiv. I am indebted for this information to the late Earl of Selkirk – then Squadron Leader 'Geordie' Hamilton, Chief Intelligence Officer of 603 (Auxiliary) Squadron in 1940 – when I visited him at his home in Wimbome, Dorset, on July 13, 1995. See also 'The Intelligence Aspect' by Edward Thomas in *The Battle Re-Thought*, p.42, passim. The reader is also referred to 'A Comparative Analysis of RAF and Luftwaffe Intelligence in the Battle of Britain, 1940' by Sebastian Cox in 'Intelligence and National Security', no. 5 (1990), pp. 425-443.

xxv. There was also, of course, the third source: the intelligence provided by captured enemy airmen. This was necessarily of a tactical nature, and of very limited use, in terms of volume, accuracy, and the time factor. To our knowledge, this source has not been studied.

xxvi. The first passage is from J.E. Johnson, *The Story of Air Fighting*, p.286; the second from Johnson and Lucas, *Glorious Summer*, p. 203.

xxvii. It is an extraordinary quality of our Commander that, in the RAF Staff College lecture that we have already quoted, Dowding, in attempting to envisage what he as the defender needs to do, puts himself in the place of a European dictator bent on attacking Great Britain. These are his words:

'Whatever may be the ultimate best air objective to bring victory, the attainment of that objective will be hampered to a greater or less extent by the enemy's air force'.

'His fighters will destroy my bombers in the air, and his bombers will destroy mine on the ground, and my air force may suffer such heavy casualties that I shall fail to attain my objectives'.

'I will therefore start by attacking my enemy's air force at his aerodromes, his reserve Storage Depots, and his factories. I will paralyse his air force and keep it paralysed.'

'I can then at my leisure adopt any of the methods of frightfulness which are most likely to bring victory in the shortest possible time.'

Here we see enunciated the principles of the defence which Dowding was to mount when the anticipated attack was launched in the summer of 1940.

xxviii. Joubert criticizes Dowding's leadership of Fighter Command by accusing him of paying too much attention to detail and not enough to principle. (*The Third Service*, pp. 129-30.) Joubert was quite wrong. Dowding had long ago established his principles. And no commander can pay sufficient attention to detail. Indeed, attention to detail is what distinguishes a great commander from a lesser one. The old adage is applicable to commanders as to corporals: 'For want of a nail, the shoe is lost; for want of a shoe, the horse is lost; for want of a horse, the battle is lost.'

xxix. I am indebted to my late friend Air Chief Marshal Sir Christopher Foxley-Norris – who was at the time a Flying Officer on 3 Squadron – for this appreciation. (Private letter, June 5, 2002.)

Envoi

Strategic Afterthoughts

Strategic Aims

—ѧ—

Introduction

In his book *Fateful Decisions* Ian Kershaw examines the likely consequences of decisions that might have been taken, had others not, during the Second World War by various authorities in the years 1940–1941. He claims that his speculations are not to be confused with counter-factual history, which attempts to answer the question: what consequences would have followed if such-and-such had happened instead of what did happen? The distinction is too subtle for this writer.

In July, as we have seen, Sinclair told Churchill that he was keen to replace Dowding. Churchill retorted indignantly that Dowding was one of the very best men he had, and that it might be a good thing to move him to a higher position than that of head of Fighter Command. The only position higher was that of Chief of the Air Staff. We examined earlier why Churchill did not pursue this idea. Now we propose to answer the questions: how were Portal's strategic decisions and policies in error? What would Dowding have done had he been appointed Chief of the Air Staff instead of Portal? Much can sometimes been learnt from post-factual historical speculation; this exercise, however, is not to be confused with it, for there is a remarkable symmetry to the answers.

In terms of strategy, and the crucial policies established for the Royal Air Force following the Battle of Britain, the appointment of Sinclair, Portal and Harris were unfortunate. The appointment of Sholto Douglas and Leigh-Mallory to Fighter Command, and of Joubert to Coastal Command, were also wrong-headed and only marginally of a lesser order of error. We do not speculate on Dowding's choice of commanders for the vital commands, for this would have hinged on particular strategic tasks. The commands which were of obvious immediate strategic importance were : Coastal Command, Bomber Command, and Fighter Command.

I. Coastal Command and the Battle of the Atlantic

The air battle won, and the immediate danger of invasion passed, Dowding turned his gaze outward – this is fact, not speculation here – and asked himself whether any other threat appeared on the horizon, or closer. Again, he saw it with his usual lucid grasp of strategic priorities. It was the Atlantic Ocean and the supply-line – the very life-line which connected the British Isles to its overseas sources of food, raw materials and munitions. Dowding had, in fact, already put his finger on its vital significance. This is what he wrote, already, in early 1941[i]:

> A grimmer spectre lurks in the oceans, more insidious and more dangerous [than air attacks] because its effects are gradual and cumulative.

The time may come when the increased efficiency of large aircraft may enable us to obtain our essential requirements by air, but throughout this war and for a long time afterwards it will probably be necessary that almost everything which we cannot produce in our own country shall reach us by sea. This means that if the rate of wastage of our shipping exceeds the rate of output of ourselves and our friends, we shall sooner or later reach a stage at which we can no longer carry on the war.

*   *   *   *   *

In the absence of any information to the contrary we must assume that the loss of shipping is the gravest remaining danger which threatens our national existence today.

*   *   *   *   *

We are as yet far from having won the Battle of the Atlantic, but if we can do that, in addition to subduing the two other primary dangers with which I have dealt, we shall have made secure a base from which our offensive may be launched.

But few people in power seemed to be listening to Dowding.

The brilliant German strategist, Karl Dönitz, also knew the vital importance to Britain's war effort and survival of the Atlantic. 'The focal point of the war against England and the one possibility of bringing her to her knees lies in attacking sea communications in the Atlantic.' Similarly, Werner Baumbach, although, like Dowding, an airman, had the same strategic grasp of things: 'the British could be defeated only if the Motherland could be cut off from her overseas sources of supply. Her dependence on such sources was the Achilles heel of British world power.' This was also the view of Clausewitz : 'The greatest secret of war and the masterpiece of a skillful general is to starve the enemy.'

The Battle of the Atlantic was almost lost and Britain was nearly starved into defeat and surrender, first in 1940, then in March–April 1942, and again the following year when 'the Germans never came so near to disrupting our communications between the New World and the Old as in the first twenty days of March 1943.' It stuns the mind to think that it took two and a half years, following the repulse of the Luftwaffe in 1940, to master the U–Boats, when this threat to survival was obvious to all possessed of a modicum of reason, and who were not bemused by siren calls to the offensive.

The secret to the successful waging of the U–Boat war lay, first, in escorting the convoys by sea and in protecting them from the air across the entire Atlantic; and, second, in developing electronic equipment capable of detecting submarines. The crucial area lay between Greenland and Iceland, an area known as the 'air gap', and within it a smaller area which was dubbed the Black Pit.

The Battle of the Atlantic was bedevilled on the British side by jealous quarrels between Navy and Air Force and between Bomber and Coastal Commands. Allies can also muddy the waters; after June 1941, when Hitler attacked the Soviet Union, the political direction of the war decreed that all possible military help be given to the Russian Allies. This help consisted largely in supplying them with war materials. When Japan attacked Pearl Harbor and the United States entered the war in December 1941, in-fighting broke out within the US Navy over the respective demands of the Pacific and the Atlantic, and squabbles erupted between the US Navy Air Arm and the US Army Air Force over the providing of long range aircraft to protect convoys. The most heinous offence was the refusal of the RAF to lend help to the Navy and to its own Coastal Command. On June 24th, 1942, when Admiral Pound served notice on the Chiefs of Staff that 'the gravity of our position at sea increases day by day', and pointed out the need for 'more land-based squadrons of heavy aircraft as a matter of supreme urgency,' he was met with a blanket refusal by Portal, who argued that Bomber Command needed every bomber available for its offensive against Germany. Portal opposed the demands of Coastal Command and the Navy throughout the war – unless ordered by higher authority. He was, of course, fully supported by Harris, who believed, and continued to believe throughout the war, that he could win the war on his own. Portal was supported by Churchill until as late as mid-1943.

For two years Coastal Command was to be denied the long range aircraft it needed. The Liberator proved to be the ideal plane: with the need desperate, the first twenty were delivered in June 1941. No sooner had they become operational, in September, than half of them were transferred to Ferry Command and British Overseas Airways Corporation – for the transport of top brass and politicians. Meanwhile Bomber Command was pressed to bomb the U-Boat assembly plants and their bases. The results were negative. 'By May 1943, when some 18,000 sorties had been made and 33,000 tons of bombs dropped, the sacrifice of 882 bombers and their crews [of the RAF and the USAAF] had not stopped a single U-boat going into service.' The story was the same with the 10-centimetre radar which began to reach Bomber Command in January 1943. Coastal Command managed to acquire an Anti-Surface Vessel (ASV) version in March; the crews were delighted by its capacity to detect submarines at night; and 'kills' increased at once. 'If just a handful of the sets had been available in early 1943, they might have been significant in the course of the battle, but Bomber Command maintained their exclusive right to the new weapon, code-named H2S.' Coastal Command appreciated the danger and saw the need; but, in view of the denial of the right weapons and the internecine strife during a protracted period of gravest danger, one cannot but question the leadership.

In the crucial period from June 1941 to February 1943, the AOC-in-C of Coastal Command was Air Chief Marshal Sir Philip Joubert de la Ferté. Joubert, although a radar man, lacked the imagination and force of character needed to do battle with the Air Ministry. Joubert was replaced by Air Marshal Sir John Slessor in February 1943, when the battle still balanced on a knife edge. A dynamic commander, Slessor began to attack the U-boat packs in the Bay of Biscay, especially with the powerful Beaufighters and Mosquitos. His hope for a decisive blow, which depended on getting more Liberators, was dashed by disputes between the Americans; and an opportunity was missed for the lack of a few extra squadrons. If ever there arose an occasion when a second prophetic letter to the Air Minister, or an intervention in a meeting of the War Cabinet, was justified, both Joubert and Slessor failed the test.

II.   Bomber Command and the war against Germany

The war of 1939–45 was to be won or lost in the spheres of science and intelligence. We have seen that Fighter Command prevailed in 1940 largely because its defensive system was based on science, and because its leader was not only an organizing genius but a man of independent mind open to scientific discoveries.

Bomber Command, for its part, did not begin to inflict serious damage on Germany until late 1943, largely because its leader knew nothing of science and cared less, and subscribed unquestioningly to the Trenchard Doctrine, which, as refined by Harris, boasted that the bomber could win the war almost unaided, even if it ignored industrial targets and aimed principally at attacking civilian morale. Harris, like Portal, with the wholehearted backing – indeed insistence – of Churchill, revelled in the government directive which guided and determined his policies: 'You will direct the main effort of the bomber force .. towards dislocating the German transportation system, and to destroying the morale of the civilian population as a whole, and of the industrial workers in particular.' This directive was sent on July 9, 1941, to the then commander of Bomber Command, Air Marshal Sir Richard Peirse, even though Bomber Command had inferior bomber aircraft totally incapable of carrying out the orders. The directive was reinforced by a further directive issued by the Government on February 14th 1942: 'In order to destroy Germany's capacity and will to make war ... the Air Officer Commander-in-Chief was to focus his operations on "the morale of the enemy civil population, and in particular of the industrial workers"'[ii] 'This instruction to undertake what was to be called 'area bombing' was now 'formally recognized as the standard basis of our policy.' Harris took over from Peirse six days later, and he made it his gospel, which he lived by religiously for the next three years.

This writer was an armourer at the bomber station RAF Upper Heyford during Harris's first year at Bomber Command. It was shortly after he took over the Command that he raised all the forces he could muster to launch the first one thousand bomber raid against Germany. The target was the city of Cologne. The damage to non-military and non-industrial targets was considerable; however, we airmen were not impressed that our skills and energies should be exploited and used against defenceless civilians. After all, had we not recently gone through the same ordeal in our cities and ports (and even villages) and had we not condemned the enemy's barbarity? Were we now to adopt the enemy's own methods of waging war, and find telling reasons – or justifications – for doing so?

The reader will be justified in asking himself: is the writer not indulging in hindsight, and taking today a moral stance that he did not feel in 1942? The answer is, no: what I feel today is what I felt then, sixty-six years ago. Today, Harris is known as 'Bomber' Harris. Then, we airmen called him 'Butcher' Harris – a title which today's admirers and apologists of Harris refute. But I was there, and his admirers were not.[iii]

At that time I applied to remuster for pilot training. I was required to show evidence of a certain standard of education and to write an essay. The sole topic given to me was, 'How can bombing shorten the war?' I recall that I argued in favour of striking targets directly related to the waging of war, above all of munitions, steel, oil, mining and transportation. The Education Officer called me two days later and asked whether I was a writer before enlisting? I said no. I was nineteen then. I was not alone at the time – though, as a humble aircraftman, I did not know it – in my disagreement with area bombing. It is all too easy to let emotions cloud reason when making decisions, even decisions that affect the destiny of nations and empires. I have suggested that the bombing policy of Germany was dictated rather by high feelings than by reason. But there were other voices, voices of reason. Conspicuous among them were Tizard and Blackett, scientists both.[iv] They argued in favour of a rational approach to the bombing of Germany. While agreeing that the RAF was the only arm capable of taking the war to Germany, they held that strictly military and industrial targets should be attacked. If, for example, the oil refining and coal producing centres, and their connecting railway networks, were to be subjected to an unrelenting assault for six months, the German industrial and military capability would be brought to a halt.[v] Harris pooh-poohed this strategy and these objectives as 'panacea targets'. Harris was opposed to scientific methods and he was hostile to operational research. He strenuously resisted efforts to set up the Pathfinders. He mocked the idea of designing special bombs to break the Mohne dam in the Ruhr. More: when he saw the results of photographic reconnaissance pictures, which showed no or little damage to the night's supposed targets, he refused to believe them.

It was the Americans who learnt the important lessons: although their bombers suffered terrible casualties in the early assaults against German targets, they learnt this lesson too. The American air chiefs were convinced of four things: i) that they had to attack strategic military targets; ii) that these targets could only be destroyed by precision bombing; iii) that precision bombing could only be carried out by daylight; and iv) that effective daylight bombing could only succeed if the bombers were protected by long-range fighters. The long-range P.51 Mustang became the offensive fighter that eventually swept enemy opposition from the skies and ensured air supremacy over Germany. This supremacy ensured two vital strategic aims: i) the precision bombing of key German targets; and ii) unopposed landings in Normandy in June 1944.

Harris's and the Air Ministry's area bombing policy failed to accomplish either of its declared objectives: a significant reduction of industrial production, and the destruction of the morale of the civilian population. The facts are that German production of aircraft and weapons continued to increase throughout 1944 and even into 1945; but oil production was ruinously and decisively low. On the other hand, under the brilliant but malign leadership of Joseph Goebbels: 'The one front which held out with incredible tenacity was morale at home.'[vi] And the cost was the loss of 55,000 lives of British and Commonwealth young men.

Some writers make the mistake of bringing in moral factors in judging the means used to defeat Nazi Germany. If a war is a just war, then the most effective means must be used to bring about the desired end. Even in war, and above all in a just war, the end does not justify the means. But surely there is another criterion at play, and that is the appeal of humanity. To lay waste a whole country as a means of destroying an evil régime, although understandable in light of the passions that ran strong at the time, is barbaric by any measure. War cannot be assessed in abstract terms of ethics. Some argue that the defence of one's homeland, and the defeat and destruction of a horrendous evil, justify almost any means. But if the critics are to use that yardstick, they must also set it beside the means and the intents of the enemy.

Do all views need to be taken into account to complete the historical record? If that is the case we should give ear to the view of Richard von Weizsäcker, who was the President of West Germany from 1 July 1984 to 30 June 1994. He became famous for his speeches. He gained wide national and international attention and respect with his speech on the fortieth anniversary of VE Day in which he referred to May 8, 1945 as 'the day of liberation from the inhuman system of Nazi tyranny.' This helped to redefine the meaning of this event as a positive landmark in German history rather than a point of agony as it was often referred to before. He specifically included in the measures used by the Allies to destroy Nazism that of their strategic bombing of the Fatherland, the cities and people as well as the industrial targets. It is an impressive statement. But Weizsäcker was speaking a good thirty years after those events, and when all the destruction had been obliterated and Germany had been rebuilt. We have the temerity to disagree. And we feel we know that Dowding would not have countenanced the inhumane, indiscriminate bombing of civilians and their homes in Germany. His vision was larger, and imbued with humanity. He would have anticipated the day when Germany was defeated with a minimum of devastation; and when above all the Allies would welcome her back into the fold of the democratic and cultural traditions to which she would have so much to contribute to the revitalization of Western Civilization.

III. The Fighter as Strategic Weapon

Having earlier excoriated Douglas and Leigh-Mallory for their unfitness for their commands and for their consequent bungling; and having exposed Portal for his failure of strategic vision, we must properly ask: what else could Fighter Command have done? An excessive amount of Fighter Command's resources were devoted to the wasteful and useless operations over Northern France. As a result, the development of a first-class night-fighter and controlling system, and the perfecting of the daytime defensive network of groups, squadrons, and controllers, were grievously neglected, especially during the first seven months of Douglas's and Leigh-Mallory's commands. Perhaps these tasks would not have occupied their resources and energies fully after May 1941. There was, however, one over-riding requirement which Fighter Command and the Air Ministry reprehensively ignored: that was the development of a long-range fighter. The pilots and squadrons complained endlessly about the limitations of their fighters – exactly as the German fighter pilots had complained about theirs during the Battle.

The failure to develop and exploit the manifold uses of the de Havilland Mosquito – in Embry's opinion the finest aeroplane to be produced – is well-known. The failure to develop the jet engine before the Germans, who accomplished it two years before the RAF, despite the intensive bombing campaign against their homeland, was a disgrace. Their joint failure to recognize that the long-range offensive fighter could be effectively – and in the event, was – a pre-eminent strategic weapon of the war, can be attributed to their inward looking habits and their endemic failure to see ahead. This judgement is not hindsight. There were in the 1930s airmen and strategists, admittedly few, who saw that the next war would be dominated and decided in the air. Most of the few, it is true, thought only in terms of attack, and the bomber; but the concept of 'supremacy in the air' must have led, eventually, to its corollary, namely, that command of the air – i.e. of one's own airspace as well as that of the enemy, which was the over-riding strategic lesson to be learnt from the Battle of Britain – could only be won by fighters. To think such thoughts, to look ahead, to learn lessons from the past, whether distant or close, isn't that the whole purpose of staff colleges and defence colleges? Is it not indeed one of the major reasons for existence of an Air Staff?

After the proving of the Messerschmitt in Spain, and the success of the Hurricane and Spitfire designs in 1936, and especially after the demonstration of radar, there was no excuse for looking for guidance to the past. For lessons, yes; but not for precepts for policy and action. The failure to recognize this fundamental reality both before and, signally, until at least 1942, is one of the gravest strategic shortcomings chargeable to the CAS and his Air Staff.

The fighter was essential for protecting and escorting bombers to their targets; furthermore the long-range fighter was essential to the perfecting of a long-range bombing strategy. The Americans rejected the RAF's night-bombing strategy. Portal denied for three years the need to develop a long-range fighter. Eventually the Americans produced the P-48 Thunderbolt and the P-51 Mustang – the latter with British help and with a Rolls-Royce engine.[vii] Thanks to these magnificent long-range fighters, and especially to the Mustang, the USAAC was finally able to escort their bombers wherever the bombers went, and thereby established domination of the German airspace.

There is little doubt that Portal's failure here was a grievous one. John Terraine has summarized the dispute between the British and the Americans in Appendix 'G' of his book, *The Right of the Line*. Terraine has been criticized by the pro-Portal (and hence the pro-Air Ministry) faction in this controversy. But Terraine's evidence, documented and impeccable, is beyond dispute. We will recapitulate the salient points; and conclude by contributing an item which may have escaped the notice of both Terraine and his critics.

When the Americans entered the war and engaged in discussion with the RAF on strategic bomber policy, they determined on daylight bombing as the best way of achieving positive results. They thought that massed boxes of their heavy bombers, with their gun positions covering all possible angles of enemy fighter approach, would 'see off' any possible Luftwaffe attack: they were sadly mistaken. Their losses were terrible. They concluded that the only way in which they could maintain their strategic bombing offensive by daylight was for their bombers to be escorted by fighters – long-range fighters, that is, capable of fighting on equal terms with the Luftwaffe fighters which had the advantage of range and warning.

The Americans – in particular, their Commander, General H.H. Arnold – looked around and saw the Fighter Command of the RAF virtually unemployed. 'He found the spectacle of a fighter force which Portal stated to consist of 1,461 RAF with crews remaining inactive while his bombers were being shot out of the sky, both incomprehensible and unacceptable.' Portal persistently opposed the idea that a fully operational long-range fighter could be produced. Terraine produces none of the evidence buttressing Portal's arguments. But he quotes the official history of the aerial campaign against the German heartland with telling, and conclusive, effect.

In 1941, 1942, and even 1943, Portal was obdurate. On May 27,1941, he told Churchill: 'The long range fighter, whether built specifically as such, or whether given increased range by fitting extra tanks, will be at a disadvantage compared with the short range high performance fighter.' Portal repeated this view one week later, when Churchill insisted that everything be done to increase the operational range of fighters. In 1942, the Air Staff, under Portal's direction, viewed with considerable scepticism – perhaps because of their 'superior experience'! – the preference of the United States Army Air Force for carrying out the bombing of Germany by daylight. This was preferred precisely because the likelihood of accurately bombing precisely identified targets increased.

> The clear realization of the limited offensive potential of Fighter Command did not result in efforts to extend the range of that force. Indeed, Sir Charles Portal was convinced that the production or modification of an RAF fighter with the range of a heavy bomber and the performance of an interceptor fighter was a technical impossibility. In 1943 there was an acrimonious exchange of letters between Arnold and Portal. But Portal remained obdurate. Webster and Frankland conclude their analysis of the situation in these terms : 'Sir Charles Portal saw no prospect of engaging the Royal Air Force Fighter Command effectively in the Point Blank campaign [i.e. the coordinated bombing of Germany industrial and military targets by the RAF and the USAAF]. He had never accepted the proposition of a long-range fighter which could effectively engage opposing short-range, or interceptor, fighters.'

Arnold had no difficulty in proving Portal wrong by having a number of Spitfires disassembled, crated and shipped to the United States, where they were modified – specially equipped – and then flown back across the Atlantic non-stop to England. Even that demonstration failed to convince, or move, the RAF's top thinker.

In fact, Arnold did not need to do even that: the feat had already, and long before, been accomplished. Wing Commander Sidney Cotton, having acquired two Spitfires from Dowding in early 1940 – a feat that did credit to both men – managed to strip and equip them so as to give them a range of 1,250 miles – which was 1,000 miles more than their normal range. Then Cotton did even better; in consultation with Supermarine's, who fitted extra tanks, he got Spitfires capable of a range of up to 2,000 miles. This was in February 1941. It is true that these long-range, reconnaissance Spitfires were stripped of all armament and superfluous weight. But how much ingenuity at Supermarine's was required to extend the combat Spitfire's range by two or three or even four times its normal fighting range, provided only that the drive to do so was exerted from the top? Did Portal know about Cotton's achievements? Of course he did. His was the decisive hand in Cotton's dismissal. Portal's failure to promote the development of a long-range escort fighter for the Royal Air Force is one of the most egregious sins of the Second World War.[viii] If the RAF had pioneered the long-range fighter, several consequences would have flowed from it: 1) Bomber Command would have been able to carry out an infinitely more accurate, sustained and scientific assault against Germany's energy resources and war industries; 2) the war might well have been shortened; and 3) Bomber Command would have been spared its terrible casualties.

The notion of the fighter as a war-winning strategic weapon is hard for some people to grasp. It was obviously hard to grasp for an avowed 'bomber man'. The answer to 'Hap' Arnold's problem was found in the Mustang, fitted with the Rolls-Royce Merlin 66 engine. 'When the sturdy little Mustang first appeared over Hanover, Goering refused to believe the reporting centre and censured its personnel; but when he was finally convinced he simply said, "We have lost the war!"'

Goering's insight is fully corroborated by the US Strategic Bombing Survey, one of whose conclusions was that their daylight bombing campaign, with fighter escort, effectively destroyed the Luftwaffe's defensive arm. The offensive fighter/interceptor thus proved to be one of the major strategic weapons of the war, for it determined the outcome of land and sea battles as well as strictly aerial battles. Few people understood this. Certainly no one in the Air Ministry understood it. Neither Douglas nor Leigh-Mallory, and not Portal either, three accomplices blinded by their ignorance of fighters, were even remotely capable of grasping that central fact.

We have demonstrated in the course of our inquiries that the Air Ministry and its planners were incapable of thinking of any other concept than that of bombers. After the Battle of Britain they had a fighter arm which kept on growing. Dowding's and Park's successors were not fighter men. They failed to perfect the night defences whose principles had earlier been laid down by Dowding; and when the night blitz came to an end they lamely continued the useless and wasteful sorties over France, for the reason that they did not have the imagination or leadership to envisage any other use for the fighter.

This attitude on the part of the Air Staff was equally disastrous in terms of its effect on overseas operations. There existed no air defence system in India or the Far East. The defeat in Malaya and Singapore, the most calamitous military defeat in

British history, coming as it did at the end of 1941, could have been averted by a few squadrons of fighters. But there were none even in the Middle East, where decisive battles were being fought out. While a thousand Spitfires, with all their pilots, ground crews, armament and other equipment sat idle in Britain, the Middle East and North African campaigns had to make do with Hurricanes, which were adequate opposition to the Me109s only in experienced hands. It appears that Douglas refused to release any of his squadrons and Portal sat on his thumbs, despite urgent and repeated appeals from Tedder throughout 1942. It was not until the time of El Alamein, in late 1942, that Spitfires began to reach the Desert squadrons. So much, once again, for the 'global strategic view of the Air Ministry'.

Conclusion
The reader may have been struck by the seeming dichotomy in Dowding's character which allows for a strong strain of both realism and idealism abiding in the same personality – abiding in harmony, as if they were but complementary to each other. On the one side he had a firm grasp of the real nature of the world, of the inconstancy and unreliability of political beings, and of the manner in which events had a way of unfolding that was often contrary to expectations and hopes – which deceive. On the other side he was dismayed with what he saw and could not fail to wonder if life and human institutions were destined to travel along the same paths of war and conflict for all time.

Strange as it may seem, it was the Royal Air Force with its customs and traditions, and a life lived in service to others and to lofty aims, that instilled in the airman both the need to have one's feet on the ground – if such a thing may be said of an airman–and the thrill and the limitless horizon open to young men and women engaged in the conquest of the air. As part of a squadron, the airman experiences solidarity with others of like mind and a sense of being bound to a common task. Be he a fitter or a rigger, an instrument maker or an armourer, he knows without acknowledging it that he works with his comrades to the same end. If he is a pilot or navigator, a wireless operator or flight engineer or parachute packer, he knows equally not only that each is dependent on the others but that if one fails, all fail. And what is that end? Why, it is to keep the peace. It is to defend the immemorial freedoms that your island race has enjoyed for centuries. It is to protect one's island home against lawless and predatory aggressors whose consuming ambition and passion is to conquer and enslave other peoples for the sheer lust of making war and subjugating others, especially if they appear weaker, and less willing to fight to defend themselves. For it is rare to find an aggressor keen to attack a neighbour if he is strong and will fight to the death.

The Dariuses, Alexanders, Caesars, Hannibals, Soleimans, Napoleons, Hitlers and Stalins are enemies of mankind – despite the magnificent human qualities that some of them possessed. Was the lust of conquest a sufficient justification for Alexander's legacy, that of spreading Hellenic culture far and wide beyond Greece's own borders? In contrast, England has had an extraordinary military history[ix] and yet has never produced a conqueror, an aggressor, a tyrant of the stamp of the invaders named above. England's policy has been to maintain a balance of power on the European continent in order to prevent the rise of a single state so powerful as to be able to dictate to the others, or, in the event of their resistance, to make war against them. Yet England acquired a vast overseas empire without a conqueror, without even seeming to be aware that she was acquiring an empire. It was not achieved without battle and revolt and bloodshed, to be sure. But it did come about without deliberate and conscious conquest. It began by trade and commerce: it was consolidated by force of arms. And it was sealed by gradual occupation, settlement, and mutual respect.

England has always tried to respect the different customs, languages, religions and social structures of the countries she colonized. She benefited much from daily contact with her subject peoples. And she gave much in return; how much England gave to the world can be gauged from the free and willing cooperation that exists today among the fifty-two independent countries that make up the Commonwealth. Those gifts can be summed up as portending towards establishing the rule of law: an independent judiciary and civil service: an educational system stressing public service, and a military arm trained to protect those institutions and to ensure sovereignty.

Britain's air force inherited the traditional role of her navy. In the nineteenth century it was to sweep the ocean seas clean of pirates and brigands in order to make them safe for legal commerce between all nations. But it has always been to protect our island race from invasion. With the advent of the aeroplane our ships became vulnerable to attack from the air, and the air force was created to protect both our homeland and the navy. This role – of defender and protector – was conferred upon the Royal Air Force and its airmen and airwomen; from the very beginning, this was an almost sacred task, and inspired thoughts and deeds which raised those in the Royal Air Force above their normal stature. To serve oneself is understandable because we all tend toward self-centredness. But all men need a larger existence. To serve others, and one's country, is noble. To serve mankind is sublime. It is the height of wisdom to live according to the ideal that to put one's labour to the service of others is also to benefit oneself; whereas to serve only one's own interest is sure to bring down the general good with it.

Dowding's life and work were devoted selflessly to the defence and well-being of his Service, his country, and to all mankind.

Notes:

i. *Twelve Legions of Angels*, p.37, p. 44. The opportunity was missed almost entirely by people who were hung up on questions of offence and defence. We have seen how stupid senior air marshals have proved themselves to be over just such an issue, where the respective needs of Bomber Command and Fighter Command were in contention. The same forces were at loggerheads in the Battle of the Atlantic, although here the forces were those of the Navy and the Air Force. This lamentable failure of the Air Ministry to tackle the menace of the U-Boats is well stated by Peter Padfield in his *War Beneath the Sea*: 'In truth there had been no reasoned basis of the policy; it had been dictated by the belligerent prejudice of Churchill, his advisers, Lord Cherwell- who before the war had advised against the development of radar - the former Air Force Chief, Lord Trenchard, and the dominant "bombing group" in the Air Staff whose tunnel vision was most notably expressed by the new Chief of Bomber Command. The failure of the Admiralty to make a reasoned case did not help their cause. They had diluted the urgency of the argument for long-range aircraft for Coastal Command by mixing it with issues of naval command of bombers operating over the sea and naval training for Coastal Command aircrews. Above all they had failed to point out the idiocy and profound historical ignorance of the bombers' claim that bombing German cities was "offensive" while protecting convoys was "defensive".' (Quoted by Cdre Toby Elliott in 'Maritime Airpower - A Dark Blue Perspective' in the RAF Historical Society Journal no. 33 (2005), p.60.) (The 'profound historical ignorance' refers, of course to the blindness of the Air Staff to a thousand years of English history.) This attachment to the doctrine of offence is enshrined in the motto of Fighter Command itself, which reads: Offence – Defence. No further commentary is needed.

The 'bomber faction' knew nothing of the history of war. Of the *Fifteen Decisive Battles of the World, from Marathon to Waterloo*, analysed by Creasy, a full thirteen are defensive victories fought and won against aggressors. Of the 'over twenty key naval and military encounters from 480 BC to 1943' in John Colvin's *Decisive Battles*, fourteen of the eighteen actions are defensive battles. And in Fuller, considering volume one alone, fifteen of the twenty decisive battles of the Western World are defensive victories. And to think that the people to whom was entrusted the formulation and implementation of 'the wider strategic view' of the CAS and the Air Ministry were hostile to the very notion of defence.

ii. Richards and Saunders, vol. II, p. 118.

iii. This is not entirely true. My friend Paul Tomlinson, himself a Battle pilot, was Harris's Personal Assistant from February 1942 to November 1943 and I questioned him about this sobriquet at his home on October 2, 2008. He told me that Harris was commonly called 'Bert'; he had heard the nickname 'Butch', and supposed it was an abbreviation of 'Butcher', but he had never heard anyone call him or refer to him by that name – the reader may well ask again, but did you not feel even then the strong desire to hit back at the Germans and to give them in spades what they had dealt out to you? Of course we did! But the passion of revenge does not win wars. Wars must be waged rationally, intelligently, scientifically. And I am trying to put forward the policy that I feel confident Dowding would have adopted.

iv. Tizard's work brought him willy-nilly into contact with political forces, which constituted further obstacles. How little did even this farseeing scientist imagine what havoc they could wreak! When his committee was dissolved in the summer of 1940, it was due to intrigue both personal and political. The intrigue was the doing of Churchill and Lindemann (the latter, later Lord Cherwell, was then, and was to be Churchill's personal scientific adviser throughout the war.) In light of Tizard's record of achievement, the news that 'he had been forced out brought despondency to the Air Force and alarm to the scientific establishment.' Among the scientists who wrote to Tizard, Egerton was appropriately blunt, and thought that his colleague's resignation made it 'quite terrifying to realize, when the country is in such danger, that things like that can be happening owing to personal intrigue.' Reaction among the enlightened air marshals was of a piece. Trenchard was aghast; Freeman was outraged; Bowhill, at Coastal Command, offered Tizard full access to all his stations to pursue his work in ship detection. As to Dowding, he resented the treatment Tizard had received, and went on to say: 'I feel that we all owe a debt of gratitude to you for the commonsense and logical attitude which you have adopted to scientific problems – in fact I always say of you that no-one would suspect you of being a scientist (and I mean that in a most flattering sense). The present witch doctor is firmly established for the time being but witch doctors lead a precarious existence.' (Author's note: The witch doctor in question, Professor Lindemann, was to lead a charmed existence during the war.) Tizard's position as scientific adviser to the Chief of the Air Staff, Air Chief Marshal Sir Cyril Newall, was only semi-official. When Newall retired and was replaced by Air Marshal Sir Charles Portal in October 1940, Portal did not see fit 'to enquire for Tizard's services.' The correspondence between Tizard and Dowding (held in the Imperial War Museum) reveals a warm and appreciative relationship between the two men on both professional and personal levels.

v. J.F .C. Fuller writes as follows: 'in 1940, he [Churchill] was *de facto* if not *de jure* head of the British armed forces, and though he was unable to take the field, he overcame this difficulty by deciding to conduct a private war of his own, with Bomber Command of the R.A.F. as his army.' Fuller goes on to quote from *Bombing Vindicated* by J.M. Speight as stating categorically that it was the British who 'began to bomb objectives on the German mainland before the Germans began to bomb objectives on the British mainland.' Fuller then adds: 'Thus, on Mr. Speight's evidence [of whom Fuller says that he 'speaks with authority, as the Principal Assistant Secretary to the Air Ministry'], it was Mr. Churchill who lit the fuse which detonated a war of devastation and terrorization.' See Fuller, *The Second World War*, p.221.

vi. Calvocoressi et al., p. 527. It was the questionable decision by Roosevelt and Churchill to insist on 'Unconditional Surrender' by Germany that strengthened Goebbel's hand, and the resolve of the German people to fight to the bitter end. The crucial question whether the Allies were at war with Hitler and Nazism, or with the German people and nation, seems never to have been asked and discussed in strategic terms, only decided unilaterally by the few people we have mentioned.

vii. Accounts of the development of the Mustang have to be read in *Wilfrid Freeman*, a biography by Anthony Furse, chapter fourteen and in *Hives and the Merlin* by Sir Ian Lloyd and Peter Pugh, chapter seven.

viii. It is pertinent to wonder whether Dowding had any views about the possibility of a long-range fighter. The answer is that he did. In his *Twelve Legions of Angels* (ch. 3) he wrote (this in 1941):

> It is not possible to make a fighter which can accompany bombers to Berlin and back unless you make it nearly as big as the bomber, and then it would lose its handiness and manoeuvrability and be at a disadvantage against enemy fighters.

To this he added: 'We have so many specialised types already that we do not want to add to them.' One wonders whether he would have changed his views as the war progressed, if he had remained in the Air Force – especially if he had remained as C-in-C of Fighter Command, or become the Chief of the Air Staff.

ix. I say England, for England I know. Much of what I say may apply equally to the Scots, Welsh and Irish. Those admirable people are quite capable of putting their own case forward to advantage.

Appendix A

Excepts from 'Dowding's Personal Notes to the Author of *Dowding and the Battle of Britain*'

—◊—

Gibraltar 1900, the Garrison Artillery, aged eighteen

One day I was detailed as Range Officer and went down early in the Morning to Rosia Bay where I was to go aboard the Range Launch.

Greatly to my surprise I found the Colonel Commanding the Artillery (the C.B.A.) there, who announced the intention of accompanying me. This was a visit of which nobody else had been informed.

As soon as we had started he said, "Now, my boy, let's have a look at your orders." After reading them he said: "All very simple. All we have to do is to steam round to the East of the Rock and then proceed Eastward, watching the flag flying from the Station at Signal Hill. Directly that is hauled down stop the launch, drop the target and take up a position to a flank to observe and record the fall of shot. When the flag is hauled up again, pick up the target and return to harbour."

When we got round to the East side there was the flag flying from Middle Hill and off we started into the Mediterranean..... (On) and on we went and on we went – 10,000, 15,000, 20,000 yards and still the flag flew, though now visible only through powerful binoculars.

At last when half the height of the Rock was below the horizon down came the flag. "Stop the launch, drop the target," cried the Colonel. Presently we saw the great clouds of black-powder smoke mushrooming up above the battery and the shells splashed into the sea so far short of us that they looked as if they had fallen just at the foot of the Rock. Presently the flag was hoisted again and we picked up the target and started on our long voyage back.

As we were walking to the Mess after landing I said to the Colonel, "You know we are going to get into trouble over this, Sir". The Colonel said "What do you mean? You carried out your orders didn't you?" "Yes, Sir" I said, "but that won't count for much when I get back." "Nonsense," the Colonel snorted, "they can't possibly blame you". "Well, Sir" I said "would you mind holding back and letting me go into the Ante Room a few seconds ahead of you, and see what sort of reception I get?" "All right, go ahead" said he.

The moment I set foot in the Ante Room there was a roar of execration. "Ah! Here comes the young .....! What the Hell do you mean by going off half way to Malta? etc., etc." In the middle of it all the Colonel sailed in. He said that he had been in the launch, that the orders had been carried out precisely and suggested that criticisms, if any, should be addressed to him. There fell a great silence!

7 Mountain Battery, Rawal Pindi, 1904

What I liked about my time in a Native Battery was the responsibility which came the way of the subaltern, so different from the lot of the junior officer in an Infantry Regiment. Twice I was sent off with my Section of two guns to work with the infantry at hill stations. I had to make all the arrangements with the local authorities for camping, rations, fodder, medical services etc., etc., with no support to fall back upon in case of disagreements. Two incidents remain especially clear in my memory. The first occurred on the return journey from Lansdowne where I had been sent to co-operate with the 3rd Gurkhas. My route lay for 3 days, through the Terai Jungle, from the foothills to the bridge of boats across the Ganges at Hardwar. This jungle short-cut saved several days on the length of the journey had it been made entirely by road. There were no provisions or fodder to be found normally.

Staff College Camberley 1912

I was always irked by the lip-service that the Staff paid to freedom of thought, contrasted with an actual tendency to repress all but conventional ideas.

A particular instance of this [lip-service ?] was in connection with the role of Cavalry in War. The predominance of the 'Arme blanche' was upheld, despite the lessons of the Boer War. Non-conformists (of whom I was one) were labelled by the Staff as 'bad boys'; and in this respect the atmosphere was rather reminiscent of that of a preparatory school with 'Wullie' Robertson as its stern Headmaster. It was quite surprising to see how childish, under this treatment, clever men in their thirties could become.

But the 'Arme-blanche' fixation went beyond a joke. In the Summer holiday period I was attached to a Cavalry Regiment, the Queen's Bays, for a period including the Army Manoeuvres. Previous to this there was a field day at Aldershot, and I heard that it had been arranged to 'down' a man called Briggs, who, at the previous year's manoeuvres, had put it across the Directing Staff by using Bays Cavalry as Mounted Infantry. Everybody knew about this. The subalterns were all talking about it. Sure enough the field day was held, and Douglas Haig came down specially for the occasion. If I remember aright Allenby was there also. Poor Briggs was given the task of attacking an entrenched enemy on the edge of a wood with guns on the flank. He was prevented by "impassable mountains" and an "impenetrable swamp" from turning either flank, so he was forced to make a frontal attack across the open. At the end of the day the 'Officers' Call' was sounded, and in their presence, plus a variegated assembly of orderlies and horse holders, Haig tongue-lashed Briggs as if he had been an offending Subaltern.

I had the greatest admiration for Briggs; he we went through this ordeal without the slightest loss of dignity or flicker of resentment. My admiration did not extend to Haig.

With the RFC in France 1916

[Major] Musgrave had the fixed idea that the R.F.C. were much too safe and comfortable and that it was his duty to impose hardships sufficient to redress the balance of suffering. The other two Flight Commanders, Lewis and James, were splendid fellows who really put wireless on a practical footing as regards observation of artillery fire. Their machines had been standing out in the open in all weathers for 5 months and the fabric of the planes had become so slack and soggy that the machines would scarcely get off the ground, let alone climb to a reasonable operating height. Repeated requests for new wings to be fitted had met with uncompromising refusal from the Major – this was a matter in which he could conveniently ensure that his officers should undergo danger approximating to that to which the Infantry were exposed.

About this time the Major returned to England on ten days' leave, leaving me in command of the Squadron. Directly he had gone I called in the aircraft from the front-line Flights two by two and fitted new wings, so that by the time the Major returned all had been so fitted.

When he found out what had been done he was furious and actually ordered the aircraft to be sent back in order that the old soggy wings might be replaced. Somebody (not I) told R.F.C. Headquarters about this, the Major was returned to Army duties and I was given command of Squadron.

Wireless Experimental Establishment Brooklands 1915

I was sent home to start a Wireless and Experimental establishment at Brooklands. ... I had one Flight Commander, two civilian assistants and no pilots, so I asked for two. The answer was that no pilots were available, but that they would send me two officers just commissioned: I could teach them to fly... I had one Maurice Farman and one single-seater Bleriot–hardly an ideal equipment for flying instruction.

One of my civil assistants was a man named Prince. He was an enthusiastic amateur (who) before the war was working part-time for Marconi's. He had all the latest developments at his finger ends, and I tried to get permission to buy the components needed to make up-to-date and efficient valve-sets instead of the out-dated and cumbersome crystal sets issued to the R.A.F.(sic) Here I was obstructed completely by Woolwich. I had no imprest account, and if I wanted half a dozen brass screws I had to put in an indent and wait days or weeks for delivery. So Prince and I used to go up to Marconi's offices in Aldwych and ... steal what we needed.

As a result Prince had made up in two or three weeks a single-valve set weighing about a quarter of the official R.A.F. set and with about four times its range.

We then reported to the War Office what we had done and asked to be allowed to demonstrate it with a view to its adoption in the Service. The first objection was that the set would be (a) too delicate to transport and (b) too complicated for use by any but exceptionally highly-trained operators.

To this I answered that if they would send us two normally efficient R.F.C. operators, after 24 hours we would send them out unsupervised in a light tender, and they would erect the station and work a dummy 'shoot' with an aeroplane. The answer to this was was to send down from Woolwich an enormous piece of furniture like a wardrobe, called a 'de Forest Audion' which requires a 70 foot mast. (We had been working with the standard 30 foot mast, easy to transport and erect.) The whole thing was obviously unsuited to front-line work; but in addition we found that although the apparatus would take a fairly strong signal and amplify it enormously, it could do nothing with weak signals. So I asked the War Office if they would send down a Woolwich team to work their Audion; they should have their 70 foot mast and we would be content with our 30 footer. I would send an aeroplane down the line to Salisbury transmitting A for the first mile, B for the second, and so on. Much to our delight they accepted this challenge, and so was born what we afterwards called the 'Priests of Baal' trial.

The first thing that happened was that Prince went off into a fit of helpless giggles when he saw the 'expert' whom the Woolwich people had brought down to operate their set. I asked him what was the matter and he told me that the expert was a man whom Marconi's had sacked for inefficiency 2 or 3 months earlier.

The arrangement was that the aeroplane should circle the aerodrome while the sets were being tuned in and should start off down the line when we gave the signal. We were ready in a minute or so, but the opposition kept saying "Not quite ready yet" – "Just a minute more", etc. etc. So we strolled across to see what was happening; and there was the expert sitting with his headphones on, twiddling the knobs frantically while the ends of the headphone leads were lying on the ground. He had forgotten to connect them to the set!

At last they were ready and the aeroplane flew off. By the letter L the Audion could receive no more, while our set was still getting good signals at S when the pilot stopped transmitting and returned.

The War Office, however, remained unimpressed.

So there we were with our offering spurned and nothing on our official programme. But, having *carte blanche* owing to the unwitting generosity of Marconi's, we decided to experiment with air-to-ground telephony, and, thanks to Prince's knowledge and ingenuity we soon had a telephone transmitter fitted up in our Maurice Farman, and I was the first person, certainly in England if not in the world, to listen to a wireless telephone message from the air. We could have fixed up two-way communication too if we had not received a directive from the War Office that radio-telephonic communication between air and ground was not considered to be practical.

About this time, Summer 1915, I was sent back to France to take command of No. 16 Squadron at Merville. I was not sorry to leave Brooklands, though I was absorbed by and interested in the work that we were doing; but we were up against the worst side of the Military Machine. It is a strange thing, but, though I served for 20 years in the Army, I never really identified myself with it. Soldiers with a capital S were on one side and I was on the other. This feeling was more or less subconscious until I went to the Staff College and there it began to filter through into my conscious mind. Brooklands brought full realization. The mental laziness which makes it always easier to say No than to say Yes, because if you say Yes you will have to think, and you may make a mistake: "Besides, what right has a barely fledged Major with a couple of civilian assistants to criticize equipment which has been recommended by our established advisors, has proved good enough for his elders and betters and has been ordered by the thousand?"

UK 1918

In the Spring of 1918 ... I was posted to York as Chief Staff Officer to Major-General Gordon. Our Headquarters were at first in the buildings of the Knavesmire Race Course, and when the war ended and the Race Course was released to its owners our officers were moved to Acomb, a suburb of York.

Thereafter most of our difficulties were concerned with demobilization. I remember being sent to Sheffield to speak to about 2,000 airmen who were reported to be on the verge of mutiny. It wasn't a very attractive prospect, but it went off all right once they were convinced that the demobilization rules had been framed on the fairest basis possible, and that the rules were being adhered to without fear, favour or affection.

This was the honest truth so far as we were concerned, but individual enterprise could not be entirely suppressed. For instance, a Stores Officer at Ayr had very grave deficiencies in his accounts. Our H.Q. read the report and ordered a Court Martial. But the Group at Edinburgh had to report that he had been demobilized and could not be traced. It transpired upon enquiry that the man had traveled to Edinburgh and from there had sent a telegram to his unit, in the name of the Group, ordering his immediate demobilization.

RAF Hendon 1926

My next appointment was the command of (RAF Station) Kenley. At this time the R.A.F. Pageant (later known as the Display) was started as an annual event at Hendon.

The first Pageant was organized by Sir John Salmond, but the second and subsequent Pageants and Displays up till 1926, and several others at later dates, were organized and controlled by me. Units came from all parts of the country to participate and aircrews were inclined to regard it as a pleasant relaxation where punctuality and discipline could be pleasantly relaxed.

Time for rehearsals had obviously to be limited, and the end of each Display found me in a state of complete physical and mental collapse. Nothing has ever induced in me a comparable state of prostration. Of course, after a few years one learned by experience how to cope with the countless emergencies which arose and the Display achieved an enviable reputation for clockwork precision.

Palestine 1929

In September 1929 I was given a more active assignment. The Arabs in Palestine had made a concerted attack on the Jews, amounting to massacre in some places. The High Commissioner in Palestine had called for a large increase in the British Garrison because he feared a general Arab uprising accompanied by a massacre of Europeans.

Trenchard's view was that this was quite unnecessary, and that Air Control supported by two or three Battalions was all that was required. He sent me out at 48 hours' notice, giving me a fortnight to write an 'Appreciation of the Situation' and to advise on the minimum force which would suffice to maintain order in Palestine. I was also in executive command of all the troops in Palestine and Transjordan, although the High Commissioner (Sir John Chancellor) was titular Commander in Chief.

At my first interview with him when I called upon him at his office, filled with nothing but polite thoughts, I was shattered by his suddenly banging the table and telling me not to forget that he was C in C. And yet he was kindness and hospitality itself.

I started my investigation with a completely open mind – in other words, in a state of complete ignorance of Jewish, Arab and Palestinian problems and politics. The first thing I did was to have a good look at the country from the air, and then to drive around it with an armoured-car escort.

I found plenty of evidence of implacable hostility to the Jews, but no apparent animus against Europeans generally.

Pursuing my enquiries in Jerusalem I very soon came to the conclusion that the chief handicap of the Government was a complete absence of any Intelligence System. They simply did not know what was going on under their noses. They relied for their Intelligence on an incredibly inefficient Police Force, which in turn seemed to have no sources of information except bazaar rumour. When I compared the Palestine Police, under their then commander, with the magnificent organization that 'Bobby' Prescott had forged in Iraq I was astounded. So there were my first two recommendations ready-made: an efficient Intelligence System and a new Chief of Police. (In one Police Post on the slopes of the Jordan Valley were found only 3 men out of a garrison of 10. The rest had given themselves leave. And guardsmen recruits for the British Section so soon lost their discipline that they could be seen sitting on the kerb-stones smoking when they were on night patrol.)

Almost everyone to whom I talked was strongly pro–Arab, without condoning their recent excesses.

I have never seen the true story told in this country. What happened in the 1914–18 War was that we induced the Beduin and Transjordan Arabs to come in on our side against the Turks by a promise that Arabs should have self-government after the war, except in the country West of Damascus. This was an obvious way of saying that we could make no promises concerning Syria, which at that time was held by the French.

This was no light-hearted promise made by an unauthorized agent like Lawrence, but a documentary promise made through Sir Henry McMahon, the British Government representative in Cairo.

Later came the shameful repudiation of that promise in the 'Balfour Declaration', a dishonesty for which we have never ceased to suffer. As I write in late 1956, the crows have indeed come home to roost and we face the hostility of the entire Arab world.

The apologists of that miserable Declaration have said, "If you draw a line South through Damascus, Palestine is to the West of it, so our promise was never meant to include Palestine."

This shame, like so many of our troubles in the Middle East, was basically due to political pressure from America, whence the Zionist movement derived almost all its funds and where the Jewish vote had a considerable effect upon Presidential and other elections.

Everything was done perfectly legally! Rich landowners, often absentees in Syria, cheerfully sold their land to the Zionists at about three times its market value, and then the Arab peasants, who had cultivated the land for generations, were given short notice to quit, without being offered any alternative tenancy or employment. And so a growing army of landless unemployed was created – the forerunners of the disposed thousands now in Jordan refugee camps. A few of them found work on the roads and other Palestinian Government works, and others took to banditry. The Palestinian Arabs as a whole saw the Jewish population growing by leaps and bounds and foresaw the time when they themselves would be outnumbered and driven out of their land. It was indeed a sad situation for anyone with the most rudimentary sense of justice.

I had several contacts who could put me into the political picture better than anyone in the Government Offices. One was an orange grower, a British subject (Maltese) who was friendly with all the principal personalities on both sides. His only wish was for peace and to be allowed to carry on his business undisturbed. Another was Colonel Shute, Commanding the Trans Jordan Frontier Force, by far the most efficient body of ground troops in the Palestine Command.

The Arab Legion, then commanded by Peake Pasha (the successor of Lawrence) was also a valuable body for the control of the Beduin.

The British Army troops were under the command of General Dobbie (later Governor of Malta in Hitler's War). They suffered, while I was in Palestine, from unfamiliarity with the country, the people and their habits and customs.

At the end of my allotted fortnight I sent off my 'Appreciation' to the effect that the situation disclosed no dangers which could not be met by the Air Force Units available locally and in Egypt, and three battalions of infantry; plus, of course, a re-organization of the Intelligence system and a big shake-up of the Police.

I was told to stay in Palestine until the end of the year to watch events in case their course should move me to modify what was of necessity only a partially-considered opinion.

Fighter Group HQ Kenley 1929

Att the end of 1929 I returned to England and was posted to the Fighter group with Headquarters at Kenley. The Group was part of the Air Defence of Great Britain at Uxbridge. The Group was not equipped in any such way as to make it a very formidable defence against air attacks, but we did have an innovation which was to prove the basis of effective Home Defence, and that was Radio Telephony between Air and Ground. (It will be remembered that we had developed a prototype of this at Brooklands fifteen years before, and had been told it was not wanted.)

For some unexplained reason the Air Ministry invited a party of German Air Force officers to come to England to see this – our one little ewe lamb of an Air

Defence secret. Milch and Udet (were) of the party; Goering wanted to come too, but he was so unpopular that the authorities drew the line at him.

During the six months I commanded this Group (there were) some rather ridiculous Air Manoeuvres. I was put in command of one side with Headquarters at Cranwell. The other side was based on the London and Kentish aerodromes.

Farcical conditions were created by the Directing Staff in which an impassable range of mountains existed in Essex and Bedford was a neutral country whose frontier must not be violated. This left a corridor about 20 miles broad through which air attacks must pass; so the first thing I did, without telling anyone else, was to collect half a dozen wireless tenders and string them across the corridor about fifteen miles South of Cranwell. So, on the first day, my fighters were able to intercept every bombing raid coming up from the South.

My only trouble was that in every combat the Umpires adjudicated that we had lost twice as many fighters as we had shot down bombers. It was at once obvious that we could not win a war against Umpires of that mentality, so we contented ourselves with making token interceptions without attack by fighters and then going and bombing the bombers on the ground while they were refueling. I had a single R.T. plane following the bombers at a distance of extreme visibility, and reporting in a very simple code when and where the bombers were landing to refuel. In this form of attack the Umpire allotted to me liberal casualties among the refueling bombers. In the end the exercise proved such a farce regarding the lessons to be drawn from it that no Report on it was ever circulated and the whole episode was decently interred.

APPENDIX B

'Too Late'

—ℳ—

[*Statement on aid to Great Britain by General Douglas MacArthur in response to a request from William Allen White, Chairman of the Committee to Defend America by Aiding the Allies, September 16, 1940.*]

You have asked my military opinion as to whether the time has come for America to give continued and further aid to England in the fight for civilization. The history of failure in war can almost be summed up in two words: too late. Too late in comprehending the deadly purpose of a potential enemy; too late in realizing the mortal danger; too late in· preparedness; too late in uniting all possible forces for resistance; too late in standing with one's friends. Victory in war results from no mysterious alchemy of wizardry but entirely upon the concentration of superior force at the critical points of combat. To face an adversary in detail has been the prayer of every conqueror in history. It is the secret of the past successes of the Axis powers in this war. It is their main hope for continued and ultimate victory. The greatest strategical mistake in all history will be made if America fails to recognize the vital moment, if she permits again the writing of that fatal epitaph: too late. Such coordinated help as may be regarded as proper by our leaders should be synchronized with the British effort so that the English-speaking peoples of the world will not be broken in detail. The vulnerability of singleness will disappear before unity of effort. Not too late, not tomorrow, but today.

Tactics in Dispute
by
Air Commodore A.C. Deere DSO OBE DFC[1]

—∿—

Public interest in the Battle of Britain having been aroused by United Artists' recent film on this famous air battle, the tactics employed in the Battle by the air defence forces of Fighter Command are again in dispute. Pilots of the time who were followers of Keith Park as AOC 11 Group and those of 12 Group who supported their Group Commander, Leigh-Mallory, are arraigned in re-awakened argument on the merits of small and large formations for defence, the root cause of the tactical disagreement between the two Group Commanders.

As a flight commander, who led both flight and squadron in the Battle, I have decided views on the subject of the tactics used. Naturally, therefore, I was interested to see if the tactical controversy was introduced into the film, and it was slanted. In the event, it was touched on only briefly in a fictitious scene – one of the few in the film – played in the Commander-in-Chief's office. Personally, I was glad that this was so because to have laid too much stress on what was, in fact, a personality clash between two commanders would have detracted from what was otherwise a magnificent team effort, and one which achieved an historic victory in the first and perhaps the last classic air battle.

However, to coincide with the film's release Robert Wright's book, *Dowding and the Battle of Britain* appeared in the bookshops. In essence a potted biography of Lord Dowding, it is concerned chiefly with the strategic and tactical issues in Fighter Command before and during the Battle. From his researches and personal contact as Aide to Dowding at the time, Wright reveals much that was not previously known about the controversy. And he confirms the belief, long held by Park's supporters, that his tactical handling of the Battle was in accordance with the aims of the Commander-in-Chief; aims with which Park had first-hand knowledge, by virtue of his previous appointment as Senior Air Staff Officer to Dowding in the formative years of Fighter Command's existence.

In the light of this re-awakened controversy and these new disclosures I have been moved to restate my views which hold firm on the side of the small formation as the basic element in fighter defence operations, at least in the conditions which pertained in the Battle of Britain. In fairness, however, to those who supported Leigh-Mallory at the time, I confess I write with the advantage of hindsight; nevertheless, hindsight has served only to strengthen a viewpoint already firmly held and not to change it.

When in May 1940, Dowding wrote his now historically famous letter to the Under Secretary of State at the Air Ministry to express his resistance to the plan to send more home-based fighter Squadrons to France, he was motivated by the necessity to have in being in the United Kingdom, the minimum number of squadrons he considered necessary 'for the defence of this Country'. He believed that 'if an adequate, fighter force is kept in this Country ... to resist invasion we should be able to carry on for some time.'

Dowding appreciated that with the fall of France imminent the full might of the Luftwaffe would be turned against England and in the time available he could not hope to match the Germans in strength. The strategic disposition of his forces was therefore of paramount importance and it must be dictated by the ability 'to carry on for some time.' In effect 'some time' was that period from the opening of an air onslaught to, in German eyes, its successful culmination as a prelude to invasion. If Dowding's fighter defence forces could hold out through the Summer the Germans would be forced to defer their plans for an invasion into the less favourable Autumnal weather period or risk a seaborne assault without having first established the necessary air superiority.

Thus time was the essence of Dowding's strategy, which resolved itself into a twofold aim:

(1) To prevent the destruction of his forces, and

(2) In the process, to inflict the maximum of destruction on the enemy air force.

To achieve this the husbanding of his force was the paramount consideration, but in order to ensure the second part of the aim it was necessary to meet the immediate threat by committing at anyone time only that portion of his force required to protect the vital targets. Only by so doing could Fighter Command still be an effective force at the climax of invasion.

It was this concept of operations which dictated Park's tactics wherein he endeavoured to combine the factors of maximum flexibility with minimum force, the latter scaled to meet the threat of his major airfields which in the context of air superiority were of vital importance and, of course, whose serviceability would play an important part in mounting around-the-clock air operations over the invasion area expected to be in the South-East; as we now know was to be the case.

His plan was simple. To use an analogy, it was based on the premise that as the lightweight in the contest he could not expect to knock-out his heavier opponent. He could but hope to win either by a technical knock-out or on a points decision. To knock-out the Luftwaffe was indeed never possible, it had too much in its armoury. A technical knock-out was possible but not probable in the expected time available. A points decision seemed, therefore, the most likely solution and this meant staying the distance. In effect this is what Fighter Command achieved.

Tactically, the Battle of Britain was a three-phase operation: the attacks on the peripheral targets including radar, on the sector airfields, and those on London. As regards the first-named it has never, I think, been disputed that the only way to combat these was by the use of small formations operating from forward airfields. The short sea-crossing to the target areas meant a minimum of radar warning and it was rarely ever possible to get more than a flight into the air to achieve effective interception. On hard-hit forward airfields, as for example Manston, a 'scramble' was always a hazardous event which usually resolved itself into an every-man-for-himself take-off as the only sure way of getting airborne before the bombs fell.

It was the two second phases which brought to light the tactical differences of opinion between Park and Leigh-Mallory. Only at this point in the Battle was there sufficient airborne time in hand to effect interception in reasonable strength before the target area was reached. Moreover, up till this time, mid-August, the 12 Group squadrons had not been called upon to take part in the fighting which continued to be concentrated in the 11 Group area.

In the meantime, back on the 12 Group airfields the pilots were persistently harrying the controllers at sectors to get them into the Battle somehow. The controllers in turn were complaining to Leigh-Mallory who was constantly ringing the 11 Group controllers for permission to send his fighters into their area. But true to his policy of containment, Park was happy that for the time being he could handle the attack with his own resources. As, however, the raids moved inland and increased in frequency and strength there was posed an altogether more serious problem, that of the defence of the Base – the sector operations room, the control link in the Air Defence System, and the sector airfields whose continued use was vital to successful air defence.

At this time, too, another factor entered into the equation, that of raid filtering. Raids of shallow penetration were easily identifiable and tracked to interception, but as they moved further inland and so out of the seaward radar coverage of our CR stations the plots became confused with those of our own fighters, both now the responsibility of the Observer Corps. With hopelessly inadequate detection devices the Corps relied mainly on visual sightings, and cloud cover quite often enabled a raid to pass by unidentified. Thus, raid filtering was early revealed as the Achilles' Heel of our air defence system, and more and more as the tracks of the enemy and those of our own fighters coalesced over South-East England, the raid picture in the Group and Sector operations rooms became one of confusion. And, moreover, one of the principle CH stations in the South had been knocked out, thus allowing undetected penetration of the perimeter defences which served to aggravate the problem confronting the by now harassed Group Controllers. Clearly, Park's chief concern, the defence of his sector airfields apart, was now one of over-commitment. He dare not take unrestrained action on the picture presented to him on the operations table because of the danger of 'spoofing' either intentionally by the Germans, who were now splitting their raids and also making diversion attacks to draw off the defences for a big raid sneaking in through the radar gap in the South, or unintentionally by wrong identification both in numbers and as between friend and foe. The only safe tactic was therefore, to operate his force in small formations which, because of their flexibility, could both delay their take-off time until raid information became more positive and yet be mutually self-supporting in the target area. Whatever tactic he adopted the problem of defence of the Base was paramount, and it was this undertaking which was assigned to the 12 Group squadrons at Park's request.

By now it was well into August, and the 12 Group squadrons, though becoming increasingly more involved in the Battle, were being used principally to defend the 11 Group Airfields and to meet 12 Group's allotted responsibility 'of defence of its own area, including some highly industrial districts'. Incursions into the 11 Group area were therefore strictly controlled by Fighter Command in accordance with Dowding's directive that Park was in sole control of the tactical battle for so long as the main weight of attack was concentrated in the 11 Group area of operations.

Circumscribed, at least as he saw it, by these instructions it is easy to understand Leigh-Mallory's feelings of frustration, and no less those of his pilots who, at constant readiness, contended they were being kept deliberately out of the Battle. It was in this atmosphere that the tactic of using big wings was first put forward by Douglas Bader in the hope, I suspect, that by adopting the large formation more 12 Group fighters would get into the Battle. It was a natural reaction from an aggressive leader of Bader's calibre who, says his biographer, 'found it intolerable that others should he plunging into the fire of battle while he was held impotently on the ground'. Bader's persuasive personality soon won over Leigh-Mallory to the concept, although, initially he reputedly countered the suggestion by replying: 'We can't put all our eggs in one basket, Bader. You've got to hang on and wait. No doubt the enemy would be delighted to draw our fighter cover away from the Midlands.' Sound advice; and based on Leigh Mallory's knowledge of his Commander-in-Chief's aims, knowledge not of course disseminated down to the squadrons; and even if it had been it was indigestible stuff to Bader and his restless followers.

By the last week of August, when fighting was at an intense stage, tempers at all levels had become somewhat frayed, and not least those of Park and Leigh-Mallory. The latter was now solidly lined up behind Bader who, to again quote his biographer, 'skulked and stormed in the dispersal hut at Coltishall'. But Park was not to he intimidated because he was both confident that the tactics he was adopting were paying off, and ever mindful of his directive to call for outside help only when absolutely essential.

More and more, Park was finding that flexibility was his chief weapon in countering new German tactics of split-raids, spoof attacks and diversions, all of which tended to swamp the raid-reporting system. Operating at squadron strength, he now introduced the tactic of using specified Spitfire squadrons to get airborne early to engage and draw-off the escort fighters and at the same time to report back on the strength and direction of the raids. This allowed him to hold other squadrons on the ground at a high state of readiness until the enemy plan of attack was established; and then to engage the bomber force under more advantageous terms. Using these tactics he quite often had all his squadrons in the air at once thus leaving his sector airfields unprotected. Now was the time to request assistance from 12 Group.

At first all this meant to the 12 Group squadrons was a higher state and longer hours of readiness, but as the weight and fury of the raids intensified they more and more got into the fighting; and with some success. Bader had, by this time, won his point, for on 7 September when in accordance with Leigh-Mallory's phoned instructions, 'Next time 11 Group calls on you, take your whole team', the Duxford wing of three squadrons took to the air. In the ensuing climb to height, the two supporting squadrons got so far behind that they virtually missed the fight. One wonders, therefore, if operating independently with less time to form-up a greater number of the fighters could have been brought to bear. The leader's answer to this was to complain on landing, 'If only we could get off earlier we could get on top of them'. A valid comment but Bader, ignorant of Park's tactics, could not know that as a reserve-cover force it would have been folly to commit the 12 Group squadrons too early in the raid build-up. Time to height when ordered off was therefore overriding, and any formation scramble greater than squadron strength would clearly operate against this consideration.

Curiously, it was on this day, 7th September, that the Germans switched their attacks to London and 12 Group was now virtually freed of its cover commitment. This fact, plus a certain amount of success – and one must be fair, the Duxford wing did have its successes[2] – led Bader to press for more squadrons *en masse* until finally the operating strength of the Wing was raised to five squadrons. Although a larger force would inevitably slow down the interception time, this factor was no longer of quite such importance because it was to some extent off-set by the deeper penetration of the raiders. If there ever was a time for using big formations it was now, and the Duxford wing certainly delivered some telling blows, albeit that a number of interceptions were made after the bombers had reached their target.

As is now known, however, the Germans had already decided that invasion was no longer a possibility. August had come and. gone, and with it the good weather; and the Royal Air Force was still a force to be reckoned with. The attacks on London were in effect the last throw of a beaten opponent, carried out as much in anger at the Royal Air Force bombing of Berlin as a desperate last attempt to deliver a knock-out blow. But the knock-out blow never came and a tired and disillusioned Luftwaffe retreated to its corner leaving the ring to Fighter Command, victors on a points decision. Thus whatever impact the Duxford Wing had on the subsequent fighting it had none on the outcome of the Battle proper which, in the words of Lord Dowding, 'ended when Hitler cancelled the orders for invasion'.

It will be argued by the protagonists of the Duxford Wing enthusiasts that because the 12 Group squadrons were held back so long before getting into the fighting, the effectiveness of the Wing concept as a tactic in fighter defence could not be proven. There is of course some merit in this argument. However, it ignores the main problem facing Park, that of fighting and surviving throughout the period leading up to and including an expected invasion, while at the same time keeping intact the sector airfields. This latter task, assigned to 12 Group when the airfields came under heavy attack, was a vital one and its fulfilment could not have been guaranteed had the bulk of the 12 Group forces been committed to the Battle from the outset.

Furthermore, and as already stated, Dowding's directive to the AOC 12 Group charged him with the defence of the Midlands as his prime task; and unrestricted entry into the fighting while it was confined to the 11 Group area and within the capacity of Park to handle, would have been in contravention of this stated task. In fact, Leigh-Mallory did partially ignore orders when, without the knowledge of Fighter Command, he sent his five-squadron Wing into Battle; thus, to use his own phrase when earlier he resisted the temptation to do so, 'putting all his eggs in one basket'. In doing so he was wrong in principle, and in the matter of tactics unsound. Johnnie Johnson had this to say on both points: 'The Duxford Wing had taken seventeen minutes to leave the ground and a further twenty minutes before it set course from base. Also, because it absorbed five squadrons from a relatively weak Group it left some highly important targets in the Midlands short of fighter cover'. A damning indictment by one who was not only a pilot in the Duxford Wing but also, at a later date, an outstanding Wing Leader under Leigh-Mallory.[3]

The Battle of Britain has gone down in history as a great victory, and it was due not so much to successful tactics as possession of an advanced air defence system backed by fine team work and inspired leadership at all levels. Tactics were of course important to the outcome, and in the finely-balanced period of fighting towards the end of August they were perhaps all important, and at that time the overriding factor that ensured final victory. Victory proved Park's tactics to be right in the particular circumstances, and however much one might lean towards the Wing concept it is difficult to envisage success other than in the way it was achieved, a combination of flexibility and economy of force.[4]

It is, I think, fitting to leave the last word on the subject with an historian, Sir Basil Liddell Hart, who wrote, 'The Germans' bid to gain command of the air as a preliminary to invasion, was frustrated by the superb efforts of fifty-odd squadrons of Fighter Command under the masterly direction of Air Chief Marshal Sir Hugh Dowding and Air Vice-Marshal Keith Park.'

Notes:

1 This article was given in typescript to the author by Alan Deere at the latter's home in Wendover, Bucks, on his visit to him of July 21st 1995. It had been published in *RAF Souvenir Book 1970* (London, 1970).

2 The reader is referred back to our chapter 3.

3 In fact Johnson flew on only one operation in the Battle and was rested for medical reasons.

4 The wing, as Dowding observed, was justified only in offensive operations.

APPENDIX D

'Where Would We Have Been. . .?'

—⚏—

There was a great deal about the Battle of Britain that has given Dowding cause to feel a pride that has never dimmed in the men who served under his command. That has always been uppermost in his mind. There were also, as was perhaps only to be expected, some aspects of the battle that have caused him to feel a hurt that has lingered, and which has attached to it an inevitable sorrow. Being of the reserved nature that he is, he has never been given to expressing himself openly or in force about his own personal feelings. To some extent that could be regarded as a pity. If he had been able to explode, the sorrow over the actions of some of those who served under his command might not have lingered on in his mind. For too long he remained silent; but it is small wonder that he did because, whether it was intentional or unintentional, the infliction of the damage that was done was of a nature that brought to him a very deep personal distress.

'Why were they all so opposed to Dowding, and why did so many people go out of their way to deny him what he was entitled to?' a former member of Leigh-Mallory's staff once asked, and without waiting for a reply added: 'Was it because they could not stand it when Dowding was proved so right and they were proved so wrong?'

It could never be said of Dowding that he ever tried to force a conclusive proof that he was right. He has always tried to arrive at a fair assessment of what he had attempted to do, believing in what he was doing, and he always fought hard for that. But the last effort that he would ever make would be to try to score off anybody at their expense, or dismiss lightly the efforts of other people, even though he might not agree with them. Everyone, in his view, was entitled to some position of attention, and no one should ever have to endure sheer neglect.

After the war, when at last it was all over and the cheering was at its height and the honours and awards to the successful commanders were being passed out thick and fast, what thought was given to the man who, nearly five years before, had laid the foundations for the great victory that was being celebrated? Two years before Winston Churchill had written to him about his acceptance of a peerage and his 'ever-memorable services to this country during the Battle of Britain'. Dowding had accepted that and had quietly gone on his own way. Now, when the huzzas were loud and those who had led us to victory were rightly being accorded acclamation, there was no mention of the name of Dowding in any of the official honours and awards and promotions. It was in the last, in the promotions, that there was a curious oversight.

Many times it had been asked, even during the war, why Dowding had not been made a Marshal of the Royal Air Force. Now others were promoted to that highest rank in the Service. There was sufficient reason, and a precedent was now established, for this reward. But Dowding remained an Air Chief Marshal.

Down through the years there have been repeated questions asked about the reason why Dowding has never received this important promotion to the highest rank in the Royal Air Force. But for all the lip-service that has been paid to the suitability of such recognition of what Dowding had achieved, twenty-eight years had to pass before a firm public statement about that was made by one of his fellow Air Marshals. In a letter in the *Daily Telegraph*, Air Marshal Sir Robert Saundby, who had been Deputy Commander-in-Chief of Bomber Command, described himself as 'no uncritical admirer of Dowding's'; but he nevertheless saw fit, quite voluntarily, to make [...] the statement: 'No one can deny that [Dowding] led Fighter Command with determination and ability in the Battle of Britain, one of the decisive battles of the world. Even at this late hour it would be a very proper act of grace and justice if Lord Dowding were to be promoted to the rank of Marshal of the Royal Air Force.' That was the expression of the opinion of a distinguished officer of air rank. It is echoed in the minds of the many who have wondered about this matter. Foremost among them are those who served under Dowding's command, and particularly his pilots. 'The treatment he received after the battle still baffles me,' Ginger Lacey once said. 'I cannot understand how the authorities were able to talk about the fate of civilisation hanging on the outcome of the Battle of Britain, and yet discard the victor.' And then Lacey asked the question that has been for so long in the minds of so many of Dowding's supporters. 'Where would we have been if Stuffy had lost the battle?'

In speaking about the resurgence of interest that has developed in what happened in the summer of 1940, Dowding had in mind the effect of the film *Battle of Britain* which was released in the summer of 1969. This contains an authentic portrayal by Sir Laurence Olivier of the part of Dowding as Commander-in-Chief of Fighter Command in that crucial time of nearly thirty years ago. But the film is more than just a story about Dowding's achievements: it is the story of the whole battle, as seen from both sides and at all levels.

Along with Tom Gleave, Robert Stanford-Tuck, 'Ginger' Lacey, and Claire Legge of the W.A.A.F. at the time of the Battle of Britain, I was asked to help with advice in the making of the film; and at the same time it became my responsibility to keep Dowding fully informed about what was being done. The producers of the film were extremely anxious that the mammoth task that they had embarked upon should meet with Dowding's approval. He was consulted, and the plans for how he was to be presented were discussed at length; and the enthusiasm of Harry Saltzman and Ben Fisz, the co-producers, and the director, Guy Hamilton, more than satisfied Dowding that they were intent upon doing full justice to the overall story.

So keen did Dowding's own interest become in the actual making of the film that he visited the Studios at Pinewood and the sites on location at the actual airfields which had been used in the battle. He watched some of the shooting of parts of the film, including those with Laurence Olivier at work in a reproduction [...] of his office as it used to be at the Headquarters of Fighter Command at Bentley Priory; and he was able to see some of the results of that work on film as it was put together.

One afternoon in the summer of 1968, on the airfield at Hawkinge, which lies above Folkestone, and from which some of Keith Park's squadrons of No.11 Group used to take off during the battle, Dowding talked with Trevor Howard, who plays the part of Park in the film. They were sitting beside one of the Hurricanes which was being used, and filming was going on only a short distance away. The weather was just as it had been in that September of twenty-eight years before: a sparklingly clear, hot, sunny day. From the direction of the Channel, no distance away, two of the Spitfires which appear in the film came hurtling in, the singing of their Merlin engines awakening strong memories in the minds of those who had known what it had all been like. The two fighters, of that slim beauty that no fashion can decry, slid easily through the air over the airfield, turned, and came in and landed on the grass in a style that marked them as part of a golden age of flying. Although Dowding watched the aircraft with intense interest, his thoughts were on the subject that we had only just been talking about. He turned to Trevor Howard, and he said: 'If it hadn't been for Keith Park's conduct in the battle, and his loyalty to me as his Commander-in-Chief, we should not be here today.'

At this moment in what we call time, nearly thirty years after the fighting of the Battle of Britain, when we stand with a threat constantly in our minds and we are so beset by fear, it is worth considering, if only for a moment, the views that were expressed by Dowding only two years after he had fought that great battle, and while the Second World War was still in full spate. We have become accustomed to military leaders expounding their views on what should have, or might have, been done, and many of them have been as tiresome as the politicians with their glib excuses and self-adulation. The airman Dowding was a military leader in every sense; but what was his outlook on the future in its relation to the bearing of arms? 'The views that I held then are the same today,' he has said. And because of what we have become those views are of interest, and value today.

'Is war a Good Thing, or not?' Dowding wrote in December 1942. 'There are those who think that war and training for war are necessary for the virility of the race, and that periods of continuous peace lead to softness, luxury and decadence. The abstract thought that war is a useful safety-valve for overpopulation may even be in the minds of some, although it rarely finds expression. If we think that war is good, we are in a happy position; all we have to do is refrain from action and we are assured of an indefinite continuance of this beneficent institution.'

But Dowding could never accept that. 'I venture to think, however, that the exponents of this theory constitute an altogether insignificant minority,' he continued; 'we have suffered too much individually and collectively. We look past the flapping of the flags, the blare of the bands, and the cheering of the crowds, and see war as a hateful remedy for worse evils, into which we have been driven with extreme reluctance.' As with everybody else, Dowding asked the age-old question: 'how is it going to be possible to stop war?' His answers rested in 'three possibilities, long, medium and short-term'.

The long term view, Dowding suggested, would be found 'if and when the standard of morality and unselfishness of the individual improves [and] this improvement will be reflected in the moral behaviour of the State'. But he could not see 'that human nature will undergo any such transformation in a period which is within the horizon of our vision today'.

The short-term measure for the control of war could be found, Dowding suggested, 'in the operation of an International Police.' He did not like that, feeling that it 'is not very practical unless the nations contributing to the upkeep of the police force think alike, and continue to do so amid the stresses and strains.' He thought of it 'at best' as amounting to 'half the world being kept in subjection by the other half', and he felt that 'it can be expected to do little more than to give us a breathing space to set our house in order.'

'Is there a medium-term policy?' he asked, for it is to the medium-term that we must look for hope and help. For that he turned to a subject which always held for him the greatest interest, and it is a strictly practical one. 'An essential step in the creating of contact between nations, and the enlargement of the political unit,' he wrote, 'must be the creation of a common language in some shape or form.' With his never-failing appreciation of reality, Dowding admitted in his further consideration that 'it is idle to discuss the question in the abstract;' but, he stressed, 'the solution depends upon what the nations can be persuaded to accept, and that is essentially a political problem.'

Immediately after any reading of the views of Dowding, and even after re-reading and studying them many times, there is an inclination towards allowing a slick question to leap into one's mind. Is this not all so very idealistic? The only answer that can be made to that is that it is, of course, idealistic. But only a cynic would belittle on those grounds these thoughts of Dowding's. Where would we be, for all the troubles that beset us today, and for all the disillusionment and bitterness which are so rife, without those whose belief in their ideals give them the courage to work for them? In his fighting of the Battle of Britain, Dowding was both a practical airman and an idealist. It is a relief to find a military leader of such stature thinking, [even] after his time in actual service has ended, in terms of the humanities rather than sheer physical deterrents as a way to the future.

But then, Dowding, the man of simple faith and such great integrity, will always be known above all else as a profound and fearless humanitarian. In this troubled world of today, torn as it is with greed and strife and near despair over man's inability to control himself and to work with any semblance of pride in self and service and manners, this airman has always pointed a way, steep though it is, to hope, and warned us of the one great danger that now so gravely besets us.

'Is it really too much to hope that . . . mankind may be induced to eschew the use of force in international relations and that he should do so from motives of altruism and brotherhood, and not from the low motive of fear?' he wrote shortly after the end of the Second World War. 'For fear is the last enemy, fear is the basis of hatred and jealousy and suspicion and cruelty; nothing good or stable was ever built on a foundation of fear.'

Appendix E

Eulogy:
Air Chief Marshal The Lord Dowding of
Bentley Priory, GCB, GCVO, CMG

—⧉—

At the Memorial Service held in Westminster Abbey, where his ashes are laid, the Rt. Hon. Denis Healey, MP, Secretary of State for Defence, delivered this eulogy:

Lord Dowding was one of those great men who this country miraculously produces in times of peril. He occupies a very special place in the hearts of the British people – and rightly so, because he was one of the principal architects of our deliverance in the Battle of Britain: a battle of supreme importance in the history of this country. Its successful outcome ensured the survival of our nation and so preserved a form of democratic society which is Britain's greatest contribution to the history of man. Here, in my opinion, lies the true significance of Lord Dowding's service to this country and indeed the world.

We should remember too that Lord Dowding's contribution was not limited to his genius as the Commander of the fighter forces engaged in the actual Battle itself: by his vision and foresight in the years leading up to our finest hour – as Air Member for Supply and Research and Development on the Air Council and in other high appointments – he contributed in no small measure to ensuring that our pilots – his 'chicks' as he affectionately called those brave and splendid young men – were equipped to the highest standards. In fact it has been said with some truth that even if Lord Dowding had not lived to fight the Battle of Britain, his work in the field of technical development alone would place him among his country's saviours. For example, he saw the tremendous potential in the work then being done of the detection of aircraft by radio beams which we now call radar. He saw clearly too the need for greater fire power and supported wholeheartedly the 8-gun fighter project. Some will feel that, historically, his sponsoring of the two principal pillars of victory, the sturdy and reliable Hurricane and its graceful sister, the Spitfire, with their Merlin engines, was his greatest contribution to the battle that lay ahead. Others will place even greater emphasis on the steadfast courage with which, at a critical moment and under heavy pressure, he insisted on preserving for the battle to come forces without which it might have ended in defeat.

He assumed command of the newly-formed Fighter Command just in time to apply the many innovations which he had foreseen in his previous appointments; he created efficient fighting formations managed by a competent team with which he could adequately defend these islands in the initial onslaught. Our success in that Battle was therefore a complete vindication of all Lord Dowding stood for...Now he takes his place in British history alongside the great Captains of the past. Like them he fought and won a battle to save Britain from destruction.

Acknowledgements

—ɷ—

No research, no work of scholarship or history, can be carried out without the help and cooperation of many people and institutions–and of course institutions means still more people. If I take the institutions first, I must record my thanks to the staffs of the libraries of the University of Victoria, British Columbia, and of the Greater Victoria Public Library, both for their own books and other resources and for the inter-library loan service they called on to fill gaps. I particularly wish to thank Ian Baird of the University Microforms Department for his help in locating and consulting his collections.

I am greatly indebted, for their unfailing courtesy and helpfulness, to the staffs of the Churchill Archives of Churchill College Cambridge; of the Imperial War Museum, London; of the Air Historical Branch, Department of Defence, RAF Stanmore; of the RAF Museum Hendon; and of the National Archives (formerly the PRO, Kew).

Friends and colleagues necessarily played a crucial part in the improvement of a text by way of critical comments and suggestions, as well as for the accounts they gave me of wartime operational flying against the enemy.

I am grateful beyond words for the friendly cooperation I received from several pilots of the Battle of Britain whom I met with over the years to discuss the stakes, tactics or air fighting, most notably 'Ginger' Lacey, Geoffrey Page, Tom Gleave, Alan Deere and Peter Townsend, all now, alas, gone from us. I am most particularly keen to express my immense gratitude to the late John Young, for long the historian of the Battle of Britain Fighters Association, who supplied me with reams of original unpublished papers bearing on various topics treated of in this book; and to Peter Brown of 611 Squadron, whose knowledge of the Battle in general, and of Bader's wings and claims and leadership in particular, is unrivalled. Both of these gallant pilots and gentlemen I have been singularly fortunate to claim as friends. I may say the same of Paul Tomlinson, of 29 Squadron, whom I had the good fortune to meet as late as June 2008, and who gave me some insights into night fighting.

I wish to record my great good fortune in counting on the friendship and help of Lady Odette Dowding and of David Whiting, the late Lord Dowding's stepson, for providing me with a number of the invaluable pictures which are reproduced in this book. It is also a pleasure equal to the duty to thank the Imperial War Museum for providing me with, and for authorizing me to reproduce, photographs identified by their reference numbers in the captions. It is also a pleasure to thank the Trustees of the Imperial War Museum for giving me access to the Tizard collection.

I also thank the Air Historical Branch (RAF) for the photograph of E J Kingston McCoughry reproduced here.

I do not forget my local friends, Hu Filleul and Derek Baker, of the Vancouver Island Branch of the Aircrew Association, for, respectively, preparing many of these illustrations for publication in this volume, and for being unfailingly helpful when my computer, or its operator, unaccountably acted up.

It is a pleasure to record my thanks to several authors who have authorized me to quote freely from their works. They are: Vincent Orange, David E. Fisher, Peter Brown, Michael Bragg, RDF 1 and Ian G. White, author of the important study of the application of AI in the battle against night attacks, for the materials he sent me to update my account of the Baedeker raids in 1942.

Finally, I acknowledge with thanks the permission I have received from the following publishers to quote from works in their copyright (see Bibliography for titles): Hodder & Stoughton (Hough & Richards), George Allen & Unwin (Charles G. Grey), Little, Brown Book Group (Robert Wright), Random House (Sir Martin Gilbert, Denis Richards), Weidenfeld & Nicolson, a division of the Orion Publishing Group (Townsend), Hutchinson (Balfour), Chatto & Windus, a division of Random House (Chisholm), Continuum Books (Geoffrey Best), HarperCollins (Sholto Douglas, Herman, Boyle), Hurst (De Groot), and Heinemann (Gilbert, Richards on Portal), and the office of Public Sector Information.

I must also mention the publishers who appear to have gone out of business since the works in question I have made use of, or for which I have been unable to trace the copyright holders. They are: Jarrolds (Dowding, Collier), Atheneum NY (H. Montgomery Hyde), William Kimber (Kent), Charles Scribner's (Churchill), Leo Cooper (Frederick Woods). Finally, and by no means the least important, it is a pleasure to express my gratitude to Jessica Mitchell, my editor at Pen & Sword, and to Jon Wilkinson, the cover designer, Sylvia Menzies-Earl, the typesetter, and Helen Vodden, production manager, for their invaluable contributions.

I regret any errors and, especially, any careless omissions from these acknowledgements. Among them I must express my regrets, and my apologies to the author of the tribute entitled 'Where Would We Have Been', which is reproduced in Appendix D, for having lost the details of authorship and source.

Jack E.G. Dixon
Victoria, British Columbia

Bibliography

—ᴍ—

UNPUBLISHED SOURCES
Documents held in the National Archives (formerly the Public Record Office), Kew, London; in the Library and Archives of the Royal Air Force Museum, Hendon; in the Air Historical Branch, Ministry of Defence, RAF Stanmore; in the Imperial War Museum, London; and in the Churchill Archives, Churchill College Cambridge, which have been quoted in this book, are identified in the Notes appended to the end of the chapters.

The Air Defence of Great Britain, vol.II, The Battle of Britain
  (Air Historical Branch Narrative, Ministry of Defence) AIR 41/15
The Air Defence of Great Britain, vol.III, Night Air Defence
  (Air Historical Branch Narrative, Ministry of Defence) AIR 41/17
The Origins and Pre-War Growth of Fighter Command, by T.C.G. James
  (Air Historical Branch Narrative, Ministry of Defence)
The All-Canadian Squadron [compiled by Wg. Cmdr. F.H. Hitchins], in the Rare Book Room of the University of Western Ontario Library, London, Canada, held in The Beatrice Hitchins Memorial Collection of Aviation History.
Dowding: 'Personal Notes to the Author of Dowding and the Battle of Britain'. Held in RAF Bentley Priory, Stanmore, under the reference OMBP/10//3/fa44. Cited in the references as 'Personal Notes'.

PUBLISHED SOURCES
Prime Documents
Dowding, Air Chief Marshal Lord. *Despatch on The Battle of Britain*.
  Supplement to the *London Gazette*, September 10th, 1946.
  — *Twelve Legions of Angels* (London: Jarrolds, n.d. [1946])
The Battle of Britain, August-October 1940 (London: Air Ministry, HMSO, 1941)
The Battle of Britain (London: Air Ministry Pamphlet 156, 1943)
Bataille d'Angleterre, La, 3 tomes, publié par Jean Lasserre
  (Paris :ICARE nos. 93, 95, 99, 1980-81-82)
Ramsey, Winston G., ed. *The Battle of Britain: Then and Now*
  (London: After the Battle Publications, 1980)

History : General (including War at Sea)
Butler, J.R.M: *Grand Strategy, September 1939-June 1941* (London: HMSO, 1957)

Calvocoressi, Peter; Wint, Guy; Pritchard, John: *The Penguin History of the Second World War* (London: Penguin Books, 1972)

Churchill, Winston S: *The Second World War, vol.II: Their Finest Hour* (London: Cassell, 1949)
— *Into Battle* (London: Cassell, 1941)

Collier, Basil: *The Defence of the United Kingdom* (London: HMSO, 1957)

Colvin, John: *Decisive Battles* (London: Headline, 2003)

Costello, John: *Ten Days to Destiny* (New York: William Morrow & Co., 1992)

Creasy, Sir Edward S: *The Fifteen Decisive Battles of the World* (London, Dent, Everyman's Library, 1912)

David, Saul: *Military Blunders.* (New York: Carroll & Graf, 1998)

Dixon, Norman F: *On the Psychology of Military Incompetence* (London, Jonathan Cape, 1976)

Fuller, J.F.C.: *The Conduct of War* (London, Eyre Methuen, 1972)
— *The Second World War* (New York, Sloan and Pearce, 1962)
— *The Decisive Battles of the Western World, vol. 1* (London: Eyre & Spottiswoode, 1963)

Gray, C.G. : *A History of the Air Ministry* (London: George Allen & Unwin, 1940)

Hackett, Gen. Sir John: *The Profession of Arms* (London: Sidgwick & Jackson, 1983)

Horne, Alistair: *To Lose a Battle. France 1940* (Boston, Little, Brown and Co., 1969)
— *The Longest Battle. The War at Sea 1939-45* (London, Weidenfeld and Nicolson)

Hughes-Wilson, John (Col.): *Military Intelligence Blunders and Cover-Ups* (London: Robinson, 2004)

Hyde, H. Montgomery: *British Air Policy Between the Wars* (London, Heinemann, 1976)

Jacobsen, H.A. & Rohwer eds: *Decisive Battles of World War Two: The German View* (New York: Putnam, 1965)

Jones, Neville: *The Origins of Strategic Bombing* (London: Wm Kimber, 1973)
— *The Beginnings of Strategic Air Power. A History of the British Bomber Force 1923-1939* (London: Frank Cass, 1987)

Jones, R.V: *Most Secret War* (London: Coronet Books, 1979)

Kingston McCloughry, E.J.: *The Direction of War. A Critique of Political Direction and High Command in War* (London: Jonathan Cape, 1955)

Luvaas, Jay: *Frederick the Great on the Art of War* (New York: The Free Press, 1966)

Macksey, Kenneth: *Military Errors of World War Two* (London, Cassell, 1999)

Peden, G.C.: *British Rearmament and the Treasury: 1932-1939* (Edinburgh: Scottish Academic Press, 1979)

Phillips, Major Thomas R. ed.: *Roots of Strategy: a collection of military classics* (London: John Lane the Bodley Head, 1943)

Pile, Sir Frederick: *Ack-Ack* (London, Harrap, 1949)

Roskill, S.W.: *The War at Sea* 1939-1945 (London: HMSO, 1956)

Sun Tzu: *The Art of War* (Oxford: University Press, 1963)

Terraine, John: *Business in Great Waters* (London: Leo Cooper, 1989)

Air Warfare: General

Allen, H.R.: *The Legacy of Lord Trenchard* (London: Cassell, 1972)

Baumbach, Werner: *Broken Swastika. The Defeat of the Luftwaffe* (London: Robert Hale, 1960)

Bekker, Cajus: *The Luftwaffe War Diaries* (New York: Ballantine Books, 1975) (London: Weidenfeld & Nicolson, 1974)

Dean, Sir Maurice: *The Royal Air Force in Two World Wars* (London: Cassell, 1979)

Douglas, Sir Sholto: 'Air Operations by Fighter Command from 25th November 1940 to 31st December 1941' (Supplement to the *London Gazette*, September 14, 1948)

Douhet, Giulio: *The Command of the Air*, tr. by Dino Ferrari (London: Faber and Faber, 1943)

Faber, Harold: *Luftwaffe: A History* (New York: New York Times Books, 1977)

Flint, Peter: *Dowding and Headquarters Fighter Command* (Shrewsbury: Airlife, 1996)

Franks, Norman: *The Greatest Air Battle: Dieppe 19th August 1942* (London: William Kimber, 1979)

Irving, David: *The Rise and Fall of the Luftwaffe* (London: Weidenfeld and Nicolson, 1973)

James, John: *The Paladins. A Social History of the RAF up to the outbreak of World War Two* (London: Futura, 1990)

Johnson, J.E. 'Johnnie': *The Story of Air Fighting* (London, Hutchinson, 1985)

Jones, Ira ('Taffy'): *Wing Commander: Tiger Squadron* (London: W.H. Allen, 1954)

Joubert de la Ferté, ACM Sir Philip: *The Third Service* (London: Thames and Hudson, 1955)

Murray, Williamson: *Strategy for Defeat. The Luftwaffe 1933-1945* (Air University Press, 1983)

Overy, R.J.: *The Air War 1939-1945* (New York: Stein and Day, 1981)

Richards, Denis: *Royal Air Force 1939-1945, vol.I The Fight at Odds* (London: HMSO, 1953)

Smith, Malcolm: 'Sir Edgar Ludlow-Hewitt and the Expansion of Bomber Command 1939-40', in *R.U.S.I. Journal* (vol. cxxvi, March 1981, pp. 52-56)

— *British Air Strategy Between the Wars* (Oxford: Clarendon Press, 1984)

Tantun IV, W.H. & Hoffschmidt, E.J., eds: *The Rise and Fall of the German Air Force (1933 to 1945)* (Old Greenwich, Conn.: WE Inc. 1969)

Terraine, John: *The Right of the Line* (London: Hodder & Stoughton, 1985)

Watt, D.C.: 'The Air Force View of History' in 'The Quarterly Review' (Oct. 1962, no.634, pp.428-37)

Webster, Sir Charles and Frankland, Noble: *The Strategic Air Offensive Against Germany 1939-1945, vol. I Preparation* (London: HMSO, 1961)

Wykeham, Peter: *Fighter Command* (London: Putnam, 1960)

Zamoyski, Adam: *The Forgotten Few: The Polish Air Force in the Second World War* (London: John Murray, 1995)

Zimmerman, David: *Britain's Shield: Radar and the Defeat of the Luftwaffe* (Gloucester: Stroud, Sutton, 2001)

Air Warfare: The Battle of Britain (including radar)

Addison, Paul & Crang, Jeremy, eds: *The Burning Blue. A New History of the Battle of Britain* (London: Pimlico, 2000)

Bickers, Richard T. et al: *The Battle of Britain* (London: Salamander Books, 1990)

Bishop, Edward: *Their Finest Hour* (New York: Ballantine Books, 1968)

Bowen, E.G: *Radar Days* (Bristol and Philadelphia, Institute of Physics Publishing, 1998)

Bragg, Michael: RDF1 (Paisley: Hawkhead Publishing, 2002)

Brown, Louis: *A Radar History of World War Two* (Bristol and Philadelphia, Institute of Physics, 1999)

Brown, Squadron Leader Peter: *Honour Restored. The Battle of Britain, Dowding and the Fight for Freedom* (Staplehurst: Spellmount, 2005)

Bungay, Stephen: *The Most Dangerous Enemy. A History of the Battle of Britain* (London: Aurum Press, 2000)

Cooksley, P.G. 1940: *The Story of No. 11 Group, Fighter Command* (London: Robert Hale, 1983)

Deighton, Len: *Fighter* (New York: Knopf, 1977)

Battle of Britain (London, Jonathan Cape, 1980)

Gelb, Norman: *Scramble* (London: Michael Joseph, 1986)

Halliday, Hugh. *No. 242 Squadron. The Canadian Years* (Belleville, Ontario, Canada's Wings, 1981)

Haslam, E.B. 'How Lord Dowding came to leave Fighter Command', in *Journal of Strategic Studies* (June 1981, pp.175-186)

Hough, Richard & Richards, Denis: *The Battle of Britain* (London, Hodder & Stoughton, 1989)

Johnson J.E.and P.B. 'Laddie' Lucas, eds: *Glorious Summer* (London, Stanley Paul & Co., 1990)

Mason, Francis K: *Battle Over Britain* (London: McWhirter Twins, 1969)

Overy, R.J.: *The Battle of Britain. The Myth and the Reality* (New York, Norton, 2001)

Parkinson, Roger: *Summer, 1940. The Battle of Britain* (New York: David McKay Company, 1977)

Ponting, Clive: *1940: Myth and Reality* (London: Hamish Hamilton, 1990)

Price, Alfred: *The Hardest Day* (New York: Charles Scribner's Sons, 1979)

Probert, Henry & Sebastian Cox, eds: *The Battle Re-Thought* (Shrewsbury: Airlife, 1991)

Ray, John: *The Battle of Britain. Dowding and the First Victory, 1940* (London, Cassell, 2000)

Townsend, Peter: *Duel of Eagles* (London: Weidenfeld and Nicolson, 1970)

Turner, John Frayn: *The Bader Wing* (Shrewsbury: Airlife, 1990)

Wood, Derek and Dempster, Derek: *The Narrow Margin* (London: Hutchinson, 1961)

The Night Battle

Chisholm, Roderick: *Cover of Darkness* (London: Chatto & Windus, 1953)

Howard-Williams, Jeremy: *Night Intruder* (Newton Abbot: David & Charles, 1976)

Johnson, David: *The London Blitz* (New York: Stein and Day, 1982)

Price, Alfred: *Blitz on Britain: The Bomber Attacks on the United Kingdom 1939-45* (London: Ian Allan, 1977),

— *Instruments of Darkness* (London: Macdonald and Jane's, 1977)

Rawnsley, C.F. and Wright, Robert: *Night Fighter* (London: Collins, 1957)

Ray, John: *The Night Blitz 1940-1941* (London: Arms and Armour, 1996)

Sansom, William: *The Blitz. Westminster at War* (Oxford University Press, 1990)

Winston G. Ramsey, ed: *The Blitz Then and Now, vol.2.* (London: After the Battle Publications, 1988)

Townsend, Peter: *The Odds Against Us* (New York, William Morrow and Co., 1987)

Whiting, Charles: *The Three-Star Blitz* (London: Leo Cooper, 1987)

See also the relevant sections in Bekker, Churchill, Collier, Douglas, Johnson, Overy, Richards, Terraine and Wykeham, above; and, below, in Churchill, Douglas, Embry, Lindemann, Tizard and Watson Watt.

Biography

Air Marshals	Andrews, Allen: *The Air Marshals* (London: Macdonald, 1970)
Bader	Michael G. Burns: *Bader and His Men* (London: Arms and Armour, 1990)
	— Lucas, Laddie. *Flying Colours* (London: Hutchison, 1981)
Balfour	Balfour, Harold: *Wings Over Westminster* (London: Hutchinson, 1973)
Beaverbrook	Taylor, A.J.P.: *Beaverbrook* (London: Hamish Hamilton, 1972)
Commanders	Probert, Henry: *High Commanders of the Royal Air Force* (London: HMSO, 1992)
Cross	Cross, Air Chief Marshal Sir Kenneth: *Straight and Level* (London, Grub Street, 1993)
Churchill	Gilbert, Martin. *Winston S. Churchill, vol.VI: Finest Hour, 1939-1941* (London: Heinemann, 1983)
Cotton	Barker, Ralph: *Aviator Extraordinary* (London: Chatto & Windus, 1969)
Deere	A.C. Deere: *Nine Lives* (London: Hodder & Stoughton, 1959)
Douglas	Douglas, William Sholto with Robert Wright: *Years of Command* (London: Collins, 1966)
Dowding	Collier, Basil: *Leader of the Few* (Norwich, Jarrolds, 1957)
	Fisher, David E: *A Summer Bright and Terrible* (Emeryville, CA: Shoemaker & Hoard, 2005)
	Wright, Robert: *Dowding and The Battle of Britain* (London: Macdonald, 1969)
Embry	Embry, Air Chief Marshal Sir Basil: *Mission Completed* (London: Methuen & Co., 1957)
Gleave	'R.A.F. Casualty' [T.P. Gleave], *I Had A Row with a German* (London: Macmillan, 1941)

Grinnell-Milne	Grinnell-Milne, Duncan: *Wind in the Wires* (London: Jarrolds, 1971)
Harris	Harris, Air Chief Marshal Sir Arthur: *Bomber Offensive*
Kent	Kent, J.A.: *One of the Few* (London: William Kimber, 1971)
Kesselring	*The Memoirs of Field-Marshal Kesselring* (London: William Kimber, 1953)
Leigh-Mallory	Dunn, Bill Newton: *Big Wing* (Shrewsbury: Airlife, 1992)
Lindemann	Birkenhead, The Earl of: *The Prof in Two Worlds* (London: Collins, 1961)
Malan	Franks, Norman L.R.: *Sky Tiger. The Story of Group Captain Sailor Malan*, DSO, DFC (London: William Kimber, 1980)
	Walker, Oliver: *Sailor Malan* (London: Cassell & Co., 1953)
Page	Page, Geoffrey: *Tale of a Guinea Pig* (Canterbury: Wingham Press, 1991)
Park	Orange, Vincent: *Sir Keith Park* (London: Methuen, 1984)
Percival	Kinvig, Clifford: *Scapegoat: General Percival of Singapore* (London: Brassey's, 1996)
Portal	Richards, Denis: *Portal of Hungerford* (London:Heinemann, 1978)
Quill	Quill, Jeffrey: *Spitfire. A Test Pilot's Story* (London: John Murray, 1983)
Richey	*Fighter Pilot* (London: Batsford, 1941)
Salmond	Laffin, John: *Swifter than Eagles* (Edinburgh & London: William Blackwood & Sons, 1964)
Sinclair	De Groot, Gerard J.: *Liberal Crusader. The Life of Sir Archibald Sinclair* (London: Hurst & Co.; New York University Press, 1993)
Swinton	*The Earl of Swinton: Sixty Years of Power* (London: Hutchinson, 1966)
Tedder	Tedder, Marshal of the Royal Air Force Lord: *With Prejudice* (London, Cassell, 1966)
Tizard	Clark, Ronald: *Tizard* (Cambridge: MIT Press, 1965)
Trenchard	Boyle, Andrew: *Trenchard* (London: Collins, 1962)
	Allen, H.R.: *The Legacy of Lord Trenchard* (London, Cassell's, 1972)
Tuck	Forrester, Larry: *Fly For Your Life* (New York: Nelson Doubleday,1973)
Turing	Hodges, Andrew: *Alan Turing: The Enigma* (London: Burnett Books, 1983)
War Lords, The	Carver, Field Marshal Sir Michael, ed.: *Military Commanders of the Twentieth Century* (London: Weidenfeld and Nicolson, 1976)
Watson Watt	Watson Watt, Sir Robert: *Three Steps to Victory* (London: Odhams Press, 1957)

Index

The names listed in this Index are sorted for the most part alphabetically. That includes the names of aircraft and of the RAF stations. Where names are preceded by a number, as in the case of squadrons, they have for the most part been assembled under 'RAF Components'. The names of people have been given the title or rank which they held in 1940, where this information has been necessary for identification purposes. Titles of books and other publications, and the names of ships, have been italicized. The abbreviation a/c identifies the names of aircraft. The mentions of Air Council, Air Ministry and Air Staff are so numerous that only the most significant occurrences have been listed.

254